CICERO
A PORTRAIT

ELIZABETH RAWSON

ALLEN LANE

Copyright © Elizabeth Rawson 1975

First published in 1975

Allen Lane
Penguin Books Ltd
17 Grosvenor Gardens, London SW1

ISBN 0 7139 0864 5

Printed in Great Britain by
Clarke, Doble & Brendon Ltd
Plymouth

To the memory of Isobel Henderson
Oxford, 1906–1967

CONTENTS

LIST OF ILLUSTRATIONS AND MAPS

Illustrations

1. Cicero from the Vatican Museum (*The Mansell Collection*)

2. The famous portrait of Pompey from the Copenhagen Glyptothek (*Ny Carlsberg Glyptothek, Copenhagen*)

3. A bust traditionally supposed to be Hortensius (*The Mansell Collection*)

4. A recently discovered head of Cato from Volubilis in North Africa (*Fototeca Unione, Rome*)

5. Cicero from Apsley House, London. Other busts of Cicero have been identified from this, the only named one (*Victoria & Albert Museum, Crown copyright*)

6. A possibly contemporary portrait of Caesar (*Deutschen Archaeologischen Instituts, Rome*)

7. A recently identified head, probably of Antony (*Studio Sallis, Narbonne*)

8. A perhaps somewhat idealized portrait of the young Octavian (*The Mansell Collection*)

Maps

Rome in the late Republic

Italy and Sicily

The Eastern Mediterranean after Pompey's Conquests

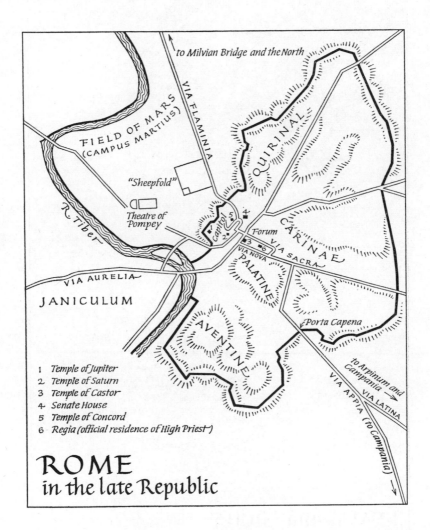

to Milvian Bridge and the North

VIA FLAMINIA

FIELD OF MARS
(CAMPUS MARTIUS)

QUIRINAL

"Sheepfold"

R. Tiber

Theatre of
Pompey

Capitol

5

4

Forum

CARINAE

3 6 VIA SACRA

VIA NOVA

PALATINE

VIA AURELIA

JANICULUM

AVENTINE

Porta Capena

to Arpinum and
Campania

VIA LATINA

VIA APPIA (to Campania)

1 Temple of Jupiter
2 Temple of Saturn
3 Temple of Castor
4 Senate House
5 Temple of Concord
6 Regia (official residence of High Priest)

ROME
in the late Republic

A*

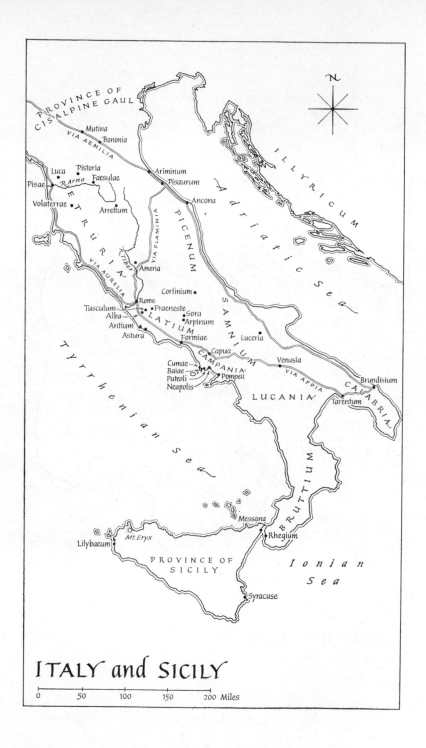

N

PROVINCE OF
CISALPINE GAUL

VIA AEMILIA

Mutina
Bononia

Luca Pistoria
Pisae R. Arno Faesulae
Volaterrae Arretium

ETRURIA

VIA AURELIA

VIA FLAMINIA

Tiber

Ameria

Ariminum
Pisaurum

Ancona

ILLYRICUM

Adriatic Sea

PICENUM

Corfinium

Rome
Tusculum Praeneste
Alba Sora
Antium Arpinum
Astura LATIUM Formiae

Luceria

SAMNIUM

Capua
Cumae CAMPANIA
Baiae Pompeii
Puteoli
Neapolis

Venusia

VIA APPIA

Brundisium

CALABRIA

Tarentum

LUCANIA

Tyrrhenian Sea

BRUTTIUM

Messana
Rhegium

Mt. Eryx

Lilybaeum

PROVINCE OF
SICILY

Ionian
Sea

Syracuse

ITALY and SICILY

0   50   100   150   200 Miles

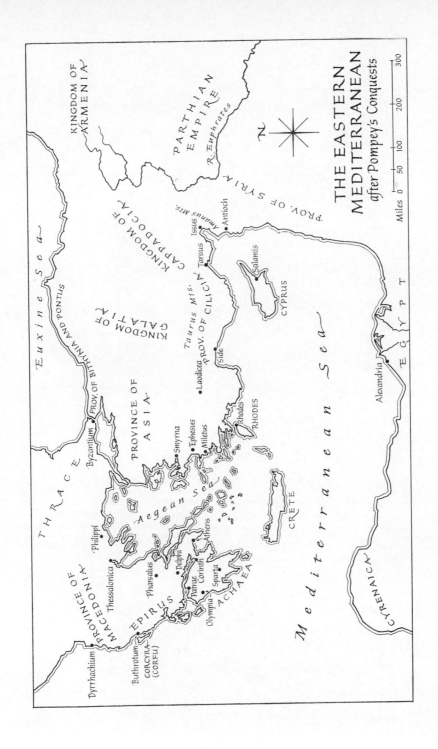

THE EASTERN
MEDITERRANEAN
after Pompey's Conquests

Miles 0 50 100 200 300

KINGDOM OF
ARMENIA

PARTHIAN
EMPIRE

R. Euphrates

PROV. OF SYRIA

Euxine Sea

KINGDOM OF
CAPPADOCIA

Amanus Mts.
Issus
Antioch
Tarsus
Salamis
CYPRUS

PROV. OF BITHYNIA AND PONTUS

KINGDOM OF
GALATIA

Taurus Mts.

PROV. OF CILICIA

Byzantium

THRACE

PROVINCE
OF ASIA

Laodicea

Side

Smyrna
Ephesus
Miletus
Rhodes
RHODES

Aegean Sea

EGYPT

Alexandria

Mediterranean Sea

PROVINCE OF
MACEDONIA

Philippi
Thessalonica

Pharsalus

EPIRUS

Delphi

Athens

CRETE

Dyrrhachium
Buthrotum
CORCYRA
(CORFU)

Patrae
Olympia

Corinth
Sparta
ACHAEA

CYRENAICA

INTRODUCTION

Cicero is almost unique among the great men of antiquity: because we know a good deal about him. We know to a great extent not only what he did, but why he did it, and how it related to his character and convictions. We have not only versions of many of the speeches that he delivered in law courts, Senate and popular assembly, but also essays, mostly in dialogue form, on political, literary and philosophic subjects; and above all we have the marvellous correspondence, which incomplete as it now is remains perhaps the most fascinating collection of documents from the ancient world. It is composed mostly of letters of all kinds from Cicero himself, running from the great series of intimate and self-revealing letters to Atticus, his closest friend, to formal notes of introduction; but there are also a few written by others to Cicero. The cautious and self-effacing Atticus himself is silent; but we hear, if only briefly, the genuine accents of Caesar and Cato, Brutus and Cassius, all well known to Cicero; and the no less informative voices of less famous men, such as the clever and amusing young Caelius, who sent on often scurrilous accounts of events at Rome when Cicero unwillingly left the city for a provincial governorship.

There is other illuminating evidence for the time: Caesar's self-justifying narrative of his campaigns; Sallust's monograph on the conspiracy formed by Catiline in the year of Cicero's consulship; a brief life of Atticus by a scholarly friend; and there is much historical writing of later date, notably histories by Dio and Appian, and Plutarch's lives of Cicero, Caesar, Pompey and others, that drew on material, including letters and other works of Cicero, that is not available to us now. It so happens, too, that towards the end of Cicero's life, portrait sculpture in Rome reached a new level of vividness and psychological penetration; we know the faces, as well as the minds, of some of the prominent men of the time. For in many fields later or 'Hellenistic' Greek traditions were coming together with Roman ones in a newly mature synthesis, a true Greco-Roman civilization, at the same time as the political system of the Roman Republic, the senatorial oligarchy re-established by Sulla, collapsed into chaos, and the lineaments of the Roman Empire, that was so deeply to influence the future of all Europe, began to emerge. In creating this synthesis, especially in the fields of rhetorical prose style, and of philosophy, Cicero played a great part; as he did also in the political collapse, and the attempts to avoid it.

It is not surprising, then, that there have been many books on Cicero in English. Why write another? The answer is that our knowledge of many aspects of the late Roman Republic has progressed considerably in the last couple of generations, and that many of the recent works, that have taken account of this progress, have not been written primarily for the general reader. The rest have tended to concentrate on a single aspect of Cicero's career – his direct political activity, or his relations with his family and friends. Though Cicero's greatness was not primarily as a politician, it was certainly his public career that he regarded as the most important part of his life; even oratory to him was not an end in itself but the weapon, indeed the supreme expression, of the statesman; even philosophy was largely valuable for its power to train and strengthen men in public as well as private life. Thus Cicero's successes and failures in politics cannot be understood without some understanding of his eloquence and the place that eloquence held in Roman life, and of his political theory and his other philosophic beliefs, as well as of his personal character. He was a man of many aspects (if also of serious limitations); and thus he is also peculiarly fitted to introduce us to his fascinating period.

This book, then, tries to give a balanced picture of the whole man, except that it says little of his strictly stylistic achievements, which cannot be conveyed in English; nor does it discuss the philosophical work from a technical point of view. Since it is for the ordinary reader, it does not hesitate to re-tell the well-known episodes and to quote the famous phrases. It aims at making Cicero and his world understandable – and here, paradoxically, it runs the risk of making them too understandable. Such a book, comparatively brief, quoting in translation and not fully annotated, must inevitably smooth out some of the most alien features of this world. In particular, readers should remember that in his letters to Atticus, who had lived long in Greece, Cicero is for ever dropping from Latin into Greek, which was also the natural language of literary criticism, medicine and other learned subjects, the language too of much of the poetry (above all Homer and Athenian drama) that he knew and loved best. I have not chosen to render this Greek by French, as some of his most distinguished translators (to whom I am in other respects much indebted) have done, feeling that in spite of the partial validity of the parallel the wrong atmosphere is evoked. But with Cicero's Greek, and with his other untranslatable allusions and quotations, some of the flavour and richness of the letters is inevitably lost. On the other hand, the speeches and treatises move too slowly and amply to be easily quotable; and it cannot be denied that a number of them are to our taste inflated and unconscionably long; that, in fact, Cicero can be a fearful bore. This cannot be, and indeed I trust is not, conveyed.

It should also be stressed that there are problems in the sources themselves. The writers of the imperial age did not understand the issues of the late Republic, and drew on bad material as well as good – for example the rhetorical invectives that formed an accepted part of political life: these violent personal assaults, in speech or pamphlet form, were not expected to aim at strict truthfulness. There is little non-literary evidence: a few, but not many, contemporary inscriptions record laws or other official documents. Too little is known of the conditions and outlook of those outside the limited circle of the oligarchy at Rome; and even of its members we not only know far less than we do of Cicero, but what we do know comes largely through him – so that it is particularly hard to say how good his judgement and policy were. And even for Cicero himself there are gaps in our knowledge, particularly at the beginning and end of his career, where the letters fail us.

Furthermore, even his surviving works are not without difficulties. Speeches delivered in court had to be rewritten for publication – and particularly if they were only published after a lapse of time, political allusions might be altered, for the publication of a speech, like its delivery, was often a political act. Anyway, like so many judicial and political documents, Cicero's speeches are often extremely disingenuous. There is much discussion, too, about the publication of the letters, though it is clear that this took place after his death and the theory that what we have is a politically slanted selection is generally rejected.

I have usually indicated what rests on good evidence, and what on less good, but I have tried not to hold the story up with argument; for I have borne in mind that I am dealing with a man who himself hardly ever wrote obscurely, and who was as capable of rapid and precise narrative enlivened by vivid detail as of the clear exposition of an intellectual position.

I

ARPINUM AND ROME
106-90 B.C.

A traveller from Rome to Arpinum takes the road that runs by an inland route south-east to Campania and Naples, and about seventy miles from the city abandons it to strike into the hills, up the narrow valley of the river Liris. The road to the little town leaves the river valley before this widens out into the fertile plain on the edge of which Cicero's estate lay; it climbs through slopes that are partly wooded, and partly set with olives and vines, often standing in fields of corn. In Cicero's day the woods were doubtless more extensive; but otherwise the country and its methods of cultivation are probably not greatly changed. And the present-day Arpino is perhaps not utterly unlike the Roman town; it clusters round a square, once the forum, on the saddle between two summits, the higher of which was once a great stronghold of the ancient Volscian people, and is still ringed with the walls, built of gigantic blocks of stone, that were centuries old even in Cicero's time. From this citadel the views are of striking loveliness, whether down to the plain and the high mountains beyond it, or over the gentler hills behind the town. But of Cicero's villa down near the falls of the Liris the exact site is uncertain and nothing remains, unless some ancient columns now in the monastery of San Domenico came from its ruins.

Arpinum was given Roman citizenship in 188 B.C., by which time it must have abandoned the Italic dialect once spoken there by the Volscians, and become entirely Latinized in speech and culture. At the time of Marcus Tullius Cicero's birth on 3 January 106 B.C., about a third of the peninsula was thus incorporated into the Roman state. Most of the other communities of Italy still had theoretically the status of allies of Rome, though with the latter's almost complete predominance in the Mediterranean world this nominal independence had become futile and indeed a source of discontent; many still spoke foreign tongues – Etruscan, Oscan, even Greek – though all were giving way before the spread of Latin. The area round Arpinum was a patchwork of communities of varying status; the Arpinates are likely to have

1

been sharply aware of the Italian allies' growing desire for full citizenship.

Cicero refers to his birthplace as a remote and out-of-the-way little town, as it still is, to which in adulthood he could come only when he had an unusual length of time free: the journey, in comfort, took two or three days. In the preface to one of his dialogues, the scene of which is set on his property down in the valley, he praises the 'charming and health-giving' countryside, with the island cutting 'like the beak of a ship' a stream flowing into the Liris, where he loved to read, write and meditate. He mentions the poplars by the river, and the oak-tree which figured in his poem on the great soldier Marius, who was born near Arpinum about half a century before Cicero himself. And he suggests that the simple beauty of the place is more attractive to him than anything in the grand villas and gardens so popular with the Romans at this time: for Nature, after all, is the basis for what is delightful, as well as of morality and law.

This is the true fatherland of myself and my brother, for we are descended from a very ancient family of this place. Here are our ancestral cults, here is our race, here are many memorials of our forefathers. What more need I say? Here you see the house, as it is now, rebuilt and improved by the care of my father, who, since his health was poor, spent most of his life here in study. But I was born in the place when my grandfather was alive and the house was a small one, after the ancient fashion, like that of Curius in the Sabine country.

It is typical of the mature Cicero that he should thus connect his experience with that of a great hero of early Roman history; as a boy he was perhaps not so aware of the austere and virtuous Curius.

Remote it may have been, but because Arpinum was the birthplace of both Marius and Cicero it is one of the few country towns of the period of which we know anything. In the late second century B.C. the chief families there were the Marii, Gratidii and Tullii Cicerones, all interrelated. Though in Roman language such men were *equites*, well-off persons outside the Senate (the name, 'horsemen', comes from the old obligation of the rich to serve as cavalry), they were also *domi nobiles*, aristocracy in their own home towns. They had in most respects the outlook of aristocrats: pride of birth, contempt for trade and business (unless on a grand scale), political interests and, increasingly at this period, a good education based on literature (Cicero's father, as we saw, was a scholar; his grandfather, like Marius, had despised such pursuits). They drew their wealth from land, and ran local politics. In short, they were not unlike the local aristocracies of small Italian towns in much more recent times; though these organized the opera season instead of the games, and prided themselves on knowing French instead of Greek. Sometimes members of Cicero's class aspired to public life in the capital, and to a certain extent they could expect to find acceptance by its great noble families; even intermarriage was not rare. These great families, whose *nobilitas* was based on the fact that a member or members had held the supreme magistracy of Rome, the consulship, might well have possessions and interest in country areas; they could not belong to one as Cicero did, and are unlikely to have had quite his awareness of small-town opinion. His Arpinate background, then, was the first of many influences that came together to form Cicero's mind and character. At all times, of course, a man's background and education are relevant to our understanding of him; but this is perhaps unusually true both of Cicero himself, who had a sensitive and receptive, but not a deeply original, mind; and of his age as a whole, in which both Greek culture and Roman *mores* laid much stress, in different ways, on tradition and example. Cicero's greatness resides, indeed, less in his creative originality than in the form and life that he could give to the Latin language and to Roman political and moral traditions, enriched by a wide knowledge of Greek civilization.

We are told that Marius first stood for office at Arpinum, perhaps around 125 B.C.; and Cicero describes his own grandfather, old Marcus Cicero, opposing the introduction there of the secret ballot, proposed by his and Marius' brother-in-law Gratidius. It is interesting to see the issues of urban politics thus reflected in the country towns. Rome had long been ruled in practice by the Senate, composed roughly of ex-magistrates and led by its senior members, ex-consuls almost entirely from a handful of leading families. But the Senate had failed to solve many of the most pressing problems of a period of great conquests and resulting social upheavals, and thus Rome had now been wracked for a generation or more by the development of an ideology that was not fully democratic, but which asserted the latent sovereignty of the popular assembly under the presidency of its traditional representatives, the Tribunes of the People. Rome had no written constitution, and these rival interpretations of her political system led to much conflict.

3

The various Roman assemblies were composed of the citizens themselves, not of elected representatives. But they were, even after the passage of secret ballot laws, far from democratic either by Greek or modern standards. Many citizens lived too far away to come often to vote; and the *comitia centuriata*, in which the higher magistrates were elected under the chairmanship of consuls or their junior colleagues the praetors, was heavily biased towards the well-off, in that there were many more voting-units, 'centuries', for the richer classes than for the much larger poor ones. The assemblies that voted by tribes, or areas, were more, but not wholly, representative; the tribes were unequal in size and there might be much noble influence, over the country tribes at least.* The tribunes presided over one form of tribal assembly, and now proposed legislation to it without, as had long been customary, clearing it with the Senate; if some were in part genuine reformers, they were also, or often, ambitious aristocrats who had quarrelled with a dominating faction in the Senate, and could only hope to gain the office and power that were a noble Roman's *raison d'être* by exploiting a popular favour sometimes acquired by merely vote-catching measures. Men who turned in this way to the people, always individuals rather than a party, were called *populares*; the greatest of them had been the two brothers Tiberius and Gaius Gracchus, tribunes respectively in 133 and 123–122. Their opponents, also, were nothing like a party; the Senate included many groups (some of which might have *popularis* sympathies), and many senators, or all senators at some times, acted in support of their own interests, or, as they saw it, their own *dignitas* – honour, rank and standing – and for the advantage of their own families, allies and dependants, with which their *dignitas* was bound up. Still, it was possible to speak of 'optimates', those who upheld the established order, the authority of the Senate and the 'best men'. And it was for his opposition to Gratidius' *popularis* activity at Arpinum that a very distinguished optimate, M. Aemilius Scaurus, who perhaps had special interests in the town, congratulated old Cicero in 115 B.C. and told him that it was a pity that he was not in politics in Rome.

In fact, some Arpinates were already ambitiously turning their attention to the capital. Marius was perhaps the first. He made his way up by the usual methods of the 'new man' – diligent

* See end of book, The Roman Political System, p. 323.

military service, patronage from a powerful Roman house, the Caecilii Metelli, and marriage into an aristocratic if somewhat decayed city family – his wife was a Julia, aunt to the great Julius Caesar. In this way he got as far as the praetorship. But the Roman nobility kept a pretty tight hold on the supreme office; and to obtain the consulship Marius had to turn against his patrons, the Metelli, and base his support on the People and the *equites*, some of whom were at this time alienated from the Senate. His military reputation, however, soon became so great that it was widely held that he alone could save Rome from the invasion now threatening of northern barbarians. In 100 B.C., when Cicero was six, Marius was celebrating their annihilation and also his sixth consulship – an unparalleled honour (though of doubtful legality).

The Arpinate upper class will have been well provided, singly and collectively, with the noble protectors – *patroni* or, more tactfully, 'friends', so vital to success in the Roman world, where a firm nexus of obligations and dependencies, created by military service, representation in the courts, marriage and so on, formed the basis of the social structure and of individual morality. Marius' brother-in-law Gratidius, author of the local ballot law, also went to Rome, where he was a friend and dependant of M. Antonius, grandfather of the man we know as Mark Antony, a distinguished politician and public speaker. In 102 Gratidius accompanied Antonius to the Eastern Mediterranean on a campaign against piracy, and with them also went his young relative, Cicero's uncle Lucius Cicero (the families must have patched things up since 115). Thus Lucius probably was also aiming at a career in Rome. But he seems to have died fairly soon, leaving a son of the same name, and a daughter who in all probability married into a distinguished, if impoverished, family of the nobility.

Lucius' elder brother Marcus, Cicero's father, was kept in Arpinum and private life, as we saw, by ill-health. He was perhaps less closely in touch with Gratidius, or with Marius, of whom our Cicero has no childhood memories to relate. Marcus Cicero did however spend some time in Rome, no doubt in order to give his two sons, the elder of whom seems to have shown great intellectual promise from an early age, an education that would fit them for the public life to which so many members of his class and family were aspiring. Arpinum was probably not a cultural desert; Cicero tells us that in his youth literature was cultivated more assiduously by Latin-speakers in Italy than in the city itself, and we know of an exceptionally learned friend and neighbour, Valerius of Sora, whose home was just across the valley. But we also know that Valerius' Latin was not considered pure. For distinction in Rome, an urban education was essential. Cicero was always to love the Italian countryside, but he will hardly have missed the country pursuits of Arpinum, though there occurs in one of his works what may be a memory of summer bathes in the cold streams by his home. He never took any interest in agriculture (confessing in a report about his brother Quintus' properties that he knew much more about architecture). An eloquent passage in one of his late essays about its satisfactions is likely to be pretty factitious.

Rome was by now a great city of several hundred thousand inhabitants. The Cicerones settled, not of course in one of the crowded, jerry-built blocks of flats in the low-lying and easily flooded areas where so much of the population lived, but in a house on the Esquiline Hill, in the district known as Carinae or the Keels – a salubrious and respectable quarter, where Pompey later lived, though not as fashionable as the Palatine. And the elder Cicero seems to have had various distinguished optimate acquaintances: contact with Scaurus, now Leader of the Senate and extremely powerful, may have continued, that with Antonius certainly did; and through his wife's brother-in-law, Visellius Aculeo, a clever lawyer, he was brought into contact with Lucius Licinius Crassus, a man of noble family and the greatest orator of the time.

The ancient world was not much interested in childhood, except as a preparation for adult life. Self-centred as he was, and sympathetic to children as he could be, Cicero does not think it worthwhile to tell us anything of his early boyhood. His mother Helvia is never mentioned in his surviving works; it is left to his younger brother Quintus briefly to recount, in a letter, an anecdote illustrating her housewifely care (how to prevent slaves stealing the wine). One of Cicero's most attractive qualities was a genuine capacity for affection, and his father, we know, encouraged his ambitions; but again, Cicero has remarkably little to say of him, and it has been suggested that an unloved childhood was at the root of some of his insecurities. Perhaps the elder Cicero's poor health made him remote; and a father's power over his children, by Roman law, was awe-inspiring. For Quintus, about three years younger than himself, Cicero for many years felt love and concern, until the Civil War brought a serious quarrel: though there had been at times tensions springing partly, no doubt, from Quintus' suppressed jealousy of his brilliant elder, and partly from his own frankly difficult character. Quintus was in fact something of a caricature of his brother, whose mobility of temperament and sense of humour in him took the form of an uncertain temper and a biting tongue, though for the most part he was indulgent and even weak with his family. It is perhaps relevant that he grew up to be a physically small man, if it is true that Marcus once said, on seeing an over-life-size portrait bust of his brother, that in this case the half was greater than the whole.

With education, if not with childhood, the ancients were however profoundly concerned. And in various passages Cicero reports a good deal about his own, thinking that the intellectual formation of Rome's great orator must be of interest, and believing that his course had been in fact in many ways fortunate and worth imitating. Of his first steps he says nothing, but he may have learnt to speak Greek from his babyhood, from a Greek slave attendant; he will then either have had a tutor (more common in well-off Roman families than in Greece) or gone to an elementary school to learn his letters. The programme was austerely logical: first the alphabet, then single syllables of increasing complexity, then words, first of one, then two and more syllables; finally pieces of poetry – made difficult by the usual lack of word-division and punctuation in written texts that made it easier to grasp the sense by reading aloud, even to oneself. The second stage of education, at school or with a tutor again, was almost purely literary; the so-called *grammaticus* concentrated on careful, all too often pedantic, reading and explanation of texts, which he would expound from the papyrus scroll that formed the usual type of book till late antiquity. In Latin, he would teach the archaic epic and dramatic poets who always remained dear to Cicero but are lost to us except for fragments – mostly quotations by Cicero himself – and for a few comedies by Plautus and Terence; and, in Greek, Homer above all, but also the tragic poets, especially Euripides, and other writers.

At the age of about fifteen Cicero will have passed on to higher education and the subject that dominated it: rhetoric. In the late 90s we find Cicero with his brother and cousins, the sons of Visellius Aculeo, and possibly other boys, frequenting the learned men who lived, as was common for those of their class,

7

as dependants in the house of a great man, Lucius Crassus. It is pleasant to picture him in Crassus' house on the Palatine, so famous in its day for elegance, though soon overtaken by the growth of luxury: there were columns of Hymettan marble – marble was still rare among the brick and tufa of Rome – and fine shady trees. Cicero often heard Crassus conversing with his scholarly friends, and met his wife too; he remembered later what pure, old-fashioned Latin she spoke.

Crassus' teachers were probably the best available in Rome; and they were probably all Greek. Cicero seems to have received most of his rhetorical training in that tongue; he says that since it was a richer language that Latin, and since the best teachers were all Greek, this was only natural. In fact his teachers prevented him from going to the newly founded school of Latin oratory run by a friend of Marius; they seem indeed to have influenced L. Crassus to close it when he became censor, though there may also have been political reasons for his action. Education at Rome was probably more Greek at this time than ever before or after; for when Cicero himself had enriched the Latin language and brought Roman oratory to full maturity there was less need for rhetorical training to use Greek models and, in the generation after his, Vergil and Horace provided the *grammaticus* too with texts that could rank with and even to some extent replace Greek literature.

Not that Cicero did not carefully study all such speeches in Latin by prominent orators as were available, especially those of Crassus. We knew that he did so. But it will have been mainly in Greek that he went through the various preliminary exercises, and in Greek that he finally attained to the practice of what was soon to be called 'declamation', the delivery of speeches on imaginary problems, legal or political. (Should Rome, victorious over Carthage, raze the city to the ground? How should Orestes defend himself on trial for the murder of his mother Clytemnestra? Or there were tricky cases like the following: suppose by law all sailors who abandon ship lose their claim to vessel and cargo, suppose that in a storm the owner of a ship leaves it to guide it from a boat attached by a rope, the owner of the cargo falls on his sword, and a shipwrecked sailor they had rescued gets the ship into port – the would-be suicide then recovers and all three claim both ship and cargo. This is plausible compared with some of the problems set at a later period.)

It is most probably of this stage in Cicero's education that

Plutarch declares that the parents of other boys came to the school especially to hear him, so remarkable was his promise. This, if true, must have fed the passion for glory that always drove him on; from a boy, he said, he was in love with Homer's line 'always to be the best and far to excel all others'. But ancient education as a whole strongly encouraged emulation, and so did many aspects of both Greek and Roman life.

Rhetoric by this time had long been reduced to a system of rules that Cicero himself later regarded as narrow and artificial. They could indeed encourage superficiality of thought and conventional forms of expression; they could also encourage elegance, clarity and a sense of proportion, qualities of which Latin literature was still in need, and like any strict literary convention they were not incompatible with, and could even give force and direction to, genuine feeling and, within limits, originality. A more serious objection, perhaps, was that the end of rhetoric tended to be persuasion rather than truth, while the extravagant subjects set for the budding orator to prove his skill on often stimulated ingenuity rather than serious thought about important problems.

Some of these very criticisms were made by the philosophers, who for centuries had fought with the rhetoricians over the education of the young. On the whole they had lost the battle, but it still swayed back and forth, each side at times annexing part of the other's territory, and occasional truces being made – Cicero was later one of those who tried to reconcile the two parties. It was when still a boy that he got his first introduction to philosophy, at the hands of a distinguished adherent of the Epicurean school; at first he was carried away by the doctrine, and though he later decisively rejected Epicureanism as a superficial, even an immoral, doctrine, he retained his respect and admiration for this first master – even though Phaedrus was prone to lose his temper when Cicero took to arguing with him (the Epicureans were always dogmatic). It is impossible to say whether he was most impressed by the Epicurean teaching on physics, with its atomic theory, on theology, according to which the gods were remote from the earth and took no care for mankind, or on ethics, which rejected public service and recommended aiming at a life of detachment from disturbing involvements, except for those dictated by mild personal affection – an ideal that was, as Cicero later pointed out, rather misleadingly claimed to be a life devoted to pleasure. Since Socrates,

9

Greek philosophy had been centrally concerned with the ethical problem of how to live; and though it is true that Cicero was interested in many technical questions of logic and epistemology, on the whole the Romans took this concern even further. The traditional, legalistic Roman religion (though it gave morality more place than is sometimes supposed) could not provide an educated man with a reason for living or help him to peace of mind; and of the Greek and oriental mystery religions now seeping into Italy most of the upper class, guardians of the national tradition, were suspicious. The mass of the people, and perhaps the majority of educated men, were pious or even thoroughly superstitious; but for many of the latter a conversion to philosophy, that often came in adolescence, fulfilled some of the functions that a conversion to religion had in later times. Indeed philosophy did not exclude a rationalized, purified religion. No doubt Cicero, in his traditionally minded family, will have been brought up to take part in the household rites of the hearth and its guardian spirits and of the family dead; he will have been present at sacrifices to the gods, where animals might be slaughtered or cakes and libations of wine or other liquids offered. The more important Roman gods had long been identified with the Greek pantheon – Jupiter with Zeus, Minerva with Athena, Venus with Aphrodite and so on; the less important were still bare personifications, without myth or character, of activities, dangers or places. But though Cicero was not an atheist and indeed thought religion had an important part to play in political life, it meant little to him in practice; his letters hardly mention the subject. For him, as for so many, philosophy filled the gap.

For all young Cicero's excitement with philosophy, some of his first ambitions seem to have been poetic. If we are inclined to think this not unusual with clever and sensitive young men, we should remember that poetry was only now beginning in Rome to be regarded as a proper subject for a gentleman's leisure. Cicero wrote a good deal of verse from the late 90s, almost all of which is lost. He was encouraged by the Greek poet Archias (whom he later defended in the courts); a famous improviser and the protégé of L. Crassus and many other nobles, whose military exploits, when appropriate, he celebrated.

But for the Roman upper class there was only one road to real distinction, that through public life; in the last resort it was only this that they took seriously, only the rewards of this that they valued: 'position, authority, magnificence at home, reputation and influence abroad, the purple-bordered toga, the ivory chair of office, the symbols of power, the lictors' rods, armies, commands, provinces'. So Cicero was to catalogue them; and these were what he set himself to pursue.

2

AT THE FOOT OF THE LADDER
90-77 B.C.

In normal circumstances, however, a young man from Cicero's background could not expect to reach the top. Marius' success had not been achieved in normal circumstances, and it also seems unlikely that the Cicerones approved of his alliance with *popularis* politicians; and most improbable that Cicero proposed to rise as a soldier. But there was another possible model. M. Aemilius Scaurus, who had been so complimentary to Cicero's grandfather, was, it is true, of a very ancient family, belonging to the earliest aristocracy of Rome, the patricians, who now formed only a minority among the nobles; but his branch had long been obscure, he had inherited a very small property (with, we are told, only ten slaves) and he had had to make his way up 'like a new man'. His political ability had enabled him to become consul, censor and Leader of the Senate (the ex-consul asked first for his opinion), and to contract a marriage alliance with the then supremely powerful Metelli, Marius' early patrons. Cicero says that it was he (or his example; his language is unclear) who encouraged him to enter political life with the hope of high distinction. And Cicero had one weapon that Scaurus lacked – the promise of high distinction in oratory.

It is possible that his family's patrons not only helped Cicero to decide on a political career, but to some extent determined his political policy and style. Scaurus was a firm optimate; he resisted attacks on the authority of the Senate for over thirty years, Cicero tells us. L. Crassus, also after a *popularis* escapade or two in early youth, had become another staunch defender of the Senate and its powers. But Scaurus had influence with the People and probably with those of the *equites* whose commercial and financial interests often put them at odds with the Senate. And L. Crassus was ready to use the popular support he had gained in early days, and to address the People in a highly conciliatory manner, employing all the resources of *popularis* oratory for conservative ends. His greatest speech was delivered in the year of Cicero's birth, and persuaded the People to end the

12

monopoly of the juries held by the *equites*, who were using it to harry senators. To Cicero in youth this speech was the high point of Roman oratory, and in old age he still quotes it with admiration: 'save us from our wretchedness, save us from the fangs of men whose cruelty can only be satiated by our blood; do not let us be slaves to others, unless to you alone, the whole People, to whom we may and should be servants'.

The stiffer optimates strongly disapproved of such language; but Cicero, though always believing that the Senate should rule, was ready to flatter the People in a similar way. And his belief that the statesman should be 'wisely *popularis* for the sake of unity', and his lifelong attempts to reconcile classes and parties, may spring to some extent from his early connections with Scaurus and Lucius Crassus. Both these men were behind the legislation of Livius Drusus in 91, which attempted to solve some of the most pressing problems of the day (notably the question of the Italian allies' desire for citizenship, and that of the juries, temporarily back in equestrian hands) in a fundamentally optimate fashion with some *popularis* top-dressing. The laws however ran into opposition and were rescinded. But before this happened Crassus was dead, having been taken ill while making a last great speech in the Senate, in which he defended the authority of that body. Cicero describes himself and his companions coming to the Senate House to gaze at the spot where that last swan-song, as he calls it, had been delivered; and later in life he frequently spoke of both Scaurus and Crassus as among Rome's wisest statesmen.

Cicero was not yet ready to follow in their path. If rhetoric and philosophy were the pillars of Greek higher education, the Romans, for those entering public life, added law. (The Roman legal system was already more developed than the Greek; 'it is unbelievable,' says Cicero, 'how confused and almost ridiculous other systems of civil law are compared with ours'; but nonetheless it was an extraordinary tangle of statutes and precedents.) As a boy, Cicero tells us, he learnt by heart the Twelve Tables, the ancient body of law – an educational custom that had died out when he wrote of it. In 90 B.C. when he was sixteen and had come to man's estate by exchanging the toga with a purple stripe, worn by children, for the plain *toga virilis* of natural wool, his father took him to the eighty-four-year-old jurisconsult Q. Mucius Scaevola (father-in-law of Crassus) who, after a distinguished political career, was, by the Roman custom, acting

as a consultant and informally taking a few pupils. The young
men would gather in his house in the early morning, when he
gave advice to all who asked for it, and would accompany him,
with other dependants and friends, if he went to the Forum, where
the courts were situated. In knowledge of law, Cicero later considered himself inferior only to the real specialists, such as Servius
Sulpicius Rufus, another early acquaintance with whom he formed
a lasting friendship; he always retained a liking for the subject,
combined with contempt for its more pettifogging aspects. One
of its attractions for him was its historical interest. All Romans
looked back to the past and were deeply convinced of the virtues
and wisdom of their forefathers, but Cicero was to develop a
somewhat deeper and more sophisticated historical interest than
most of his compatriots, who contented themselves with praising
the past in general terms and studding their speeches with acceptable historical anecdotes and examples. At some time in his
youth he laid the foundation for this interest by studying with
the first prominent Roman-born grammarian and antiquarian,
Aelius Stilo, who not only explained obsolete words but, himself
a strict optimate in sympathies, provided his noble friends with
historical information for their political speeches – the contemporary political crisis, with its rival interpretations of the
ancestral constitution, was partly responsible for this first flower-
ing of antiquarianism. It was, it should be noted, the past of
Rome which inspired Cicero and with which he enthusiastically
identified himself; in spite of his Italian ancestry, he never cared
for the traditions of other peoples in Italy, unlike for example his
friend the learned Nigidius Figulus, who was an expert on Etruscan religion.

Scaevola, it used to be thought, helped Cicero in another way
to find inspiration in the Roman past, by reminiscences of his
youth in the circle of Scipio Aemilianus, the destroyer of
Carthage in 146 B.C., who united traditional Roman virtues
with a newly thorough Greek education. But it has recently
been argued that this circle was much less extensive and intellectually dominating than has been thought, and Scipio himself
less influenced by his Greek friends and less concerned with the
values of *humanitas* or civilized behaviour; it has also been
claimed that although Cicero was undoubtedly interested in
Scipio and his generation he only acquired detailed knowledge of
them fairly late in life and on the basis of literary records. So it
may well be that others, particularly L. Crassus, should be re-

garded as having more part in Cicero's intellectual formation than the 'Scipionic Circle'.

Among the other pupils with Scaevola (who seems to have been an agreeable and humorous old man) there was, in all probability, a young man two or three years older than Cicero, T. Pomponius, later to be called Atticus from his long residence at Athens. He came from an old Roman family, some branches of which were active in politics if not strictly 'noble', though he was himself to stay in private life like his immediate forebears. Like Cicero (as his biographer, Nepos, reports) he had excelled in his studies; they had listened to Phaedrus together (Atticus was to remain nominally an Epicurean); and the friendship that sprang up between the two was to endure till Cicero's death, though it is clear that in the earlier years the bond between them was nothing like as close as it later became, and was certainly weakened when young Pomponius settled in Athens in the early 80s to avoid the political dissensions of Rome. Marius' son was also studying with Scaevola, but of him Cicero has nothing to tell us and it seems unlikely that the families were encouraging contact. Several other friendships, however, mostly with young men of high but not supremely grand birth, may have been made at this time. At any rate, the upper-class world in Rome was a small one; we know that Caesar, for example, six years Cicero's junior, had been known to him and his brother from early days; the two families lived fairly near each other, and indeed were connected through Marius. There was probably also a remote connection with Cato's family. Arpinum, we should notice, has faded into the background: Cicero's education and early life place him firmly in a Roman, and an aristocratic Roman, milieu; though it is true that some of his most relaxed friendships, as we can see from the letters, were to be with men of the equestrian status and Italian background from which he sprang himself. He was to write that like all Italians with Roman citizenship he had two fatherlands, one by nature and the other by adoption, and that though both were dear, the greater must also be the dearer.

Cicero's life of study was rudely interrupted. When L. Crassus' protégé Drusus failed in his attempt to enfranchise the Italian allies, they turned in desperation to revolt. By a mixture of concession and brutality the Romans succeeded in suppressing the movement, but there was a couple of years' hard fighting. The old regulation that every aspirant to office had to do several

15

campaigns' military service had fallen into disuse; but in the War of the Allies Cicero served on the staff of Pompeius Strabo, where he perhaps first met two of the men who were to have most influence on his life: his general's son, almost exactly his own age, whom we know as Pompey, and his future opponent, Catiline; these were both serving with Strabo, as a famous inscription records. Cicero was certainly present at a conference with an Italian leader who expressed his regret at having to meet the Romans as an enemy. After this he joined Sulla and his army in Campania; it is noteworthy that he did not serve with Marius, who was also employed in the war, but with Sulla, the dissipated but able patrician who had for some time been Marius' bitterest enemy. This was Cicero's only experience of warfare until he went out, unwillingly, to govern a province in 51; a good deal less than most of his contemporaries had.

The war had transformed the political situation by equipping all prominent politicians with an army apiece, and close to Rome at that; while Marius' previous (and inevitable) army reforms, by which landless peasants eager for booty while under the standards and for allotments of land on discharge, came to form the backbone of the army, had led to a dangerously close link between soldiers and their general – for it was the general, not the State, who was responsible for fulfilling their demands. When Marius, again in alliance with a tribune, attempted to replace his rival Sulla in a great command to chastise King Mithridates of Pontus on the Black Sea, who had overrun Asia Minor and the Roman province there, Sulla set a terrible precedent. He marched on Rome with his army – though most of his officers refused to follow him (Cicero was probably no longer with them) – and forced the restitution of his command. Marius fled, to return with another army after Sulla's departure to Asia. The old man initiated a massacre of his enemies in Rome, but died after a few days of his seventh consulship in 86, leaving affairs in the hands of his friends, led by Cornelius Cinna.

Cicero was in Rome when Marius returned from exile, for he heard a speech to the People in which Marius described his sufferings and boasted that they had not broken his spirit. But the family was not likely to approve of the new régime. Various distinguished friends, including M. Antonius, perished horribly in the massacres of 87; and there was an attempt to assassinate Q. Mucius Scaevola, the High Priest, to whom, on the death of his cousin of the same name around this time, Cicero had transferred himself as a pupil. Even more learned than his cousin, Scaevola had been a close friend of L. Crassus.

It has recently been claimed that the rule of Cinna and his friends was more reputable than scholars used to believe, and that fewer nobles fled to join Sulla in the East than his propaganda made out. This may to some extent be true; but looking back at the period Cicero saw it as a grim and lawless epoch, though for three years free from actual fighting. As Mithridates was thrown back from Greece and the Aegean coast of Asia, and consequently Sulla's return with a victorious army became imminent, Scaevola, who advocated negotiation, saw his own position in Rome increasingly precarious; but he refused to leave the city to take refuge with the invaders. 'He used to say that he foresaw his fate, but that anything was better than to join an army marching against his country'; the words came back to Cicero as Julius Caesar prepared to march on Rome nearly forty years later. Indeed in 82 Scaevola was successfully murdered. Cinna and his friends tried to exploit the magic of Marius' name, making his son, who was well under the proper age, consul; but their position began to disintegrate and more and more prominent men, among them, in spite of a somewhat *popularis* background, the young Pompey, seeing the way things were moving, went to join Sulla, who was able to crush his enemies and take supreme power in Rome, claiming to represent 'the cause of the nobility'. He initiated a massacre, soon formalized into proscriptions, in which many more perished than had died at Marius' hands.

In these years Cicero had not attempted to enter public life. He was too young for important elective office, but many Romans started activity in the law courts, where political support was built up and political alliances and feuds pursued, at a very early age. His family seems conspicuously not to have tried to make political capital out of their links with the younger Marius, or with a closer relation, a Gratidius adopted into the Marian family, who as Marius Gratidianus was one of the most powerful and most thoroughly *popularis* politicians in Rome in the mid-80s. The stories Cicero tells of him all illustrate his dishonesty, and he was deeply implicated in the Marian massacres. At any event, when Sulla made a clean sweep of his enemies the Cicerones do not seem to have been in danger. (They were incidentally also left as indisputably the most important family in Arpinum.)

Later Cicero was grateful for the delay that prolonged his education: 'I came to the Forum not, like most men, for my training, but, in so far as I could be, already trained.' Meanwhile he listened eagerly to such speakers as were still active, above all the highly promising Hortensius, eight years his senior. He continued his rhetorical exercises: 'I declaimed, as they call it now, often with M. Piso or with Q. Pompeius [two young nobles], at any rate with somebody every day, and I did this a great deal in Latin too, but even more in Greek.' Above all, this was the period in which he really fell in love with philosophy. In about 87 Philo of Larisa, the head of the Academy, the school founded by Plato 300 years earlier, came to Rome with other prominent Athenians as a refugee from Mithridates, and Cicero, 'inspired by an extraordinary zeal for philosophy', sat enthusiastically at Philo's feet; a close relationship between master and pupil was an essential part of ancient higher education, and especially of philosophic education. The views of the Academy had moved a long way at this time from those of their founder, though its radical scepticism could and did claim some affinity with the inquiring spirit of Socrates and the early Plato. Although Cicero called Plato his god, adoring him above all for his moral and political seriousness, and for his eloquence and vaulting imagination, there were many aspects of his work, such as the famous theory of Ideas, which he did not accept; while Plato's stress on mathematics, not a subject pursued in its higher reaches by the practical Romans, would have rapidly got him out of his depth. Scepticism, with its habit of arguing both sides of a case, was perhaps naturally attractive to one trained in rhetoric; though Philo was not the complete Sceptic that some of his predecessors had been, and had come to argue that probable, even if not certain, views can be formed and acted on. Unusually for a philosopher, he did himself teach rhetoric, and though we do not know that Cicero studied this with him, Philo's influence may have helped Cicero to his belief that the true orator should also be a philosopher.

At about the same time or a little later Cicero also learned the rival doctrines of Stoicism; the Stoic Diodotus was or became a direct protégé of his and lived in his house to the end of his life, impressing his pupil with the way he managed, after becoming blind, to continue his varied interests, even his teaching of geometry, with greater energy than ever. Stoicism was perhaps the most vital school of the day, and in a somewhat adapted form it had already for a generation inspired some of the best of the Roman aristocracy. In its original purity, with its dogmatic tenets on cosmology and divine providence, and with its utterly un-compromising ethical teaching, centring in its picture of the wise man indifferent to all worldly fortunes and unmoved by emotion, it impressed Cicero, but he could not make it his own. But he was much influenced by many aspects of the modified Stoicism of his day. He also owed to Diodotus a training in dialectic, the art of philosophical debate, that had been so important a part of Greek philosophy since Socrates. It was 'to be considered as compressed and concentrated eloquence', he thought, and with-out it true eloquence could not be attained.

Some time in the 80s, he planned a large work on rhetoric, of which he wrote only the first part, that on 'invention', the finding of arguments and ideas in a speech (the other standard divisions of the subject were organization, style, the training of the memory and delivery). It was one of the first technical works on rhetoric in Latin, and is the earliest of his own writings to survive. He later dismissed it as immature, and much of it is in-deed dry and conventional, with its fifteen topics that can inspire indignation and sixteen that evoke pity. But if the general intro-ductions to the two books that he actually wrote were not added later (and however much they owe to Greek prototypes), they show that Cicero formulated very early in his career various ideas that were to remain important to him. In the first, he asks whether oratory does more harm or good. He answers that it can do more good than anything else: it was responsible for the creation of society and civilization, by urging primitive men to band together; but it must be united with wisdom, that is, with philosophy, as it was in Scipio Aemilianus and others. In the second book Cicero declares that he will take his material from all the writers of the past, from Aristotle down, who have dealt with the subject; but that for his own part he will not be dogmatic and stands ready to be corrected. The lofty task of eloquence, the supreme im-portance of social and political matters, the value of tradition but also of independent judgement, the possibility of error: all this is fundamental to the outlook of the mature Cicero, and was probably largely taken over from Philo.

He was also still writing poetry: mythological narratives, possibly about this time his poem on Marius, a translation of the Greek poem on astronomy by Aratus; he always remained proud of this last, and may even have produced a revised version con-siderably later. His work was much admired at the time, which happened to be very barren of poets; it was probably handed round privately rather than published, though the distinction, before the invention of printing, is a fine one. Although, on account of certain unfortunate passages in later works, and the immense developments of the late Republican and Augustan ages in poetry, his verse ultimately became something of a laughing-stock, the fragments that remain – mostly because he was prone to quote himself – suggest that it was technically accomplished for its day and even, possibly, influential in refining the language and developing some of the characteristics, notably an infusion of personal feeling, later typical of Latin as opposed to Greek poetry. It was of course, like most verse in this period, heavily influenced by rhetoric. But even the Aratus translation is, com-pared with its original, inclined to be over-explicit; and Cicero's basic impulse was perhaps not really poetic at all. Significantly, he is said to have remarked that the Greek Lyric poets were not worth serious study as they dealt with trivialities; this may have been spoken by a character in one of his dialogues, but he cer-tainly shows little knowledge or love of these writers. He seems to have regarded his own verse as an exercise in linguistic virtu-osity, a possible path to the glory he so desired, or at most as something to inspire himself or others to moral or political excel-lence. He wrote much too easily – 500 lines a night, says Plutarch. Tacitus was to observe that 'Caesar and Brutus also wrote poetry, not better than Cicero, but with better luck, for fewer know that they did so'.

It is a picture of a well-spent and studious youth that Cicero draws. The picture may not be too one-sided. In one of his speeches he asks why there are so few good orators: 'it is because one must despise every pleasure, abandon the search for enjoy-ment, renounce all frivolity, amusement, social occasions, almost the very conversation of friends and family'. He was always hard-working in the extreme, though he was sociable and at times high-spirited. He may have allowed himself in youth a few of the dinner parties that later on he so enjoyed; the letters reveal no very serious interest in the food and wine, as opposed to the company and conversation (his digestion is said to have been delicate); and when once, in late years, he found himself in fast company at a dinner party, notably that of a notorious actress and courtesan, Cytheris, whose very name evoked the goddess of love, he wrote to a friend that 'as you know, even in my youth I was not attracted by this sort of thing'. While in middle life at least he was handsome and elegant, we know of no affairs of the heart, though it is not very significant that in his late philosophic work he agrees with at any rate some Stoics in attacking the irrational and irresponsible passion of sexual love. Whether he had felt it we cannot say; though he would have been thought by most an odd, and not an especially admirable young man, had he had no sexual experience before marriage.

Equally clearly he had never cared for sport, though it is probable that for a year or so, as was usual, he participated in the physical training, seen mainly as a preparation for military life, that young Romans went through outside the city walls on the Field of Mars beside the Tiber. Here they ran races, practised javelin throwing and swam in the river. However boring he found this, Cicero is likely to have been conscientious over it; physical fitness was vital to the strenuous life of the orator, and in one of his rhetorical works he speaks of it as gained on the playing-field or even by the practise of arms. There is no sign that he was any more interested in the common country pursuit of hunting. And what he enjoyed at the 'games' that formed part of various religious festivals or special celebrations was not the gladiatorial combats – though he once tried tentatively to justify these, at least as they had existed in the past, as a way of hardening the spectators' nerves – or the wild beast shows, but the theatrical productions; he often quotes plays or refers to events on the stage. The most creative period of the Roman theatre was over, though Cicero was able to know the last of the famous tragic authors, Accius, by then a very old man; but there were many opportunities to see the best tragedies and comedies of the second century B.C., adapted from Greek originals, while there were also less literary but more indigenous forms of comedy. There were sometimes also performances in Greek. In these early days Cicero also knew the famous Roscius, who appeared with immense success in both tragedy and comedy, and who, most unusually for a Roman actor, was of free birth and accepted in good society (to maintain his position there he took no fees in his later years). This interest on Cicero's part is not surprising; the actor's art was agreed to be in many ways similar to that of the orator, who not only used all the resources of his voice – including, to some extent, mimicry, as some figure of the past or present was summoned up in imagination to address the audience – but also movement and gesture. Plutarch says explicitly that Cicero modelled himself on Roscius and the other great actor of the day, Aesopus, with whom he was also acquainted; though

21

Cicero himself was repeatedly to insist that the orator's style should not be identical with the actor's. He may perhaps not have used – he certainly never discusses – the whole language of gesture described by a later Roman writer, who tells us for example that 'amazement is shown by turning the palm slightly upward and closing the fingers one by one, the little finger first, and then opening them in the reverse order'; but he certainly thought that in the right place the speaker might stride up and down, or strike his brow or thigh. (His actual delivery, we are told by a later source, was, by comparison with some, slow and distinct.)

It is worth noting that Cicero would not seem, however, to have fully understood the important musical aspects of the theatre. In many plays much of the dialogue was sung; but a character in one of his philosophic works is made to speak wonderingly of those who can recognize a tragedy from the first notes of the accompaniment, and we may assume Cicero was not among them. Indeed at this time music was not so highly regarded an art, and not so recognized a part of a liberal education, as it had been in archaic and classical Greece. Gentlemen no longer automatically learned to play the lyre or flute. True, Cicero's Stoic teacher Diodotus practised music in the old fashion of the Pythagorean philosopher–mystics, as a purificatory ritual; but his pupil clearly thought this rather strange, and did not emulate him.

Under Sulla's dictatorship Cicero, now twenty-five, at last began his public career; not that he gave up study – his first lessons with the rhetorician Molon of Rhodes, who was visiting Rome on an embassy, date from this period. From the year 81 comes the first of his speeches that survives, though incompletely. When their usual advocate proved to be unavailable, Roscius persuaded his brother-in-law, who was engaged in a suit over some property, to give young Cicero an opportunity. The other side had retained Hortensius and a prominent ex-consul, and in a Roman court the prestige or *auctoritas* of an advocate was as liable as his arguments to win him his case. It is probable then that the modest nervousness that Cicero professes in his opening is genuine enough – indeed he claimed towards the end of his life always to have been nervous before a big case. He now begged the presiding magistrate not to be influenced by eloquence or the personal authority of an arrogant noble rather than by equity; and against the charge that his client and his client's agent had been Marians he retorted that so had his opponent – only *he* had changed his coat; but all such matters ought now to be forgotten. Already, perhaps, we hear his desire for unity in the state and for mild government. He probably won his case, and published his speech to mark his success.

In 80 came the speech for Roscius of Ameria, with which at one blow Cicero made his name. His brief was to defend Roscius, the son of a landowner in Umbria (no relation of the actor) on the charge of parricide, which as he argued had been trumped up by private enemies, themselves (he ingeniously insinuates) guilty of the murder. These, with the aid of an influential freedman of Sulla's, had also got hold of the man's property by having it sold up as though its late owner had been on Sulla's list of the proscribed.

This was the first murder trial since the proscriptions had ended, and many people were eager to see law and order reasserted by a condemnation. It was also Cicero's first appearance in one of the 'public' courts: criminal courts presided over, usually, by a praetor, but where verdicts were given by a majority of the large jury of fifty or more, which was since Sulla's victory composed again of senators. They were situated out of doors in the Forum, the official centre of Rome – the advocate, we are told, had to be prepared to speak in sun or wind, rain or cold – and they attracted crowds of onlookers of all ranks, amateurs of rhetoric or politics. What shouts of applause there were, Cicero complacently recalled later, at that rather exaggerated and juvenile passage of mine about parricide!

The said passage reminds us how far ancient rhetoric relied, in its most studied parts, on effects of repetition, balance and rhythm, here admittedly employed in a somewhat forced and mechanical way; but already in this speech Cicero shows that he could be plain and rapid where necessary. But if it had a great artistic success, the *pro Roscio* was also a political speech, though its precise importance is difficult to assess. Roscius, though himself a quiet countryman, had been able to mobilize various great nobles, patrons of his father, in his support. It is certainly to some extent as their mouthpiece that Cicero uses his opportunity to attack the arrogance and lawlessness of jumped-up foreign hangers-on, slaves and freedmen, of great men, a class that the Romans always hated and despised. Sulla himself is absolved from every breath of blame, and indeed compared to Jupiter Best and Greatest, while his cause is described as the rightful restoration of due rank and honour. Cicero also veils his disapproval of the proscriptions themselves, but he openly deplores the possibility that persecution may be extended to the children of the proscribed, and at the end he warns the nobility that only by being 'watchful and upright, strong and merciful' will they keep their restored privileges; and in a passage of simple eloquence, very different from the artificial conceits of the bright purple patch about parricide, he stresses the need to cure Rome of her recent disease of cruelty, which corrupts those citizens it does not destroy. When one recalls the sad fate of Cicero's early mentors – and that of Scaevola is referred to in the speech – it is hard to believe that this is not as sincere as it sounds.

Cicero declares that the great nobles who are present in court do not dare to speak out themselves, feeling that their views will be exaggerated and over-publicized; and he represents the other side as being thrown into disorder by the boldness of his attack on adherents of Sulla and on the state of the times. It is hard to say, however, how much courage Cicero really needed to show; Sulla had apparently already resigned from the dictatorship and many of the nobles closest to him disapproved of the proscriptions, while some at least wished to conciliate the people. How much influence the speech had it is also hard to say. As far as Cicero himself is concerned, he may well have hoped that by attaching himself to a group of nobles whose rights over him, springing from their 'benefits' and 'friendship', he eagerly proclaims, he had found successors to Crassus and the Scaevolae. Whether they helped him in the early part of his career it is impossible to say; there is no evidence that these particular connections meant much to him later.

Cicero took part soon afterwards in another important case with political ramifications, again as a critic of Sullan excesses, though this time the speech is lost. Much of Italy had been hostile to Sulla, and in revenge he had attempted, in the case of several communities, to reverse the enfranchisement granted to all Italy as a result of the War of the Allies. This was dubiously legal, and Cicero in representing a woman from Arretium (now Arezzo) in Etruria successfully challenged it. The decision did not entirely settle the general question; but by this act, and his defence of Roscius, Cicero may have gained the sympathy of many Italians and laid the foundations of his later following in Italy; though, now that the old distinctions in status were gone, the very fact that he came from a country town might influence Italians in his favour.

A third step also prepared his political career. It was perhaps in 79, to judge by the age of his daughter Tullia, that Cicero, now about twenty-seven years old, married. We know little of Terentia's immediate family, except that she had a half-sister (or conceivably cousin) who was a Vestal Virgin and who from her name was probably of patrician descent; and there had been Terentii of some distinction in Rome since the third century, one branch even rising to the consulship and thus technically noble. Terentia herself was undoubtedly rich; she is said to have had a great dowry, and her property is a recurrent theme in the letters. If she was an heiress, that would help to explain why we do not hear of male relations. Such a marriage into an urban family was almost *de rigueur* for an ambitious 'new man' from outside Rome. For many years the marriage, though doubtless not a love-match, was successful enough. Terentia, who was probably very young at the time of her wedding, developed into a strong-minded woman who, according to Cicero himself as quoted by Plutarch, took more interest in her husband's political career than she let him take in household affairs. There is some indication that she was pious; none that she cared for poetry or philosophy, as a few women of her time did (rhetoric and law were subjects for the men alone).

Almost at once, however, Cicero seems to have parted from his wife in order to go abroad. Plutarch says that it was through fear of Sulla that he left Rome; if so, he is perhaps wrong in singling out the case of Roscius rather than that of the Arretine woman. But it is not clear that these episodes were so very important; and Cicero is probably his own best witness, in a passage of intellectual autobiography to which there are no real earlier parallels in surviving classical literature.

I was at that time very slender and not strong in body, with a long, thin neck; and such a constitution and appearance were thought almost to promise danger to life, if combined with hard work and strain on the lungs. Those who loved me were the more alarmed, that I always spoke without remission or variation, using all the strength of my voice and the effort of my whole body. When my friends and doctors begged me to give up speaking in the courts, I felt I would run any risk rather than abandon my hope of fame as a speaker. I thought that by a more restrained and moderate use of the voice and a different way of speaking I could both avoid the danger and acquire more variety in my style; and the reason for my going to Asia was to change my method of speaking. And so, when I had two years' experience of taking cases and my name was already well known in the Forum, I left Rome.

It seems that he took with him his brother and his much younger cousin Lucius Cicero; they possibly also travelled with Cicero's friend Servius Sulpicius, and were doubtless accompanied by a number of slaves and freedmen. They will have stayed, on their journey, mostly in the houses of local notables, since inns were generally poor and disreputable places; we even hear of distinguished men camping on journeys. Probably the party travelled on horseback, unless Cicero's state of health was thought to warrant a carriage; older men often used litters. It is not surprising if Terentia was left behind; free as Roman women were in some respects compared with their Greek counterparts, they rarely ventured abroad.

Cicero had special reasons for visiting the East, but a grand tour of sightseeing and study in Greece and the Greek cities of Asia Minor was becoming common with young Romans of the upper class. We know what excited Cicero most in what he saw. He and his contemporaries were not visually insensitive; but the profoundly literary bias of education meant that for them the real thrill came from seeing places described by or associated with great men of the past. In Athens, where the party spent six months, it was not the sublime works of architecture, sculpture and painting that inspired them so much as the fact that for them the whole region was haunted by the famous figures of earlier days. Much later in one of his philosophical dialogues Cicero remembers or imagines himself and his friends, including Atticus whom they re-met in Athens, walking one afternoon a mile or so out of the city to Plato's school at the Academy, in hopes of finding it deserted at that hour. There, deeply moved by the scene, they talk of the other places rich in associations that they have visited. Quintus (who later wrote tragedies) speaks of the village of Colonus, with its memories of Sophocles and his play *Oedipus at Colonus*; Lucius, shyly, of going all the way to the beach where Demosthenes was said to have practised speaking, and of seeking out the tomb of Pericles. Marcus himself thinks of the places where the great philosophers lectured, and of how once, when he came to Metapontum in southern Italy, he could not wait to pay his respects to his host before rushing off to find the house where Pythagoras the mathematician and sage had died 400 years before.

The city of Athens was now in decay, and bore the marks of its recent siege and storm by Sulla. But it was not only the home of the great philosophical schools – independent, well-endowed institutions that appointed their own heads – but a centre for other teachers as well, with students coming from all over the civilized world. Here Cicero devoted himself chiefly to philosophy, studying with Antiochus, the new head of the Academy, who, partly under Stoic influence, continued the retreat from Scepticism further than Cicero altogether approved; but 'I loved the man, and he me'. He also accompanied Atticus to listen to the Epicureans. They will not have quarrelled on the subject; Atticus' Epicureanism sat lightly on him, and he never quarrelled with anybody. In fact much of Atticus' interest in the last few years had been directed to Athenian politics, in which his financial generosity and obliging nature had made him a great figure; he will have been able to introduce the visitors into all the best Athenian society. There is, indeed, a hint that they stayed in his house.

Cicero also kept up his practice of oratory with a good teacher. He was initiated, as Atticus had been, into the Eleusinian mysteries; he later wrote of their civilizing influence and their promise of bliss after death, but he may also have been stirred by the thought of the great Athenians who, too, had been initiates. According to Plutarch he not only visited Delphi but consulted the oracle, which was now far less influential than it had been. He certainly went south to tour the Peloponnese, where many of the famous cities now lay depopulated or in ruins. He was moved by the sight of Corinth, whose destruction by Rome seventy years previously, together with the last flickers of Greek independence, he later lamented: and he even saw a few of the inhabitants enslaved at the time and bought up by neighbouring communities. In Sparta, now of no importance except as a tourist draw, owing to its ancient and peculiar customs, he saw the notorious ceremony at which boys showed their power of enduring the lash, and the violent battles between bands of youths in which no holds were barred; in both events deaths were not rare.

Afterwards, with Quintus, he travelled through many of the great Greek cities on the coast of Asia Minor and studied with various leading rhetoricians. At Smyrna they visited Rutilius Rufus, an elder statesman and one of the first Romans to be a serious student of Stoicism, who had been driven into exile some fifteen years before by a notoriously unjustified condemnation. He had a link with Cicero through Scaevola the Augur. Much later Cicero pretended, in his dialogue 'On the Republic', that Rutilius had recounted to him this conversation of Scipio Aemilianus and his friends; he was of course here only using a literary convention. But it is difficult to imagine that Rutilius, who was or had been writing his memoirs, did not speak of the great men of the past whom he had known and lived among.

Finally Cicero came to Rhodes. Here he met and heard Posidonius the Stoic, a scholar of encyclopaedic knowledge and an influential figure in the intellectual life of the day. But his real purpose was to study with his old teacher Molon, who cultivated a somewhat more restrained style than most of the rhetoricians of the Asian mainland. He was

not only a pleader in real cases [most Greek rhetoricians were not] and an admirable writer, but excellent as a judge and critic of faults and a very wise teacher and adviser . . . And so I came home after two years not only more experienced, but almost another man; the excessive strain of voice had gone, my style had so to speak simmered down, my lungs were stronger and I was not so thin.

Indeed his physical health was never seriously to trouble him again. Plutarch says that he was fussy about taking walks and having massage at set times but, except in periods of distress, when anxiety invariably made him ill, the letters complain of nothing worse than occasional digestive trouble or sore eyes – the latter probably the result of incessant work at night, by an inadequate oil lamp. And in spite of such work he was able until old age to do without the usual afternoon siesta.

He came back to Rome to pick up his career where it had been broken off.

3

POLITICAL APPRENTICESHIP
76-7O B.C.

The political world to which Cicero returned was one beset with problems. Sulla had enlarged the Senate and reasserted its traditional power. All the weapons that had served to challenge that power were to be blunted or torn from its opponents' hands. He returned the courts to senatorial control; he bridled the tribunate, hamstrung the provincial governors, and seems to have decided to manage without censors (an occasional but very senior magistracy) or a permanent Leader of the Senate. He laid down a strict time-scheme for holding the main magistracies, forbade re-election to the consulship within ten years, and by increasing the number of praetors made it unnecessary, though not impossible, for a consul to control an army during his year of office, or for ex-consuls and ex-praetors, who usually proceeded after their magistracies to govern a province, to do so for more than a single year. On retiring from the dictatorship, and soon after from Rome, Sulla handed the machine over to his political allies, informally led by the respected Catulus. Everything was to work smoothly and automatically, giving no opportunities to over-ambitious men; though the Senate, indeed, retained the right to confer special commands in an emergency.

Sulla's work was more than a simple putting back of the clock; but it failed in its prime purpose. If the magistracies were all strictly regulated, the Senate itself, in the absence of censors, was entirely uncontrolled, and many of its members were soon to be found thoroughly misbehaving themselves, especially in their capacity as jurors. Sulla did little for the poor of Rome, who were left to nostalgic memories of the tribunes who had helped them, and to more than usual distress and fear of starvation owing to the plague of piracy throughout the Mediterranean and the expenses of the great wars on hand. Sulla's harsh measures in Italy, especially his forcible settlement of his veterans in many places, left the peninsula in turmoil. He had departed from the East without thoroughly defeating Mithridates, and had made for Rome before dealing with the Western provinces, occupied by

29

Marian governors. His own irregular career hardly encouraged the humble subordination to constitutional restrictions that he proposed for others. He exploited the loyalty of his own veterans and clients (perhaps also the wealth he had acquired) without attacking the institutions that allowed individuals to amass such resources till they could overshadow the state. He did not provide Rome with the police force she needed, whether because the treasury could not afford it or because he feared the power its commander might acquire. And finally, his constitution was simply too much of a straitjacket. If it suited someone like Cicero well enough – he could fill the gaps between office by activity in the courts and the Senate – it did not suit an ambitious soldier, who was condemned to repeated spells of unemployment between magistracies. In these circumstances it was not surprising that the ambitious young Pompey succeeded in bypassing the ladder of office entirely, extorting from Sulla and his political heirs an almost continual series of special commands – in Sicily and Africa, in Italy after Sulla's death against a Marian rising, and then in Spain against the ablest of the Marian generals, Sertorius; nor that Pompey, by 75 B.C., anxious that his coming return to Rome should be a beginning and not an end, and doubtless aware that he would get no more from the oligarchy, should be beginning to put out feelers towards its increasing vocal *popularis* opponents in Rome. Julius Caesar did not try to avoid the regular *cursus honorum*, but he chose to revive his Marian connections, no doubt judging that by acting as a *popularis* he would gain influence more rapidly than by orthodox measures, and perhaps also being genuinely disgusted by the corruption but too characteristic of the Sullan oligarchy.

Though Cicero may have realized that many senators were not heeding the warning he had given in the *pro Roscio*, he was fully occupied in building up that network of personal supporters essential to a politician in Rome, but to which he, unlike the great nobles, had not been born. (These called such activity 'the new man's industry', and despised it.) On his return from Asia he pleaded, he says, for a year in important cases: the tie of gratitude that bound a defendant to his advocate or patron (who received no formal fee) was one of the strongest in Rome, and one that the patron regularly exploited at election time. For this reason, Cicero, like most 'new men', confined himself to the defence. A prosecutor made enemies (all prosecutions were private, there being no state prosecutor). Thus the accusers in

important cases were usually either young nobles attracting attention or pursuing family feuds, or obscure near-professionals of
whom Cicero speaks with contempt and whose motives were
suspect to him, being either the rewards and privileges held out
by the laws to encourage such action, or the harrying of prominent men. No speeches survive from this stage in Cicero's career,
unless that in which he represented his old friend Roscius the
actor is to be dated here. The speaker he chiefly emulated and
began to rival was Hortensius, the dominating figure in the
courts at this time and a connection of many leading nobles.
Hortensius' style was what Cicero later called 'Asianic', showy,
rhythmical and pointed; it displeased the older generation in
Rome, and indeed, as Cicero came to think, was only suitable
for a young man. According to him, Hortensius was further remarkable for his outstanding memory, his fine voice and his
perhaps over-studied movement and gesture (which led to him
being compared, by adversaries, with an actor, and even, once, very
rudely, to a dancing-girl or mime). It is possible that the speech
of Cicero for Roscius the actor, mentioned above, and rather
unlike his other works in style, is closely based on the manner,
or rather one of the manners, of Hortensius. As a property suit
pleaded before a single judge, it cannot be grand, but it is full
of point and antithesis, rather than ample and flowing as Cicero's
style usually is. But of Hortensius' own work we have only
negligible fragments, as is the case with the other orators of
Cicero's day. Hortensius, it is true, was better heard than
read; but for some of Cicero's younger contemporaries there was
a fashion under the Empire. In the end, however, Cicero utterly
eclipsed them all.

On reaching the earliest possible age, that of thirty, Cicero
stood for the quaestorship, the first magistracy on the regular
ladder of office (he seems to have omitted the optional minor
magistracies). There is no evidence that he expected or found
any difficulty in securing election from the assembly of tribes.
The elections were held in July each year; harvest was over,
travel easy, and games and festivals helped to lure voters to Rome
– especially, this year, we may be sure, the people of Arpinum
and neighbouring districts, whom Cicero describes in one of his
speeches as gathering to support another favourite son. But since
their tribe, the Cornelian, was made up of various scattered areas,
there can be no absolute certainty that Cicero carried it with a
larger majority than he did the rest. Much would depend on

his and his friends' contacts of all kinds, and especially with the tribes' headquarters and officers in Rome, though it is unlikely that Cicero used these, as was often done, to distribute bribes, or gifts and favours equivalent to bribes. The elections themselves took place in the Field of Mars, where a roofless wooden structure stood, with divisions for each of the thirty-five tribes. Over the quaestorian elections a consul would preside, seated on a platform in his ivory chair of office, attended by his lictors, an augur to pronounce on omens, the tribunes, and probably also the candidates in their specially whitened togas (whence the name *candidati*). After a prayer, the voters were dispatched to the 'sheepfold'; most of them doubtless to the divisions that served the four urban tribes (indeed perhaps not all who belonged could get in, though many landowners who lived in Rome will still have been registered in rural tribes); some of the enclosures for the larger and closer rural tribes might be well filled, but those for small or distant ones might be almost empty. In their enclosures the voters, shepherded by tribe officials and by 'custodians' of high rank from other tribes, received wooden ballots covered with wax, on which they scratched the names, or perhaps only initials, of the candidates they favoured; one by one they crossed a raised gangway or 'bridge' to drop the ballot in a basket, and left the enclosure. There was a long delay while the custodians counted the votes; apparently next year's candidates seized the opportunity to do some canvassing. It must have been an excited and, in a Roman July, a very heated gathering. Ultimately the herald announced the successful candidates of each tribe, the order of announcement of tribes being determined by lot; as soon as a candidate was known to have carried eighteen tribes, a majority, he was considered elected, took an oath to observe the laws, and was formally returned.

There were at this time twenty quaestors a year, severally attached by lot with financial responsibilities to the treasury and to provincial governors; they could also act for the latter as deputies in other matters. It seems that the young gentlemen often did not take the financial side of their work too seriously, leaving it to the clerks of the small permanent civil service. Cato, who did fling himself into his duties, caused astonishment and confusion.

Cicero entered on his office on 1 January 75; he had been allotted Western Sicily. The island was the oldest of Rome's provincial conquests, and one that supplied much corn and other foodstuffs, partly exacted as tribute, to the city. Greek was generally spoken, both by the inhabitants of the old Greek colonies on the coast and the by now largely hellenized natives. Although the West of Sicily, before Rome's day, had long been controlled by Carthage, Punic traditions were probably now weak – except perhaps at the sanctuary of Astarte or Aphrodite on the lofty citadel of Eryx, where, among the slaves attached to the goddess, there were temple prostitutes; this practice was very rare in the Greek world, and was in fact now declining at Eryx, but a Sicilian historian remarked a few years later that when Roman officials visit the place 'they lay aside the severity of office and enter with great cheerfulness into play and intercourse with women'. Cicero must undoubtedly have visited the famous shrine, for it was particularly honoured by the Roman state, and one trusts he enjoyed himself.

He naturally also spent some time at Syracuse on the eastern coast, where his governor, who became a real friend, and another quaestor, resided; and he tells us of the pride and pleasure he took in discovering the tomb of Archimedes, the great Syracusan mathematician and scientist of the third century B.C.,

surrounded and covered with briars and thorns; the Syracusans did not know it, they even denied its very existence. But I knew some lines of verse, which I had heard were inscribed on his monument, showing that a sphere and a cylinder had been placed on the top of the tomb.* When I had run my eye carefully over the whole area – for there is a great mass of graves outside the Agrigentine Gates – I noticed a small column projecting a little way from the bushes, on which there was the shape of a sphere and a cylinder. I at once told the Syracusans (some of their leading men were with me) that I thought that was just what I was looking for. A number of men with sickles were sent in to clear the place; when a way in had been opened, we approached the front of the base: the epigram was visible, though the latter half of each line had been eaten away. And so one of the most famous of Greek cities, and once one of the most learned, would not have known the grave of its most brilliant citizen, if it had not learned it from a man of Arpinum.

One notices that Cicero's knowledge of a great scientist is literary; though only a junior magistrate, he is respectfully attended by leading Syracusans; and they none of them dream

---

* Archimedes had discovered the relation of the volume of a sphere and cylinder of the same height.

of pushing through the brambles, but summon workmen to clear the path.

The only other anecdote recorded of Cicero in Sicily comes from Plutarch, who says that he dedicated to the gods a piece of silver plate, with the name 'Marcus Tullius' engraved on it, and then a picture of a *cicer*, or chick-pea, by way of a pun on his surname. This had faintly comic overtones, and Cicero had apparently been urged to drop it; but Plutarch says that he replied that he would make it as illustrious as those of Scaurus and Catulus, which, as respectively meaning 'swollen-ankled' and 'puppy', were scarcely more flattering.

In his own part of the island Cicero devoted himself to his task of dispatching corn to Rome and saw to it that his clerks behaved themselves, or so he says. His main concern was still to extend his connections. Sicily was, it is true, particularly well provided with hereditary patrons at Rome – especially the Marcelli, descendants of the general who had conquered Syracuse in the Hannibalic War (and failed to prevent Archimedes' death in its sack). The Marcelli, said Cicero, had honorific equestrian statues in every town in the island. But there was always room for more *patroni*. The speeches against Verres, a few years later, show how many prominent Sicilians Cicero claimed as his friends, and how many communities paid him honours. He continued to make use of his skill as a speaker; Plutarch says that he defended various noble Romans in the court presided over by his governor, though it is not clear who these can have been. Certainly he divided attention between the provincials proper and the large number of Romans who had settled in the island to make a living by business or farming, and were known as *negotiatores*. It was presumably to these last, since it was in Latin, that he addressed a lost speech in which he promised his hearers friendship and protection.

Many of these Romans would have been rich enough to count as *equites*. Cicero's relationship with this class is one of great importance. He was, of course, the son of an *eques Romanus* himself, but apart from members of senatorial families who had chosen not to enter the senate, the name covers both local aristocrats and the businessmen and financiers as well (even the wealth of these last would be largely invested in land, however). It is true that new men from the country-town aristocracy do tend to become the mouthpieces in the Senate of those Roman contractors and financiers whom we tend to think of as the *equites par excellence*, since both classes may easily get a grudge against the optimates, who could block their ambitions. This was the case with both Marius, in his time, and to some extent Cicero. But, while Cicero's grand early friends may possibly have wished to conciliate the leaders of the *equites*, on the whole these had been bitterly hostile to Livius Drusus and probably, in a great degree, to Sulla, who had cut down their privileges – though in expanding the Senate he had to put into it men, including recently enfranchized Italians, who were rich enough to keep up the position and thus were themselves *equites*. So Cicero had probably little to do with representing the interests of *negotiatores*, till his time in Sicily; and he was probably still not much concerned with the great businessmen in Rome, and particularly with the big companies of tax-farmers, who had fewer opportunities in Sicily than in some provinces; but will have dealt rather with the smaller traders and immigrant landowners. Many would be of Italian, especially south Italian, origin, the enfranchized descendants of the so-called *Italici* who swarmed over the provinces in the wake of the great conquests of the second century; so that Cicero's new supporters have links with his existing Italian ones.

Such a *clientela* as Cicero's in Sicily, though too distant to come often to vote for him (and in the case of the native provincials not entitled to do so) could nonetheless be of value in many ways to a Roman politician. Fame and honour, complimentary statues and inscriptions, clients thronging his house when on a visit to Rome, or sending to ask him to do business or exert influence for them, all redounded to the prestige or *auctoritas* so important in the political world; and there could be more concrete benefits.

Cicero returned from Sicily well pleased with himself; but he was to receive a shock, if we may believe a story he later told against himself (it rings true enough, but it is sometimes forgotten that in making a point in a legal speech he is hardly on oath about such a matter).

To say the truth, I believed that people at Rome were talking of nothing but my quaestorship. At a time when the price of corn was very high I had sent over a large quantity; I was thought to have been civil to the men of business, fair to the traders, generous to the tax-farmers, upright to the provincials and everyone thought I had been most conscientious in all my duties; the Sicilians had devised unparalleled honours for me. So I left my province expecting that the Roman people would rush to reward me in every possible way. On my journey home I happened to reach Puteoli [on the Campanian coast near Naples] just at the time when it is full of fashionable people. I almost fainted, members of the jury, when someone asked me when I had left Rome, and what was the news there. I told him that I was on my way back from my province. 'Oh yes,' he said, 'from Africa, I think.' I began to feel angry and said proudly, 'Not at all, from Sicily.' Then someone who thought he knew everything interrupted 'Don't you know our friend here has been quaestor at Syracuse?' I swallowed my irritation and became an ordinary visitor to the waters. But I believe the incident did me more good than if everyone had congratulated me. When I realized that the Roman People was hard of hearing, but had sharp and observant eyes, I stopped caring what people might hear of me, but took care that they should see me in the flesh every day. I lived in their sight, I was never out of the Forum; neither sleep nor my doorkeeper prevented anyone from gaining access to me.

He never left the Italian peninsula again (apart from a brief visit to Sicily on business) until dispatched against his will to Cilicia in 51. Perhaps for him this decision was right, though had he spent more time in the provinces he might have taken a longer view of Rome's interests, and had some of that sense of the pettiness of the squabbles in the capital that Caesar seemingly developed to excess.

Looking back, Cicero considered that it was after his return from Sicily that he came to the full maturity of his powers as an orator. There is only one partially surviving speech before the year 70, however, interesting for the glimpse it gives us of the world of the great cattle-ranches of southern Italy, run by large gangs of armed slaves, among whom violence and murder were endemic. This was a socially unhealthy phenomenon, as Cicero realized; so indeed must anyone have done who had lived through the dangerous slave rising of Spartacus in 73–71.

But Cicero was now automatically also a member of the Senate. The rank in itself was a great mark of distinction; so far, so good. But he was unlikely to be called on to speak by the presiding consul, since seniority of rank was strictly observed. Most of the 600 or so members of the house never got beyond quaestorian standing. They would busy themselves, if at all, on the juries or on committees. We have a chance sight of Cicero thus at work: in 73 he was among those who assisted the consuls to decide whether certain temple lands belonging to a city in Greece were liable to pay tax to Rome or not. The city won its exemption, and set up an inscription recording the decision on stone, as was normal Greek practice. By such activities Cicero will have made more useful connections abroad; we know, for example, from a late letter, that he was a patron of Sparta.

The next stage in a political career was to become one of the four aediles or ten tribunes, though neither office was in fact compulsory as the quaestorship was. An imperial historian, Dio, tells us that Cicero did not wish to antagonize the nobility by seeking the tribunate; but it was always possible to use a tribunate in the conservative interest. Cicero was perhaps influenced rather by the fact that the aedileship gave great opportunity for making a man known to and popular with the People without arousing political controversy; the aediles (two 'curule', two less grand, 'plebeian') were responsible for games, the food supply, and general conditions in the capital. Few ex-aediles met with a repulse in standing for the praetorship. So in 70 B.C. Cicero stood for (probably) the office of plebeian aedile.

It was a year of crisis. For some time the agitation for the restoration of the full rights of the tribunes had been growing in force; there was more real anger, Cicero was to claim, over the prevalent corruption, especially on the senatorial juries; he tells us, in speeches of this and subsequent years, horrific stories of the courts, involving men as distinguished as Hortensius, while Plutarch decribes the intrigues to which the proud and able Lucullus was said to have had to stoop to get the Eastern command against Mithridates, who was still restive (they involved a politically minded courtesan and her lover, a disreputable wire-pulling senator). There was feeling also about the conduct abroad of generals and governors, unchecked as they now were by fear of hostile equestrian juries.

At first the agitators were unimportant tribunes; but soon it was clear that Pompey was behind them. As it turned out, Pompey, on his return to Italy with his army from Spain, had to be called on to help the ex-praetor Marcus Crassus to save Rome from the serious slave revolt led by Spartacus, and in the circumstances it was not easy to oppose their joint candidature for the consulship of 70; though Pompey had never sat in the Senate at all. Pompey made his position clear in his first speech to the People as consul-designate: he would restore the powers of the tribunes, by which was meant primarily their right to propose legislation to the People without senatorial authorization, and to veto decrees of the Senate and the actions of other magistrates; and he was applauded when he touched on the question of remedying the scandals in courts and provinces. Probably he was already hoping to get a new command from the People in return; its right to grant emergency powers would become important again as soon as tribunes could legislate freely.

What sort of a man was Pompey? It is hard to tell, since Cicero, who was for many years closely associated with him, repeatedly complains of his disingenuousness: he simply cannot make out what Pompey would be at. In his earliest campaigns Pompey had been cruel and treacherous, earning the name of the 'boy executioner', as well as that of Magnus, the Great. But later he seems to have been by Roman standards humane, as well as fairly honourable in money matters, in spite of the huge wealth he amassed in the East and elsewhere. He was also thought to be genuinely fond of at least one of his wives, Caesar's daughter – though he had a tendency to change wives whenever he changed political direction, which he did repeatedly and entirely from calculation as to who would give him employment and influence. But he was not at home in the political intrigues of the capital; when he became consul, his scholarly friend Varro had to provide him with a special handbook on senatorial procedure, while he was embarrassingly prone to blush in public, especially in the assembly. No wonder then that he acted in Rome mostly through others. Indeed Pompey is always apt to disappear behind a smokescreen of both Greek and Roman friends, who represented his deeds as those of a second Alexander. Though he was determined to be the greatest man in Rome, he seems to have had no conscious desire to overthrow the constitution. Probably he may be summed up as a fundamentally decent man, a very able soldier and organizer but (as Cicero complains) without profound political views or principles, who was ruined by the temptations of ambition in a period when these were virtually overwhelming.

Marcus Crassus is the least attractive, and for all his disastrous end in the East the least truly tragic, of the dominating figures of the late Republic. He was of noble birth, and his father, a relative of Cicero's admired L. Crassus, had been a distinguished man, who was killed by the Marians in the 80s. The son fled to Spain and was hidden in a cave by friends (who provided him with two compliant slave-girls, one of whom was interviewed in extreme old age by a historian of the Augustan period). He returned to join Sulla, and was largely responsible for his victory just outside Rome over the Samnites of southern Italy. Plutarch traces his deep-seated jealousy of Pompey to this period. But he also alienated the Sullan oligarchy; he made too much money in the proscriptions, buying up property cheaply and, it was rumoured, even getting an innocent man on to the list for his wealth. His ruling passion indeed was a desire for money, perhaps not unconnected with his somewhat impoverished youth; but for him wealth was primarily a means to power. He is famous for his dictum that a man could only be called rich if he could maintain an army on his income. It has been said that he was one of the only two or three people whom Cicero really hated. At a late date, disclaiming all prejudice against a man long dead, Cicero painted a vivid picture of an unscrupulous figure ready, for example, to inherit money under a will he knew to be forged – why, he would have danced in the Forum for the opportunity (the last word in scandalous behaviour by Roman standards). Plutarch's biography adds such notorious but perhaps unreliable tales as that of the private fire-brigade, brought into action only when its master had bought up threatened property cheaply. He was an assiduous if uninspired advocate for the defence, wide-ranging if less than lavish in his hospitality, an agreeable and flattering companion (himself very susceptible to flattery), and ever ready to disburse his wealth in gifts and loans to embarrassed or ambitious politicians. Thus he put a great number of men under obligation to him, and was gradually building up influence in the Senate, at least in its lower ranks, and perhaps already among the *equites* too. His ambition for the consulship had probably recently been fired by his victory over Spartacus; he had restored discipline among his own troops by severe punishments, and marked his victory by crucifying 6,000 of the slaves along the Appian Way. Thus, though he hated Pompey and had no political convictions (he changed his friends, views and policy as his interest demanded, says Plutarch) he was ready in 70 to join Pompey in actions that would gain him popular support and damage the nobles who eyed him askance.

A law introduced by both consuls restored the tribunes' powers, and the consuls had censors elected, partly to purge the Senate: seventy-two members were thrown out, mostly it seems fairly obscure men, perhaps genuinely disreputable types thrust in by Sulla as a reward for services rendered, whom the great nobles could watch go without too much regret; while they must have been glad to see that the consuls were soon on poor terms with each other. In spite of this, however, some sort of proposals for reforming the juries seem to have been on the stocks by the summer.

Among the worst of the scandals of the late 70s had been Verres' three-year governorship of Sicily. Recent prosecutions for extortion had often come up against the senators' reluctance to condemn their peers, and their readiness to accept a share of the illgotten gains of the accused. Young Julius Caesar had twice failed in this way to get a condemnation. Nevertheless, late in 71 the Sicilians decided to sue Verres for the recovery of their losses. They got in touch with Pompey, the reforming consul-designate, and asked their new patron, Cicero, to take their case. Verres had powerful friends among the optimates, who prepared for a trial of strength over the issue and obtained the services of Hortensius (who received an ivory sphinx, one of the works of art removed from Sicily, for his trouble). It was clear that, in the excited state of public opinion, the case would make a great deal of noise.

Cicero could hardly have refused the formal request from his Sicilian protégés, and the case might bring him support from other provinces, most usefully that of Roman settlers – those in Sicily had suffered badly at Verres' hands. In the shorter term participation might reflect favourably on his prospects at the aedilician elections. Furthermore, though he had appeared both with and opposite Hortensius before, his comments in the *Brutus*, his history of Roman oratory, show that he regarded the case as a challenge to Hortensius' primacy in the courts. It has been suggested that Cicero also hoped, by a successful prosecution, to succeed to the rank in the Senate that Verres, an ex-praetor, would lose. Such rewards for prosecution were available under certain laws. It was however an invidious way to rise, especially for a 'new man', and it is perhaps unlikely that Cicero accepted his opportunity; it was possible to waive the rewards, and he declares in one of the published speeches that he is not prosecuting Verres in order to gain his 'spoils'.

In addition it is likely that Cicero's heart was to some extent in his case. It was not necessary to be an extreme *popularis* to think some reform needed. It is disputed to what extent the reforms of 70 were agreed to by optimate leaders, or constituted the real destruction of the Sullan system. But a number of prominent men who are seen cooperating with Pompey about this time may not have had personal motives only; and Cicero claims that the nobles were privately admitting that the situation was untenable, and that the eminent Catulus agreed that what the People wanted was simply honest government.

The nobles did not however intend to leave Verres in the lurch. They had a number of tricks up their sleeves. First of all a rival prosecutor appeared, according to Cicero intending collusion with the defence, and especially to make the case drag on into the following year, 69, when a number of Verres' most powerful supporters expected to be in key positions, and Hortensius indeed to be consul. Cicero however successfully pleaded his prior right to prosecute, and left for Sicily with his cousin Lucius to collect evidence. He was in a hurry, for Verres and his friends were now trying to get the extortion court occupied by another trial; and if Verres' case were not over by the middle of August, it would run into a series of festivals that made the later part of the year virtually useless for judicial business. In a much later speech Cicero represented himself in Sicily as seeking out witnesses in their distant cottages and at the tail of the plough, in stormy weather. After a whirlwind tour of fifty days, only half the time allotted to him, but productive of the most damning evidence, and after (he says) a dangerous voyage home in a small boat, he was back in Rome; to find that his opponents, in order to blunt the Sicilians' ardour, were declaring that he had been bribed not to fight the case seriously.

The dates of the next events are not quite clear. But on 27 July Hortensius was indeed elected consul, together with Verres' patron Q. Metellus. This shows how the nobles could keep their hold on the consulship even when public opinion ran against them – a matter partly of availability of qualified candidates and partly of the bias of the *comitia centuriata* towards over-representation of the rich, though in this case Verres' newly gained wealth also played a direct part. The result was equivalent to his acquittal, a friend told him in open congratulation. A few days later a brother of Metellus was elected praetor for 69 and assigned to the extortion court, where he would be able to hamper the prosecution (one may wonder if the lot was operating entirely unhindered). A third brother had already succeeded Verres in Sicily, where he could put pressure on the witnesses. Cicero had been torn between the preparation of the case and his own election campaign. In spite of Verres' money, which he claims was being spent heavily against him, he was elected aedile with gratifying ease, and this strengthened his position. But it was now quite clear that he must make haste. By, probably, almost superhuman efforts he got his case prepared, and on 5 August the trial began. A vast throng from all Italy and perhaps beyond was in the city for the elections, the census and Pompey's games, and the case opened in a blaze of publicity. With the permission of the presiding praetor Cicero self-sacrificingly omitted the lengthy opening speech, which the defence could have answered at equal length. He presented a short introduction, revealing (and perhaps exaggerating) all his opponents' recent machinations, and stressing that if the court had the face to absolve, the law to reform the juries, which had already been announced, would pass at once. He also threatened himself to prosecute any juror guilty of bribery. He then plunged straight into the evidence. This was so devastating that Hortensius refused to reply. Verres fled from Rome (with some of his looted valuables, which he kept till Antony, supposedly coveting them, put him on the proscribed list in 43), and the jury had no choice but to condemn him. It was 14 August; the games began on the 16th.

This dramatic story rests on Cicero's own account alone, but in its main lines it must be true. Probably as soon as he could, he published a written-up version both of what he had said and of what he might have said had the trial run its course, incorporating such masses of detailed evidence that his political purpose, of providing support for reform, is as obvious as his rhetorical one, of illustrating his own brilliant and varied handling of intractable material. He never did anything on the same scale again. The *Verrine Orations* are a mine of information on Roman maladministration, covering Verres' entire career (the courts at Rome were very lax about standards of relevance). They go into details as to his misdemeanours over the export and requisitioning of corn, his supposedly treacherous and lucrative dealings with pirates and his sweeping removal of all the best works of art from the temples, thus outraging the provincials' religious susceptibilities and entirely disrupting the tourist trade; the guides at Syracuse were reduced to showing people where the masterpieces had once been. Cicero moves from a solemn and poetic description of the spot near Enna where the god of the underworld carried off Proserpina, to pungently satirical narrative or detailed technical accounts of financial iniquities. Rome must have been dazzled. The trial of strength with Hortensius had ended in decisive victory, and Cicero must have become one of the most talked-of men in the city.

The speeches are not entirely disingenuous; it seems likely for

42

one thing that Cicero is covering up for those of his friends among the Roman settlers who had connived at or collaborated in Verres' misdeeds. From the political point of view he spoke, or at least wrote, moderately, not attacking prominent nobles by name or praising *popularis* politicians, and declaring that he wished the senatorial juries to clear their name by a just condemnation; it was only the few who were corrupt. This, to a senatorial jury, was only tactful; but the praise of the great days and great men of old is very Ciceronian, and he even approves the equestrian juries of the past, brazenly asserting that they never took bribes (in fact, they had never been made liable to prosecution on this charge). And some time in the autumn a law passed, which left one-third of the seats on the juries to senators, and may have been a modification of the earlier proposal, for the *Verrines* speak of transferring rather than sharing the juries. The author of this law, the praetor L. Cotta, was probably a genuinely moderate optimate; his brother Gaius had already in 75 passed some legislation favourable to the tribunate, though he was regarded as one of the ruling clique, and had originally been a pupil of L. Crassus. Cicero calls L. Cotta a friend of his, and probably approved of his action now.

Thus the constitution of 70 as it finally emerged may have been close to Cicero's ideal. The *equites* had recovered a voice in politics, the tribunate, which he later at any rate thought a necessity, if a regrettable one, was restored, and the censorship, which he was to consider a vital weapon in the cause of order and morality, had been revived (Scaurus and L. Crassus had both been censors and may have thought highly of the value of the office). The instability of the balance established in 70 was at first not revealed; the next few years were quiet ones. The *equites* did not use their strength in the courts to persecute the nobles, the *popularis* were content to act as watch-dogs, and Pompey bided his time.

4

THE BID FOR THE CONSULSHIP
69-64 B.C.

These were also years very satisfactory to Cicero and his family. His aedileship passed off successfully in 69. It gave him, as he said in the *Verrines*, a purple-bordered toga and an ivory curule chair and, more permanently, a higher place in the Senate (and his son the right, after his death, of placing a bust of his father in his hall: though this room with its solitary portrait would draw attention to the contrast with the *atria* of the great families, crowded with the smoke-stained memorials of dozens of ancestors who had held high office). Cicero was not rich enough to make a great splash with the games, for which the aediles were accustomed to supplement the official allowance from their own purses, but his grateful Sicilian clients apparently saw to it that such quantities of foodstuffs were sent to Rome that the cost of living was kept very low, at a period when piracy in the Mediterranean probably usually made it high. Cicero gained much popularity in consequence. His brother Quintus had started auspiciously on his career, being elected quaestor probably for 68; he was not without ability, though he understandably avoided courting comparisons by public speaking (one orator was enough for a family and almost for the city, said Marcus), and though he probably owed much of his advancement to his brother's influence. Cicero himself returned to his pleas for the defence, making yet more useful contacts, senatorial, equestrian and Italian, or on occasion representing even humbler men. In speaking for a prominent Etruscan, he reasserted the Roman citizenship of his town, one of those which Sulla had tried to disenfranchize; the new censors probably accepted his arguments, and the question was henceforth closed, but it is not surprising that we find Cicero later enjoying great support in parts of Etruria.

One of the senators he defended was a governor accused of extortion in his province of Gaul, and Cicero has been, perhaps a little unfairly, criticized for palliating what he had denounced in the case of Verres; certainly he was willing to play on Roman contempt for barbarians in denying the Gauls' testimony all weight in comparison with that of the Roman settlers, who were on suspiciously good terms with the governor and may have been given by him far too free a hand. But the Gauls would not make Cicero such useful clients as the settlers; and the accused had links with Pompey, the most valuable of all possible allies.

Cicero was now the unchallenged master of the courts. Hortensius, he tells us, relaxed his efforts after his consulship, to enjoy a luxurious private life: 'the first few years took from his powers, as though from the colour of an old picture, which the ordinary man does not notice, only the expert and understanding critic', but later his decline was visible to all. Rather remarkably, Hortensius and Cicero were, or came to be, on fairly good terms; Atticus, who was a close friend of both, was in all probability largely responsible for this.

Cicero, unlike Hortensius, continued to study and improve himself. There was no one to compete with him in knowledge of literature, philosophy, law and history, no one who could raise laughter, anger or pity in the same way, no one who could vary a speech with an agreeable digression or raise a particular question to a general level, as he could; or so, certainly rightly, he later indicated. He himself describes the atmosphere in a public court when a fine speaker is pleading:

When it is known that he is going to speak, the benches are crowded, the tribunal full, the clerks are influential in giving or allowing space, there is a crowd of bystanders, the jury is all anticipation. When the speaker rises, the bystanders signal for silence, there are frequent expressions of agreement and admiration. They laugh as he desires, they weep as he desires. Even from a distance it is possible to tell, though one does not know what is going on, that the speaker is a success, and a Roscius is on the stage.

Dramatic, as this comparison suggests, many trials certainly were. Large delegations from distant towns or provinces came as character witnesses, the accused man's aged parents, or even better his small children, appeared in mourning dress and weeping to implore the court for pity. Cicero tells us that he once made his peroration with a baby in his arms. He excelled in such pathetic finales, in which, as he said, his intellect was less involved than 'a strength of feeling that makes me unable to control myself'; he also writes of giving the impression, by his passionate look and gesture, that he was unconscious of what he did.

As we have seen, standards of relevance were far from strict;

the whole life of a defendant was ransacked for scandal, and the various advocates, if as so often they were prominent politicians, might use the opportunity to justify their own activities or recommend their own policies. And elegant digressions, moralizing or descriptive, were prescribed by the rhetorical authorities. It must however be remembered that in his later cases Cicero was usually one of several advocates and speaking in the place of honour at the end, and that such mundane matters as refuting the actual charges in detail had already been dealt with; also that such refutation might seem of little permanent interest and be much condensed in the published version.

These versions were written, Cicero claims, when others were celebrating festivals and holidays. He brought with him into court only a fully written exordium, and for the rest of the speech mere notes. He took pains to use pure and correct Latin, avoiding archaic or dialect, poetic or slang terms, and any word that seemed heavy or clumsy. Latin, like French or English in the seventeenth century, at this point needed to develop such a smooth and lucid prose. But Cicero's Latin is rich too, with the long and well-constructed periods on the Greek model, which were his greatest gift to the language, their balancing phrases and words, and melodious cadences – an aspect of style to which listeners in ancient times were far more sensitive than we are; Cicero tells us of audiences that were moved to applause less by an orator's sentiments than by his rhythms. Contrary to popular opinion, however, it is only at appropriate places that these effects are used by Cicero, at least in his best speeches; in his best works, too, his flowing amplitude is not simply a preference for two words where one would do – an apparent synonym will add either a nuance of meaning or an improvement of rhythm.

By this period Cicero was also introducing others to political life. Just as he had been entrusted by his father to Scaevola, so in 66 a prosperous *eques* called Caelius sent him his clever and ambitious young son – to get experience rather than formal teaching no doubt. It seems certain that young Marcus Caelius must have been a responsive and enjoyable pupil, and he was sufficiently satisfied with Cicero to stay with him longer than was customary. There were, it seems, other young men in a similar position; it would be interesting to know if they included youths of noble family. Probably they did; M. Crassus' son Publius, who was devoted to Cicero, had perhaps been associated with him in this way, and the younger Curio, later so notorious.

With all this success, Cicero was subject to certain criticisms. His reputation as a 'philhellene' was not entirely in his favour, for many Romans still despised and distrusted Greeks and Greek culture; the fact that when collecting evidence against Verres he had made a speech in Greek to the city council of Syracuse was considered undignified by the governor Metellus, and in the *Verrines* Cicero finds it wise to pretend that he cannot remember the names of Greek artists such as Polycleitus. In addition, as Plutarch tells us, his irrepressible wit and irony, as exercised on his opponents in court, got him a reputation for being malicious. The jokes, as retailed by Plutarch – mostly personalities and puns – do not for the most part survive translation.

At the end of 68 the extant letters to Atticus, who was still living mainly in Greece, begin. They are thin on the ground at first, and some may be lost, though both correspondents complain of the other's negligence in writing. They deal mostly with family and business matters: Atticus' sister Pomponia had recently married Quintus Cicero; she was probably older, and richer, than her husband and they were not getting on very well – Cicero, who reputedly was responsible for the match, tries to smooth Quintus down, and reports that Pomponia is expecting a child; the baby was probably Quintus' only son, named after his father. Cicero also keeps an eye on Atticus' mother, and writes that Terentia has rheumatism but sends greetings, and is on excellent terms with Atticus' female relatives. Atticus has promised 'my darling little Tullia' a present, and she is dunning her father for it. In 67, when she can have been little over ten, Cicero announces her engagement to a young noble, Gaius Piso, who proved to be an excellent young man, quiet and serious. Cicero also expresses his grief at the death of his young cousin Lucius, whom we have seen with him in Greece and helping to collect evidence against Verres. (One of his Visellius cousins, a lawyer like his father, was to reach the aedileship some years later but to die thereafter; he is the only one we can trace at all.) A bald statement – 'my father died on 28 December' – has been used as evidence of Cicero's heartlessness; but he is probably giving a precise date for something announced in an earlier letter that is lost. (Or possibly, if we emend *pater* to *frater* – the word, 'brother', was used of first cousins – the death of Lucius. It does however seem that Cicero's father may have died about this time.)

It also emerges from the letters that both Cicero and Atticus

have just bought estates, Atticus in Epirus, on the coast opposite
Corcyra (Corfu). Here he raised huge flocks of sheep and herds of
cattle and horses, a fact we do not learn from Cicero, who was
not interested in these matters, but from his encyclopaedic contemporary Varro, who was. Cicero had acquired a country place
or *villa*, once Sulla's, at Tusculum in the Alban hills, just south-
east of Rome; in the Renaissance, too, villas sprang up here, at
Frascati, to enjoy the cooler air and fine views. Cicero also mentions a property at Formiae on the coast south of the capital,
another fashionable area. He took special pleasure in his *Tus-
culanum*, and commissioned Atticus to ship him suitable works
of art for the adornment of a 'gymnasium' there, which was to be,
like Plato's Academy, originally a real gymnasium, after which
he named it, a layout of halls and walks for intellectual rather
than physical relaxation. He later had a second 'gymnasium' at
the villa, called the Lyceum in memory, this time, of Aristotle;
such reminiscent names were very fashionable. But now it is in
his Academy that he sits to write to Atticus: yes, a set of marble
herms with bronze heads will be very suitable, and 'I also want
you to get some reliefs for the walls of the small entrance-hall,
and two carved well-heads'. Though there were Greek and other
artists at work in Rome, Greece and especially Athens were still
the best place for such objects, and Atticus, whose judgement of
art was entirely reliable, also succeeded in getting Cicero things
cheaply. Taste at this time was eclectic, pieces in classical or
sometimes even archaic style (often copies) being as much
favoured as the more realistic or dramatic works typical of the
more recent or Hellenistic period. But Cicero says nothing of the
style or quality of the works he wants, though something of their
subject (a Minerva, goddess of wisdom, will do nicely to preside
over the Academy – in fact he always had something of a cult
for this divinity) and in this omission one perhaps again sees how
his literary bias affects his approach to the visual arts. In a letter
written probably many years later, to another friend who had
been buying works of art for him, he says that more has been
spent than he feels all the statues in the world are worth; and
what is he to do with Bacchants and a statue of Mars? He also
remarks that if anything of this kind really gives him pleasure, it
is painting. Perhaps we may connect this interesting statement
(possibly borne out by his use of similes from the art in his discussion of literary matters, though this is not untraditional) with
his love on the one hand for beautiful landscapes and on the other

for lively scenes such as he watched at the theatre or portrayed in his speeches; while it reminds us that the visual arts in antiquity were less dominated by sculpture than, with the loss of all but minor decorative painting, we are inclined to believe. (We should like to know if the picture Sulla had had painted in the Tusculan villa, of himself receiving a military decoration from his troops, was still there now that the villa had passed through several other hands into those of Cicero.)

It may be that Cicero could, in spite of his disclaimers, be guilty of extravagant expenditure on *objets d'art*; there still existed in the late first century A.D. a fine circular table of citrus wood, which was much prized for its beautiful figuring and colour, for which he was said to have paid a very large sum – larger indeed than one can easily believe he had to spend at any time in his life, though such tables were becoming wildly fashionable. Books he certainly collected.

But purchase of his villa now at any rate strained Cicero's resources and left him unable for the moment to buy from, or through, Atticus a collection of books he wanted 'as a resource for my old age'. But it is likely to have been politically necessary. Tusculum was a place where many prominent men, including Hortensius and Lucullus, had villas, and private discussions in the country were almost as much a part of political life as they were in the Whig England that Ciceronian Rome sometimes resembles – not least in its passion for building and improvement on country estates. The comparison should not be pressed too far; we may concede that the taste for watching animals massacred in the arena and for gladiatorial combats was marginally less civilized than that for fox-hunting and prizefighting, as that in Rome the technological level was a little lower, and the incidence of crude superstition a little higher, than in eighteenth-century England.

But at any rate, in both, politics were only for the rich; perhaps more particularly in Rome, where the level of luxury among the upper class had soared in the last decades, where every politician needed a large house in the city to receive the mass of his clients and callers, and where, there being no printing and no public post, a vast staff of secretaries, copyists and messengers, mostly of slave or freedman status, had to be kept – and the chief of them ultimately pensioned off, usually by the gift of that one safe investment, a farm. Though Cicero was not allowed, as an advocate, to take fees, he accepted legacies and loans from those under an obligation to him in the usual Roman fashion.

Some of the legacies he received, often from *equites* with business interests, were very large. Senators were theoretically forbidden to engage in trade; almost all Cicero's income appears to have been in rents (from Italy; senators, unlike *equites*, seem rarely to have invested in land in the provinces). Being an absentee landlord, he let his farms at Arpinum to tenants, rather than exploiting them directly by slave labour, as was often found most profitable; he made improvements at his Tusculan villa, to get a better rent from the market-gardener who leased part of the ground; towards the end of his life he inherited shops and other property in the flourishing Campanian port of Puteoli, in which Hortensius also had investments. Terentia owned woodlands, rented grazing from the state, and had house-property in Rome itself, a risky but profitable investment. This diversity is noteworthy; the Romans often preferred it to owning one large estate, and for various reasons, including political instability as well as the absence of rules of primogeniture and entail, they were prone to buy and sell frequently, and not to identify themselves closely with any particular piece of property. Here the parallel with eighteenth-century England breaks down – though doubtless Cicero would not have parted lightly with his Arpinate estate. By contrast with Cicero, Atticus the *eques* not only owned real property in town and country, some of it outside Italy, but was a money-lender on a big scale (not that Cicero and other senators disdained to lend money on occasion) and engaged in various profitable concerns; he had slaves educated to increase their value, may possibly have sold the fine books his copyists made, and at one time owned a troop of gladiators which he let out for hire. It does not appear, however, that he had any shares in the companies that farmed state contracts, especially for tax-collection (in which again senators were not supposed to invest): these were the nearest thing to modern companies that existed.

Though Cicero ultimately owned half-a-dozen fine villas (not to mention several small lodges to rest in on the way to them, inns being so inadequate) and though he kept up his great position, his personal life was considered simple, and his finances were always a preoccupation, in spite of the care that Atticus came to give them and the fact that he did not spend money on the lavish bribery that so many politicians employed at election or other times. He was often in debt, a condition endemic among the upper as well as the lower classes in Rome, though he was perhaps never seriously in danger of the disasters that threatened so many of his contemporaries. The law of debt was severe; the Romans disliked any defaulting on contracts, and for the poor a form of private debt-bondage still existed. Bankruptcy involved *infamia*, the loss not only of reputation but of actual political rights, and a man merely suspected of insolvency might be thrown out of the Senate by the censors. No wonder men piled debt on debt to conceal the true state of affairs until they became utterly desperate.

In 67 Cicero's letters show him completely confident about his candidature for the praetorship: Atticus need not bother to come home to help (he seems often to have returned to Rome for elections; this was but one of the services he made it a point of honour, and the chief business of his life, to render to his friends, who included many distinguished men). This confidence was justified, for Cicero was returned at the head of the poll by the centuriate assembly – three times, for the elections were twice interrupted. One reason for this remarkable result may be that the censors of 70, the first since the early 80s, had perhaps inscribed on the rolls of the centuriate assembly for the first time a mass of Italian voters, including well-off men full of goodwill to friends of Pompey and often to Cicero himself; the increase in bribery in elections from this period may indicate that the old noble houses had less control than before.

Cicero had written briefly of the campaign, saying that candidates were being harried by unreasonable demands, and the polling put off. This is certainly a reference to the *popularis* tribune Cornelius, whose reforming proposals included a fierce one about electoral bribery. Many of these proposals were admirable, and Cornelius seems to have been a serious and reputable person, but he alienated the Senate by his revival of the old Gracchan tradition, especially in attempting to depose another tribune, who vetoed him in the optimate interest; and most of the nobles were disgusted by proposals that cut down their freedom to use their influence. We know that Cicero joined the optimates in the Senate in opposing the demands that public money appropriated by Sulla and his supporters should be refunded; after so long a time this was perhaps, as Cicero's learned commentator Asconius says, an impracticable proposal – though Cato, from a political standpoint opposite to Cornelius', was to do something of the kind. Cicero's over-cautious attitude to reform was perhaps in evidence. To Atticus he complained that he was fed up with public life: 'it's incredible how much worse you will find things have become in the short time since you left them'. He must have been dismayed by the breakdown of the comparative unity of the last few years.

Cornelius had been Pompey's quaestor, a relationship that set up a particularly close tie of obligation. The increasing use of dependent tribunes by great soldiers was to be a disturbing phenomenon. Cornelius' colleague Gabinius was almost as extreme as himself. His main object was a proposal to give Pompey a great command against the pirates, who had become intolerably well-organized and successful; their fleets attacked Greek cities, and prominent travellers were kidnapped even on the Appian Way near Rome. Among those who had had to be ransomed were Julius Caesar and the man who was later to be Cicero's bitterest enemy, Publius Clodius. Cicero did not openly support Gabinius, but he was moving towards him and his friends at this time, partly for the sake of the business interests that suffered from the unreliable state of transport, and partly to gain the favour of the people, to whom the high price of imported food was a burden. He probably also had an eye to the favour of Pompey, with whom he had been brought into touch again in 70, over the Verres case. An alliance with Pompey and his present friends might push Cicero too far into the *popularis* camp, but Pompey himself was clearly no extremist, and his influence was great; while Cicero was doubtless already aiming at that prize so elusive for a man of his background, the consulship. But according to his statement a year later, even leading optimates like Catulus found it hard to speak openly against Gabinius' proposals, so clear was it that drastic steps needed to be taken. The bill passed in a crowded and enthusiastic assembly, though Gabinius had to go very near deposing a hostile tribune. Pompey, on getting the command he wanted, behaved moderately, choosing his officers with tact, and refraining from arming all the troops he had been allowed. In three months, by sound organization and rapid movement, he swept the Mediterranean clear, resettled the surviving pirates in a humane manner, and became the idol of the People and the *equites*.

The next step soon followed. In 66 one of the tribunes, Manilius, proposed that Pompey should receive the command against Mithridates that had recently been taken from Lucullus and split between two incompetent nobles. Pompey, still in the East, claimed that he did not want it; he had been hoping to live quietly at home with his wife. But to such protestations from

Pompey the Romans were perhaps already accustomed; they were always contradicted by his friends' actions.

Cicero, now praetor, supported Manilius' bill (explaining that Pompey had not asked him to do so) in the first speech that he had ever made to a popular meeting. The published version is a very careful piece of work, constructed according to the rules and largely consisting of a eulogy of Pompey. It is aimed largely at the commercial classes, including humble people on the vast staffs of the tax-farmers and businessmen, who were all impatient with the continued disorder in the East; the province of Asia had been the scene of their greatest profits, and indeed as Cicero points out it was also the only one whose taxes represented a real surplus to the treasury – if too many individual Romans, both officials and private citizens, sucked the blood of the provincials, the state itself had not so far done so too badly (after the original conquest). There are echoes in the speech of the reform programme of 70, especially on the need for clean provincial government: Pompey is irreproachable in such matters (so, it seems, had Lucullus been, but Lucullus had been too intent on defending the provincials against Roman tax-farmers and businessmen to please that class). Cicero indeed talks in a very *popularis* way at times in this speech, as he was always to do when addressing the People. But he remains polite to the leading nobles, especially Catulus, Hortensius and Lucullus, and he points out that they have in fact backed all Pompey's earlier commands (that they unwillingly acquiesced in them would be nearer the truth). The imperial historian Dio, possibly using invectives against Cicero dating from a later period of his career, does call his support for Manilius deserting the optimate cause; but there seems to be no contemporary echo of this charge, and much was allowed to those with elections before them. It is clear however that we cannot altogether absolve Cicero from responsibility for encouraging the habit, fatal to the Republic, of letting the People confer vast extraordinary commands. He argued, as he was so often to do, that the immediate public interest was more important than precedent, though he could find precedent. It was a claim to which he had recourse rather easily; one reason for this we shall see when we consider his political theory.

In a speech delivered in court the same year, in defence of Cluentius, Cicero displays another side of his political beliefs. For the first time he openly formulates the programme with which his name is always associated, that of the 'concord of the orders', or

unity between the Senate and the *equites*. This was an alliance
of the well-off in defence of law, order and property against
revolutionary movements. The two classes did have much in
common – some scholars even treat them as two parts of the same
class. But at times the ruling clique in the Senate alienated the
tax-farmers and businessmen who represented the *equites* in
Rome, or individual governors clashed with the same tax-farmers,
or with the *negotiatores* in the provinces: and then the situation
might be exploited by *popularis* politicians and enmities flare up
in the law courts. And at times the non-senatorial landowners
opted out of politics altogether. Cicero was right, from his point
of view, to be aware of the dangers. The best senators, he says,
desire the unity he advocates; only greedy or haughty ones resent
the *equites'* position. Concord was an old ideal; it is likely that
in this special form too it was not Cicero's invention.

The speech for Cluentius deals for the rest with an incredibly
complicated tale of murder in a south Italian town, which Cicero
carefully does nothing to simplify, and goes back over one of the
worst legal scandals of the late 70s. This time it suits Cicero's
book to play down the bribery, however, and he later congratulated himself on having 'wrapped the jury in darkness'. As a result, he received support from the well-off in a number of areas
of southern Italy, and the speech was immensely admired by later
critics. Some now may be inclined to consider it a masterpiece
only of exaggerated rhetoric and perverted ingenuity, but there is
no denying that Cicero did the best he could for his client.

As praetor, he presided over one of the courts himself, that for
extortion. He was much embarrassed by the trials of various
popularis politicians which happened to come up before him.
He wrote to Atticus how thankful he was that in refusing to
prevent the condemnation of one (an ally of M. Crassus rather
than Pompey) he had not in fact damaged himself with the
people; but in putting off till his own year of office had expired
the trial of Manilius, who had terrorized the courts and the city
with his gangs, it seems that he did offend the People, and to
placate them had to promise that he would be Manilius' advocate
instead. This trial never came off; but next year we find Cicero,
who had refused a province (doubtless because he preferred to
stay in the limelight at Rome rather than to take the opportunities
for gain, legal and illegal, that a province supplied) actually defending Cornelius on a charge of treason; it was the old business
of his ignoring a tribune's veto.

Asconius' commentary, with its brief quotations from the two speeches involved, is all we have of what later writers show was a famous performance, greeted at the time of its delivery with applause and cries of acclamation. It is said to have had regard to the *dignitas*, the rank and position, of all the great optimates who appeared as witnesses against Cornelius, and to have treated a difficult subject with moderation. Cornelius' connection with Pompey, we are told, influenced in his favour all the jurors except a few who had close ties with the leading optimates. Nevertheless, Cicero was later blamed for taking the case; but it may be that this charge was only made much later, when opponents felt that older, like more recent, charges of inconsistency might be made to stick. At the time of his fight for the consulship, as we shall see, it seems that his enemies found little to say except that he was a 'new man'.

And there were *populares* in this year, 65, whom he was perfectly ready to attack. Not all the politicians playing that game were Pompey's former or would-be officers like Cornelius and Gabinius; there were also independent and potent nobles: Caesar and Catiline, furtively backed by M. Crassus. Caesar at least (who had just given magnificent games and was perhaps already in financial straits and in debt to Crassus) openly supported Pompey, as anyone courting the People's favour at this time was bound to do. But Cicero did not trust them. And he seems gradually to have become determined that Pompey should owe them nothing. He hinted later that Crassus and possibly Caesar had been behind the violence of Cornelius and the rest, but of this we cannot be sure; and some murky events following the unseating for bribery of the successful candidates for the consulship of 65 probably did not involve Catiline (who had wished to be a candidate himself but had had to stand a trial instead), let alone Caesar and Crassus; these events were probably only blown up by Cicero and others a few years later into the 'First Catilinarian Conspiracy'. At the time Cicero, as he said afterwards, was not in the counsel of the leaders of the state, and nothing was made public.

At all events, in 65 Cicero joined Catulus and other optimates in successful opposition to the proposals (whatever exactly they were) of Crassus, now censor, to annex the immensely rich country of Egypt, which had been left by the will of its last king to Rome, but which not everyone there was at all keen to take over. Crassus' proposals doubtless involved far too great opportunities for himself and his friends; and thus as so often in Rome fear of the influence a measure might give its proposer completely inhibited action. Cicero's lost speech to the Senate on the Egyptian question seems from its fragments to have included a violent attack on Crassus' itching palm. This, as we saw, reflected his considered opinion.

However, as the few letters of 65 show, Cicero was now mainly preoccupied with his prospects for the consulship. Sulla's law laid down that two full years must pass between the end of the praetorship and the start of the consulship. Cicero therefore could not hold the latter before 63; but it was inglorious for a candidate not to get in in 'his' year, though with eight praetors a year and only two consuls competition was stiff. In 65 Cicero was already going through the possible candidates for 63, chiefly those who had been praetor with him; none were too formidable, one was starting his campaign too early and finding people say they were bound to Cicero. 'I hope it will be to my advantage when the rumour gets round that I have much support.' The immediate elections, for 64, were important, as rejected candidates might stand again (Cicero's prophecies, incidentally, as to who would win were mistaken). He was planning to work very hard in 64, even spending the whole of the period between September and January, when as we saw there was little legal business, drumming up support in northern Italy, a rich and prosperous area. He had not, he said, yet discovered the nobles' intentions, but people thought they would be against him. Atticus, in Greece, was to make sure that Pompey's staff supported him (perhaps by persuading them to write to their friends and dependants?). 'As for my friend Pompey, tell him I shan't be cross if he doesn't come home for my election.' This is obviously a joke, but perhaps implies that Cicero by now was an acknowledged ally. Finally, will Atticus forgive him for not acting for his uncle against a man who was an invaluable agent in the praetorian elections and is a friend of Domitius Ahenobarbus 'on whom all my hopes depend'? Why this young noble was likely to favour Cicero we do not know – his own speeches were without literary pretensions. His later career reveals him as a proud and sometimes unscrupulous optimate, vastly rich, popular and influentially connected and not particularly close to Cicero, who was inclined, indeed, to think him stupid.

In another letter, announcing the consuls for 64 and the birth of his son, Cicero mentions that he is considering defending

Catiline on his trial for extortion (though he was sure of his guilt), in return for which Catiline might cooperate over the canvas. Such combinations between two candidates were often made, but in the end Cicero seems to have remained independent. He begged Atticus to return quickly to use his influence with the nobles. Sufficiently well-born himself, clever and agreeable, tactful and helpful to all, but strictly optimate in convictions, Atticus might well have considerable powers of persuasion; we know him to have been on close terms with Hortensius and Lucullus, the Metelli and others. But we do not know how successful he was in winning them over, for he answered his friend's appeal and the letters stop. What we do have is what purports to be a long letter from Quintus Cicero (who had become aedile in his turn in 65) to his brother, calling itself 'a brief handbook on electioneering' and full of advice on how to run the campaign. Many scholars do not believe it genuine, and it does perhaps seem an unlikely document, more plausibly to be regarded as a rhetorical exercise of imperial date. But it is probably well informed on Roman elections in general and Cicero's in particular. Its picture of the way the candidate should collect support at all levels and take care never to commit himself to a particular line is certainly true to conditions in Rome, where office was rather a reward for previous services, personal or ancestral, to classes or individuals, than an opportunity to put a programme into effect. The little work stresses Cicero's influence with the country towns, the *equites* and Pompey; explains that in the circumstances it is not considered disgraceful to make up to the most dubious personages, including political agents who boast that they can swing the votes of their tribe or century. It tells us that several of the popular associations or guilds (which we shall meet again) are bound in honour to Cicero, since he has defended members; and suggests that clever young nobles, if not their elders, are friendly to him. (Cicero's patronage of bright young men is attested from his letters only a few years later, and it does sound from the *Brutus* as if the 60s was the period in which 'the novelty of style' of his oratory most impressed the young – later there was a reaction against his domination.) There is little suggestion that the nobles' opposition is based on anything except Cicero's status as a new man.

There is another, and a very amusing, source for consular elections in Cicero's speech for Murena, dating from his own year of office. It dilates on the importance of knowing everybody and being polite to everybody, and of going around looking optimistic with a great train of supporters. In fact a prominent Roman seems hardly ever to have appeared alone; the more important he was, the greater the number of servants, friends and clients who accompanied him; but as a candidate, he needed a great procession with him. As for knowing everybody, Cicero excelled at that; Plutarch says that when he travelled in Italy he knew to whom every property he passed belonged, and he was doubtless less dependent than most politicians on his *nomenclator*, the slave who whispered in his ear the names of the men he met.

In the event, it seems that Catiline, who had escaped condemnation at his trial, without Cicero's help, but perhaps with Crassus' money; and another candidate, C. Antonius, who had been expelled from the Senate in 70 and managed to get back by re-election to the praetorship (with Cicero's help), raised such suspicion by their *popularis* language and disreputable life that, though nobles themselves, they caused most of the nobles to come round to Cicero as the only candidate in a not very strong field with enough support to defeat them. As Sallust says, 'When danger came, envy and pride took second place.' Asconius' commentary on the speech 'In the white toga' (i.e., as a candidate) delivered by Cicero in the Senate, shows the position just before the elections. The optimates were trying to tighten up the penalties for bribery in order to thwart Catiline and Antonius, and when these got the proposal vetoed by a tribune, Cicero attacked them in the name of the Senate. Invective was an art and a convention in Rome – the obverse of the elaborate courtesy practised to friends and allies; we need not take seriously all that is said of Catiline's crimes, which supposedly include murder, especially of Cicero's cousin Marius Gratidianus, with whom in his life he had had little sympathy; treason, in the 'First Catilinarian Conspiracy'; and incest with his own daughter by a previous adultery. But the sinister insinuations against Crassus and Caesar are at least interesting (it was perhaps Crassus' money that was being used for bribery).

Both Catiline and Antonius abused Cicero in their turn, but according to Asconius all they could find to object to was his lack of nobility. The outcome was that, as Cicero himself and other sources agree, he was elected 'by general acclamation'; his name was greeted with applause before ever the votes were cast. Antonius, who had some support for the sake of his father, the distinguished orator of Cicero's youth, just defeated Catiline for second place. Cicero had in some ways been lucky, but his achievement was nonetheless a very remarkable one: a 'new man', he had been elected consul in first place and punctually in 'his' year, without bribery or violence and with the support of many of the nobles. Even Marius had not managed that.

5

THE FATHER OF HIS COUNTRY
63 B.C.

The poor of Rome lived always on the brink of disaster. The free-born seem largely to have subsisted by casual labour in the docks or the building industry; freedmen, who might have a patron's capital behind them, and Greek as their native language, probably dominated trade and much of such industry, always small-scale, as there was. All lived crowded into blocks of flats, without decent sewage, water or cooking facilities and susceptible to frequent and disastrous collapses, floods and fires. They were sometimes liable if they could not pay their rent or other debts to forfeit their personal liberty. The State took no responsibility for their plight (nor was it asked to) except to see that they did not actually die of famine, by subsidizing corn and organizing its import; but prices and supply still fluctuated. In 63 the situation was particularly desperate, owing to the loss of the Eastern revenues and the expenses of the Eastern wars, which had made money scarce and probably caused unemployment (as a result, the Jewish colony at Rome was prevented from sending money to Jerusalem). Things were perhaps even worse in the countryside; many of the veterans whom Sulla had settled in Etruria and elsewhere had either received poor land or proved themselves poor farmers, or from whatever cause were in financial difficulties. Even though some of those they had dispossessed may have gone either as volunteers or conscripts into the army, there were plenty of peasants left with old grievances or new troubles. As a result brigandage was common. The slave war of Spartacus, in which a few free men had, exceptionally, joined, had left conditions unsteady in the South and shown once more the dangers represented both by the bands of slaves trained to fight as gladiators and those who, often armed ostensibly against beasts or robbers, worked as herdsmen on the great estates.

And the desperate might well find leaders. The sons of those proscribed by Sulla had a serious grievance – their political rights had never been restored. Many nobles were themselves in debt, ruined either by a life of dissipation, marked perhaps by the very

Roman vice of extravagant expenditure on rare foods or by the new mania for huge and luxurious villas on the coast or in the hills; or else brought to bankruptcy by the ever-growing expenses of the political race – games, shows, dinners and outright bribery. In this race, since Sulla had enlarged the Senate, many more were entered than could hope to excel; furthermore, numbers of those thrown out by the censors of 70 were now trying to get back by election to office. At present the low prices, caused by the shortage of money, made it particularly hard to sell land to pay outstanding debts.

Thus revolution – a revolution aimed primarily at abolishing debt – was on the cards. And yet the revolution that almost came with Catiline's second rejection at the polls and subsequent conspiracy late in 63 was not really the dominating problem of the year, though our sources may mislead us into thinking so. What many Romans at least were most anxious about was the imminent return of Pompey from the East. Which way would he jump this time? With whom would he ally himself? With whatever group was most influential, of course. The year 63 is, to put it rather over-personally, a duel between Caesar, who now comes to the fore as far and away the most brilliant of the new *populares*, and Cicero, himself with support from the People and representing himself as in some sense a *popularis* too, but acting in the interest of the Senate: a duel for the prizes of the People's support and Pompey's alliance – preferably on fairly equal terms. Could Cicero show that he was able to act as well as speak; could he so control the situation, retaining the People's favour, saving the pockets of the *equites*, who made up many of the creditors, and asserting the Senate's authority, that the revolution should come to nothing and Pompey have no interest in cooperation with the enemies of the optimates? Or could Caesar and his friends use the excited temper of the People to force through measures that, while perhaps benefiting the voters too, would give themselves power and influence and put Pompey under an obligation to them? Caesar and Crassus themselves are unlikely to have wished for revolution; for one thing it could only mean Pompey sweeping home, as dictator if he wished, to restore order (though the conspirators are said to have intended to guard against this danger by seizing his children as hostages) and, for another, Crassus was a great creditor (though there might have been opportunities for him in an unsettled time, as there had been under Sulla). But Caesar and Crassus might use attempted revolution; might see to it that the optimates either failed fully to cope, or that in doing so they discredited themselves in the eyes of the People.

The details of this fascinating and important year are all too uncertain. Sallust, who wrote his monograph on the Catilinarian War some thirty years later, is theatrical and inaccurate, especially in chronology; and for his own purpose, which is primarily that of illustrating the moral and political corruption of Roman society, he isolates the conspiracy artificially from the fabric of events. There are no letters from Cicero (Atticus stayed in Rome); and he only published his speeches three years later, when some young friends asked for them and he had a fancy to emulate Demosthenes' *Philippics* with a collection of orations on a weighty political theme. It is reassuring that he does indicate to Atticus that they may be treated as a source for 'what I did and what I said'. But what he said at least had been at times brilliantly disingenuous. Worse still, some details in later accounts seem to depend only on his own poem about his consulship. In short, this is a year in which we see Cicero from a distance only, and in full dress – the heavy formal toga (not to mention the famous cuirass in which he presided over the elections) rather than the easy tunic worn at home. But it is a year too important in his life to be skimmed over.

As for Cicero's chief opponent, Caesar, his earlier career was probably considerably romanticized when his biography came to be written. But there can be little doubt of his personal fascination, his extravagance and huge debts, his generosity to dependants, his cool courage and his complete belief in his own ability (and perhaps in little else). He had distinguished himself on military service at an early age, and his enormous ambition was probably directed towards a great military command; the memory of Alexander the Great and his conquests perhaps haunted him as it did Pompey and too many others in later antiquity, if it is true that, a year or two after 63, he wept at seeing a statue of Alexander, who had conquered the world at an age when Caesar himself, he felt, had achieved nothing. But there can be no doubt either of his brilliant skill in the political game that he seems to have despised. He came from an extravagantly ancient, though somewhat decayed, patrician family, which traced its origins to the Trojan prince Aeneas and his mother the goddess Venus. He was a fine speaker, noted for the purity and elegance of his language, and like Cicero had studied with Molon at Rhodes. Also like Cicero he was an occasional poet, but unlike him no philosopher, though possibly a good deal of a sceptic in religion; unlike Cicero again, he had some interest in science, at least astronomy, and was a dashing horseman, a successful lover, and probably incapable of laughing at himself. In most respects indeed the two men, the cleverest of their day, present an extreme contrast: the one devoted to and an interpreter of the traditions of the past, emotional, often hesitant, willing to compromise; the other shackled by no prejudices, scruples or superstitions and ready to go straight to his goal. Late in 64 Caesar as special judge presided over a trial of Catiline for murders carried out under Sulla; perhaps with the president's assistance, Catiline got off, and could prepare for his renewed attempt on the consulship.

What *he* was really like it is much harder to say. We have two eloquent – over-eloquent – set character-sketches, one from the pen of Cicero and one from that of Sallust. When Cicero came to compose his portrait he was trying to excuse a client for his past association with the conspiracy without playing down his own achievement in overcoming it, and so he represents Catiline as a contradictory, dangerous figure, with high abilities and specious virtues to balance his fearful vices. Sallust portrays him schematically as a monster of luxury and avarice, greed and dissimulation, who rejoiced in civil strife and discord – the product and embodiment of an age characterized by these particular vices; in addition he had perhaps been influenced by the striking antitheses of the Ciceronian passage, and may not be an entirely independent source. One may cautiously accept that Catiline had dissipated his fortune both by riotous living and by generosity to allies and dependants, that he was remarkable for boldness and above all for extraordinary powers of endurance, and that he had as much force of mind as body. Most of the information on his early or private life comes directly or indirectly from invectives by Cicero and others and is as highly coloured and unreliable as possible; and we need not, for example, accept the picture found in Sallust and elsewhere of the conspirators sealing their bond by quaffing human blood. But we do know that Cicero seriously believed Catiline to be guilty of extortion in the province he had governed, and it was at one point considered appropriate to prosecute him, vainly as it turned out, for seducing a Vestal Virgin (Terentia's half-sister, in fact).

Cicero entered on his year of office at a moment of great uncertainty, with rumours and suspicions rife. The new tribunes, who had come into office, as was normal, on 10 December, were solidly supporting the bill promulgated by one of their number, Rullus, for a far-reaching distribution of land in Italy, financed by public money. It is usually thought that Cicero was right in seeing Crassus and Caesar behind this measure. The other consul, Antonius, was expected to support it. Ten commissioners, elected for five years, were to be given sweeping powers to settle colonies where they pleased, raising the money by selling public land in Italy and the provinces, by imposing special taxes on such land, by requisitioning booty from generals (Pompey being excepted) and by using any new sources of revenue to hand; this would include the income from the newly annexed territories in the East. In many respects an agrarian law might have been socially valuable (there had been none for a long time), and with Pompey's veterans to provide for it was indeed necessary; and some of the bill's provisions were moderate – for example, it did not try to upset the title of Sulla's assignees or to expropriate private property. But such a bill would in sober fact have given its authors and executors, by Roman tradition, such enormous influence that Cicero had little choice but to oppose it. On 1 January he called the Senate to meet in the Temple of Jupiter on the Capitol and sketched out his programme for the year. The speech as we have it is unfortunately incomplete, but he says that he will use his consulship to oppose violence and revolution; peace and harmony are what the People really want, what is really *popularis*. He paints an alarmist picture of the operation of Rullus' measure – the state deprived of all its revenues, the provinces beset by corrupt commissioners, colonies planted in strategic positions to threaten Rome, even Egypt annexed on the sly. To show his own integrity, he declares that he will refuse to take a province when his consulship is over – he would otherwise have been to some extent dependent on the goodwill of the tribunes – and he begs these to think again what they are doing and to unite with the respectable classes – the 'good men', or the *boni*. Peace and concord, and the idea that the only danger to Rome now comes from within: these strike a very Ciceronian note.

Shortly afterwards, Cicero addressed a popular meeting. He began with the usual expressions of gratitude for his election, and declared that he intended to be a *popularis* consul and regularly address the People, adding a reference to the illwill that he might incur on their behalf as a result. He then turned to the subject of Rullus' proposal. He represented himself as the one true friend of the People, whom Rullus and his allies were deceiving. He had tried to help the tribunes in drafting the bill, and been rudely repulsed. He went so far as to praise the Gracchi, those great *popularis* tribunes of old, and their agrarian legislation; but Rullus and his friends are not true *populares*, rather Sullans, confirming the title of Sullan profiteers, notably Rullus' own father-in-law, or giving them an opportunity to sell at a good price the lands that made them so hated. It appears that Rullus, to conciliate the Senate, had rashly told it that the *plebs urbana*, the urban populace, had too much power and should be 'drained off'; Cicero unkindly reported, and perhaps exaggerated, a remark likely to alienate its subject. He claimed that the commissioners, those 'ten kings' (the word 'king' was one that roused hatred and fear in the Romans) were all set for a power equivalent to tyranny; indeed that by the peculiar form of election proposed in the bill, involving only seventeen out of the thirty-five tribes, its backers were preventing the Roman People from expressing its will.* Worst of all, they were enemies of Pompey, the People's darling, and Cicero's friend. This was disingenuous: the bill was perhaps a bribe. if also a trap, for Pompey, who would have to cooperate if he wanted his veterans settled, but could not be one of the Ten, who were to be chosen in short order from men on the spot in Rome. Most of the colonies, too, Cicero claimed, would be settlements of criminals, threatening Rome and the Roman People from every direction. He ended, again, with the idea of peace and harmony, and professed to have made his colleague Antonius (who, Plutarch states, intended to be one of the commissioners), a loyal collaborator with himself.

Cicero harangued the people probably twice more on the subject; we have a very fragmentary speech, made after the tribunes had accused him of Sullan sympathies, in which he reiterates the same horrific picture of the bill. In the event it probably never came to the vote. This was possibly because the People's support was clearly lacking – Cicero had urged them not to forego the advantages of life in Rome to follow Rullus to some unspecified waste, and many of the urban voters may really not have wanted land; and it also seems that already on 1 January one of the tribunes had backed down and announced that he

---

* The seventeen tribes were to be chosen by lot. The provision was perhaps designed to make optimate bribery difficult; or, if the lot were really to be rigged, to make it easy for the sponsors themselves. This form of election was used for religious reasons in the election of the high priest.

would veto. How he had been persuaded we do not know. This first round, then, was Cicero's.

His analysis of the social and political situation is already clearly expressed in his speeches on the agrarian bill. On the one side are the *boni*, 'good men', the respectable of all ranks, who stand by the laws, peace, the authority of the Senate and the rights of property; on the other are the 'seditious', the 'wicked' and also the 'ignorant' whom they have misled. This strikes us as a lamentably inadequate diagnosis of the situation; Catiline, who talked of the 'many' and the 'wretched', and their opponents the 'few', came nearer reality. But a strongly moralizing interpretation of what was basically a class conflict was of great antiquity in both Roman and Greek upper-class thought (as it has been in some more recent societies) and undoubtedly normal among the optimates in Cicero's own day.

Dates are uncertain; but it was probably in the early part of the year that there was a good deal of competition as to who should pay honours to Pompey. Caesar got his proposals through (they included the right of appearing at the Games in the robe worn by a general at his triumphal celebration) in spite of opposition from Cato, who now first comes to the fore. Caesar was assisted by the tribune Labienus, a competent person who was later his lieutenant in Gaul, but who came from Pompey's home area in Italy and was probably his protégé, holding the tribunate this year specifically in his interest; one notes that he must have supported Rullus' bill. Cicero however got the Senate to vote a public thanksgiving of unprecedented length on the news of Mithridates' death. So Pompey was obliged to both sides, and honours in every sense were equal. Cicero also pursued his self-imposed task of uniting the different classes in the state by giving a great extempore lecture to the *plebs* for whistling in the theatre at a praetor who was a friend of the *equites*; he called a public meeting at a nearby temple and persuaded his auditors to cheer the man instead. The speech is lost. He seems also to have frustrated other tribunicial proposals referred to by a late historian, including one directly aiming at the cancellation of debts, and one to restore the rights of the sons of the proscribed. The latter at least might seem only just; but in practice it would strengthen the hands of Cicero's opponents. Later sources say that his speech on the subject was particularly clever.

We know rather more about the prosecution of Rabirius for high treason, mounted by Labienus and probably inspired by

Caesar. Rabirius was an elderly and inconspicuous senator who was supposed, thirty-seven years previously in 100 B.C., to have killed the *popularis* tribune Saturninus after the Senate had passed a decree enjoining the consuls to look to the safety of the state. The so-called Last Decree had been devised to get rid of Gaius Gracchus; it had since been used several times against the Senate's enemies. The optimates held that by this means the Senate had the power, in a crisis, to declare certain persons not citizens but enemies of the State and to underwrite the magistrates and those assisting them in the ordinarily illegal action of putting such persons to death without trial. The *popularis* view on the other hand was that the Senate had arbitrarily assumed a power that contravened the old laws of appeal, according to which citizens of any standing could only be condemned to death by the People, or a court specially set up by it, as the ordinary criminal courts were.* (And in practice those condemned in these courts could now avoid the death penalty by retiring into exile.) This is the clearest example of the fatal fact that in Rome there were always two possible interpretations of the constitution, an optimate and a *popularis* one.

The prosecution of Rabirius involved some splendid antiquarian play-acting of which it is tempting to suppose Caesar the author. After much debate (including a speech by Labienus to the people in which he produced a portrait of Saturninus) a praetor was made to create two special judges: the lot conveniently selected Caesar himself and a cousin. They pronounced the grim sentence of death by scourging and crucifixion according to an archaic formula of which we have a version in Livy's account of early Rome (it is unlikely that Caesar really intended poor old Rabirius to suffer this fearful fate). The subsequent course of events is much disputed. Rabirius was expected to appeal to the People, meeting in the Field of Mars outside the walls, apparently with executioner and cross in attendance. But, probably before it did so, Cicero intervened, persuading the Senate to declare that the whole procedure was unlawful, having been abolished long ago as the law became more humane. Nonetheless, Labienus persisted with the case under a different procedure and a trial before the People

* Labienus was probably not objecting only to private individuals like Rabirius taking action, or to a case where the victim had been given a promise of safety on surrendering as Saturninus had; rather the Senate was being warned that the *populares* did not recognize the 'Last Decree' as giving any special powers at all, even to magistrates. See note at end of chapter.

did take place, in which Rabirius was only threatened with the usual capital sentence that could be escaped by exile. The defence – severely circumscribed for time – was undertaken by the Senate's biggest guns, Hortensius and Cicero.

Hortensius argued only that Rabirius had not in fact killed Saturninus. Cicero, who spoke in the place of honour after his old rival and whose speech survives in a curtailed form, took as so often the more general aspect. He stressed the great importance of the case and grasped the nettle firmly, becoming very eloquent on the need to uphold the Senate's authority by obeying its decree, and the necessity for some final sanction in political crises. (He later described the speech as entirely in the grand style.) Would that Rabirius *had* killed Saturninus! – at which there were howls, though not, he claims, very loud ones. Labienus, of course, is represented as a false *popularis*; the procedure he has dug up from the history books and the archives dates from the time of the kings and is savage and tyrannical; it is Cicero, who got it quashed, who is the real friend of the People (Labienus had clearly been calling *him* bogus). In the year 100 all 'good men' of every class had backed the consul – who was no oppressive noble, he points out, but Marius himself, inspired by that desire for the immortality of fame that moves all politicians and proves that there is something more than mortal in us. Cicero says openly that he would do what Marius did; and again the People is warned to beware of the internal dangers of sedition that threaten Rome now that her external wars are over. It is clear that both sides realized that the Last Decree might be called on in the near future.

Our sources differ as to whether the People had been influenced towards acquittal by Caesar's too-obviously partisan behaviour, or were, unmoved by Cicero, on the point of condemning, when the praetor Metellus Celer, who was perhaps presiding, broke up the assembly on the score that the red flag on the Janiculan hill had been hauled down. In early days this had been flown when-ever the assembly met outside the walls, to show that a watch was being kept against Etruscan attack. Celer had connections with Caesar and Pompey and this last piece of antiquarianism was probably intended either to save Rabirius, now that the *popu-lares'* point had been made, or to prevent a formal acquittal, which would gravely weaken that point. At any rate, the warn-ing to the optimates still stood. We may agree with Cicero that a state must hold some sort of sanction in reserve; Caesar, at any rate later, admitted it. We may agree, too, that with all its faults the Senate was the body to deploy it. But the opimate position, with its easy destruction of all right to a trial for its enemies, was a dangerous one.

One round, and that important for his future, was won by Caesar. Labienus, with his support, passed a *popularis* law restoring to the People the right of electing members of the priestly colleges; and this strengthened Caesar's hand in canvassing for the office of High Priest – though curiously enough the *pontifex maximus* had long been elected and even remained so after Sulla. The office was for life, and it was one of immense prestige: the *pontifex maximus'* official residence was the ancient palace of the Kings of Rome on the Sacred Way, and he presided over the College of Priests, who gave expert advice on matters concerning the rites on which the safety of Rome depended; he also had authority over the Vestal Virgins, who tended the fire on the public hearth. His position was also politically a strategic one, and was usually held by senior statesmen: in Rome as in Greece, there was no special priestly caste, and members of the upper class held both political and religious power, the boundaries not always being clear-cut. Laws and appointments could be annulled, business held up, on the excuse of religious flaws in procedure or other technicalities.

Caesar's competitors were the elderly and influential Catulus and another almost equally respected optimate; and while Caesar was already a member of the College of Priests and gloriously descended from gods, his comparative youth and his manner of life hardly fitted him for the post he sought. According to a well-known story Caesar kissed his mother before leaving home on the morning of the election and said that she would see him again as High Priest – or not at all. He probably meant that, if he failed, his creditors would close in and exile be his only hope. He returned as *pontifex maximus*. The rage of the optimates may be imagined; but no one apparently dared to prosecute the High Priest for the bribery that had probably been employed.

As it turned out, the consular elections, in July, were finally Cicero's round again; but they brought the crisis closer. Cicero claims to have been partly responsible for getting Lucullus' triumph – the grand military procession to the Capitol in celebration of his victories – over just before the poll, so that large numbers of veterans were at hand to vote for Lucullus' lieutenant Murena. Cicero, at first at least, supported his old friend Servius

Sulpicius Rufus, the famous jurisconsult; and Sulpicius persuaded Cicero to put through (somewhat unenthusiastically and minus some rather *popularis* clauses) a new law against bribery, by which both parties to the bribe were to suffer. This was aimed chiefly at Murena, whom Sulpicius hoped rather to unseat and replace than to defeat. Catiline was meanwhile still in high hopes, and went about escorted by a motley crowd of smart young men, Sullan colonists from Etruria, and those ruined in Sulla's time. He may still have enjoyed the support of Caesar and Crassus, as it is unlikely that he yet had plans for open revolution; he certainly boasted of the support of the consul Antonius. Antonius however had been pretty inactive all the year; his hands were to some extent tied by his zealously loyalist quaestor, Sestius; and Cicero now made, or completed, a bargain with him, reiterating in a speech to the People his own refusal of a province, and handing over Macedonia, which had been allotted to him, to his colleague.

Catiline himself was threatened with prosecution, like all the other candidates, for the use of bribery, by Cato. He replied that he would meet any attempt to make his expectations go up in smoke not by dousing it with water, but by pulling down the whole building over everybody's head. He also, if we may believe what Cicero later said, talked very wildly in private of the qualities needed by a leader of the wretched; he should himself be in distress and have the courage of desperation. This, and all Catiline's subsequent actions, were reported to Cicero by Fulvia, the aristocratic mistress of one of Catiline's most rackety supporters, Curius, famous as a dicer and spendthrift, who had been expelled from the Senate in 70; her suspicions are said to have been aroused by her lover's sudden wild promises, which led her to get in touch with Terentia, and according to Sallust ultimately Curius himself turned informer. Cicero indeed got the Senate to postpone the election, in order that it might discuss the report of this speech of Catiline's; or, as he declared later, because he had heard of a plot against himself, though without proof he dared not mention it in the Senate. At the meeting he called on Catiline to explain himself. Catiline faced it out boldly; he said that the state had two bodies, one weak and with a feeble head, one strong but headless; to this, if it desired it of him, he would provide the lacking organ. One catches an echo of the dash and allure that attracted to him many young men of his own noble class, whom he is also said to have attached to himself by every sort of favour. But it is not possible to rewrite history and make

Catiline into a serious reformer, though the task has been attempted; the unscrupulous and disreputable past history of himself and his chief lieutenants stands in the way. His main aim was clearly power for himself, his programme simply the abolition of existing debt; there is no word of more fundamental measures. Nor can it seriously be maintained that it was Cicero's persistent opposition that drove Catiline into violence, as some claimed even at the time; for far too long Cicero was simply a voice crying in the wilderness.

For the crowded Senate, though it groaned at Catiline's words, was not ready for action; Catiline left the house in triumph. It was one thing to fear that he would be an unreliable consul; it was another to take strong action against a noble, with many high connections, on the demand of a consul who did not belong to the charmed circle and was probably already exciting irritation and jealousy; also, Crassus had immense influence in many parts of the house. If Cicero had hoped to get the elections further delayed, or himself given an official bodyguard, or even Catiline's candidature disallowed, he was disappointed. The elections took place in due course, under his presidency; he was ostentatiously clad in a cuirass and accompanied by a strong body of armed supporters (the lack of a police force led disastrously to self-help of this kind). He said later that the cuirass was less to protect himself than to awaken the *boni* to their danger. In the event Murena and the equally safe Silanus – distinguished only by being the husband of Servilia, who combined the positions of Cato's sister, Brutus' mother and Caesar's mistress – were elected without trouble; according to Cicero, there had been a last-minute swing away from Sulpicius Rufus to Murena. This second rebuff for Catiline spelled the end of his hopes of legal power; it was probably only now that he turned to thoughts of armed insurrection. From this point we may be pretty sure that Crassus and Caesar had dropped him.

About the same time, Caesar became praetor-designate, as did Quintus Cicero. One of Pompey's officers, who was also his brother-in-law, Metellus Nepos, was elected tribune; so was M. Porcius Cato, who, some months before, on his way to a philosophic retreat on his estates in southern Italy, had met Nepos coming back from the East; he immediately determined to return to Rome and stand himself in order to oppose Nepos' plans.

Cato was related to all the dominating optimates of the 70s and 60s – Catulus, Lucullus, Hortensius; he was to be the most formidable of their successors, for long implacably hostile, on both private and public grounds, to Pompey's ambitions. He was the great-grandson of one of the most famous personages of the second century, Cato the Censor, whose force of character he perhaps inherited and whose political and moral attitudes he to some extent imitated – the Romans believed that one should emulate not only the *maiores*, the men of old, in general, but also one's own ancestors in particular. The younger Cato may well have conceived his role as watch-dog over senatorial behaviour, especially where finance and provincial government were concerned, in imitation of his great-grandfather. Unlike his predecessor, however, who roundly condemned Greek philosophers, he was greatly inspired by Stoicism, chiefly, as Plutarch says, by its ethical and political aspects. Plutarch describes his mind as slow to learn but retentive; the recently discovered portrait bust, however, suggests a keener quality than perhaps many would have given him credit for.

Since Cato was to become the martyr of the Republic and a figure enormously discussed after his death, much of our information about him comes from hagiography or invective. But we may believe that from his orphan childhood he was obstinate and passionate, and remarkably able to impose his authority on others. He was deeply attached to a half-brother who died young, and is said to have had a great regard for his half-sister Servilia, who helped to bring him up. As he grew older his way of life became increasingly independent and austere. As a young man he served in the army, and then did the tour of Asia – travelling on foot, while his friends and servants rode, and firmly refusing gifts from a friendly king. He married, for celibacy was not a virtue and parenthood was a duty to the state (but he was notoriously to divorce his second wife so that she could marry his friend Hortensius, only to take her back after Hortensius' death). In Rome he often carried his austerity to the point of going without shoes; he was renowned for his rigid observation of the laws and his strict regard for justice – in a society where many of the ill-known and uncodified laws were flagrantly disobeyed and personal favour and obligation considered as reputable motives. He was a forceful, if harsh, and totally inexhaustible speaker (who never published his speeches), without care for his personal safety in riotous popular assemblies. He treated the Senate, says Cicero, to philosophic harangues, and was to be seen sitting reading philosophy while waiting for it to assemble. In 63 he was still little over thirty, but had already made his mark as quaestor, by taking his financial responsibilities with a seriousness that appalled his clerks and almost led to quarrels with optimate friends, including Catulus himself; and we have seen him active in the Senate's interest in the last months.

Meanwhile Cicero remained, as he claimed, ceaselessly on the watch. His anxieties, his hopes and fears in this supreme test, as he must have felt it, can be imagined, but they cannot be documented. He continued to receive information from Fulvia, now to the effect that Catiline was preparing a rising in various parts of Italy, above all in Etruria, where his chief agent Manlius was enlisting Sullan veterans, peasants and brigands at Faesulae (modern Fiesole). It is possible that on 22 September the Senate discussed the affair, but refused again to take strong action. Cicero was considered an alarmist, and there was merriment over his cuirass at the elections, and his perpetual, mysterious 'I have been informed' (it was to this meeting that the senator Octavius is said to have come late, owing to the birth of a son who was to be the Emperor Augustus). But on the night of 20 October Crassus and two other prominent nobles came to Cicero and showed him anonymous letters warning them to avoid a massacre of optimates. Cicero called the Senate next morning and read the letters out. A praetor also produced messages from Etruria about the concentration of troops in the area. Cicero was even able to say, or so he later claimed, that Manlius was to rise on the 27th and the massacre in Rome to take place the next day. The Senate was at last impressed, and passed the Last Decree, about which there had recently been so much argument.* Some nervous senators seem to have left Rome. Probably at this point Cicero armed a strong force, while the companies of gladiators in Rome, of which there were suspicions, were removed from the city and dispersed. Nothing happened on the 28th. Catiline was still in Rome and attending the Senate, while Cicero's opponents continued to declare that he had invented the whole thing for his own greater glory. But a few days later a senator read out a letter showing that Manlius had indeed risen on the 27th, and there were other reports of unrest and of slave movements in the South – not necessarily the result of concerted conspiracy, as Cicero claimed. Magistrates were now dispatched in various directions to levy troops and suppress disturbances, and all Italian communities

* It is possible that there were two meetings of the Senate; thus Dio as opposed to Plutarch and Sallust.

were warned against surprises. Praeneste, near Rome, in fact repulsed an attempted *coup* on 1 November.

There was much alarm in Rome, and as always in such conditions prodigies of all sorts were reported to the Senate as signs of divine anger. But Catiline remained calm; there was no absolute proof that he was implicated in Manlius' actions. When an attempt to prosecute him for violence was made he offered, in order to repel suspicion, to place himself in the custody of any senator – that of the consul Cicero, perhaps? Cicero, and several others, refused to have him, and he went off to the house of a friend and probable confederate of his own, who did not prevent him from attending a conference with his chief allies on the night of 6 November at the house of M. Porcius Laeca in the Street of the Sickle-makers. Here he agreed plans for the rest of Italy and proposed that he himself should leave Rome for Manlius' army, which in the last resort could not do without his leadership. The others were to seize the city. First Cicero was to be murdered; two of the conspirators offered to do this, entering his house on the excuse of the customary early morning call. But when, at dawn on the 7th, they came to Cicero's house, they found the place strictly guarded. Cicero had learnt everything, as usual, through Fulvia, and had discussed the coming attempt with a number of leading senators.

He called the Senate next day to a temple near the Palatine, easier to guard than the Senate House, and surrounded it with loyal *equites* and other citizens. He probably supposed that Catiline had left the city and hoped at last to get support for action against him. But to the general amazement Catiline appeared. If Cicero's picture is to be trusted, no one greeted him, and all shrank away from the bench where he sat. But it was not likely that in the circumstances either his fellow-*nobiles* or any senators with *popularis* links or doubts about the Last Decree would give Cicero full backing. In the famous speech known as the First Catilinarian Cicero turned on his enemy and did his utmost to shake his nerve and drive him from Rome to open revolt, and to stir up the Senate. Its brilliantly vehement opening used to be known to every schoolboy:

How far, then, Catiline, will you go on abusing our patience? How long, you madman, will you mock at our vengeance? Will there be no end to your unbridled audacity? Is it nothing to you that there is a nightly guard on the Palatine, that there are patrols throughout the city, that the populace is in terror, that all honest men are rallying together, that the Senate meets in this stronghold, that the senators look on you with expressions of horror? Do you not see that all your plans are discovered? Do you not realize that you conspirators are bound hand and foot, by the knowledge that every man here has of you? Which of us do you think is not aware of what you did last night, or the night before, where you were, whom you summoned, what plans you made? Oh, what times we live in, what scandals we permit! * The Senate knows these things, the consul sees them; yet this man lives.

Cicero goes on (in the published version; but how close any of it is to the necessarily improvised speech of 8 November is impossible to tell) to show that he knows all about the meeting at Laeca's house, the abortive attempt at his own murder, and the state of Etruria; he gazes round the Senate and declares that he recognizes the other conspirators; he threatens to take action on the Last Decree, as he should have done long ago, as has so often been done before. But

there are not a few members of this order who either fail to see what hangs over us, or pretend that they do not see it; who have built up Catiline's hopes with their mildness, strengthened his plot as it grew by their scepticism; whose authority is such that had I dealt with this man many people, the ignorant as well as the wicked, would say that what I did was cruel and tyrannical.

Catiline seems to have interrupted to demand a vote as to whether he should leave Rome for exile; but Cicero could not risk that. Was it not enough, he asked, that no voice was raised in Catiline's behalf? If the consul were to ask the Senate about any other member, whether he should leave Rome, a great outcry would arise. It is uncertain whether Catiline answered the speech, as Sallust declares, accusing Cicero of being a mere 'immigrant to Rome'; Cicero himself and Plutarch record that he left the hall without a word. And he also left Rome. How far the speech contributed to that result we cannot say. But he was off to Etruria, where he raised the silver eagle that had been the standard of Marius, and kept all the pomp of a legitimate general of the Republic. He had, according to Plutarch, 20,000 men, He left letters for leading men in Rome, however, in which he stated that he was going into exile for the sake of his country's peace – presumably he wished to gain time and raise odium, even

---

* Somewhat more economically, in the Latin, the famous *o tempora, o mores!* which pleased Cicero so much he used it elsewhere as well.

if only temporarily, against Cicero. But Sallust reproduces the text of a letter to Catulus, in which, if only ambiguously, he admits the truth. In it we hear the proud and selfish tones of the Roman noble writing to his equal.

Inspired by wrongs and insults, failing to gain the due position and dignity in the state that I had earned by my toil and labours, I took up the cause of the poor and wretched . . . because I saw men unworthy of it honoured with office and felt myself avoided through groundless suspicion. For this reason I am pursuing the hope, honourable enough in the circumstances, of preserving what remains of my position. I would write further, but I am told violence is being prepared against me. Now I commend my wife Orestilla to you and entrust her to your honour. I implore you in the name of your own children to keep her from harm.

Next day Cicero reported to the People. He urged them to stay quiet, representing Catiline's departure as a great victory for the *boni*, and claiming that everything was under control in both Italy and Rome. He describes Catiline's confederates in Rome as 'those men whom I see circulating in the Forum, standing about by the Senate House, even entering the Senate, gleaming with unguents and glowing with purple', and claims that his supporters are made up of seven groups, rich men who will not pay their debts, ambitious men who cannot gain power in ordinary circumstances, debauched and effeminate youths, Sullan veterans run into debt who can only recover 'if Sulla rises from the dead' (a hint of proscriptions, this); and at a lower level the failures, the outright criminals, the slaves. This is of course a biased analysis; but Cicero was trying to persuade the mass of the urban *plebs* that it could have nothing in common with the revolutionaries. For the same reason he made much of the supposed plans for massacre and arson, and talked of himself as running into unpopularity with certain nobles in his attempts to protect the People. There is no doubt that this language had a certain effect.

When Catiline's presence in Etruria became known, the Senate declared him and Manlius public enemies and warned his men to leave him within a given time (there was little response). The consuls were to levy troops, and Antonius to march against Catiline, whom he should not have too much difficulty in subduing, while Cicero remained in the city. Here the position was much as it had been, in spite of Cicero's promises in the First Catilinarian that on Catiline's departure all would be rapidly cleared up. Catiline's associates were led by the praetor Cornelius Lentulus; an imposing figurehead at first sight from his name and rank, as from his dignified person and fine voice, but slow and superstitious; he had received an oracle to the effect that three members of the patrician clan of the Cornelii would reign in Rome, and imagined that he, after Cinna and Sulla, was to be the third. He had actually been consul in 71, but had been thrown out of the Senate by the reforming censors; he had made his way back, but could hardly hope for the standing and influence he doubtless considered his right. Also prominent were the fat and stupid ex-praetor Cassius Longinus, like Catiline a defeated candidate for the consulship of 63, and the violent Cethegus. (These hostile characterizations are of course Cicero's.) Their plan, though Cethegus apparently thought it too dilatory, was that Rome should be attacked simultaneously from within and without, towards the end of December, during the festival of the Saturnalia. Rome's walls were old and useless – though the stretch that still stands beside the main railway station has proved durable enough. And the inhabitants would be off their guard and making merry. But for the moment no move was made, and many people still held that Cicero was to blame for the unrest in the city and the warfare in Italy. The tribune-designate Metellus Nepos was taking this line; and some of the optimates had clearly relaxed, and allowed their ordinary feuds to come into the open. It was about now that Cato and Servius Sulpicius kept their promise and prosecuted the consul-designate Murena for using bribery at the election.

Murena was pretty obviously guilty. His prosecutors were both men of the highest integrity; Cato had already acquired a remarkable ascendancy, based on his force of character as well as his family connections, while Sulpicius was of course a friend of Cicero's. The law under which the accused was charged was Cicero's own. But Murena was an experienced soldier, who might be useful if Catiline were still at large in the new year; and the situation would be dangerous if, owing to a tribunicial veto on elections, there were to be only one consul on 1 January. Murena also had influential friends, including Lucullus, whom Cicero may have wished to conciliate. He determined, among his other distractions, to take the defence.

Hortensius and Crassus, who were also retained, spoke first. Plutarch tells us that Cicero was so anxious to excel Hortensius (who, since Cicero had reached the consulship, had begun to exert himself again for fear of being overshadowed) that he worked all night on his speech and seemed tired when he spoke. He had been up a good many nights round this time, by his own account: it was on his perpetual vigilance in the crisis that he most prided himself. But there is no sign of tiredness in the published speech. If the Catilinarians themselves are sometimes strained and verbose, the *pro Murena* is one of the wittiest and most agreeable of his orations. He excuses his action elegantly and politely, representing the prosecutors as high-minded but impractical idealists, in contrast to himself as a down-to-earth politician (this was, at least as far as Cato was concerned, his real opinion). Sulpicius had failed to be elected? Well, bribery was not the only possible explanation. Legal learning does not impress the people as much as military glory like Murena's; and has a less striking and noble function than oratory. And Cicero has great fun with pedantic and ludicrous legal terminology and the ingenious ways it takes to get round people's plain intentions. And then, Sulpicius went about his campaign in quite the wrong way: Cicero tells him what he should have done – but anyway, the electorate is totally unpredictable. As for Cato's Stoicism, what an impractical and improbable creed! Cato should read Plato and Aristotle instead, who recommend forgiveness and reconciliation. But Stoicism holds that the wise man is never influenced by favour, never changes his mind, never forgives, is never mistaken; he alone is handsome, rich, a king – even if others see him as hideous, poor and a slave. All sins are of equal gravity to the Stoic: it is as bad to wring a cock's neck as your father's. (This of course is a travesty, as Cicero later admitted: 'I was speaking before men unskilled in philosophy; I even conceded something to the general public.') But Cato will be mellowed by age. Indeed even now he is inconsistent, he does campaign for office, pretending he knows people when he has merely been prompted by a slave, and showing himself much more cordial than usual.

Cato himself is reported to have said, as the speech went on to the accompaniment of waves of laughter, 'What a comic consul we have' – perhaps with a hint of ambiguity. But Cicero ends on a serious note. Cato is short-sighted: the state needs Murena. There may be little danger from Catiline, but the Trojan Horse is within the walls, and Cicero must watch day and night for the safety of the Republic. There must be two consuls on 1 January, as Cato himself, as tribune, will find. Catiline is surely praying for Murena's condemnation. The speech also reveals Cicero's conservative acceptance of Roman institutions that even to some Roman tastes smacked of undue influence, especially the weighting of the *comitia centuriata* to the rich, and the whole client–patron system; let us not, he said, deprive the poor of their right to wait on us and attend us in return for our benefits to them – they cannot plead or go bail for us, or invite us to their homes, as we do for them.

Some days later the conspirators in Rome, with incredible folly, gave Cicero the opportunity for which he had been waiting so long; 'no burglary of a private house was ever made so obvious', he commented. They got in touch with the envoys of a Gallic tribe, the Allobroges, who were in Rome vainly seeking redress from the oppression of Roman governors in southern Gaul; and asked them to support Catiline with their admirable cavalry, and to effect a diversion by raising a revolt in the province. The Allobroges were uncertain what to do, and at last told their story to their hereditary patron, the senator Fabius Sanga, who informed Cicero. They were told to continue negotiating and to get documentary evidence. In the event the praetor Lentulus, Cethegus and others gave them letters, and a guide, Volturcius, to take them to Catiline. Volturcius had messages for Catiline from Lentulus, which are said to have included an injunction to enlist slaves – something Catiline had hitherto refused to do. On 2 November Cicero sent two of the praetors to conceal armed men (part of a body of supporters from Reate in the Sabine country, of which he was patron) at both ends of the Milvian Bridge across the Tiber outside Rome, across which all travellers going north must pass. Of the ensuing events he gave a precise report to the People in the Third Catilinarian Oration. In the night the Allobroges' party was caught on the bridge; their letters were seized, and Volturcius and others were handed over to Cicero just before dawn. The leading conspirators were summoned to the consul's house, came – Lentulus last of all – and were detained. A number of other prominent senators had also come to him, hearing the news. Still sceptical, they advised Cicero to read the letters before calling the Senate. But Cicero knew well enough what they contained, and was anxious to cover himself with the Senate's authority in every respect. 'I said that in a matter that concerned the public safety I would not deprive the public council of the right to be first to consider it.' He summoned the Senate to the Temple of Concord. Meanwhile, on a tip from the Allobroges, a praetor searched Cethegus' house and discovered a large quantity of arms. Cethegus said he had always been a collector of fine weapons.

Cicero himself led Lentulus into the temple where a crowded Senate had hurriedly convened. Four senators, at Cicero's instance, took down all that was said, though there was usually no verbatim record of proceedings. Volturcius was rapidly persuaded to turn state's evidence, and announced Lentulus' wish to arm slaves, and that as Catiline attacked Rome fires were to be lit at various points in the city and leading optimates killed. Then the Gauls were brought in, to tell of their meetings with Lentulus, Cethegus and the rest. At last the letters were produced; the writers were forced to acknowledge their seals, the contents were read out, and their authors, one after another, after a few vain denials, confessed. The idea of a few moderns, that Cicero had organized a plant, as well as a trap, is quite untenable. For one thing, Cicero's pride, to the end of his life, in his achievements this year, rules out any large-scale falsification on his part. The Senate, at all events, so long hesitant, now hastened to give Cicero all the backing he could desire. It passed a vote of thanks to him, and also to the praetors and Antonius (for dropping his old associate); it decided that the conspirators were to be kept in private custody for the time being, since Rome's prison facilities were inadequate – the senators who took charge of them included Crassus and Caesar. Lentulus had been persuaded to abdicate his praetorship, and lay by his purple-striped toga, conveniently as there was no good precedent for deposition, though there was some for ignoring an office in such a case. A public thanksgiving was decreed, something that had never been done before except for a general's victory in war. It may have been at this same sitting that Catulus called Cicero 'Father of his Country' and another ex-consul declared that he deserved the Civic Crown, the highest military decoration, which was given for saving the lives of fellow citizens.

The moment the Senate dispersed, before even the decree was recorded, Cicero reported to the crowds waiting in the Forum. He stressed again that all was under control. He was able to make the most of the threat of widespread conflagration, slave revolts and barbarian invasion. Any fire in the crowded, partly timber-built city was liable to be disastrous; many shopkeepers and artisans had much of their capital locked up in a slave or two; and the Romans always tended to hysteria about the Gauls,

never forgetting that 300 years earlier they had sacked the city,
and not distinguishing them from the Celtic or Germanic tribes
who had only forty years before destroyed several Roman armies
before being annihilated by Marius. From this point, at latest,
most of the urban *plebs* turned definitely against Catiline, and
Cicero's struggle for their allegiance was, for the moment at least,
won.

It was always useful to talk of religion to the *plebs*, but Cicero
may have felt in his exalted state that the gods had indeed been
with him. He said that the many signs of divine intervention in
his consulship had now been justified; the aid of Jupiter was
shown by the fact that at the very moment that the conspirators
were led across the Forum, the great statue of the god vowed
by the consuls two years before he was being put into place. It was
Jupiter who was to be thanked that, in this greatest of all wars
in history, the consul had been able to save the citizens without
bloodshed. What a contrast to the dreadful years of Marius and
Sulla! Even Pompey's deserts, Cicero added, were no greater than
his own. But all the reward that he desires, he says, is glory;
and he dismisses his auditors to rejoice quietly and thankfully,
continuing to keep guard against malefactors.

The people responded to the speech with unbounded enthusiasm. It is Sallust, no great lover of Cicero, who tells us this.
But he is surely right in saying that 'immense joy and anxiety
together filled the consul'. Whether the passage near the end of
the speech, begging for protection against those who wished him
ill, was inserted a few years later or not, Cicero must have been
looking back to what he had promised at Rabirius' trial, and
wondering if he dared put the conspirators to death on the
basis of the Last Decree of 21 October. There was no doubt of
their guilt, and a public trial would mean dangerous delay and an
invitation to violence. But there were nobles, indeed two patricians involved. And Cicero had always boasted of his mildness.
He spent the night at a friend's house; in his own the rites of the
Good Goddess, held every year in the home of a magistrate, were
being celebrated, and no man might be present. With a few
friends, including his brother, he discussed the situation. If we
may believe a story that apparently derives from Cicero's poem
on his consulship – and he did not think that strict historical
accuracy was required in such a work – Terentia came to them,
bringing a message from the Vestal Virgins. A sign had been
given to them at the sacrifice to the Goddess, a great flame leap-

ing up on the apparently dead altar, which should encourage Cicero to persist in his patriotic course.

Next day, 4 December, the Senate reconvened to hear a spectacular piece of information. A prisoner, caught on the road to Etruria, declared that he had been sent to hurry Catiline on – by M. Crassus. This is not likely. We know that Crassus had given Cicero information six weeks earlier; and the Senate as a whole refused to believe the tale, for whatever reasons. One theory, according to Sallust, was that the conspirators wanted to implicate Crassus and thus force him to use his immense influence to save them as well as himself. Sallust also says that he actually heard Crassus remark that Cicero had engineered the affair on purpose to embarrass him, but it is usually (and surely rightly) believed that Cicero would not have been so foolish. He had been doing his best to isolate the conspirators, not to involve others, and he refused, at this same sitting, to help Catulus and another ex-consul to implicate Caesar on dubious evidence. It seems that Caesar at some point had also given the government useful information. But Catulus had doubtless not forgiven Caesar for filching the high priesthood from him. There are those who still believe that Crassus and Caesar really were involved, and that Cicero knew it; partly on the basis of a fragment from the frank historical memoir that Cicero later wrote. But what this apparently said was that they were *responsible* for the conspiracy, as in a sense, by their long support of Catiline, they were.

While the Senate still sat, there came news that there had been an attempt to free Lentulus and Cethegus; their freedmen and clients had been trying to persuade the People to use force. Cicero set guards on the Capitoline Hill and in the Forum, and summoned all citizens capable of bearing arms to make oath that they would come to the aid of the state in need. The quaestors' clerks were too few, he later said, to take down the names of all who offered themselves. Above all the *equites*, with Atticus among them and urging them on, congregated on the Capitol in arms.

It was now urgent to decide what to do with the conspirators. On 5 December – the Nones of December – the Senate met again, surrounded with guards. Crassus, it appears, was absent; Caesar, with his usual courage, was in his place. The course of this most famous meeting is not known to us in all its details. We have Cicero's speech as published, and those of Caesar and Cato in the compressed but perhaps not wholly unfaithful versions of Sallust. Since Cicero had set shorthand writers to work, Sallust and the later historians could have had good material to work on. But the rhetorical tradition of historiography permitted great freedom in the reworking of speeches. Sallust simplifies the debate to make his contrast of Caesar and Cato stand out, and has little interest in constitutional niceties; and the later historians differ in various details. The real trouble is that we are not sure of the order in which the various interventions were made.

Cicero, as the only consul in Rome, necessarily presided and put the question to the Senate, which was theoretically his body of advisers, though their advice had long been considered binding. He called first on the consul-designate, Silanus, who declared that the five men in custody and four others still at large deserved 'the extreme penalty', which was understood to mean death. The other consul-designate, Murena, and all fourteen of the ex-consuls present agreed. Then Caesar, as praetor-designate, spoke. According to Sallust he begged the Senate to judge coolly, and this seems wholly in character. He agreed that no punishment could be too harsh for the prisoners, but he insisted that to put them to death without trial would be a disastrous precedent. 'Though I have no fear of this with Marcus Tullius', he said, on another occasion another consul might be encouraged to act tyrannically. Also, it would cause disorder. The laws were wise in allowing exile as an alternative to death. Let the prisoners' property be confiscated, let them be confined in various strongly fortified Italian towns ('a new form of penalty', though foreign princes and hostages had been so confined). Anyone attempting their release should be seriously punished, and to propose it to Senate or People should be treason. Was not such a penalty worse than death?

This was a very clever and a very brave speech. By it Caesar dissociated himself entirely from the conspirators, and yet dared to maintain, if perhaps in rather veiled form, the *popularis* principles with which he was associated. The proposal, if successful, would have made the Senate look indecisive, and there could be no security that the prisoners would not be released in time. But the speech had an effect. It was probably at this stage that an ex-praetor proposed that a decision should be put off until Catiline was defeated. Various opinions were put forward, and it seems that Cicero found it necessary to intervene, demanding a rapid decision between Silanus' and Caesar's proposals. He begged the senators not to worry about his own position if they declared for death; he had always been in danger in his consulship. In fact this was probably not the only thing the Senate was anxious about, but Cicero's egotism had a strong hold on him in this supreme moment. He was ready for, he would even prefer, he said, a decision for death,* relying on the unity of all classes that had been achieved and the support he was sure the Senate would give to one who had deserved a place above the great heroes of old, above even Marius and Pompey. But he would carry out Caesar's proposal, difficult as it would be, if it got a majority vote. Silanus now turned round and said that by the 'extreme penalty' he had meant prison. And except probably for Catulus, everyone, including Quintus Cicero, supported him, in part at least, as Plutach says, to spare Cicero responsibility and danger – until it came to the turn of the tribunes-designate and Cato. According to Plutarch, Cato fiercely reproached his brother-in-law Silanus for changing his mind, and attacked Caesar savagely (Sallust, who admired them both, has nothing of this): Caesar was lucky not to be in danger himself, and it was ludicrous that he should influence the Senate. According to Sallust, Cato went on to say that the prisoners would not be safe outside Rome. Pity was wholly out of place; the Senate must recover its senses and make a firm decision, which would have an effect in Catiline's army. Men of noble family had planned to fire Rome, had called Gauls to their aid, Catiline was in the field, yet still the senators hesitated. But the conspirators had confessed. They must die, like criminals caught in the act, as ancestral tradition demanded in such cases. The Senate burst into applause. It seems that Cato altered the whole course of the debate. It was extraordinary that someone so junior should have such an effect.

A piece of by-play between Cato and Caesar is also recorded. According to Plutarch a letter was brought in to Caesar in the course of the proceedings, and Cato accused him of being in communication with the conspirators, challenging him to read the note out loud. Caesar instead passed it across to him; it was a love-letter from Cato's sister Servilia. Cato threw it aside in rage.

Cicero finally put the question on Cato's motion. He explains

---

* This is made clear in the published version of the speech, the Fourth Catilinarian. Plutarch says it was not clear in the Senate; but in the letter to Atticus quoted below Cicero insists that it was. Some hold that he spoke at the end of the debate, but if so the speech must have made some reference to Cato, since it was his motion rather than Silanus' that was ultimately put to the vote. Other scholars arrange the debate differently in other respects.

why in a letter to Atticus of 45 B.C., in which he complains of the account given by Brutus in his memoir of his uncle Cato.

Brutus is shockingly ignorant on this point; he thinks that Cato was the first to propose the death penalty. Everyone who spoke before Caesar advocated it . . . Why then was it Cato's motion that was voted on? Because it comprised the same meaning in grander and ampler language. Then Brutus praises me for bringing the matter before the Senate – not for discovering the plot, not for urging the Senate on, not for making my own decision before consulting the Senate! It was because Cato had praised all this to the skies and moved that it be officially recorded that it was on his motion that the vote was taken.

It was overwhelmingly for death.

Caesar dared to argue that in this case the conspirators' property should not be confiscated. His suggestion, perhaps because it seemed to imply that his first proposal had not been serious in its claim to severity, was greeted with uproar, and Caesar begged in vain for the protection of the tribunes. The *equites* outside were ready to lynch him and Cicero had personally to escort him out of the temple.* He himself however saw to it that the prisoners' property was spared.

For the rest of the day's events we must turn to Plutarch, though his account may be elaborated with rhetorical commonplaces. Cicero gave order that all should be made ready at once for the execution. He went in person to fetch Lentulus from the house on the Palatine where he was under restraint, and four praetors brought the other prisoners. The leading senators and armed guards accompanied them across the Forum, while the people watched in silence. One after another the prisoners went down into the subterranean vaults of the Tullianum, the ancient prison of Rome below the Capitol; one after another, they had their necks broken by the executioner. When all was over the consul announced loudly to the crowd in the Forum, where some were still meditating rescue, '*Vixere*' – 'They have lived', in other words 'Their lives are over'. It was now evening; and as Cicero was accompanied home by all the chief men in the state and a mass of other followers, the streets of the city, usually dark, were illuminated, women crowded to wave from the roof-tops, and the people acclaimed him as the saviour of the state.

---

* According to Sallust this had occurred rather on 4 December. After this Caesar kept out of the Senate till the end of the year.

We should perhaps remember that while our sources, all steeped in rhetoric, may have edited and improved on reality, all the participants in the events, too, had been formed by the same educational and political tradition and fell by second nature into striking poses. This is one of the reasons why the history of the period is often so exciting. The last scene of Cicero's consulship was as dramatic as any that had gone before. On 10 December the new tribunes, including Metellus Nepos and Cato, came into office. On the last day of the year Cicero went to the assembly to pronounce the usual oath of a retiring magistrate, that he had obeyed the laws, and to take his farewell as consul of the People. Nepos refused to allow him to do anything more than take the bare oath, on the ground that one who had put citizens to death without trial should not himself be allowed to speak to the People. But when silence was obtained, Cicero was heard to swear, not the ordinary formula, but that he had saved his country and maintained her supremacy. And to the chagrin of the tribune the People greeted his words with enthusiasm.

In Etruria, as Sallust reports, Catiline had taken to the Appenines, where he avoided battle, in hopes of hearing of success at Rome; he was still refusing to recruit slaves. When the bad news came that the conspirators had been executed, many of his troops deserted; with the rest he determined to flee to Gaul. But his movements were forestalled, and early in the new year, being hemmed in to north and south by mountains and enemy forces, he staked everything on a pitched battle against Antonius near Pistoria, the present Pistoia. His opponent and old associate, on the plea of gout, handed over the command to his lieutenant, who was an experienced soldier. Catiline placed his few well-armed troops in front across the narrow valley, and, dismissing his horse, took his stand by the eagle of Marius. It was a grim hand-to-hand combat; Catiline was unremittingly active, 'carrying out at once the duties of a brave soldier and a good commander'. But the issue could not be in doubt. Sallust declares that the rebel troops were killed where they stood, and not a single free man was taken alive. As for their leader, when all was lost, 'mindful of his descent and of his previous standing', he flung himself where the enemy was thickest; his body was later found far within their lines, 'his face still showing the ferocity of mind that had marked him in life'.

So Sallust tells us; but had he good information, or did he simply think that this was how the reckless conspirator should have, must have died? Catiline disappears, in the end, into the haze of rhetoric from which he has never really emerged.

*

Note: The Trial of Rabirius

My reconstruction of the trial differs from that now most usually accepted, which rests on the great authority of Mommsen and Gelzer. The latter holds that there was a popular trial on appeal from the sentence of the Duoviri, broken off just before the voting by the affair of the flag; and that later there was another trial, with only a fine as penalty, under Labienus' presidency and thus in the Forum (since tribunes could not preside in the *comitia centuriata*). At this Cicero delivered the speech we have, which shows that there is now no danger of crucifixion.

But it seems impossible that Cicero in his speech could completely ignore the first trial, which on this hypothesis was only broken up when all the arguments had been presented; indeed, for obvious political reasons, he would surely have taken the defence in it; but the opening of our speech shows that this is the first time he has appeared for Rabirius (and when in 60 he lists the speeches he made as consul he only mentions one for Rabirius). I assume then that he and the Senate quashed the first trial before the start; and this perhaps does better justice to his language than the supposition that they merely altered the savage penalty, or even that they simply prevented Rabirius' arrest and thus left exile open to him.

But we must have one trial in the *comitia centuriata*, in the Field of Mars, for the flag scene. So I would assume a second trial for *perduellio* (the first actually to take place), by a more ordinary process, with a praetor presiding. (A trial with a fine is referred to by Cicero, but it is not clear that this is the trial at which he is speaking. He seems to imply that Rabirius is still in danger of exile, though Mommsen and Gelzer think his language exaggerated and misleading here.) This reconstruction has the merit of fitting Dio, admittedly a poorish witness, who does say categorically that Labienus did not take up the case again after the flag scene, which he has to do in Mommsen's and Gelzer's view. Mine is closer to those of Rice Holmes, Hardy and Ciaceri, also now A. H. M. Jones (who believes Labienus presided).

Somewhat similarly, the political situation makes it more likely that the *populares* were issuing a general warning about the *senatus consultum ultimum* than that they were arguing simply that in the peculiar circumstances in which Rabirius acted (he was not a magistrate, Saturninus had been given a pledge of safety and was still tribune) the *senatus consultum ultimum* had been misused. Cicero who, unlike Rabirius, acted as a magistrate and with full senatorial backing, knew that what he was doing was nonetheless disputed. True, Caesar in the Senate on 5 December seems to have admitted that death would be justifiable; but he would really have been lynched if he had not, and certainly would not have had the influence on the debate that his moderation gave him. In his account of the civil war he accepts that the *senatus consultus ultimum* may be rightly used – but here, many years later, he is trying to recommend himself to politically *bien pensant* readers.

What the *senatus consultus ultimum* really meant is debated. It has been argued either that it created a state of war thus giving the consul wider powers (so Mommsen) or that it was mere advice that could make no legal difference. In fact the distinction is not clear-cut. The Senate's advice, no more than advice formally, was supposed to be binding, and for a consul to take strong action without the Senate's support would be insanity. (Thus Cicero could not possibly have acted, in December, simply on the strength of a six-week-old *senatus consultus ultimum* that did not name anyone but Catiline and Manlius.)

6

POMPEY'S RETURN TO ROME
62-60 B.C.

In a strictly political sense the whole of Cicero's life, hitherto so remarkable a success story, is from this point one of failure. This was not at first apparent. On laying down the consulship he became one of the elder statesmen, the *principes civitatis* or chief men in the state, with whom lay supreme influence, especially in the Senate. He felt that he deserved in every way to rank with or before the great nobles in this position. Indeed it is likely that in 62 the consul regularly called upon him to give his opinion in first place in senatorial debates – to judge by his complaints next year, when he only came second, yet still before Catulus and Hortensius.

At first the old political alliances were still in being, as the cooperation of Pompey's new tribune Nepos with the praetor Caesar shows. Promptly on 1 January Caesar accused Catulus of embezzling money granted him as overseer for rebuilding the temple of Capitoline Jupiter, which had been destroyed in a fire some years earlier, and proposed that Pompey's name, not his, should be inscribed on it. Nepos had, it appears, originally intended to get permission for Pompey to return to a second consulship, to which he should be elected in absence and before the statutory ten years' interval was up; but now, with Caesar at his side and slaves and gladiators round the platform, he put forward a proposal for Pompey's immediate recall to deal with Catiline. In the disorderly scenes that followed, Cato and another tribune got knocked about in trying to interpose their veto. The Senate had rapid resort to the Last Decree, and suspended Nepos and Caesar from their functions. Nepos departed East, probably after the news from Etruria came in, declaring that Pompey would avenge the insult to the tribunicial office. Caesar accepted the situation, and by quelling a riot in his own favour quickly earned his reinstatement; he then devoted his energies to repelling attempts to involve him in the trials of minor conspirators that now began. In this Cicero bore him out. All these trials ended in condemnation, except that of Publius Sulla, a nephew of the

Dictator, who was supported by influential nobles and defended by Cicero himself. The damning evidence that Cicero gave at the other trials was naturally conclusive.

Yet, though perhaps no one realized it, initiative had passed out of his hands, even before the end of his consulship. It fell, in some part, into those of Cato. It was Cato for example who tried to safeguard the People's favour by increasing the number of those eligible to receive cheap corn – the only reform that any of the optimates thought to propose. But Cato was a bitter enemy of Pompey; there was no use in Cicero detaching Pompey from Caesar and the other *populares* if the optimates were not willing to receive him. True, the Senate in the spring passed a new vote of thanksgiving to Pompey (partly at Cicero's instance) and put off the elections so that his lieutenant M. Pupius Piso could stand for the consulship, though they would not delay them until his own return; and they also affronted him by giving a triumph to a rival. In a sense the problem of Pompey's alliances, that so preoccupied Cicero, was a secondary one, but it was nevertheless genuinely important. Cicero was equally aware of one of the more basic problems, that of holding the classes together. But he hardly seems to have realized that only in an emergency could eloquence draw very different interests together. No more than others among the optimates did he make any attempt to instigate far-reaching reforms at this point: indeed he later says that on the suppression of the conspiracy it proved that all debts could easily be paid in full – doubtless a complacent reaction to a serious problem; if what he says is true, it was probably due to Pompey's victories establishing credit.

And Cicero's personal influence was itself threatened. Attacks from *populares* such as Nepos were to be expected; but at the trial of P. Sulla he had to repel a bitter personal assault by the young optimate prosecutor, who described his position in Rome as tyrannical and himself as an 'alien despot', and further accused him of falsifying the official report of the evidence given by the Allobroges, to incriminate or exculpate whom he pleased. He spent much of the time allowed him in court in meeting this attack; but it was prophetic of his inability, in the next few years, to find full cooperation among the great nobles.

To some extent this was undoubtedly Cicero's own fault. And yet, though he was certainly self-centred, the charge of vanity commonly made against him is not exactly correct; for he was sometimes able to laugh at himself, and in moods of depression his self-criticism was as excessive as was his self-satisfaction in periods of exaltation, while his judgement of others was often very generous. He did, during and after his consulship, boast unconscionably of his achievement, even if with occasional apologies, and he had, even by Roman standards with their high value for glory, an insatiable thirst to hear others praise him – the result, perhaps, of an underlying insecurity rooted in both his origin and temperament. But two things must be remembered. One is that *dignitas*, position, and also office, depended in Rome directly on a man's achievements or those of his ancestors, and on public recognition thereof; thus 'new men' in particular tended to extol their own acts, though nobles too might write apologetic memoirs, like Caesar, or get literary men to expatiate on their deeds, like Pompey. The alternative was the haughty assumption of some of Cicero's high-born correspondents, that everyone is aware of the merits of their forefathers. Certainly, the language of the 'new men' might disgust such nobles; and in particular Cicero's enthusiasm for the Roman tradition, in so far as it led him to claim a place with the heroes of old, will have seemed to those heroes' descendants intolerable in a man from Arpinum. Secondly it must be remembered that there was, especially after 61, a real prospect that the question of the death-sentence on the conspirators would come up again; and if Cicero then disseminated a flood of information in Greek and Latin, prose and verse, about his aims and achievements, this is at least understandable.

But there were other ways in which, as we saw, he stood apart from the average noble: his deeper intellectual interests, his lack of military experience, his whole mercurial temperament and in particular the wit, unusual and somewhat suspect in a Roman, that was often turned against individuals. He could never control his tongue; and he lacked, many may have felt, the *gravitas* proper to a leader of the state.

In 62 self-satisfaction did not entirely blind him to the need for tact and conciliation. When Metellus Celer sent a laconic note, full of family pride, reproaching Cicero and the Senate with neglect of himself and with daring to oppose his brother Nepos, Cicero wrote back to justify himself firmly but politely, even laughing at his own desire for congratulations from everybody, and admitting that on one occasion the Senate had laughed too. He was also disappointed at not getting them from Pompey. Early in the year he had sent off a tremendous letter 'the size of a book' (and 'somewhat arrogant' according to a later commentator) on the subject of his consulship. It seems to have been an open letter; at least the prosecutor of Sulla quoted it. It is lost, but we have the short answer Cicero wrote to Pompey's reply, which it is clear that he considered sadly cold. Pompey was perhaps still keeping his alternatives open, and may not have liked the way Cicero had tried to commit him. Cicero in this second letter expressed the hope that they would be close cooperators on Pompey's return; he hoped, he said, to play Laelius to the other's Scipio – referring to the close friend and respected adviser of the great soldier Scipio Aemilianus. He also got in a dig about 'those new friends and old enemies of yours', by whom he certainly meant Crassus and Caesar, indicating their unreliability. These are the first letters of his to correspondents other than Atticus to survive.

The only preserved speech, besides the one for Sulla, made in this year is one on behalf of his old teacher the poet Archias, whose status as a Roman citizen had been attacked. Archias, he hoped, would write a poem on his consulship, and he may also have wished to oblige Archias' patron Lucullus; he made the speech an expression of gratitude to the poet and an eloquent panegyric of the delights of literature. Towards the end of the year Cicero, who by now owned several country properties in Latium and Campania, bought from Crassus a splendid house on the Palatine Hill, overlooking the Forum and most of Rome. It was much less costly than those of the most extravagant of his contemporaries; but still it was doubtless to some extent one of those palaces he describes as 'built of marble, gleaming with ivory and gold, full of statues and pictures, embossed gold and silver plate, and Corinthian bronze vessels'. It got him so heavily into debt that, as he cheerfully wrote to a friend, he was ready to join any conspiracy going – but no one would have him; however, he went on, the other result of his recent activities was that the money-lenders regarded him as a good risk.

His grand house, however, was not likely to still jealousies, and the fact that one of the loans that had financed it came from P. Sulla was susceptible of an unpleasant interpretation – that Cicero would take money to protect conspirators (in fact there seems to have been little hard evidence against Sulla). There was also trouble over his former colleague Antonius, now misbehaving himself in the province of Macedonia. It seems that another loan was in question, and Cicero heard ('I do not dare to say, "I have been informed" ') that it was being put about in the province that Antonius' extortions were made on Cicero's behalf. Such financial assistance in return for benefits – and both Sulla and Antonius were morally deep in Cicero's debt – was not unusual in Rome; but in both these cases Cicero had probably been foolish to accept it. Next year however he reported that the new consul, a noble, had also bought a house with loans from his friends (getting a bad bargain) and that people were now less critical of his own action.

At the end of 62 the calm that had apparently descended on Rome came to an end; also we know more about events, since Atticus had left Rome for his estate in Epirus across the Adriatic. Unfortunately Cicero found it hard to get messengers who would not 'lighten the weight of a letter of any substance by a perusal', and so is often elliptical, or probably downright silent, about important matters. As well as politics his letters are full of detail about financial affairs, in which Atticus had clearly begun to assist him, and about literary and other subjects. It is plain that the last years of Atticus' presence in Rome had cemented their old friendship.

About the time that these letters open Pompey landed in Italy. He dismissed his army, since there was now no possible excuse for intervention. He also dismissed his wife, which, as she was half-sister to Celer and Nepos, and as Caesar was it seems thought to be her seducer, was also a political act, a divorce from his recent *popularis* associates. 'Mucia's divorce is strongly approved of,' wrote Cicero. Pompey had often marked his changes of policy by a new marriage – that to Mucia had been his third. According to Plutarch he now or a little later actually applied to Cato himself for an alliance with his niece. But Cato refused the offer, and in the Senate obstructed other requests of Pompey's. As for Cicero, Pompey could not persuade himself to enthusiasm. 'As you said, he began to praise me when he found he did not dare to criticize . . . he pretends regard, intimacy and affection for me, and praises me in words, but underneath it is easy to see that he is jealous. There is nothing courteous, nothing straightforward, nothing politically superior, nothing honourable, nothing courageous, nothing generous there.' It is the first of many complaints of Pompey's disingenuousness.

Meanwhile Rome was distracted by a spectacular scandal. 'I expect you have heard that Publius Clodius, son of Appius, was caught dressed as a woman in Caesar's house at the national sacrifice and that he owed his preservation and escape to the hands of a slave girl; a tremendous scandal. I am sure you are much distressed.' Clodius was supposed to have been present on an assignation with Caesar's wife; the sacrifice was the exclusively feminine celebration to the Good Goddess, which had been held as we saw in Cicero's house the year before, and this time was taking place in that of Caesar as praetor; the fact that he was also *pontifex maximus* simply made the position worse. The affair had political ramifications, for young Clodius, who was just about to enter on his quaestorship, had enemies, especially his brother-in-law Lucullus, and was already something of a demagogue. Though he used a popular version of his name, he belonged to one of the most illustrious houses in Rome, that of the patrician Claudii, which had produced consuls in every generation since the foundation of the Republic – a house, too, with a remarkable tradition of arrogant and individualistic behaviour (and family tradition, as we know, was important to the Roman noble) as well as vast patronage in the Greek East. Many tales were told of them, and particularly of this branch, the Claudii Pulchri; it was a Pulcher who, when the sacred chickens failed to give a favourable omen before a naval battle, by turning up their beaks at the corn offered them, is said to have flung them into the sea, saying, 'If they won't eat, let them drink'. It was a later Claudius Pulcher who, when refused a triumph by the Senate, celebrated it on his own account, taking his daughter, a Vestal Virgin and sacrosanct, in the chariot with him to discourage forcible intervention. Like others of his name, this man had been a politician of formidable stature and ambition, with policies not confined to a single line, whether reactionary or demagogic, as later historians tended to suppose.

In the present generation the Claudii Pulchri were represented by a family of three brothers and three sisters (unusually large for the Roman upper class), all of dubious reputation. They stuck together, to the extent that P. Clodius, the youngest brother, was regularly accused of incest with one or more of his sisters. Ordinarily one would say that such charges told us more about the standards of political debate at Rome than their subject's morals (Cicero was to be accused of incest with Tullia), but in this case the rumours were very persistent and came in part from those who should have known, particularly (in a statement on oath) Lucullus, who married and divorced the youngest Clodia. The second sister, the wife of Metellus Celer, was also guilty, at least according to Cicero, and is the one most usually identified with the woman whom the poet Catullus addressed under the name of Lesbia, and who caused him so much unhappiness by her promiscuity. The eldest brother and head of the house, who bore the unusual forename of Appius like his father and numerous ancestors, had had to pilot his brothers and sisters through an impoverished youth, was rapacious, entirely without shame, a great collector of works of art, profoundly supersititious, and a repository of the civil and religious traditions of Rome. Cicero's relations with him were not so singlemindedly hostile as those with his youngest brother soon became.

The optimates were much concerned about the Bona Dea affair. Could Caesar or Clodius or both be discredited? How would the somewhat *popularis* consul, Pupius Piso, a friend of Clodius and already at odds with his colleague, react? What would Pompey's attitude be? The matter was referred to the Vestal Virgins and the College of Priests, who ruled that it was a matter of sacrilege. Some optimates pressed hard for a trial.

Cicero says that he began by great severity; he seems to have taken a high moral line about the degeneracy and irresponsibility of the younger generation. But seeing how much influence Clodius had with some of the nobles and how he was preparing gangs, he began to fear that the affair might have disastrous repercussions, since the *boni* had rashly chosen to try their strength on the issue; and for a while he drew in his horns. In the event, Caesar parried the blow cleverly by divorcing his wife without admitting her guilt ('Caesar's wife must be above suspicion'); thus no one was able to say he was condoning sacrilege, yet he was able to remain on good terms with Clodius, whom he may have envisaged as an ally in politics. As for Pompey, the first speech he had made on his return had pleased nobody, it was so noncommittal: 'it was a frost'. But now, under a tribune's questioning, he came down 'very aristocratically' and at great length against Clodius and for the Senate – thus alienating his own friend the consul Pupius Piso. He also spoke in the Senate in general commendation of its recent policy and said to Cicero as he sat down that he thought that was enough on that subject. We may imagine Cicero bridling; we may also imagine Pompey's hurt feelings that nobody in Rome seemed the least interested in his immense achievements abroad. Crassus then rose and praised Cicero to the skies, clearly in order to show the Senate that Pompey was only a lukewarm supporter of both it and Cicero, and thus to prevent the threatening alliance between them.

In short, his speech developed that whole theme which I am accustomed to illustrate in my speeches, of which you are such a revered critic – fire, sword and so on – you know my palette. It was very impressive. Pompey was sitting next to me, and I saw he was annoyed, whether at Crassus gaining the credit he could have had, or that my achievements are so great that the Senate is pleased to hear them praised, and that by one who owes it to me the less, in that in all my writings, whenever I praise Pompey, it is at his expense. Today has brought me close to Crassus; not but what I was glad to take whatever Pompey openly or covertly granted me. As for myself, good gods, how I showed myself off before my new hearer, Pompey! If ever I had well-rounded periods, cadences, arguments of all kinds at my call, I had them then. In short, I brought the house down. For this was the theme, the dignity of the Senate, the unity of Italy, the dying remnants of the conspiracy, the price of corn, peace at home. You know how I can thunder on those subjects; the rolls were so loud that I need say little, you must have heard them over there [in Epirus].

The speech was probably published, but its loss can be borne with equanimity. We, like Atticus, know how he could thunder on these subjects.

After disorderly scenes in the assembly, in which Clodius attacked his optimate enemies, primarily Cato ('of me he only complained that "I had been informed" '), an extraordinary court was successfully set up some time in the spring of 61. The original idea of specially selected jurors was given up, for the optimates under Hortensius thought that 'a sword of lead would do to cut Clodius' throat', in other words that acquittal was inconceivable. Cicero believed this to be a mistake, but he did not refuse to give evidence, breaking the alibi put forward by the defence by stating that he had seen Clodius in Rome on the day in question. The story that Cicero acted under pressure from Terentia, who was jealous of Clodia, is certainly no more than typical Roman gossip.

The trial seemed to start well; the jurors were not a very reputable lot, but when Cicero was called they rose and surrounded him in a demonstration, which pleased him intensely, of protection against Clodius' violent supporters; next they even asked the Senate for a guard so that they could deliberate in security. But then, according to Cicero, Crassus got to work;*

* Cicero does not name him in his letter to Atticus, and it is not quite beyond doubt that the man he describes as distributing money is Crassus.

and Clodius was acquitted by a majority verdict. 'Meeting one of them later, Catulus asked "why did you want us to give you a guard? Were you afraid of your money being stolen?" '

Cicero regarded the verdict as the death-knell of that unity in the state established by himself in 63 and as a great victory for the 'scoundrels'. But, he wrote to Atticus,

It was I again (for I don't think that I am boasting objectionably when I talk about myself to you, especially in a letter which I don't want others to read) it was I, as I say, again who revived the drooping spirits of the *boni* . . . deprived the consul Piso of the province of Syria which had been promised him . . . Clodius I crushed in the Senate in a set speech of great solemnity and also in a sharp exchange, of which you may taste a few points; most of it loses its force and savour when the excitement of battle is over.

The exchange centred on such subjects as the propriety of Cicero visiting seaside resorts and buying his great house.

'You would think he was saying I'd bought a jury,' I said. 'The jurors gave no credit to your sworn testimony,' he said. 'No,' I said, 'twenty-five of them did give me credit – but thirty-one gave you none, for they got their money in advance.' Overwhelmed by roars of applause he collapsed into silence.

Flushed with a success that perhaps was not as important as he thought, Cicero goes on to tell Atticus that his own position is all he could wish, indeed recent jealousies have been reduced by the 'painless blood-letting' of the defeat inflicted by Clodius' acquittal; and the People, believing him to be close to Pompey, with whom he has indeed much personal contact, 'gives me wonderful applause at the games and gladiators, without a single shepherd's whistle'. But in fact, perhaps by his language in the Senate rather than his mere evidence, he had made of Clodius a dangerous enemy. He had also attacked a prominent noble, Curio, who had defended Clodius at the trial; but Curio and his son forgave him, where the arrogant Claudian did not. It is possible that, having supported him in 63, Clodius regarded Cicero's conduct to him as ungrateful; anyway he had already shown a liking for spectacular pieces of revenge: when Lucullus in the East had treated him with what he saw as insufficient honour, he promptly fomented a mutiny of his troops. Able and ambitious, the young man now had his eye on the tribunate, undeterred by the fact that as a patrician he was ineligible for it – ways round that could be devised. And he let it be known that when tribune he would proceed against Cicero for putting the conspirators to death in 63.

The excitement of 'the Clodian drama' had held up all business, even preventing the ex-praetors being allotted their provinces (this sort of thing was all too prevalent in the last years of the Republic, and led to serious neglect of, in particular, foreign affairs). But now Caesar went off to Spain, and Quintus Cicero to the province of Asia (western Asia Minor). He avoided seeing Atticus on the way, since to Cicero's grief he was on bad terms with his brother-in-law. Atticus wrote to exculpate himself, and in reply Cicero begged him to do nothing so unnecessary; and for, as is plain, the first time put into words the affection and respect that he felt for his friend. Though their ways of life were different 'in the things that truly deserve praise, in uprightness, honesty, conscientiousness and sense of duty I put you second neither to myself nor anyone, and in affection for me, leaving aside my brother and family, no one is your equal . . . indeed in your absence I badly miss not only the advice you give so well but the pleasure of our conversation together'. On these two pillars the friendship was to rest for many long years. Cicero indeed often clamoured for advice – largely on politics, for he held Atticus to be 'a politician by nature', however carefully he avoided personal involvement, and Atticus' contacts with leading optimates, and also with many of the most influential friends of Pompey and (later) Caesar, were of great value to Cicero in his own somewhat isolated position. He also greatly respected, and even feared, Atticus' literary judgement, especially as to what constituted pure latinity; he often wrote or tried to write to his friend's suggestion, and was overjoyed when Atticus praised his writings – chiefly the speeches and political philosophy, for Atticus was less able to criticize the strictly philosophic works to which Cicero later turned, and is perhaps significantly not discovered complimenting his verse – though (or because) he was himself a great lover of poetry; it is recorded that he read it aloud beautifully. He was also a great lover of the past, and himself a historian; but although often called on by Cicero to do historical research for him, Atticus never succeeded in his plan to get Cicero to write a full-scale history. By contrast, Cicero never gave advice, going only so far once or twice as to suggest that Atticus ought to think carefully about his own position; for this the self-sufficiency of the latter was quite as much responsible as the self-centred nature of the former.

For the rest, Atticus' main business in life was to look after his fortune, and help his friends, of whom he had many, of all ages and, in spite of his strictly optimate beliefs, of all shades of opinion. In Cicero's case he finally took over responsibility for his financial affairs and saw to it that his new works were disseminated in correct and handsome copies made by his own well-trained slaves (even his footmen, we are told, had a literary education). He had the strictest regard for truth and obligation, and lived with striking simplicity in spite of his wealth, which after the death of his difficult uncle was very great; scorning in particular the rage for building and collecting, even though he was a noted connoisseur (his Epicureanism probably meant little more to him than a warrant for devotion to friendship, private life, and simplicity). He was an amusing conversationalist with idiosyncratic turns of phrase, and (to judge by the portrait in some of Cicero's dialogues) at times a pleasing tartness of judgement. To Cicero he was the embodiment of *elegantia*, good taste, and *humanitas*, a quality possibly better conveyed in English by the word 'civilized' than by 'human' or 'humane'. There was more in Atticus, then, than the caution and compliance that have disgusted some scholars: though he was cautious and compliant, and rewarded for it by surviving all turns of the political wheel with position and fortune intact. He soon came to be remembered simply as Cicero's friend; but where his relationship with Cicero is concerned, we should always remember that he was the elder, richer, socially more secure and emotionally more independent of the two; and that he was not only thought to deserve in his own right a place in the series of short lives of Roman historians by his friend Cornelius Nepos, but that, in his contacts with Greek and Roman scholars and writers of his day, his encouragement of their works, his complete mastery of Greek and many aspects of Greek culture due to his long residence in Athens and his firm rejection of some tendencies of Roman life, combined with a deep love of Rome and her past, he held a very notable place in the cultural life of his time.

Cicero had hoped that Atticus would have accompanied Quintus to Asia, where in his governorship, prolonged against his will for three years, he in fact gave his brother much anxiety. Quintus was thoroughly honest, but irascible; his rash letters about burning people alive were hardly to be taken literally, but he did want to sew a parricide into a sack and throw him into the sea, the old-fashioned punishment for such a crime. And he made himself disliked by relying for advice on a confidential slave, one Statius, whom he soon freed, instead of on men of suitable rank. Cicero felt that Quintus' unpopularity would damage himself too; indeed, he long thought and spoke of himself and his brother almost as a single political unit. At some point he was moved to write an admirable treatise on the proper duties of a governor, in the form of a letter to his brother; to this we will come back.

Meanwhile the question of Pompey's veterans and his arrangements in the East was becoming urgent. And the optimates were not in conciliatory mood. Had they been so, Pompey, still not himself eligible to stand again, would probably not have been bribing heavily to get an insignificant friend of his own, Afranius, into the consulship for 60. 'Here, do you observe that if he gets in, the office I make so much of, which Curio used to call an apotheosis, won't be worth a thing? So I suppose we must take to literature, like you, and not care for their consulships.' Afranius did get in, but Cicero needless to say did not abandon public life, though he was distressed by the Senate's loss of authority.

In the autumn of 61 Pompey was at least finally able to celebrate his triumph. He allegedly drove into Rome dressed in Alexander's cloak. Fantastic treasures from the East were carried in procession, including a portrait of himself made entirely of pearls. A new rage for precious stones developed in fashionable circles. Pompey might hope that the People at least had been impressed. He was clearly now pinning his hopes to independent action next year by a friendly tribune and to the aid of Afranius.

Early in 60 Cicero found further cause for distress. He wrote to Atticus,

I suppose you have heard that our friends the *equites* have practically broken with the Senate. First they were much annoyed when the Senate authorized the promulgation of a bill for inquiry into the conduct of jurors who have taken bribes. I happened not to be present when the decree was passed, but realizing that the equestrian order took it amiss, though they said nothing openly, I took the Senate to task in what seemed to me a most impressive manner, speaking with weight and eloquence in a not very honourable cause. And now the *equites* have another pet notion, really almost unbearable – but I have not only borne it, I have spent my eloquence on it. The tax-farmers who bought the Asian taxes from the censors complained in the Senate that from over-eagerness they bid too high a price, and asked for the cancellation of the contract. I was their chief supporter, or rather their second, for it was Crassus who pushed them into this impudent demand. It is an invidious business, a disgraceful claim, and a confession of recklessness. But there was the gravest danger of an open breach with the Senate if they were flatly refused.

Ultimately Cato got both demands rejected – after business had again been held up for a long time – and the threatened breach took place; henceforth, too, the *equites* would look as much to Crassus as Cicero. ' "Well," you will say, "are we to pay your friends for their support like hired servants?" What else are we to do, if there is no other way?' Apart from anything else Cicero believed that the *equites* could provide a defence against the slave and freedman rowdies of such as Clodius.

He went on to say,

So I maintain my established policy and defend as far as I can that alliance I put together. But as all this is so uncertain I am paving a way, which I hope will be a safe one, to protect my influence. I can't explain it properly to you in a letter, but I'll give you a small hint. I am on the closest terms with Pompey. I know what you will say. I will look out for the dangers and I will write at another time more about my politicial plans.

Atticus, always prudent, did write back urging caution; and Cicero agreed that he must not retreat from the optimate position he had taken up and that 'the man you speak of has no large and lofty views in politics, nothing but a mean desire for popularity'. But he insisted that it would be advantageous to the state as well as a protection to himself to keep close to Pompey and thus cut him off from disreputable allies.

He complained of his loneliness.

I am so abandoned by all that the only relaxation I have is the time I spend with my wife and little daughter and my darling son; for those grand and superficially flattering friendships of mine look impressive in the Forum, but are no use in the home. And while my house is crammed with morning callers and I go down to the Forum surrounded by droves of friends, in the whole crowd I can find no one to whom I can make an unguarded joke or let out a friendly sigh.

He begged Atticus to come home. Later it appears that antiquarian and literary studies are taking up all the time he can spare from the legal work with which, to maintain his support, he still busies himself; and he asks Atticus to see that he gets safely a collection of books that he has been given. He continued to complain of the 'fishpond fanciers', the rich nobles who took more interest in their villas and their tables than in politics, and of the spoiled younger aristocrats, and as a result continued to range himself with Pompey, who was now at least praising him properly: he said that salvation had twice come to Rome from Arpinum; and that though he himself had served, Cicero had saved, the state. This was just what Cicero wanted to hear. And he probably felt the easier with Pompey, that the latter, in spite of his vast wealth, lived fairly simply, and his family's nobility was of recent date.

Many of the nobles were doubtless as selfish and short-sighted as Cicero thought them; and the temptations of a rapidly rising standard of wealth and luxury, or, in better men, disgust at the state of politics, were encouraging an opting out of public life that was profoundly opposed to old Roman traditions, and of which Cicero, however tempted at moments by a life of retirement, at bottom deeply disapproved. But there were special reasons for the combination of weakness and intransigence that the optimates showed in these years. Death and age were making ravages among the group of *principes* who had so long claimed to guide the state as Sulla's heirs. Catulus died in 61 and with him, Cicero believed, his own best ally. Lucullus had retired into a private life of legendary luxury, from which he emerged only to oppose Pompey; he was a tired and ageing man. Hortensius had real reason to be jealous of Cicero. These two were the fishpond fanciers *par excellence*: we have a vivid contemporary account from Varro of their desperately expensive salt-water tidal pools in Campania. Hortensius personally fed his fish on expensive food and was as concerned over a sick fish as an ailing slave. Lucullus' gardens in Rome passed to the emperors and even in that period were considered magnificent. His villas at Tusculum and in Campania showed his rage for building. He was a great collector and connoisseur of paintings and statues, but especially of books, and opened his library to all scholars. He was reputed to dine, even when alone, in fantastic state. There is a story that Cicero and Pompey (who was clearly still on superficially polite terms with him) one day insisted on taking pot luck with him, and prevented him from giving his servants any special orders; they let him however tell one of them that he would dine that day 'in the Apollo' and were thus outwitted. It proved that each of his dining rooms had a fixed allowance for a meal served there, and special equipment: the usual cost of a dinner in the Apollo room was 50,000 *denarii*, a huge sum, and the feast was prepared with a speed that amazed the guests.

To succeed these men in politics there were Cato and his associates, all much lesser men than he: Bibulus, Domitius Ahenobarbus, once Cicero's stay in his consular elections, and 'Cato's Ape' Favonius. But they were relatively junior. And 'you have not a greater regard for our friend Cato than I have; but with all his good intentions and complete integrity he sometimes damages the public welfare; for he gives his opinion in the Senate as if he were living in Plato's Republic, not on Romulus' dungheap'. Cato might have retorted that Cicero was too ready to adapt himself to Roman conditions; but in fact Cato usually had to do so in the end too. And if we can understand better than Cicero seems to have done why the idea of cooperation with Pompey stuck in Cato's throat, it was foolish to think that the great man would stand his isolation indefinitely, even if Crassus now seemed to be needling, rather than angling for, his old rival.

Pompey's hopes for 61 were proved vain. One of the consuls was Metellus Celer, now, owing to his sister's divorce, Pompey's bitter enemy, and the other, Afranius, though known as a good dancer, proved a very inadequate chief magistrate. A tribune however put forward a bill in Pompey's interest for distribution of land. It was fiercely opposed in the Senate, and in the struggle the tribune even imprisoned the consul Celer, though Pompey himself felt this was going too far; to Cicero's distress the *equites* did not lift a finger to protest. Cicero himself tried to help the bill through by deleting all the clauses prejudicial to private interests: 'the well-off, as you know, form my army'. Unfortunately at this point there was trouble in Gaul, and the bill was dropped. Some think that Pompey may have been offended by Cicero's less than wholehearted support. When lots were drawn for an embassy to Gaul, Cicero was flattered that the Senate declared that he, like Pompey, was needed in Rome; but in the case of Pompey at least the Senate must have had ulterior motives for this assertion.

As for Clodius, Cicero could not stop sharpening his wit on him. Once, in the course of a harmless conversation about providing room at the games for clients, Clodius complained that his sister Clodia, the consul Celer's wife, would not give him a foot. 'Don't complain about one foot,' Cicero replied, 'you can lift the other', referring to the supposed incestuous relations between

them. 'You'll say it wasn't a remark worthy of a statesman of
consular rank; I admit it, but I hate that woman, who isn't
worthy to be a consul's wife.' Efforts were being made to let
Clodius become a plebeian by adoption, so that he could hold the
tribunate. Perhaps partly in fear of this, partly in pique at what
he saw as optimate ingratitude to himself, partly in disappointment that Archias had not (it seems) produced the hoped-for
poem, Cicero started a propaganda campaign about his consulship. He wrote out and published the speeches of 63; he produced
a memoir in Greek, which he sent to Posidonius of Rhodes, who
was a historian as well as a philosopher, to work up into an
account of his own – Posidonius tactfully refused, on the grounds
that he could not improve on Cicero's version; the author was
cock-a-hoop at this. Atticus wrote a simpler account in Greek.
Cicero further mentions a Latin memoir, as well as his epic
poem in three books, which was adorned with all the regular epic
machinery, such as a Council of the Gods. This work was a mistake; it was a laughing-stock to the end of antiquity, for its poor
verse as well as its self-praise, and the notorious line beginning
'Let arms to the toga yield' was not calculated to please Pompey.

Though there is no reference to it in Cicero's letters, this was
also the period of the long struggles over the ratification of
Pompey's Eastern arrangements. Lucullus reappeared in the Senate
to defend his own enactments there, which Pompey had annulled,
and to insist that the latter's decisions should be discussed one
by one. Celer and Cato backed Lucullus; so did Crassus. It was a
painful position for Pompey, whose honour to his dependants was
involved. In the summer of 60 Cicero was still writing to Atticus
that his influence with Pompey had detached that great man from
unworthy allies and strengthened his principles; and that one
might try to do the same with Caesar, who was now on his way
home to Rome and an inevitable consulship. Cicero should have
remembered how misleadingly Pompey was given to talking and in
what direction his immediate interests pointed him. At the same
time Cato made it clear that Caesar had nothing to hope for
from him; he talked out a not unreasonable request, which most
senators were ready to grant, for a technical allowance enabling
Caesar to apply for a triumph as well as stand for the consulship; and Cato was perhaps also behind the Senate's decision
that the next year's consuls should ultimately proceed not to
provinces abroad, but to a minor policing job in Italy – a decision
that, if left to stand, would frustrate all Caesar's ambitions. Cato

also agreed to the use of bribery at the elections, in order at least to counter-balance Caesar by bringing in a stiff-necked optimate, his own son-in-law (though his elder) Bibulus. The outcome was exactly what Cicero had spent so many years and such torrents of words in trying to avoid. Caesar was not repulsed when he put out feelers for an alliance with Pompey, and undertook to reconcile his new friend with Crassus. The triple alliance is what is known, too officially, as the First Triumvirate.*

* A triumvirate was properly a formally constituted board of three men, as a decemvirate was of ten. I shall call them, therefore, the Three.

FROM OPPOSITION TO EXILE
59-57 B.C.

Caesar had high hopes that Cicero would follow Pompey into the new partnership. Before the end of the year 60 it was known that one of the Consul's first acts was to be the long-delayed agrarian law, and Cicero considered his own position very carefully (in the first letter to survive since the previous June). After arguing with Atticus, now home or nearly so, about the best size of windows from which to enjoy the view from one of his houses, he goes on:

I come now to the month of January, and my political position; I shall argue on both sides in the fashion of the Socratics, but in the end, as they do, come down on one. It is certainly a question that needs careful thought. For either I must stoutly resist the agrarian law, which means something of a battle, but a glorious one, or I must keep quiet, which is tantamount to retiring to one of my houses in the country, or I must actually help it through, which they say Caesar has no doubt I shall do. For I have had here Cornelius, I mean Caesar's friend Balbus [the first reference to Caesar's invaluable factotum, from the Phoenician city of Gades in Spain, who had won the citizenship by his services to Pompey in the war against Sertorius]. He assured me that Caesar will take my and Pompey's advice in everything and will do all he can to bring Pompey and Crassus together. On this side there is close association with Pompey, and with Caesar too if I want it, reconciliation with my enemies, peace with the populace and quiet in my old age.

But he remembers how in his poem 'On his consulship' he made the Muse Calliope advise him to pursue the course on which he had entered in his earliest youth and followed as consul, and also the other aristocratic sentiments in the work, and says that he does not think that he can hesitate to enter on the 'struggle for my country'. Thus the unfortunate poem perhaps justified its existence after all. It should be noted that Cicero at least believed his career hitherto to have been a model of consistency; and that it was from shame and principle alone that he stood out of the alliance. About this time, too, we find him reading works of

Greek political philosophy, and perhaps already beginning to think a little more deeply about the subject.

For the first months of 59, when as usual most of the legislation was introduced, Cicero and Atticus were together in Rome and we are reduced to the inadequate accounts of later historians, one of whom specifically declares that there were many laws passed which he will not trouble to mention. As a result the order of events (as well as many other things) is unclear. The first step was the agrarian bill, which was to benefit *plebs* and veterans alike. It was so tactfully framed (had Caesar learnt from the Rullus fiasco?) that only the bitterest optimates, led by Cato and Bibulus, could oppose it; but their opposition was enough to break down any pretence of harmony between the consul and the Senate, his theoretical advisers. Cato was briefly marched off to prison, and Pompey and Crassus had to be brought on the scene. Pompey said threateningly that if anyone raised a spear, he would use his shield; and called up his veterans to see the bill passed. Veterans had not been visible in Rome for many years; it was an ominous development.

At first Cicero probably did, as he intended, show some fight. He refused the place offered him on the board administering the law, and he seems to have attacked Caesar in the speech he made while unhappily and unsuccessfully defending Antonius in March; precisely which aspect of Antonius' disreputable career his enemies had singled out for prosecution is unclear, but on his condemnation flowers were laid on Catiline's tomb. Cicero later claimed that it was in anger at this speech that Caesar and Pompey put through the long-delayed adoption of Clodius by a plebeian (half his age). But possibly he did himself too exclusive an honour; Caesar is said to have been in debt to Clodius over his legislation. Whether through fear of the latter or because he saw the Three were ready to use violence and had no intention of being balked, Cicero became more cautious, and his subsequent letters are full of complaints about Cato's intransigence, which had ruined everything; while it appears that he persuaded Cato and others to take the oath to observe the law which (on the precedent of the best *popularis* tribunes) Caesar had appended to his agrarian bill.

Caesar had won over many at least of the *plebs* by the agrarian bill; he attached the *equites*, or at least the tax-farmers, by finally annulling the notorious tax-contract; he ratified Pompey's arrangements in the East, without opposition even from Lucullus;

and the tribune Vatinius (a connection by marriage of Caesar and a man much attacked by Cicero, with frequent insulting reference to the boils on his neck) passed a special law giving Caesar the provinces of Cisalpine Gaul and Illyricum for five years with three legions. There were other laws too, most of them combining *popularis* allure with patent reasonableness, like the one providing for the publication of senatorial debates, or that regulating the conduct of provincial governors. But Cicero complained that every possible political and religious regulation was ignored in the passing of them. Many of these were mere technicalities designed to give opportunity for blockage by the optimates; but enough violence and constitutionally dubious behaviour remained for Cicero to have some justification for feeling that, if this was what the coalition of Pompey and Caesar meant, he had been right to oppose it.

When the curtain goes up for us, in April, Cicero with his family has left home for his house at Antium on the coast south-east of Rome – it was usual to go to the country at this time of year, when the Senate went into recess for a month or more. He is trying to write a work on geography, which does not get on in spite of Atticus' encouragement; he prefers to read or 'count the waves', the weather being unsuitable for fishing. Finally however he turns to the still rather dilatory composition of a frank and bitter political memoir, his *Secret History*, destined for the moment for Atticus' eyes alone, though it was in fact published posthumously (it is now lost). Meanwhile he is replying eagerly to Atticus' letters from Rome, which he awaits with uncontrollable curiosity, in spite of having decided as he claims to think no more about politics.

He still intended to refuse all offers from the Three; there was some questions of an embassy to Egypt, whose king Caesar and Pompey had agreed to recognize, for a huge bribe. Cicero longed to visit the country – to the Romans it was an exotic and fascinating place, rich in monuments of extraordinary antiquity, and there was a fashion for things Egyptian that could be compared to the eighteenth-century taste for *chinoiserie*. But what would Cato say? And what the history books a thousand years hence? 'I am much more afraid of that, than of the gossip of the men of today.' He would wait and see. The vacant place in the College of Augurs – priests of high rank and much political importance – might tempt him: 'see how irresponsible I am!'

He maintained that it was largely the ingratitude of the optimates ('if there are any still') that kept him out of politics; but in spite of declaring that Antium, not Rome, was the place in which to hold a magistracy, he drank in all Atticus could tell him, especially what he learned of Clodius through the latter's sister Clodia, and he was much put out when a letter got lost *en route*. Clodius wants the Egyptian embassy? Well, he is being treated rather badly, and the one hope is dissension between the members of the alliance of which this is one of the signs. Perhaps they will quarrel over the augurate too. 'I hope I shall send you many splendid letters on these matters.' Soon young Curio calls and says that the younger generation is very angry about the present state of affairs; but what hope is there in *them*? People however will soon be regretting 'my time'. Cicero still expects to be prosecuted by Clodius, and professes to foresee that he will have great fun with his enemy; but he recurs to the subject so frequently as to betray his apprehension. But then – here are the Three declaring the adoption illegal! And now he hears that Clodius intends to devote his tribunate to overturning all Caesar's measures! He was afraid that this sort of thing might exasperate Pompey into proscriptions or massacres. But 'I see it's as you say, things are as uncertain in political matters as in your letter, but it is just this variety of talk and comment that amuses me. I feel I am in Rome as I read your letter, and, as happens in a crisis, hearing now this and now that.' He was still being idle, and in excusing himself was very funny about various unwelcome callers (he had now moved to his villa in fashionable Formiae). Arpinum is the only refuge – better the country people than such intolerable visitors.

At the end of the month came news that excited him into sleeplessness: a new agrarian distribution, which he hoped would fail to satisfy the people while it would inflame respectable opinion yet further. 'What our friend Gnaeus* would be at now I really do not know . . . seeing that he has agreed to go to such lengths; hitherto he has prevaricated: yes, he approved of Caesar's legislation, but Caesar himself must answer for his methods; he was in favour of the agrarian bill, but whether opportunity for a veto had been given was no business of his,' and so on. A little later Cicero decides that he agrees with Atticus: Pompey is now ready for anything, and aiming at a tyranny. In fact the Three, in view perhaps of optimate threats to rescind all the legislation

* Pompey (Gnaeus Pompeius Magnus).

next year, seem to have tightened up their alliance and prepared to keep long-term control of the state. Pompey married Caesar's daughter Julia (the most politically significant of all his marriages); plans were probably made for the elections, which Bibulus in the event succeeded in getting delayed, and money, according to Cicero, was being spent like water. He claimed a philosophic indifference: 'indeed the foolish streak I have, of desire for glory (it's nice to know one's faults) is rather pleased. I used to be tortured by the thought that the services of Sampsigeramus [this oriental potentate's name was one of his soubriquets for Pompey] to his country might in the remote future seem greater than mine. I certainly do not worry about that now.'

Whether the friends met at Arpinum – Atticus was ready to go to this rustic retreat though Cicero had hesitated to invite him – or only on Cicero's return to Rome, the letters stop here, to pick up in June; coming now from Cicero in Rome to Atticus in Epirus. Now that he was actually on the spot Cicero could pretend to philosophic indifference no longer. By this time Caesar had extorted from a Senate whose members were literally in fear of their lives yet another province, Transalpine Gaul, where there was a possibility of some good fighting. And Bibulus, after being considerably knocked about, had retired to his house to 'watch the heavens' for omens, on the (possibly rather dubious) theory that this would entitle the Senate to rescind all Caesar's legislation next year on religious grounds. No one dared oppose the Three save the clever and spirited young Curio, who thereby got much approval, according to Cicero, from the People and the *equites* (possibly mainly country gentlemen in for the games, rather than the tax-farmers) as well as senators. 'This causes me not hope, but greater grief, to see that the country's wishes are free, but its courage is in chains.' There were demonstrations in the theatre, however, and the biting, not to say scurrilous edicts or proclamations that Bibulus issued from his self-enforced isolation made him so popular, and caused such congestion when stuck up at street corners, that Cicero was clearly a little jealous. He himself was still superficially on friendly terms with Pompey; and Caesar offered him a post on his staff in the provinces. But though this would protect him against Clodius, 'I don't think I shall use it; but no one knows about it. I don't want to run away, I'm eager to fight. People are very zealous on my behalf. But I don't promise. Keep this to yourself.' In spite of such indecision, he rejected firmly a seat on the agrarian commission, which fell vacant, as likely to damn him with the *boni*. His ultimate rejection of all Caesar's offers may have been contrary to Atticus' advice, for there is some evidence that he recommended prudence.

He begged that Atticus would hurry home as soon as requested. Pompey 'insists that Clodius won't say a word about me; in this he does not deceive me, but is himself deceived.

'What else? Let me consider: this, I think. I am sure Rome is done for. Why pretend so long?'

He was soon frightened of writing plainly of politics. 'I am terrified now that the very paper may betray us'; and he proposed to use the name Laelius, showing he still hankered after the role of friend and adviser to Pompey, the new Scipio. But at times he was afraid that his optimism was groundless, and that Pompey's asseverations that Clodius would attack Cicero only over his own dead body, and that both Clodius and his brother Appius Claudius had pledged their word to him, were actually insincere. At the same time Cicero was very sorry for Pompey:

Our friend, unaccustomed to unpopularity, always surrounded with praise and glory, is now physically altered and broken in spirit, with no idea where to turn. He sees that to go on is disastrous, to turn back inconsistent. Decent people are his enemies, the ruffians themselves not his friends. See how soft-hearted I am: I shed tears when I saw him addressing a public meeting on 28 July about Bibulus' edicts. How magnificently he used to bear himself on the platform, adored by the people, admired by all! How humble and crestfallen he was now, how wretched a figure he cut in his own eyes, not only those of the audience! A sight that could please only Crassus, no one else.

Pompey indeed lamented his situation to Cicero, who was of opinion that there was no cure for his malady. He was still afraid that the intense unpopularity of the Three would lead to an outbreak of violence on their part; he had hoped for the 'painless death' of liberty, or even for 'the storm to pass over'. But now he was not so sanguine.

Meanwhile he was very busy amassing support by work in the courts – so busy that for the first time Atticus received a letter in a secretary's hand, dictated while taking a constitutional. Cicero now asked Atticus to come home, as he had warned him he would; for Atticus would be able to find out from Clodia what her brother was planning; and he would be able to get more help from Varro, Pompey's friend and ex-lieutenant, who was already a prolific author but not yet a famous antiquarian (and

111

according to Cicero, who respected but never really felt at ease with him, was as devious as his patron); Varro was perhaps also a relation of Terentia's.

Some time in the late summer, Cicero wrote summoning Atticus even more imperatively than before. It seemed that the crisis was coming at last. An unsavoury informer, who had earlier been active in the aftermath of the Catilinarian conspiracy, had now accused a number of young nobles of a plot to murder Pompey. Cicero thought that Caesar had set the man on in order to discredit young Curio. There were various improbabilities in the tale, and the Senate scouted it, but Caesar made its author repeat it to the People, with certain improvements. Young Marcus Brutus was left out (Cicero suggested that his mother Servilia had intervened overnight with her lover Caesar) and there was now a reference to an 'eloquent consular' who had said that a tyrannicide was needed; ultimately Cicero's son-in-law Piso and another young protégé were added to the list. Cicero was afraid that there would be prosecutions. What was really behind the affair is hard to say. Was Caesar aiming not merely at Curio, but at preventing a possible reconciliation between Pompey and the optimates? Or even, as has been suggested, at making Pompey distrust Cicero? Cicero declared that he himself, for one who did not make light of dangers, was not much alarmed; people assured him of their goodwill, and anyway he was sick of living – Catulus' death had been as enviable as his life. In fact a few days later the informer was found dead in prison and the affair lapsed. Cicero later declared that Caesar or his ally the tribune Vatinius had killed him to prevent his being convicted of falsehood.

One last letter Cicero sent off before Atticus arrived in Rome. It was written after he had been defending one of the praetors of 63, Flaccus, who was probably guilty of the extortion with which he was charged. Cicero seems to have got an acquittal by representing the prosecution as part of an attack on the men and policies of 63 (as well as by impugning the trustworthiness of Asian Greek witnesses) and was pleased to report that he himself and his deeds had been highly praised by Hortensius, who was again sharing the brief. In October the much-delayed consular elections were held, probably under the threat of force, and resulted in the victory of Gabinius, who as tribune had given Pompey his command against the pirates and had since served under him, and Lucius Piso, a noble who had recently become, or was soon to be, Caesar's father-in-law. The tribunicial elections, held some time earlier, had inevitably resulted in Clodius' designation as tribune; but the rest of the college was favourable to Cicero, and so were most of the praetors, while indeed the consuls did not appear hostile. Gabinius was, it is likely, an old acquaintance; and Piso was related to Cicero's son-in-law of the same name.

Cicero envisaged that Clodius, as tribune, would prosecute him, as Rabirius had been prosecuted, before the centuries, where the well-off had influence, and he believed that 'all Italy will come together' to vote in his defence. If all men of any substance had openly committed themselves to his cause, and if throngs of supporters accompanied him wherever he went to repel violence, he was surely safe. But it proved that Clodius had much more far-reaching plans. Immediately on entry into office on 10 December he promulgated four bills: one to make grain distributions to the People, for the first time, completely free; one to restore the popular right of association in local or trade clubs or *collegia*, which the Senate had abolished six years before; one to cut down the higher magistrates' power to block tribunicial legislation on grounds of ill-omen, as for a hundred years they had been able to do; and one limiting the censors' right to expel senators from the House – which may have won him the support of members who felt their position uncertain. He seems to have had the duplicity to promise to spare Cicero if he did not oppose these laws; and Cicero, forgetful now of the welfare of the state (for he must have considered all these bills pernicious) persuaded a tribune devoted to his interests not to veto them. He was blind enough to suppose for a time that the law about the clubs would be to his advantage, since he had formerly had some influence in them. On 3 January 58, after the statutory interval, the bills consequently passed. In insolent anticipation Clodius had already encouraged a client of his to celebrate the Compitalia, the games held by one of the best-known clubs, which had lapsed when they were banned. Now he began to organize the revived associations, and possibly new ones too. He enrolled and armed slaves and freedmen – as we saw trade seems to have been largely in the hands of the latter, who therefore naturally dominated the *collegia*. According to Cicero, the Temple of Castor in the Forum was his headquarters and armoury, and he even destroyed the steps in front to turn it into a stronghold. What he was doing was, it seems, something much more thorough than had ever been done before when violence was used in Rome.

For the course of events we are again reduced to late sources, and to Cicero's retrospective references, which are here unusually unreliable. In writing from exile his state of mind was such as to make him a very uncertain witness; and his speeches on his return are highly rhetorical apologias, further influenced by the desire to attack some, and the necessity of sparing others, among those he saw as responsible for his exile. In the first weeks of the year L. Piso, who as senior of the two consuls presided in the Senate for the first month, treated Cicero with great respect, calling on him to speak in third place (after Pompey and Caesar? or, if Caesar had already left to collect his troops, Pompey and Crassus?). But at some time, late in January or early in February, Clodius announced two more bills. One bought the consuls' support: Piso and Gabinius were to get, on leaving office, special commands in the attractive provinces of Macedonia and Cilicia (later changed to Syria); and simultaneously another bill reasserted the *popularis* gospel, denying fire and water to anyone who had put citizens to death without trial. Now that Clodius by his various measures had made himself the idol of an armed and organized *plebs* and guarded against interference from above, Cicero could dispose of no force that would stop the bill passing. The consuls might make it difficult to summon the Italians; and there was a real or fancied danger that Caesar, lingering outside the gates with an army, might intervene if there were disorder – though sooner rather than later he must leave to deal with the threatening movements of population in Gaul.

Cicero later thought that he should have ignored, or welcomed, the last bill as not touching him at all; though there can be little doubt that Clodius intended to proceed promptly to personalities. In fact Cicero changed his dress for mourning – a recognized means of bringing odium on one's enemies and accumulating sympathy for oneself – and went round 'day and night', according to Dio, imploring support, meeting as he went with mud and stones from Clodius' gangs. Soon a demonstration of *equites* from all over Italy was held on the Capitol, and sent to the Senate a delegation which itself included such distinguished senators as Hortensius and the elder Curio; meanwhile the Senate met in the Temple of Concord and voted that it too should put on mourning. The consuls however jointly issued an edict forbidding this, while Gabinius, now presiding consul, firmly repressed the *equites*, even relegating one of their leaders, Aelius Lamia, to a distance of 200 miles from Rome. Cicero says that the *publicani* were intimidated, and that the praetors were alienated from him.

He went to visit L. Piso, taking with him his son-in-law, C. Piso. The consul received them 'all muffled up and wearing sandals' (he seems to have been ill, though Cicero later publicly represented it as a hang-over) and said, according to Cicero himself, that he must support his colleague, who needed a rich province and would not get it from the Senate – justifying himself with a reference to Cicero's own behaviour to Antonius. He added that everyone should look after himself. Piso was a person of austere appearance interested in Epicurean philosophy, and the rest of his career seems to have been moderate and even statesmanlike; but it is hard to justify his actions now, and Cicero had some reason for his violent anger.

Clodius had been loudly asserting that he was supported by Caesar with his actual, and Pompey and Crassus with their potential, forces. He now held a public meeting outside the walls, so that Caesar, who was technically on active service, could attend. He called up L. Piso, who said significantly that he did not approve of cruelty – meaning Cicero's action in 63; Gabinius, who more openly attacked both Senate and *equites*; and Caesar, who said that as all knew he disapproved of the executions, but also of a retrospective bill. This typically reasonable remark was probably disingenuous; he needed Clodius' support, especially in preventing the annulment of his laws of 59, which two praetors were at this very moment trying to get a frightened Senate to discuss; and he may have preferred to leave Pompey in Rome without his perpetual tempter towards the *boni*. At any rate, he did nothing to help Cicero. Pompey was not present at the meeting.

He was in a great state of embarrassment, and according to Plutarch retired to his villa in the Alban Hills. Cicero and his son-in-law came out to plead with him, but he refused to see the former at all; though Cicero does refer to an occasion on which he fell at Pompey's feet, and Pompey, refusing to raise him up, said that he could not oppose Caesar's will (Cicero also says later, perhaps simply as an excuse for Pompey, that the consuls had been declaring that he himself was plotting against his life). He did see a deputation of leading men of the Senate, to whom he talked of being bound, as a private citizen, to obey the tribunes and consuls. The optimate envoys went on to L. Piso, who said that he was not as brave as Cicero had been: let him save the state again by departing, or there would be a terrible bloodbath; he himself could not betray the tribune, and neither would his colleague Gabinius or his son-in-law Caesar. The envoys returned very angry, according again to Cicero, and at a conference held in Cicero's house they, led by Hortensius, advised him to leave Rome, holding out hopes of a quick and glorious return. Cicero was to regard this advice, probably quite unfairly, as the blackest treachery, and to wish that he had followed Cato's instead. The obvious interpretation is that Cato wanted him to stand out, but Plutarch says that it was Lucullus (possibly the great man's brother) who alone advised resistance, while Cato was for departure. And it is true that Cato was not his most rigid self: at just about this time, Clodius (needing cash for his corn law, ever prepared to intervene in the East, and wishing to get a formidable opponent out of the way and stop his tongue about the illegality of his own and Caesar's acts) passed a bill dispatching Cato to annex Cyprus and its King's treasure; and Cato obediently went. It is hard to suppose that, if Cicero had stayed in Rome, there could have been a fortunate outcome, unless Pompey and Caesar had ultimately relented; but his departure certainly meant a shattering loss of face, of the prestige or *auctoritas* so vital in public life.

It was now some time in March 58. One day Cicero went up to the Capitol, where he dedicated a statue of Minerva Protectress of the City; then he slipped out of Rome by night. Next day Clodius' bill passed; and Caesar rushed north to deal with the threatening migration of the Helvetii – he had cut his programme very fine. Clodius promptly promulgated another bill outlawing Cicero by name and confiscating his goods, accusing him also of falsifying a decree of the Senate. This was presumably the old slander about the Allobroges' evidence; to suggest that Cicero had been responsible for the death of innocent men would create even more odium against him than executing confessed conspirators could do. The bill also forbade Senate or People to discuss the matter further, and Clodius stuck up a copy by the door of the Senate House. The same day the grand mansion on the Palatine of which Cicero had been so proud was burnt down, and his beloved Tusculan villa looted; even the trees, he later complained, had been uprooted and carried off. On the site of the house in Rome Clodius dedicated a shrine to Liberty. Terentia, doubtless with her son at least, had taken temporary refuge with her sister in the house of the Vestal Virgins.

Cicero probably went first to one of his properties well away from Rome. On the news of the second bill it became plain that he must leave Italy. He thought of Macedonia, or Sicily and Malta, and moved south to a friend's house near the toe of Italy. Hearing of an emendation to the bill barring him from any place less than 400 miles from Italy* ('I am allowed to live, at a distance of 400 miles, but not allowed to get there'), and that the governor of Sicily, though a man with whom he had ties, forbade him the province, he left his friend's house, to spare him danger, and decided to make for Brundisium (Brindisi) and then Macedonia; he must avoid Greece, where a number of exiled Catilinarians were living. His journey was made through stormy weather; Marius and his exile were much in his mind, which explains a dream he may have had *en route*.† At Brundisium he was kept waiting for a suitable wind, and we have a miserable letter bidding an affectionate farewell to Terentia and the children and expressing his gratitude to the friend who is putting him up outside the town in spite of the penalty threatened by the law. Indeed all along his route friends assisted him, while Plancius, the quaestor in Macedonia, an old acquaintance and a 'new man' from a country town near Arpinum, came to meet him on landing, wearing mourning, and escorted him to Thessalonica, the capital of the province, not quite the specified 400 miles from Italy. They arrived at the quaestor's official residence there on 23 May.

We possess a number of brief notes written to Atticus at various stages of this journey. At first Cicero begged his friend to overtake him, but it was soon agreed that he would be of more use in Rome. Cicero told him of Terentia's gratitude for his help, regretted that he and the family had dissuaded Cicero from suicide, implored him not to change his friendship now. Cicero was also in very real distress of mind about Quintus, who was on his way home from Asia, in all probability to face prosecution by his brother's enemies. They did not meet.

My brother, my brother, my brother, were you really afraid that it was from anger that I sent slaves to you without letters, or even

---

* Later sources say 500. The Roman mile was rather shorter than the English one.

† According to Cicero's treatise on divination, he was cheered by a dream in which Marius encouraged him and led him to the temple he had built; but this is presented as a prophetic dream, since the vote for Cicero's recall was in due course voted in this temple – and it later emerges that Cicero did not believe in prophetic dreams. The account of this one therefore has probably been at least improved.

was unwilling to see you? I angry with you? Could *I* be angry with *you*? I suppose it was you who brought me to disaster, your enemies, your unpopularity that ruined me, and not I, who ruined you in the most miserable fashion. That much-praised consulship of mine has robbed me of you, my children, my country, my possessions; you I hope it may only have robbed of me . . . I not want to see you? rather I did not want to be seen by you: you would not have seen your brother, the man you left, the man you knew, the man you took leave of in mutual tears on setting out, not a trace or semblance of him but only the likeness of a breathing corpse.

At Thessalonica Cicero avoided all company, could hardly write even to Atticus and the family, wept frequently, and grew thin and changed. He now accused himself continually of folly and cowardice in leaving Rome, his allies, especially Hortensius, of treachery, and even Atticus of shortsightedness and timidity, and of not loving his friend enough to have really put his mind to giving the right advice. He continued to threaten suicide. It seems likely that, even with due allowance made for a tendency to theatrical language, he was very near a real nervous break-down. No reversal of fortune, he repeated, was ever so great as his. Atticus kept urging him to fortitude, excused the optimates, and tried (as others did) to send hopeful reports of the political situation, which met with incredulity. Cicero did rouse himself to suggest that a speech against Curio, which had got into circulation most inconveniently (for Curio was now one of his leading supporters), might be passed off as a forgery 'since it is not very carefully written', and he agreed to send off a few letters, including one to Pompey; whom he never included in his bitterest recriminations, speaking of nothing worse than his 'ungenerous reply'. He knew no doubt that it was on Pompey that he must depend for his recall, and was unable to admit that his whole policy had broken down through the great man's suspicious-ness and unreliability. In fact Pompey, on whose reputation the whole affair certainly was a blot, was soon talking in a way that made Cicero's friends hopeful; for Clodius not only kept Rome in a state little better than chaos, but rapidly and inevitably quar-relled with Pompey over Eastern affairs. In the summer a tribune was encouraged by Pompey himself to propose Cicero's recall to the Senate; he was vetoed, but Pompey suggested that some-thing might be done after the elections. And at least nobody moved against Quintus, who joined Atticus and the family in working for recall.

Though miserable at Thessalonica, where, he said, there was no one to talk to and nothing to think about, Cicero hung on there rather than cross into Asia, where he would be off the direct route to Rome and less in touch with the capital. He was furious to hear that in Rome people were reporting that he had gone mad with grief. Now he bombarded Atticus with questions and advice. The second, not the first, bill must be repealed (though there were doubts whether it was legal at all, as a *privilegium* or measure directed against a single individual). But how could this be done? What did Domitius (Ahenobarbus) mean by promising it? Could his house be restored – 'if not, how can I?' He sometimes thought that in Italy, which so favoured him, he might be safe. His agony was long-drawn-out, for various attempts at raising the matter in Rome failed; public business came almost to a standstill, and all the latter part of the year Pompey spent shut up in his house for fear of Clodius. In the autumn, however, after much hesitation, Cicero moved to the town of Dyrrhachium (now Durazzo) on the Adriatic coast, of which he was patron – partly because the now bitterly hated L. Piso would soon arrive at Thessalonica as the new governor of Macedonia, and partly because there was hope that the new year and the new magistrates might bring better things. He even apologized to Atticus for his recent reproaches (though he returned to them again later); they do not seem to have left any mark on his ever-patient friend. There was this much of truth in them, that Atticus was by a long way the more detached of the two. But his friendly offices were beyond criticism now. On inheriting a large fortune from his 'extremely difficult' uncle, with whom nobody else had been able to get on at all, he wrote that it was all at Cicero's disposal; and he was incessantly busy with Cicero's affairs and prospects at Rome. Cicero wrote to Terentia about the house, affectionately, and appreciated the competence that she had been showing in spite of ill-health; but she complained of the brevity of his letters and urged him to write to others too, and it is possible that she had little sympathy with failure and depression. For his brother's affection Cicero was genuinely grateful, and he wrote to him of how he missed Tullia, 'so devoted, so modest, so clever! In face, speech and mind my very image'; but it is clear that, from this crisis of his life at least, in many respects his deepest emotional dependence was on Atticus.

Before the year 58 was out he heard that an attempt had

been made by eight of the tribunes to revoke Clodius' second bill. Cicero complained that it had been ill-drafted; it made no reference to his house and property, and did not get neatly round Clodius' cause forbidding the subject to be raised at all. The attempt, as might be expected, ran into a veto. Cicero also criticized the tactics of the group working for his recall in other ways; an opportunity had been lost of getting the new consuls into the debt of the incoming tribunes, who were favourable (one of these, Sestius, the pro-Ciceronian quaestor of 63, in fact went all the way to Gaul to see Caesar, from whom he did not receive much encouragement). However, one of the consuls-designate, Lentulus Spinther, a friend of Pompey, proved to be a whole-hearted supporter, and the other, Metellus Nepos, had to some extent been persuaded by Atticus and others to forget the quarrels of 63–62. A very favourable vote was passed by the Senate on 1 January 57, on the proposal of the new consul Lentulus; Cicero thought for a moment of returning on the strength of it. But soon there was renewed disappointment, renewed laments and complaints to Atticus. Clodius' violence had prevented a bill from passing the assembly, and Quintus and the friendly tribune Sestius had been hurt in the struggle – indeed left for dead, Cicero later alleges: the Tiber was choked with corpses, the sewers blocked, sponges were used to mop up the blood in the Forum. Perhaps it was not quite as bad as that; but Clodius was, as Cicero had feared, still at the head of his bands, and this ability to maintain control of the streets even after his tribunate had expired, which was clearly due to his organization of the *collegia*, contributed very materially to the downfall of the Republic. For his opponents could do nothing but organize armed gangs them-selves, a work in which the tribunes Sestius and Milo were promi-nent; and these were personal, rather than official forces. Public business was again almost at a standstill.

Cicero retained enough hope to think it worth writing to Metellus Nepos to add his prayers for a reconciliation; but Atticus soon came out to Epirus, and for the next months we have no letters to members of the family either. In the summer the situation changed. Milo and Sestius were containing Clodius; Caesar, on Pompey's urging, apparently signified his assent to a recall; Quintus probably gave a pledge that his brother would not oppose the Three. At the end of May the Senate, on Lentulus' proposal, formally thanked Plancius and others who had assisted Cicero, recommended him to other magistrates abroad, and summoned the inhabitants of Italy to Rome. In July, 417 senators, which must have been almost all who were not bedridden or on service abroad, passed a decree which was not vetoed, and was opposed by Clodius alone; it directed the magistrates to propose a bill for Cicero's recall; anyone opposing it was declared a public enemy, and if it did not get through Cicero was to return anyway. The magistrates *en masse*, with the exception of two tribunes and the praetor Appius Claudius, Clodius' brother, obeyed. Their bill assumed the legality of Clodius' legislation and formally repealed only his specific banishing of Cicero, thus implying that his more general measure had not touched Cicero at all. A powerful collection of leading men addressed the People, in particular Pompey, who praised Cicero's record in 63 and said that the Senate, the *equites* and Italy were all for recall. Indeed various bodies, from the companies of tax-farmers to numerous Italian municipalities, had passed resolutions to that effect. Pompey, who had been busy organizing Italian opinion, called up his veterans. The normal summer influx into Rome was this year enormously swollen. The bill passed by unanimous vote of the centuries, in the presence of Milo's toughs and gladiators and with distinguished senators overseeing the voting and the ballot-boxes. All these demonstrations were unparalleled; Cicero had some reason for elation. He was already on his way home.

8

RETURN AND RECANTATION
57-52 B.C.

The next letter to Atticus is a triumphant account of his return. His first thought was to congratulate his friend on the success of his efforts (though he spoilt this gesture by a glance at what he still thought of as Atticus' original bad advice). Then:

What I thought would be the most difficult part of my position to recover, my fame in the Forum, my prestige in the Senate, my influence with the *boni*, I have regained better than I hoped; but my private affairs – you know how my property was damaged, scattered and pillaged – are in a bad way, and I need not so much your resources, which I consider as my own, but your advice in collecting and organizing what is left.

Then the details: he had left Dyrrhachium on 4 August, the very day on which the law was voted, and reached Brundisium on the 5th, to stay with his kind host of the previous year. Tullia, recently widowed, had come to meet him; it happened to be her birthday, and also the anniversary of the town's foundation, and the festival of the goddess Salus, Safety or Prosperity; great celebrations were held. Soon letters from Quintus announced that the law was through. All along his road through Italy Cicero was met by congratulatory embassies from the towns. On the outskirts of Rome

nobody of any rank, whose name was known to my *nomenclator*, failed to come to meet me, except for those enemies who could not conceal or deny the fact. When I came to the Porta Capena the steps of the temples were thronged by the common people, who welcomed me with great applause; the same throngs, the same applause, followed me to the Capitol, and there was an amazing crowd in the Forum and on the Capitol itself.

Here, no doubt, he gave thanks to the gods for his return. 'Next day, 4 September, I made a speech of thanks to the Senate.'

This speech was carefully written and read out, so that Cicero should not forget to mention any of those who had put him under obligation; it stressed his gratitude to his brother, and is to our

122

taste fulsome in its thanks to Pompey and Lentulus ('parent and guardian god of my life'). It elaborates the version of his exile that he was often to put forward for public consumption: he had left Rome to prevent violence in which he, a private citizen, might have been forced to kill the consuls. The liveliest part of the speech is the abuse against Piso and Gabinius, now in their ill-gotten provinces: a brief and vivid piece of invective, in full accordance with the rules of the genre – imputations of low birth, caricature of physical appearance, and so on. The People too received their speech of thanks, briefer and as ever somewhat *popularis* in colour, with mention, here, of the treacherous optimates who had betrayed him.

Two days later there was a debate on the high price of corn. Clodius worked up a crowd to demonstrate against Cicero on the grounds that he was responsible for the throngs in Rome and thus for the shortage. Stones were thrown at the consul Nepos. Another crowd called on Cicero to propose that Pompey should be given a special command to deal with the problem. He was so deeply indebted to Pompey now that he could not refuse. He successfully proposed in the Senate a five-year command, with the right to appoint a large staff. 'When the Senate's decree was at once read out the crowd applauded in this silly new fashion, by reciting my name. I then addressed the People.' He wrote that the *boni* as well as the poor supported his action; but most of the consulars had stayed away from the meeting of the Senate on the plea of danger, and it is clear from his report of the crowded meeting next day that it was only because a tribune made a second proposal, giving Pompey vastly more extensive powers – a fleet, an army, and the right to override provincial governors – that Cicero's seemed at all tolerable to the optimates. 'Pompey says he wants the first , his friends say he wants the second; the consulars are seething.' This was perhaps partly because there was a fear that, with these augmented powers, Pompey might establish his influence in Egypt, that great corn-growing region, by restoring its king, who had now been thrown out by his subjects and sought refuge in Rome. If a case can be made out for giving Pompey a fleet and regulating his status *vis-à-vis* provincial governors, he could hardly want an army for legitimate purposes. In the end Cicero's proposal was put to the People by the consuls and passed. 'I keep quiet,' Cicero goes on, 'particularly because the priests [mostly influential optimates] have not yet given me an answer about my house; if they annul

123

the consecration, I have a magnificent site, and the consuls, in accordance with a decree of the Senate, will estimate the value of the building.' If the priests found they could not annul, they would pull down Clodius' temple to build another one, and compensate Cicero for the site as well as the building. As usual, he begs Atticus to come home, to help him in this 'second life' that is beginning, for already 'those who supported me while I was away are starting, now that I am here, to show secret resentment and open jealousy'. Inevitably; as before, Cicero was balanced precariously between Pompey and the optimates, pleasing neither completely. Clodius tried to drive the wedge in further, representing Cicero as no sooner recalled than betraying the Senate and betaking himself to the People. And Cicero, too, was what he had ever been, or even more irritating in the extravagant elation that followed on his generally known collapse, so incomprehensible to the average tough Roman and so shocking in one who claimed to be a philosopher.

However, Pompey professed great friendship and the matter of the house ended well.

After I sent that letter there was a great battle over my house. I addressed the priests on 29 September. I dealt carefully with the subject, and if ever I was anything as a speaker, or even if I never was before, now indeed emotion and the importance of the subject gave me a certain force of eloquence. And so the younger generation cannot be deprived of the speech. I shall send it to you shortly, even if you feel that you can do without it.

It may seem extraordinary that even Cicero should believe that 'all the prestige of the state, safety of the citizens, their lives, liberty, altars, hearths, household gods, fortunes, homes' were at stake. But it has been pointed out that at Rome the majesty of the Roman state was very directly embodied in the various magistrates and ex-magistrates. And there was further the question of whether 'wicked' tribunes could successfully use religious sanctions. The speech remains to our eyes too high-flown; but it is interesting that Cicero should feel it necessary to spend the first part of his time defending his recent proposal on Pompey's behalf. It is ironic, too, in the light of the events of 63, that it should now be he who is arguing that a citizen's rights and property could only be removed by the formal trial he had not had.

In the absence of their president, the *pontifex maximus*, in

Gaul, the priests found that the site could be restored to Cicero without sacrilege if Clodius had not been properly authorized by the People to dedicate it. Cicero received general congratulations. Clodius however interpreted the decision in his own favour and urged the *plebs* to defend their shrine of Liberty by force. The Senate met, to decide the point of law in Cicero's favour, and though Clodius tried to talk the subject out, he failed to get the decree vetoed. The consuls however assessed the compensation for the house and the two damaged properties at Tusculum and Formiae at less than Cicero had hoped – owing, he thought, to the old jealousies. The last-named villa was being repaired: 'I can't bear either to let it go or to see it. I am selling the Tusculan property, though I need a place near Rome.' In fact he did not succeed in selling it, and kept and enjoyed it to the end of his life. To Atticus he also hints discreetly of troubles at home, which are the first signs of the rift with Terentia. Money may have been at the bottom of it. Cicero was very short of this, and especially anxious to repay what Quintus had disbursed on his brother's account – though Quintus was not pressing for repayment.

Cicero had accepted an appointment on the staff of Pompey (who soon went abroad on his commission for the corn-supply) on the understanding that he should not have to leave Rome; he was at this time thinking of standing for the censorship, if an election were held next year, though he felt that in some ways it would be to his advantage to be away for a while. In fact the elections even for some of next year's regular magistracies had not yet been held, and Cicero's belief that his return had been the return of order and legality was soon shown to have no foundation. On 3 November Clodius' gangs invaded his house, already rebuilding, and damaged and set fire to that of Quintus, who now lived nearby. On 11 November Cicero himself was attacked on the Sacred Way leading to the Forum ('I retreated into Tettius Damio's courtyard, and those with me easily kept the gangsters out'). Next day there was an attack on Milo's house, which was repelled by force. Even sittings in the Senate were disrupted. Clodius, who was standing for aedile, wanted the elections to take place; Milo wanted to prosecute him first, and in this was supported by Cicero, who shortsightedly applauded all Milo's achievements in the field of counter-violence, and expected, almost hoped, that he would succeed in killing Clodius. 'He has no hesitation about it, he talks openly of it, he doesn't fear my fate. For he will never take the advice of envious or treacherous friends or trust an inert noble.' In January 56 the delayed elections were held and the magistrates appointed at once entered office, Clodius among them. Not long after, Atticus returned to Rome, and there are only sporadic letters to him to throw light on an uncertain and important period of Cicero's career; there are however some important ones to Quintus, who was now serving in Sardinia on Pompey's staff.

During the early part of the year 56 the Egyptian question was again distracting Rome. Ptolemy XII, in 59 recognized as king by the Three, had been, as we saw, turned out by his subjects – before he could raise the money for the bribes required for his recognition. He was in Rome begging to be restored. He would have liked Pompey to go. But an oracle was produced (possibly with the aid of Clodius and Crassus as well as some of Pompey's optimate enemies) declaring that the king must not be restored with an army. Even so Pompey's friends still pressed for the job to be given him. But Cicero, who was not indebted for his recall to Pompey alone, supported the claims of the consul of 57, Lentulus Spinther, who was now governor of Cilicia; Lentulus was also the candidate of Hortensius and Lucullus, but not of Cato's friends, who wanted a board of three (excluding Pompey). Pompey felt that in public at least he must support Lentulus, who had put to the People the bill granting him his present office. 'As for Pompey,' Cicero wrote to Lentulus, 'I never cease pressing and urging him, even openly upbraiding and warning him to avoid what will damage his reputation. But . . . not only in private conversation but also in the Senate he presses your claim with eloquence, weight, zeal and eagerness such as no one could outdo.' Two days later he wrote again after dining with Pompey: 'when I listen to him, I acquit him entirely of all suspicion of self-seeking; when however I see his friends of all stations I realize, what is now clear to everyone, that the whole affair was arranged long ago by certain persons, with the concurrence of the King and his advisers.' But in the event the Senate passed a decree shelving the business, and the fact that the decree was vetoed had no effect. The forces against Pompey had been too strong: they included not only Clodius and his supporters, who abused him at a trial that Milo was standing, and declared that they wanted Crassus to go to Egypt, but also the optimates, who listened complacently in the Senate to Clodius' attacks on Pompey (which included the charge that he had betrayed Cicero). Pompey told

Cicero that he himself was in danger of assassination – he seems to have had a morbid fear of plots – and that Crassus was behind Clodius: 'and so he is preparing himself and getting in men from the country.' Cicero wrote further that he and Pompey felt that if Lentulus was certain he could manage it successfully he might restore Ptolemy and present Rome with a *fait accompli*; Lentulus clearly thought it wiser not to do so. But in the event Gabinius as governor of Syria did just that, at Pompey's instigation – and with the army forbidden by the oracle, too.

In February Sestius, who had been so warm in Cicero's cause as tribune in 57, was charged with using violence at that time. 'He was unwell; I went to him at once at his house, as I ought, and put myself wholly at his disposal. People were surprised, as they thought I had good reason to be angry with him.' Cicero made some comments relevant to Sestius' case at another trial, and was encouraged to find a favourable hearing. In his next letter to Quintus he was able to write that Sestius had been unanimously acquitted, and that he himself had taken the opportunity to 'cut up Vatinius [who had been Caesar's tribune in 59 and was now a prosecution witness] to the applause of gods and men'. The speech for Sestius was published separately from the attack on Vatinius and all his works; as it turned out, both had to be toned down for publication at least so far as attacks on Caesar were concerned. But the *pro Sestio* in particular recalls old Ciceronian themes: there is now no danger from without, only from within. The People wants peace, and *otium cum dignitate* – tranquillity for the People and honour for the senators, as the famous but ambiguous phrase is probably best translated – is Cicero's object. Men like Clodius are not true *populares*, their following is unrepresentative of the People. There is no narrow faction of optimates, as Vatinius claims; honest men of all ranks are optimates, as they showed at Cicero's recall – and here he extends the significance of the term, and his own programme, considerably. There was in fact remarkably wide support for Sestius as the list of his advocates and witnesses shows. Cicero may have felt that, now that Pompey had broken so openly with Clodius and Crassus, he might abandon his alliance with Caesar too, and that his own way to revive his old policy was clear. True, the letter recounting Sestius' acquittal states reassuringly that Cicero is keeping out of politics and the Senate; but this would seem not to have been wholly true, for in early April he got the Senate to put on the agenda for 15 May a discussion of Caesar's law for the division of state lands in Campania, which the optimates had always particularly disliked. Atticus, later letters suggest, was urging caution. But by now Pompey's veterans had doubtless been settled, and he no longer seemed to have much need of Caesar; while a tribune friendly to Pompey had actually been the first to raise the reconsideration of the law in the Senate, at the end of the previous year. So Cicero had no reason to think he was offending Pompey. He mentions the matter of the debate in the Senate quite casually in a letter to Quintus in which he gives the news that Pompey is leaving for the north and he himself going, as usual in the spring, to the country. It shows that he and Pompey parted on friendly terms.

After dinner I was taken in my litter to call on Pompey at his house in the suburbs. I had not been able to meet him during the day because he was away – I wanted to see him because I was leaving Rome next day and he was going to Sardinia. I did find him, and asked him to send you back to us as soon as possible. 'At once,' he said. He was leaving, he said, on 11 April, and taking ship at Labro or Pisae. So, my dear brother, as soon as he arrives take the first passage that offers, provided the weather is fair.

But in fact Pompey went to Luca (Lucca) where he met Caesar, Crassus, who had already been with Caesar, and a large number of other senators. The cracks in the alliance were pasted over. It was apparently decided that Pompey and Crassus should be consuls for the next year, 55, and should afterwards have five-year commands in Spain and Syria respectively; while Caesar himself should have another five years in Gaul to finish and consolidate his conquests. Pompey then went on to Sardinia where, according to Cicero's later, apologetic version, as soon as he met Quintus he said, 'You're the man I'm looking for; if you don't deal carefully with your brother Marcus you will forfeit the pledge you gave me for him.' He also sent a messenger to tell Cicero to leave the Campanian question alone.

In this later account Cicero wrote as though the Conference of Luca was simply an answer to his own initiative. This is incredible, though scholars, in reaction against Cicero's own estimate of himself, often tend to regard him as of less importance than he was. Caesar still needed Pompey, to safeguard his position in Gaul, and was obviously worried by the possibility that he might defect, especially in view of the fact that Domitius Ahenobarbus, the powerful optimate, a close connection of Cato, was standing for the consulship and intended if elected to press for a new governor of Gaul. (Doubtless Domitius had himself in mind, as he had an inherited *clientela* in the southern part of the country.)

However exactly they were worded and conveyed, Cicero obeyed Pompey's commands. We find him in fact dispatching, either to Pompey or to Caesar, a somewhat mysterious document, perhaps an open letter, committing himself entirely to support of the Three. He had not sent it to Atticus to vet, as he usually did with his writings.

I had no second copy. And then – for I have been nibbling at what I must swallow down – my recantation seemed to me just a little disgraceful. But farewell to straight, true, honourable policies. It is unbelievable how much perfidy there is in your leading optimates . . . I felt it, I knew it; I was led on, abandoned, cast out by them; yet I intended to take the same path with them in politics. They remain what they were. Finally, at your urging, I have barely come to my senses. You will say you tried to persuade me to a certain line of action,* not to make a written confession of faith. I really wanted to commit myself to this new alliance, so that I could not fall back to those who, even when they should pity me, continue to be jealous. But I was moderate on the theme, as I wrote to you I should be. I'll write more fully if *he* likes it and if it annoys those who are angry that I should own a villa that Catulus once had . . . who say I should not be rebuilding my house but ought to sell it. But what is that to the fact that they were glad that in the speeches I made in the House, which they themselves approved, I turned out to be acting against Pompey's will? Enough; since those who have no power will not love me, let us see that those who have it do. You will say, 'I wish you had thought so long ago'. I know you wanted me to, and that I was a thorough ass. But now it is time I should look after myself, since they won't look after me.

This time, then, he did not listen to the imagined voices of the muse Calliope, of Cato or of posterity, as he had done when the triple alliance was first formed. His debt to Pompey and to Caesar for his recall was too deep, his disillusion with the optimates, some of whom were now backing Clodius against Pompey, was too great, the experience of his exile, with continuing fear of Clodius, was too traumatic. But the pill was a very bitter one. When the discussion of the Campanian law came up, he was not present and nothing was done. But he had very soon to rise in the Senate and declare his change of colours by supporting Caesar's demand that his extra levies be ratified, and then by opposing an attempt to include Gaul among the provinces to be distributed to the

* Or perhaps 'to keep silent', an alternative reading.

next year's magistrates. This speech included an eulogy of Caesar. The optimates were furious, the consuls surprised, but the motion went through. All these demands of Caesar's Cicero had earlier called monstrous. It can have been only partial comfort that he was still free to attack Piso and Gabinius, and to suggest that it was they, not Caesar, who should be superseded; that he could publish his speeches for Sestius and against Vatinius, though shorn of all criticism of Caesar; and that he was able to repel another attack by Clodius, who declared that a prodigy which the soothsayers had interpreted to mean that sacred places had been defiled referred to the destruction of his shrine to Liberty, and who tried again to pull down Cicero's house. Milo came to the rescue, the Senate passed a decree condemning Clodius' action, and Cicero retorted, in a lengthy speech to the Senate, that the prodigy in fact referred to Clodius' own shocking behaviour as aedile. He declared that unity – unity, presumably, now between the optimates and the Three – was necessary, to prevent the quarrels between leading men that the soothsayers had also spoken of; it was primarily being undermined by Clodius. By this argument he tried to give the impression that he had changed his political programme very little.*

Indeed he tried in every way to set his change of course in the best possible light. He wrote a letter, which he described to Atticus as 'very pretty', to a friend of Pompey's, Lucceius, begging him to lay aside the general history on which he was engaged, and produce as quickly as possible a monograph, more laudatory than accurate, on his own consulate, exile and return, 'bringing out the intrigues of certain persons against me'. Lucceius agreed, but the work apparently never materialized. Cicero also stressed the ingratitude of the optimates in writing to Lentulus Spinther, who, he thought, had also been badly treated, over Egypt. He added that

those who are stronger in wealth, arms and power seem to me to have managed, through the folly and levity of their enemies, to acquire more prestige as well. And so, with little opposition, they have got from the Senate what they did not think they could get even from the People without violence . . . I write briefly of this, for the present state of the country does not please me.

---

* The date of this speech (De Haruspicum Responsis) is uncertain; it may have been earlier than the speech openly supporting Caesar, and some hold it to be earlier than the news of Luca: in this case the unity hoped for is that between Pompey and the Senate.

Atticus wanted him to write something himself about his position; but this time he replied that he hesitated to bring up old grudges against Hortensius. Late in 54 however he wrote a long formal letter to Lentulus Spinther, probably designed also for other eyes; this again laid great weight on the optimates' ingratitude, the way they had supported Clodius, and his own mistaken idea of what Pompey really wanted. It expatiated on what Pompey and Caesar had done for him. Times, he said, had changed, and his policy had changed with them; what was reprehensible in that? But his end, *otium cum dignitate*, was still the same. He hardly succeeded in persuading people; during these years he was the subject of many attacks. Everything doubtful or ridiculous in his past was brought up against him, from his poem on his consulship or the boastful letter to Pompey written at the end of 63, to his collapse at Thessalonica and his recent volteface.

It was time, no doubt, for a reaction against his rhetorical style; but it is a fact that, around this time, Cicero sometimes wrote almost badly, in something of a parody of his own manner: his tone can be shrill and unpersuasive, his mood monotonous, while an automatic reliance on technique covers a certain emptiness of content, and his amplitude at last becomes genuinely long-winded.

His own true feelings can be seen from a letter to Atticus either of summer 56 or the following spring:

What is more shameful than our lives, especially mine? For you, though you are a political creature by nature, share only the slavery that is common to us all. But I, who if I speak as I ought on public matters am thought mad, if I say what expediency demands, appear a slave, and if I am silent, seem oppressed and crushed, how much pain must I feel? As much as I do, the more bitter for the fact that I cannot even grieve without seeming ungrateful to you. What if I choose to give up and take refuge in a life of leisure? Impossible. I have to take part in the fight. Am I to be a common soldier, after refusing to be a general?* I must; for I see that you, whom I ought always to have obeyed, decree it.

In fact the Three intended to make use of his still considerable influence not only in the Senate but in the courts. Cicero soon had to defend the first in a procession of their friends: Pompey's and Caesar's confidential agent Cornelius Balbus, who had been given citizenship by Pompey many years earlier, illegally as was

---

* In reference to his refusal, in 60–59, to make a fourth with the Three.

now alleged. This was an easy case: a clear exposition of the principles governing Rome in her relations with allied and other foreign states, sandwiched between praise of Pompey and Caesar, and the thing was done. Worse was to come.

Cicero was not alone in his distress. In the autumn of 56 he suggested that Domitius' case was harder to bear than his own.

For what can be more wretched than for him, who has been consul-designate from his birth, to be deprived of the office, especially when he would have had no competitors or only one at most? If it is true, as I daresay it is, that their notebooks contain as long lists of future consuls as they do of past ones, what could be more pitiable than Domitius – unless it be the state, for which we can expect no improvement?

In this pessimistic conclusion, as in his rush to commit himself entirely, is expressed all Cicero's impulsive and emotional nature. Domitius was to be consul only one year late; and the alliance of the Three was to break up in due course.

The elections for 55 had been postponed by tribunicial vetoes till the winter, so that the obstructive consuls of 56 should be out of office and some of Caesar's troops could come home on leave (and exert pressure?). Pompey and Crassus were naturally successful; Cato, now back from annexing Cyprus, could not persuade Domitius to persist to the end with his obviously point-less candidacy, and he himself was deprived of a praetorship to make room for Vatinius. The new consuls, with a friendly tribune, carried the measure agreed at Luca – five more years for Caesar in Gaul, five years in Spain and Syria for themselves. Cicero hoped for tranquillity at Rome at least: 'it seems that those in power will give it us, if people can endure their rule quietly'. He still traced the whole disaster to Cato and his friends for having alienated the *equites* and Pompey from the Senate in the late 60s. Pompey and Crassus were gracious to Cicero, and with Pompey at any rate he was still on friendly terms, writing in the spring from one of his properties in Campania, 'I was with Pompey here; he spoke much of politics with me, regretting his own position – so he said, for one must always add that, in his case. He expressed contempt of Syria and extolled Spain. Here too one must append "so he said", as, I think, everywhere in speaking of him.'

For Cicero it was a year of inglorious personal squabbles, the bitterness of which perhaps reflects his frustration; he even clashed with Cato. Cicero removed from the Capitol the inscribed version of Clodius' law against him, which for some reason had never been destroyed. Clodius put it back; Cicero carried it off again, this time to his house. The Senate was concerned in the matter, and Cicero argued that all Clodius' laws were wholly invalid. Cato was precluded from accepting that by his recent mission, and a coolness sprang up between him and Cicero. Then, when Piso returned from Macedonia, where he had been superseded, in the summer, he and Cicero exchanged fire in the Senate. Cicero was able to write up his invective for publication; it ploughs through the events of 63 and 58 yet again, but it has its vigorous and amusing moments; the swarthy Piso, with his remarkable eyebrows and his secret Epicurean orgies, and the elegant curly-haired Gabinius, a crack dancer, form a memorable, if of course unfairly portrayed, couple. Cicero wrote complacently to Quintus that the young were learning the work by heart as a lesson. It long kept its place as a fine example of that favourite genre, invective, but it seems to have had little effect on its victims' position; and Cicero admitted in it that, for Caesar's sake, he would not actually prosecute Piso. Piso, not unfairly, jeered at Cicero for not daring to attack those really responsible for his exile.

There was however a quarrel with Crassus himself – over Gabinius, who was now known to have invaded Egypt. But that could not be allowed; Caesar wrote from Gaul, and Pompey forcibly reconciled Cicero and Crassus. A dinner party given by Cicero's new son-in-law Crassipes (of whom we know very little) sealed the reconciliation. But when, towards the end of 55, and after leaving the citizens a huge donative to ensure that he was remembered, Crassus set off for Syria pursued by a tribune's curses for ignoring the omens, Cicero remarked in a letter to Atticus, 'What a villain he is!' He was nonetheless about to write the villain an effusion which he wished, he said, to have the force of a treaty, not a mere letter. Pompey for his part delayed setting out to Spain, where he put his lieutenants in charge – a development that paved the way for Augustus' solution of the problem of provincial commands. With the recent death of his wife Julia, Caesar's daughter, whom he had really loved, and with Crassus far away, he clearly felt it wiser to remain in Rome. Though there was no open rift yet with Caesar, he refused suggestions for a new marriage alliance with his family.

While Pompey and Caesar were drifting apart, Cicero's relations

with the latter were becoming closer. For one thing Quintus transferred early in 54 from Pompey's staff to Gaul, in order to gain
friendship and protection and to get out of debt – Caesar was
known for his liberality and Gaul offered rich booty and other
opportunities even to men considered honest. To judge by what
we hear of his building operations in the country Quintus must
have needed money badly: he was in process of acquiring two
elegant villas within a few miles of each other and Arpinum. He
was not wholly happy in Gaul, and had to be urged to patience
by his brother. He accompanied Caesar to Britain, fought gallantly
for him when the Nerveii suddenly revolted, but on a later
occasion let a force and his camp be surprised by the Germans.
He also at one point wrote four tragedies in sixteen days, which
even his fluent brother thought rather rapid, though in a fit
of modesty he once confessed that he sincerely believed Quintus
the better poet. With Cicero himself in Rome Caesar carried on a
correspondence which is unfortunately now lost. It seems that
each was susceptible to the charm and brilliance of the other, and
for a while the relationship flourished. Caesar appears to have
promised Cicero some great prize – a priesthood, the censorship,
or a second consulship, possibly with himself (less probably a
consulship for Quintus)? It was the Three, now, especially with
their grip on the provinces, who controlled patronage; Domitius,
who had won an empty consulship for 54, would think, says
Cicero, that anyone applying to *him* for a job was mocking him.
And at some point Caesar also made Cicero a large loan. In his
letters to Quintus, Cicero is careful what he says, since they went
by Caesar's courier service, but the sincerity of his praise of his
new friend is to some extent guaranteed by his words to Atticus
on 'this most delightful connection'. To Quintus he wrote

My zeal will perhaps have an effect like that of travellers who
rise later than they intended, but by making haste reach their goal
more rapidly than if they had been up before dawn. Thus, though I
was asleep for so long to the advantage of cultivating him, though
you indeed pressed me to do so, I will catch up by riding posthaste,
or, since you write that he likes my poem, in my poetic chariot.

This seems to refer to an epic poem on Caesar's victories and
the invasion of Britain; Cicero wrote anxiously to find out what
its hero thought of it. In return Caesar dedicated to him a work
on the fashionable subject of grammar, with a preface of elegant
compliment. The two men's views on the matter were highly

typical: in the dispute between 'analogy' and 'anomaly' as principles of language, Caesar was all for logic and the first, Cicero for the second, for following usage and tradition, however irregular and irrational it might be.

Cicero seems also to have been in contact with, and indeed helping, Caesar's agent Oppius, a man from a banking background with a taste for writing biographies, and who is usually found coupled with the invaluable Balbus. He was at this point in control of the huge programme of works in the Forum and the Field of Mars that Caesar was now financing out of the spoils of war, to rival Pompey's theatre. 'In the Field of Mars we will build enclosures for the Assembly of Tribes, made of marble and roofed, and we will put a colonnade round it, a mile long, and also build official offices.' By these and other means Caesar was collecting a large body of supporters, while his victories did indeed bring him much of the *auctoritas* that his opponents were forfeiting. The expedition to Britain – always remote and romantic to Roman eyes – and the crossing of the Rhine made a special impression.

Cicero felt assured that the goodwill of Pompey and Caesar would keep him safe from Clodius; but he still tried to make sure that everyone of importance, and especially all consuls, should be favourable to him. He spoke in the Senate, but, as he wrote gloomily, 'rather that others shall agree with me than that I myself shall'. His moods varied; sometimes he wrote, as he did to Atticus, that 'I find no recreation in other pleasures on account of the state of public affairs, but I am sustained and strengthened by literature, and prefer to sit in your little chair under the bust of Aristotle than in our consuls' chairs of office'. But once, late in 54, he permitted himself an outburst. Quintus had written asking for some verses. Cicero replied that he had neither time nor spirits for poetry, and would confess what he had intended to conceal.

I am tortured, dearest brother, tortured, by the fact that we no longer have a constitution in the state or justice in the courts, and that at my age, when I ought to be at the height of my influence in the Senate, I am distracted by legal work or sustained by private study. And the eager hope I have had since I was a boy,

Always to be the best and far to excel all others

has been destroyed. Some of my enemies I could not attack, others I have defended. I am unable to give free rein to either my opinions or my hatreds. And Caesar is the one and only man who loves me as I wish.

The summer and autumn of 54 had been exceptionally hot, and Cicero was very busy in the courts, where Cato is said to have appeared without a tunic under his toga, on the grounds that there was ancestral warrant for the mode. Cicero doubtless defended M. Scaurus' son out of old loyalty, and Plancius in gratitude for his hospitality at Thessalonica (the speech dilates yet once more on the events of 57–56, to the obvious irritation of the prosecution). But he also had to represent Vatinius, whom he had only two years previously attacked so violently; Lentulus Spinther for one showed his disapproval. And then came a yet bitterer draught. On Gabinius' return from Syria he clashed with Cicero in the Senate, calling him to his face 'a banished man', to the anger of the Senate as a whole. 'Pompey has been trying hard to effect a reconciliation, but so far he has made no progress, nor will he while I retain a shred of freedom.' Cicero yearned to prosecute in the trial for treason that Gabinius was facing (for his unauthorized restoration of Ptolemy); he contented himself with giving evidence for the prosecution, and was disgusted at the verdict of acquittal. But soon there was a second trial, for extortion. What persuasion or what threats Pompey used we do not know, but Cicero took the defence. Worse, he was unsuccessful. He must have seen Gabinius go into exile with mixed but wholly unpleasant feelings. He also had subsequently to defend a rich financier friend of Caesar's, deeply involved in the Egyptian affair. In this speech he protested, presumably quite falsely, that his reconciliation with Gabinius had been spontaneous; Pompey would never have asked, could not have forced, such a thing. It is clear that there had been much talk about the episode.

Meanwhile, politically things were going from bad to worse in Rome. Complete demoralization seems to have seized many of the now futile ruling class. Those accused in the courts failed to answer to their summons. The exclusion, especially from the consulship, of various expectant nobles by the dynasts and their dependants exacerbated the struggle for office, which was now carried on without any kind of scruple. The consuls of 54, Domitius Ahenobarbus and Appius Claudius, took money to declare certain candidates elected for the next year whatever the actual result of the poll. The compact was revealed in the Senate – to the embarrassment of Domitius, who as a connection of Cato's had a reputation to keep up, but not at all to that of Appius, whose brazenness was proverbial. Scandalous and open bribery occurred in the other election campaigns, though Cato, who had now got his praetorship, tried to stop the rot. There was fear of a dictatorship by Pompey: soon a tribune known to be friendly with him proposed the appointment. 'It's hard to say if he wants it or not; but with Hirrus backing it he will not be able to persuade people he doesn't.' Public business was apparently completely suspended. The year 53 opened without consuls and with all candidates for the office on trial for bribery. Consuls were not elected till July, and were faced at once with the elections for next year. Since Milo was standing for the consulship and Clodius for the praetorship (an office which a hostile consul could reduce to ineffectiveness) trouble was inevitable. But by now all the candidates depended on force as well as bribery.

Pompey had candidates of his own for the consulship, but Cicero was heart and soul for Milo, with whom he had long been on the friendliest terms, though alarmed at the extravagance with which he poured out money on his political ambitions. In spite of this he maintained in the Senate that Milo should be accepted as a suitable candidate. He never wavered in his gratitude to Clodius' enemy – though we may be able to see little else in Milo to recommend him. We have few letters for 53 or 52, but there is one begging young Curio to support Milo's candidature: 'I have concentrated and invested all my zeal, effort, care, industry, thought, my whole mind indeed, in Milo's consulship.' But Curio preferred to stand by his old friendship with Clodius, and Cicero's hopes here too were to be frustrated.

The year 52 again opened without consuls. A friend of Pompey's as tribune vetoed even the appointment of an *interrex* (recourse was had to a series of these temporary magistrates in such an interval or *interregnum*). The immediate motive was a manœuvre against Milo, but it is little wonder that Cato accused Pompey of 'promoting anarchy to achieve monarchy'. On 18 January Clodius and Milo, both travelling with armed escorts as usual, but Milo with the bigger, if the less warlike, met on the Appian Way some miles from Rome. Their slaves clashed; Clodius was wounded, and carried into an inn. Milo had him dragged out and killed.

Later in the day a senator travelling to Rome came upon the body; he sent it on to Rome in his litter. Clodius' corpse was laid out in his house on the Palatine, where the lamentations of his wife Fulvia* stirred up the throngs of his supporters as they

* Not Cicero's informant of 63, but a formidable heiress, married in turn to Clodius, Curio and Antony.

gathered through the night. Next day the body was transferred to the Rostra in the Forum, and two tribunes, who had been Clodius' allies, addressed the crowd. This bore some resemblance to the honours regular for one who had taken part in public life. But it was hardly regular that the crowd carried the body into the Senate House next door and burnt it on a pyre of furniture and official documents. The building itself caught fire and was destroyed. The crowd then attacked the houses of the *interrex*, who had at last been appointed, and of Milo. A demonstration called for Pompey to become consul or dictator, offering him the *fasces*, the bundle of rods that formed the insignia of high office, which had been stolen from their place of safe-keeping. The consular candidates continued to demand elections, but to make them impossible by their bands of roughs. The optimates could hold out no longer. The Senate passed the Last Decree, calling on the only magistrates available, the *interrex*, the tribunes and Pompey the proconsul, to restore order, and authorizing Pompey to levy troops. Pompey did so, but still delayed intervening, until, on Bibulus' motion, the then *interrex*, who happened to be the lawyer Servius Sulpicius Rufus, declared him sole consul, thus avoiding at least the name of dictator. To the general surprise, Cato supported the appointment; any government, he said, was better than none. In assessing Pompey's position, we may remember that for some time now it had been known that Crassus was dead, killed at Carrhae in a disastrous battle against the Parthian Empire, which he had wantonly provoked in hope of wealth and glory; and also that Caesar was struggling with serious revolts in Gaul.

In declared fear of Milo, Pompey collected a large force. He saw to it that Milo was put on trial (two nephews of Clodius prosecuted) and special precautions taken against tampering with the jury. After the first day of proceedings, he found it necessary to post troops in the Forum and all the temples round it; before one of these he took his own seat. Cicero, who had been eagerly active on Milo's behalf – at the cost of his popularity with a section of the People, threats of prosecution, and probably Pompey's wrath – took part in the cross-examination. He proposed to argue in his final speech, not simply that Clodius' death had been for the public good (as Brutus did in an imaginary oration for Milo) but, not very convincingly, that the accused had acted in accordance with the natural law of self-defence. But when the day came, the Clodian tribunes had urged the People to see that Milo did not escape, and impressed on them that Cicero was responsible for Clodius' death. When Cicero rose he was greeted with uproar, and between the sight of the mob and of the soldiers he lost his self-command and 'spoke with less than his usual firmness' and quite briefly. His commentator Asconius at least, to whom we owe an admirable account of the background of the trial, thought it very courageous of him to have persisted so far. Milo went into exile at Massilia (Marseilles); and when Cicero sent him a copy of the speech he had worked up, which Asconius considered his best, Milo replied that he was glad it had not been delivered in that form, for he would have had no opportunity to taste the seafood of Massilia.

Cicero had subsequently more luck with a supporter of Milo's, whom he got acquitted, and one of the Clodian tribunes, Bursa, whom he prosecuted for violence.

You say that you think [he wrote to a friend] that because he is a low fellow I make little of my success. Believe me, I rejoice more at this verdict than at my enemy's death. I prefer the operation of the courts to violence . . . I was especially delighted that the *boni* felt such zeal for me in spite of the intense pressure exercised by a most distinguished and powerful man [Pompey]. Finally, though it seems improbable, I hated him much more than Clodius himself. I had attacked Clodius, Bursa I had defended. And Clodius aimed at something big, since the whole constitution was involved in my danger.

At last, then, Pompey and the optimates were, if uneasily, in alliance. But the coalition, as Cicero must have reflected bitterly, owed nothing to him. In fact at this point he was closer to Caesar, who seems to have summoned him to Ravenna to ask him to prevent Caelius, now tribune, obstructing his interests. However, Pompey, who was not ready for an open breach with Caesar, did not object to this and he did, as Cicero later said, forgive him his defence of Milo. And Cicero received some satisfaction when Pompey and Hortensius proposed him for young P. Crassus' vacant place on the board of augurs – a priesthood which, as a letter of 59 showed us, he had long hankered after. He did not believe in augury (the interpretation of omens given by the flight of birds and other events) but such an office was an almost essential decoration for a distinguished consular, and an important component of *auctoritas*, as well as a position of some power. Cicero's colleagues included, besides his sponsors, some of the noblest names in Rome; almost the noblest of them all,

Appius Claudius, was to pay Cicero the compliment of dedicating to him a work on augury – in which he at least implicitly believed; but then Appius believed in everything, and even practised necromancy. (Cicero was also to write on augury, but the book is lost.)

There was a solemn inaugural ceremony, and Cicero will also have had to give the college an inaugural banquet. Presumably the members were still arrayed in their official dress, the *trabea*, a mantle striped with purple and scarlet, though it is probable that the dinner provided was less extravagant than had been that of Hortensius, at which roast peacocks were first introduced to Rome; or than the inaugural banquet of a priest in 69 B.C of which an amazed later scholar has preserved the menu: *hors d'œuvres* of oysters and other shellfish, with asparagus, fattened chicken; small birds, loin of goat and boar, fattened fowl in pastry, more seafood; and a main course of sow's udders, boar's head, fish, duck, boiled fowl, hare, roast fowl, pudding and 'Picene bread'.

Pompey meanwhile set about clearing up the political mess. He had recently pleased the optimates by a safe marriage, to the intellectual but charming daughter of the highly aristocratic Metellus Scipio, and now took his father-in-law as colleague in the consulship. And he passed a certain amount of reforming legislation, directed primarily against corruption. Cato, though not in close collusion with him, as his failure in the consular elections for 51 shows, seconded him; he sat regularly on the juries, shaming his fellows into integrity; the eulogistic tradition shows him running his friend Favonius' aedilician games as he thought games should be run, without buying favour by extravagance or expensive prizes (he gave wreaths not of gold but fresh leaves, on the Greek model, and cheap presents, mostly of food: 'to the Greeks beets, lettuces, radishes and pears', says Plutarch, 'to the Romans wine, pork, figs, cucumbers and bundles of wood'). Fortunately the populace was amused; as it had been impressed a few years earlier when Cato walked out of the theatre as a protest against the nudity on stage traditional at that particular festival. With rare abnegation, on his rejection for the consulship he declared he would not stand again, for which Cicero blamed him. But these efforts to shore up the Republic came too late and were too superficial. Some of the nobles vital to the new alliance, like Domitius and Appius Claudius (who had recently married one daughter to Pompey's son and one to the rising

young optimate, M. Brutus, Cato's nephew) were hopelessly
discredited. Cato and his friends were not conciliatory, and they
were a narrow group. There were plenty of people to attack his
'faction' as harsh and oppressive, and to feel that Caesar, generous, reasonable, with all the prestige of a great conqueror, offered
them, and even Rome, a better hope for the future. The alliance
of Pompey and the optimates did not rest, as Cicero's policy had
demanded, on the 'concord of the orders'. The Senate itself
was now deeply divided; the *equites* were still unenthusiastic
about the optimates, while they were indeed actively hostile to
Gabinius if not to Pompey himself. And Caesar's following continued to swell.

One of Pompey's new laws laid down that no governor should
go out to his province till five years after his magistracy. The
intention was probably to discourage a candidate from spending
huge, frequently borrowed, sums on election to office in the
knowledge that he could soon recoup in the province to which
he would proceed immediately after his year of office. As a result
of the law there would for several years be a shortage of qualified
governors. Ex-magistrates who had refused to take a province had
to be deployed. Consequent to Crassus' disaster at Carrhae, trouble
was looming in the East, and the most senior men available were
called on. In spring 51 Bibulus was sent to Syria, where Crassus'
quaestor C. Cassius, later to be one of Caesar's assassins, was
hanging on; and Cicero was dispatched protesting to Cilicia, where
Appius Claudius had for the last two years been oppressing the
provincials.

These years had been in many ways deeply depressing ones
for Cicero. But, with his family and friends at hand, and work
to occupy him, his private life was not wholly unhappy. In February 56 he helped to celebrate the wedding of Atticus, now in his
fifties. There are henceforth brief but friendly references to his
wife Pilia in the letters. There were frequent reciprocal visits and
dinner parties. Atticus' house in Rome was an old building on
the Quirinal hill, to the charm of which Cicero was as alive as its
master, who refused to modernize it; Atticus' dinners were so
simple that Cicero occasionally laughed at him for preferring
vegetables to meat, and water to wine; and when he commissioned
Cicero, on his departure to the East, to get a special dinner service from Syria, the abandonment of precious metal for earthen-
ware, however exotic, elegant and expensive (Cleopatra is said
to have spent a fortune on the same gaily painted ware) was

probably most untypical of the Roman rich. We know that Atticus liked having his guests at dinner entertained with reading aloud – later on, they sometimes heard selections from Cicero's still unpublished works; but he was also a lover of good talk. He was particularly fond, however, of walking as he talked; there was a walk to be taken on his property at Rome, presumably in the grove that formed its chief attraction; and Cicero's grander mansion had a doubtless colonnaded *palaestra* or courtyard, while he once mentions Pompey's portico and the Field of Mars as suitable places in Rome for a stroll; one of his dialogues shows himself, Quintus and Atticus walking and talking in the grounds of his property near Arpinum. Even in that unsophisticated place one must not think of rough scrambles or tramps; the gentlemen doubtless promenaded sedately along well-smoothed paths. Atticus himself had only a couple of farms in Italy, though he kept his estate in Epirus; by descent and outlook he was more strictly Roman and urban than his friend, and when in Italy liked to be in the capital.

Cicero's relations with Quintus also remained close; though it seems that the latter was not always quite at ease with his famous brother, for before he left for Gaul Cicero had to write in some distress, insisting that he could never feel that Quintus was interrupting him or taking up his time.

The letters show Cicero busy with his own and Quintus' building and rebuilding projects; Quintus bought a new property near Arpinum and was on the lookout for a place near Rome. Cicero himself had the library of one of his seaside houses reorganized, with the help of Tyrannio, one of the leading Greek scholars of the time, and some well-trained slaves or freedmen of Atticus. He sent both his friend and his brother reports on the progress of young Quintus (who was of course Atticus' nephew) who was being educated with his cousin Marcus Cicero. Quintus was the elder and apparently the more gifted of the two (though he is reproved for greed) – a fact that Cicero, who was at this time very fond of the boy, does not seem to have grudged. He did not want to interfere with the plan of rhetorical study laid down by the boys' master; but he more than once proposed, if he could get the lad into the country, to take him off declamation and introduce him to his own more scientific and theoretical approach. There was certainly an element of the gifted teacher in Cicero; and in this period we have glimpses of his relations with several young protégés.

Of his old pupil M. Caelius he had clearly not seen much recently; the young man had gravitated towards Catiline, though avoiding his disaster, and then Crassus. Caelius had made his name by prosecuting important men, and had developed very much his own style in speaking, harsh and vigorous. He was now, or was soon to be, regarded as one of the leading orators of the age. Handsome and dashing, he lived in a strategically placed flat on the Palatine rented from Clodius. He was, it is fairly plain, for a time the lover of Clodia, since Metellus' death a dissipated widow living a gay life in her suburban mansion on the Tiber or her house in the resort of Baiae on the Bay of Naples. In the spring of 56 however Cicero answered an appeal to help Caelius defend himself on a charge of trying to poison her – thrown in with some even more serious accusations. This Cicero success-fully did, in an exceptionally lively and varied speech, which moves rapidly from avuncular considerations on the morals of young men to vivid and ironic evocations of Clodia's awesome ancestor, the blind Appius Claudius, on the one hand, and of her cynical brother Clodius on the other, together with a slapstick account of the bungled rendezvous at the public baths at which, according to the prosecution, the poison was to be handed over to Clodia's slaves; not to mention a pathetic description of the deathbed of her husband, himself poisoned, so Cicero insinuates, by his wife, that 'Medea of the Palatine' or, as Caelius had himself called her, 'sixpenny Clytemnestra'. Whether Caelius, whose wildness and vindictiveness are as certain as his wit and charm, was wholly innocent, must remain unclear; but he was certainly grateful for the assistance of Cicero (who once described him, in a rare sporting metaphor, as having a good right but a bad left) and we see them henceforth on the easiest terms.

Another young friend was the promising lawyer Trebatius Testa, whom Cicero recommended to Caesar. Trebatius did not much enjoy Gaul, and Cicero wrote repeatedly, scolding him and telling him to stick it out, in view of the opportunities open to him there, and pursuing him with legal jokes. A third was Publius Crassus, Marcus Crassus' son, who fought with courage and enterprise for Caesar in Gaul, and tried to reconcile his father and Cicero; he was to die with his father at Carrhae.

There are references in these years for the first time to Tiro, the highly educated slave, and soon freedman, who acted as Cicero's secretary and of whom the whole family seems to have been fond. The evidence as to his age is contradictory, but he was probably a young man at this time. Indeed a later writer quotes some erotic verses supposedly addressed to him by Cicero. If these are genuine they are probably, like most Roman love-poetry addressed to young men, a mere *jeu d'esprit* on the Greek model; the Romans in general and Cicero in particular disapproved of homosexual affairs, and there is no hint of such a relationship in the surviving letters to Tiro, affectionate and concerned for him as they are: 'such a well-behaved and conscientious young man' is what he remarks to Atticus, while extant letters from Quintus and Cicero's son as well show similar regard and respect. The attitude to slavery of the better Romans – and its limitations – can be shown by two quotations; one from Cicero some years earlier on the death of a young slave he employed to read to him: 'I am more upset than I ought to be at the death of a slave.' The other comes from a letter of Quintus to his brother on Tiro's enfranchizement: 'I am so grateful to you for feeling that he did not deserve his station in life and for preferring that he should be a friend to us rather than a slave.' Quintus adds, perhaps rather defiantly, that this was how he regarded his own freedman Statius, of whose influence Cicero continued to disapprove. Tiro was an invaluable assistant; apart from his scholarly accomplishments and interests, he invented or popularized a form of shorthand that made him famous, and could work to Cicero's most rapid dictation.

There are a number of references in these years to Tullia also, for whose sake, since she is nervous and unwell, Cicero once refrains from taking a brief that would irritate Clodius. We know little of her second marriage, her husband Crassipes, a young noble, apparently leaving much less impact on his father-in-law than the talented, respectful, hard-working Piso. But she seems to have been friendly with Atticus' wife Pilia, who was probably young. There is no mention at all of Terentia, apart from an early suggestion of a quarrel between her and her sister-in-law Pomponia.

One of Cicero's most attractive letters during this period was written partly as a literary exercise to a friend who, staying in the country in ill-health, had missed the festivities accompanying the opening of Pompey's theatre, the first permanent theatre in Rome, in autumn 55; he had asked for something to console him for his absence. Cicero assured him that he had missed nothing worth seeing; the comeback of the famous old actor Aesopus had been a pathetic failure. The plays did not have the charm that mediocre performances generally have, for the grandeur of the production prevented one laughing . . . What pleasure does one get from 600 mules in *Clytemnestra*? . . . in addition there were two shows of wild beasts lasting five days, magnificent, no one denies that, but what educated man can take pleasure in seeing a helpless man savaged by a beast far more powerful than himself, or a fine animal transfixed with a spear? The last day was that of the elephants, by which the crowd was much impressed, but hardly amused; rather they felt pity and a sense that the monster has something in common with man. Do not think however that I had all the leisure in the world to enjoy my good fortune on the days of the dramatic productions: I almost burst my lungs at the trial of your friend Caninius Gallus. If I had an audience as ready to let me retire as Aesopus' I would give up my craft with pleasure to live with you and those minded like us. I was sick of it already, when youth and ambition spurred me on and I did not need to defend those whom I did not like; but now it is no sort of a life. For I expect no advantage from my work and I am sometimes forced to defend men who do not exactly deserve well of me at the demand of those who do.

But these court cases were not his only work in these years. As he told Quintus, he could not be idle, and to him and Atticus he wrote of the literary work on hand. Apart from the poem and the book on grammar sent to Caesar, there was another epic poem, *On his Times*, dealing with his exile. It was to have the usual Council of the Gods in it, this one featuring Apollo describing the inglorious return to Rome of Piso and Gabinius. Fortunately Cicero decided not to publish it, professedly because he had not been able to mention in it all who helped him, in fact perhaps because he had been warned by the reception of the poem 'On his Consulate', and Atticus probably advised against it. Far more important were the two long prose dialogues *On the Orator* (*De Oratore*) and *On the State* (*De Republica*), which Atticus read and praised highly. But these need closer consideration.

9

CICERO ON THE REPUBLIC
56-52 B.C.

The 50s, so unhappy and chaotic politically, were in other respects the most brilliant age that Rome had yet seen; indeed
political and social troubles appear, as sometimes happens, to
have stimulated intellectual and artistic activity. Not that it would
be remotely plausible to interpret the great poets, Catullus and
Lucretius, to any significant extent by this principle, concerned
as they so largely were, the one with his private experiences and
with the inspiration of Greek poetry, and the other with that of
Greek philosophy; yet there are Catullus' political and social
verses, ranging from scurrilous invective against Caesar and his
friends to amusing anecdotes about prominent persons, while his
own experiences themselves were to some extent determined by
the hectic, cynical society in which they were lived; and among
the evils from which Lucretius the Epicurean wished to free
his contemporaries were not only religious fears, but the desperate
social and political ambitions that he has described so memorably.
And the progress of the other arts was certainly partly dependent
on social factors. The grandiose building plans of so many rich
men, however deprecated by the moralists, gave an impulse to
architecture and other forms of art; for example, the fashion for
richly coloured wall-painting representing architectural motifs,
familiar to us from Pompeii under the name of the Second Style,
has its roots in this period, and the rampant individualism of the
time perhaps had something to do with the efflorescence of portrait sculpture.

The breakdown, too, of republican government did produce
some effort at diagnosis and prescription. There was probably
an element of these in the histories of recent events, such as that
of Lucceius whom Cicero had wished to narrate his own vicissitudes; we have seen how Cicero himself recorded in various forms
his own version of these events, and shall see how he was himself tempted to write a formal history. There was also some
attempt to go further back; if the Roman tradition was in danger,
it was necessary to be sure what this tradition really was. The

early 50s are probably the time of Varro's first big antiquarian works, that take up a subject that had recently been neglected, though earlier activity in the field had been in part provoked by the political crises of the late second century. Some of Cicero's own works of this period, as we shall see, have antiquarian as well as historical aspects, and it was these elements of his work *On the State* or *De Republica* that inspired Atticus to turn to chronological researches. Atticus' protégé Cornelius Nepos, who subsequently wrote his patron's life, also embarked on a historiographical career. (Nepos is also known as the dedicatee of Catullus' poems; the Roman literary world was small – Cicero was the recipient of a versified compliment, whether sincere or ironic, from Catullus, and passed a favourable verdict on Lucretius' poem in a letter to his brother; indeed there is a late and uncertain tradition that he corrected the work, and it is known that he encouraged poets.) Also perhaps to some extent a conservative reaction to the troubles of the 50s was the work on augural law by Appius Claudius, dedicated, as we saw, to Cicero.

Most of these reactions, as one would expect of the Romans, were very concrete, and looked to the past. It was only Cicero, so far as we know, who went a little further towards the theoretical in his dialogues *On the Orator* and *On the State*, though here too there is a feeling for history which is not only Roman but Cicero's own. The dialogue tradition, as it happens, did not encourage historical accuracy, but Cicero seems to have satisfied his love of the manners, and the great men, of the past by reconstructing as carefully as he could the milieux of his central characters, in the one case L. Crassus and in the other Scipio Aemilianus; though at the same time he often echoes the dialogues of his beloved Plato (and probably those of Aristotle, which have not survived), such echoes being sought, not avoided, by ancient writers. The frameworks to his dialogues are delightful illustrations of Roman aristocratic manners, for all that they are less lively and dramatic than Plato's. The *dramatis personae*, prominent Romans together with their young relatives or protégés, assemble in a palazzo or a country villa, on a festival when they have leisure for conversation, and decide, in a graver and more formal manner than Socrates' friends in the Platonic dialogues, to debate some serious question.

Both the dialogues of the 50s are dedicated to Quintus. They are set among men to whom Cicero looked back with admiration, and in years in which the unity of classes on which he set so much store had been challenged; both the protagonists are represented as enlightened champions of the *boni* and the Senate. In the *De Oratore* Cicero opens by looking back to the flourishing days of the Republic when distinguished men might either engage in public life with safety or live in tranquillity without loss of standing – *in otio cum dignitate*. The body of the work is concerned not only with technical and artistic questions, such as the proper role of humour in oratory, but in a sense with the whole problem of political education. For Cicero argues that the only man worthy of the name of orator, and thus of the influence in the state that oratory gives, is the one who unites formal rhetorical training with legal and historical learning, civilized values or *humanitas*, and above all philosophy, which means primarily ethical principles. L. Crassus, if he does not quite attain this encyclopaedic ideal, approaches it; and in the proem to Book III his last political intervention, in support of the tribune Livius Drusus, the optimate demagogue, and of the rights of the Senate, with his subsequent illness and death, are eloquently recounted as a tribute to the true statesman. Cicero modestly declined to claim originality for the work; writing to Lentulus Spinther that his books on the Orator, in the Aristotelian style, would be useful for Spinther's son, he says that 'they are different from the usual rules, and embrace the whole oratorical theory of the ancients, especially Aristotle and Isocrates' (the latter in particular had defended rhetoric against Plato's contempt for an art he put on a level with cookery, by giving it a wide political and moral content). But the Roman dress that Cicero had given them so successfully was his own; the work is full of quotations and anecdotes from Roman legal cases and thoroughly adapted to Roman conditions.

The *De Republica* (the title is really untranslatable and means something like 'On State and Society') also made few conscious claims to originality. Cicero indicates elegantly that Plato and certain other Greek writers are his sources, and scholars' attempts to reach greater precision have been notably unsuccessful. He took a lot of trouble over the work, 'a heavy and laborious task indeed', as he called it in a letter, and he plainly read a great deal of Greek political theory and many historical and antiquarian studies in preparation for it, borrowing Varro's works from Atticus when his own library gave out and probably using a learned freedman of Atticus' as adviser and research assistant. But again he may well have been the first to discuss political theory at any length in Latin, though in this case some of the adaptation to Roman circumstances had been done by Greek writers living in Rome in the second century B.C. and closely associated with the aristocracy, especially with Scipio himself; if not by yet earlier Greek authors.

Cicero defines his subject in a letter to Quintus as the Ideal State and the Ideal Citizen; well-worn problems, certainly. But how relevant a discussion that at first sight looks abstract could be may be shown from the unfortunately very fragmentary introduction. This includes an urgent defence of the life devoted to public service against the Epicurean view that the wise man will preserve his freedom by remaining in a private station. Cicero argues that the desire to make life better for others is implanted in human nature; that the labours and dangers of political activity are outweighed by the honour and satisfaction it brings; that we owe a duty to our country even above that to our parents, while if there are worthless men in politics, this is one reason the more for good men going into public life. And he ridicules the Epicurean concession that in a crisis the wise man may step in to preserve the state; how, without experience or standing, could he possibly do so?

The problem was entirely topical; the Epicurean view had just been restated by Lucretius with burning eloquence, and perhaps by other Epicurean writers, Roman and Greek, now in the city; and there were certainly many able men, such as Atticus, to look no further, who in the present state of things preferred tranquillity to glory and quoted Cicero's own misfortunes as an example of the ingratitude and disappointments to be met with in public life. Not all of these were Epicureans. On the other hand, at the time of the Civil War and later, a number of Epicureans were to be found active in politics, the best known being Cassius. Popular as Cicero's work apparently was, we need not ascribe too much influence to it; but it is clear that it reflected a real situation. And the work as a whole is an elaborate theoretical justification of Cicero's long-established policy of aristocratic but conciliatory government.

Scipio and his friends are first seen talking of a prodigy recently observed in the sky, which leads them on to astronomy and the claims of the theoretical as opposed to the practical life – an old dichotomy. Laelius insists that nothing is so important as politics. Finally Scipio is asked to tell his auditors what he considers the best form of government. He describes the three basic types distinguished by Greek thinkers: kingship, aristocracy and democracy, which can degenerate respectively into tyranny, rule by junta, and rule by the mob. Following in the steps of many masters, he claims that the rapid change of one form into another can be arrested by a well-regulated mixture of the three pure types. This is the famous doctrine of the mixed constitution, which was to have an even longer and more glorious career in the future than it already had behind it when expounded by Cicero. To be found in embryo in Plato and Aristotle, and then in many writers of the Hellenistic period, it was to dominate the political thought of Aquinas, Machiavelli, and much English political theory into the eighteenth century. Cicero was not the first to see Rome, like Sparta and Carthage, as an example of the mixed constitution, with the consuls, who had succeeded to many of the powers of the kings when the last Tarquin was exiled in the late sixth century, representing kingship, the Senate aristocracy and the People democracy. The Romans could hardly think their ancestral constitution other than perfect, so great was their veneration for their deified ancestors; and by this theory it seemed that the best Greek thinkers had endorsed their view. To us the mixed constitution may appear a Procrustean bed into which the Roman system had been forcibly fitted; for example it took no account of the *equites*, who had developed as a factor in politics after the theory had already been applied to Rome; and we may be less impressed with its stabilizing and conciliatory effect than Cicero was – we may indeed see in the overlapping and ambiguous powers of the various elements a positive invitation to faction, and the right of veto chiefly as a means of paralyzing all government.

But not only was the prestige of the theory in Cicero's time enormous; it was the only reputable, more liberal, alternative to monarchy or aristocracy. Democratic theory, which had rarely attracted intellectuals after the fifth century B.C., declined further with the political decline of Athens, and the increasingly unequal distribution of wealth all over the Hellenistic world.

It had probably already been claimed in the second century B.C. that the Roman mixed constitution had come to perfection through long years of trial and the contributions of many wise men, instead of springing fully armed, as the Greeks tended to believe their systems had done, from the head of a single legislator such as the Spartan Lycurgus or the Athenian Solon. This view Cicero accepted. And so his discussion of the Ideal State becomes a brief history of Rome, founded on a perfect site and gradually emerging to perfection. (In spite of a natural tendency to formalism here, Cicero's narrative of an extremely obscure period of history is not wholly uncritical of its sources.) Plato's Republic, as a rival Ideal State, is rejected as impracticable as well as imaginary.

The fact that Cicero accepts such Roman features as the weighting of the Centuriate Assembly towards the rich and the aristocracy's control of politics through religion does not of course mean that he approves of injustice. To him, as to Plato, justice is involved in the preservation of proper ranks and hierarchies, though there is a sympathetic insistence on the equality of all citizens before the law – something that was to disappear under the Empire, when there came to be different penalties for rich and poor. In fact, refuting an old and paradoxical argument that injustice is necessary to the state, and proclaiming a somewhat Stoic belief in Natural Law, Cicero virtually identifies Law and Justice. By defining Law in this fashion, rather than as the pronouncement of the People, as the jurists did, or of any other body or individual, Cicero opens the way to something we see him doing in his public life, where, for all his professed devotion to law and legal procedures, he is able to sweep aside, rather too easily, laws that he regards as unjust or inexpedient; it is also one of the roots of his belief that it is necessary to consult the People's good, but not necessarily its wishes. He insists however that government must be gentle, the People not irritated; the Romans are wise in making the death penalty rare, statesmen should seem sympathetic to the People for the sake of Concord. And he approves the traditional institution of clientship on the grounds that the upper class is thus encouraged to protect the poor and help them with advice, support and money.

The latter part of the De Republica has come down to us in a very fragmentary condition. It seems to have discussed education and the influence of the arts; Cicero defended the Roman upper-class system of centring education on the family, in opposition to the state system for which so many Greek philosophers hankered. He thought both women and children should be disciplined in the home alone; but there should be strict laws to control the stage, especially to avoid the personal attacks for which early Athenian comedy was notorious. There was also a long discussion of the Ideal Citizen. Here there has been much dispute as to Cicero's intentions. It was natural that, in the 50s, he should consider the proper norms and limits of the power of

151

the individual. Some used to believe that he envisaged a quasi-monarchic protector of the constitution, such as Augustus later became; it is true that Scipio had said that kingship, the rule of one wise man, is the best of the simple forms of government, but this is an academic admission, for it is also the least stable, lapsing easily into tyranny, the worst of all forms. Cicero would not thus have contemplated monarchy as a practical proposition, and it is now generally agreed that there may be more than one *rector* or *gubernator* in the state, at one time, and that he has none of Augustus' solid (and mainly military) powers but depends wholly on example, knowledge of the laws and influence over public opinion. Nor was Pompey the model; we know that Cicero felt that military prowess was outmoded now that Rome had no dangerous enemies, and Pompey certainly did not have the learning he demanded instead. Rather, the models are the great men of old, Scipio, his friend Laelius and others, and also surely Cicero himself as he might, he felt, have been in happier circumstances, given his capacity to unite theory and practice in politics. Cicero is however here sharply aware of the dangers of eloquence: corruption by eloquence, he holds, is worse than corruption by money, and his *rector* is apparently to cultivate a laconic brevity of speech, a different solution from that in the *De Oratore*, in which rhetorical skill is developed alongside moral qualities.

In a crisis, however, Cicero certainly thought a dictator was permissible – he uses the word of course in its traditional Roman sense of a magistrate with overriding powers appointed for a definite, usually a very short, time. He suggests that Scipio might have become dictator in order to set the state on its feet in the disturbed period after Tiberius Gracchus' death. Had Machiavelli known the *De Republica*, which was almost entirely lost until the nineteenth century, he would have seen here something like his own doctrine of the *riordinatore*.

A fragment describes the fundamental object of the statesman: that the citizens' lives shall be fortunate – 'secure in prosperity, ample in resources, great in glory and honoured in virtue'. Most earlier thinkers, with the exception of the Epicureans, to whom the state was only there to provide minimal safeguards, pitched its aims equally high. Such views must lead to strong and interfering government; they help to explain why Sparta, the state that regulated every aspect of her citizens' lives, was so admired.

The statesman's proper recompense for what he does is glory,

Cicero declares; this was the motive for the great deeds of the early Romans. But let us turn to the famous *Dream of Scipio*, with which, in imitation of the myth of Er at the end of Plato's *Republic*, Cicero finishes, and which for many centuries, until a re-used manuscript originally containing the *De Republica* was found in the Vatican, was all that could be read of the work. Taking up, so carefully is the dialogue constructed, the themes with which the work began, astronomy and the justification of political activity, the Dream transports Scipio to the heavenly spheres. Here he meets his grandfather, the elder Scipio Africanus, the conqueror of Hannibal, who proclaims that the statesman's real reward is the favour and immortality given by the gods, who are pleased by well-ordered societies. From the heavens Scipio can see how insignificant the earth is, and how small a part of it his glory can fill, and for how short a time – since the conflagrations and floods postulated in Stoic cosmology repeatedly wipe out all living creatures. If he will think of these things, he will not be influenced by popular repute or put his hopes in human honours. In this life, political activity should be altruistic – and about the other, Cicero was never dogmatic: this scene is no more, perhaps, than the dream it is represented as – with some sceptical words on the origin of such phenomena.

In autumn 54 Cicero wrote to Quintus that he had originally planned nine books (nine papyrus rolls, each the equivalent of a long chapter), and had finished two, but that a friend had suggested that he would write with more authority in his own person, and that it was true that, though he had avoided a contemporary setting to escape giving offence, it was inconvenient not to be able to treat events more recent than Scipio's death. And so he would recast the work as a discussion between Quintus and himself. In fact, he compromised; the *De Republica* finally consisted of six books, set in the past, but we also have substantial fragments of a work, possibly also in six books, *De Legibus*, or *On the Laws*, which takes the form of a conversation between Cicero, Quintus and Atticus at Arpinum. It is explicitly a continuation of the *De Republica* and lays down detailed regulations for the ideal state, after the model of Plato's *Laws* (though that was not closely connected with his *Republic*); but with, this time, an explicit claim to originality of content. It was perhaps never finished, and almost certainly it was not published in its author's lifetime; but it clearly owes its existence to the impulse which created the *De Republica*, and it is likely that Cicero was working on it in the late 50s, to be interrupted by his forced departure for Cilicia; though he may have at least planned to take it up again after the Civil War. Apart from its pleasant framework, it is a less readable work than the De Republica, consisting as it largely does of dogmatic rules announced in archaic, legalistic language and then commented on by Cicero, who takes un-ashamedly the leading part in the conversation. But it is our best evidence for the reforms that he would have liked to see introduced at Rome.

The De Republica says nothing, in surviving parts at least, of the causes for degeneration in the perfect mixed constitution; the only hint we are given is a lament for the vanished manners and virtues of the old days. Such a moralizing explanation of decay was exceedingly common among historians and politicians of an-tiquity; we should rather wish to explain demoralization itself by social or economic developments (though the ancients did lay stress above all on one economic factor, the introduction of luxury). But the De Legibus suggests that Cicero could get a little further than vain laments, though it was profoundly difficult for a Roman to subject his constitution to radical criticism. He makes proposals inspired by three sources: Greek theory, ancestral practice now vanished, and his own experience of contemporary problems. Often all three converge behind a single law.

The De Legibus begins by reformulating the theoretic basis of his thought, already expounded in the De Republica. Law is de-pendent on Natural Law, which is Natural Reason; it is in some sense the reasonable mind of God, and to this wisdom human wisdom is related. Cicero's conviction that the laws of Rome are consonant with the laws of nature perhaps helped to prepare the way for the extension of Roman institutions over the whole Empire. This conception of Natural Law also explains why his laws cover custom and morality (as the Greek word nomos did in ordinary usage) and also why he now begins, as the Greek works he used generally did, with religious law.

His main interest in religion is in its direct social and moral value. He declares that the conviction that the gods care for social health, and reward and punish political acts, is both true and useful. (Certainly the advantages of popular superstition were a commonplace in aristocratic Rome.) Since divine and human wisdom concur in preferring the rule of the optimates, it is perhaps logical to believe that traditional religious usages working to the preservation of aristocratic influence are justified, even though it is admitted that in these days at least the augur's science is an empty cheat. Indeed, Cicero even makes disobedience to an augur's ruling a capital crime, something probably quite new; and not only are ancestral rites, especially the cults of the family, to be piously preserved, but a number of public rituals, extinct or nearly so, are to be revivified – for example, those carried out by special priests in charge of the making of war and peace. He insists also that no private rites may be carried out without official priests in attendance (they were of course drawn from the nobility) on the grounds that it promotes social cohesion for the people to be dependent on optimate assistance. Cicero speaks of the various colleges of priests, but nowhere singles out the *pontifex maximus*; religion is the organ of a class, not an individual. On the other hand Cicero requires simplicity in ritual, not only to curb the luxury of the rich (and thus vice and so political decay) but to ensure equality before the gods as before the law. Simple funerals, in particular, are enjoined; it is 'most natural', the final touchstone, that differences in wealth should cease with death. There are other interesting social preoccupations: with the rarest exceptions, sacrifices and other rites held at night, as was the case chiefly in certain Greek and oriental mystery religions, are banned as conducive to immorality. The consecration of land is forbidden, as it damages agriculture, and fertile land may also not be used for graves. Collections of money for religious purposes are mostly to be stopped, since they encourage superstition and impoverish whole families. Cicero is also anxious to put the calendar right (it had got badly out of step with the seasons) so that festivals shall fall in the idle periods of the agricultural year; the rest that slaves get by such holidays is pointed out (there was no equivalent to the later Sunday, though market days fulfilled some of its functions). The games celebrated at these festivals are to be athletics, chariot-racing and musical competitions; there is no reference to the gladiatorial shows and beast-hunts that occurred on special occasions, but we cannot be certain that Cicero wished to do without them. The musical events are to be severely controlled, as Plato recommended, since nothing has so much influence over young minds, and such power to corrupt, as soft and licentious music. This was a well-established belief. The other main innovation is the abolition of cults to such evil abstractions as Fever; only good powers, like great and good men, should be regarded as divine. Here Greek as well as Roman practice, if not philosophic tradition, is left behind. In this as in his insistence on purity of mind in the worshipper, it is clear that Cicero wants to refine and increase the moral content of traditional religion; but he did not go as far as Varro, who, also under Stoic influence in a huge work on religious antiquities published a few years later, regretted the use of images and animal sacrifice.

Book II deals with the magistrates, who are the law given voice. It lays down in some detail the powers of the Senate, which are to be great. Its decrees have the force of law and it alone can create a dictator in a crisis (though in early days the consuls had nominated to the post and Sulla had been theoretically elected). The consuls themselves can take exceptional action at such times however, and it is not clear whether the Senate has to pass the so-called Last Decree beforehand. 'The people's welfare is the highest law.'* But Cicero's Senate, however powerful, is not, like Sulla's, uncontrolled. The great constitutional innovation of the *De Legibus* is the extension of the censors' powers. Whether this idea is Cicero's own we do not know, but it seems possible. There is always to be a pair in office (traditionally they were elected every five years for a period of eighteen months, but had recently been appointed very irregularly). They are to be the guardians of morality, especially senatorial morality; so much was traditional. But they are also to pronounce on the behaviour of magistrates as they leave office, though prosecution remains the right of individuals, and in this they bear a close resemblance to the boards set up to oversee the behaviour of officials that were common in the Greek world. Finally, the censors are to be given a general guardianship of the laws, such as Greek philosophers from Plato on had advocated. Under this they are to see that the laws are available in correct form, perhaps actually published, and that they are obeyed by magistrates and private citizens alike. This proposal might have raised the standards of public life and indeed to some extent, by creating a single supreme authority, obviated the rival interpretations of the constitution that plagued Rome. There are also minor reforms, such as one originally advocated by L. Crassus, holding the presiding magistrate responsible for violence occurring at a popular assembly. Another does away entirely with laws directed against individuals; this is aimed against such measures as Clodius' final bill against Cicero.

* *Salus populi suprema lex.*

Cicero does not find it necessary to argue for any of these proposals at length. It is different when he comes to the People's share of power, embodied in the tribunate and secret ballot. He puts forward arguments for retaining the tribunate as a check on the consuls, who might sometimes challenge the Senate's will. The tribunes could control them with their veto; and he thought them likely to be more responsible than the People, left leaderless, would be. When first instituted, he claims, the tribunate itself had a conciliatory effect; it gives satisfaction to the People, and anyway it cannot now be quietly abolished. As for the vote, Cicero's Senate, like Sulla's, is to be composed of those who have been elected to office by the People, and the latter is still responsible for legislation. But if there is no bribery or intimidation secret voting will be unnecessary. So let the ballot survive to please the People, but let it be open on demand, so that the People should be ashamed to vote 'badly' and should try to win the favour of the optimates. Cicero's methods of binding the classes together are prone to be over-optimistic.

None of this sounds dangerously *popularis*. But Cicero represents himself as quite unable to win over Quintus and Atticus. ' "You are aware, my dear brother, that in dialogues of this kind it is customary to say 'certainly' or 'quite true', so that a new subject can be introduced."

"As a matter of fact I do not agree at all, but please go on to the next subject nonetheless." ' They want, clearly, to see the tribunate cut down at least to the Sullan level, and voting by word of mouth to be restored. Probably most of the optimates felt that there would never be quiet while tribunes and assemblies retained any real power; and Caesar as Dictator and Augustus were to agree with them.

In the fragmentary state of the *De Legibus* we must beware what we say that Cicero left out (we know that there was more on the powers of individual magistrates, probably a section on the law courts, and a further discussion of that subject which the ancients recognized as crucial to society, education). Thus a final judgement on Cicero's analysis of Rome's troubles is hardly possible. All we can say is that nowhere in his surviving works does he explicitly consider what seem to us some of the most urgent problems of the day, for example, the too great dependence of armies on their generals. This was partly solved, in a sense easily, by Caesar who doubled the rate of pay, thus reducing reliance on booty and special donatives, and by Augustus,

157

who instituted a military treasury so that it was the state that settled claims to land or cash on discharge. These measures, however, cost a lot of money, and it is doubtful if Cicero would have contemplated the increase in taxation that was forcibly imposed even on citizens in the Civil Wars (though the final annexation of Egypt also helped Rome's finances) and the closer control over the provincial governor's expenses, that proved an essential preliminary. His belief that foreign affairs and warfare were no longer of first importance perhaps helped to blind him to the interdependence of military and political problems.

Nor does he seem to consider the difficulty that we identified as one perpetuated and aggravated by the Sullan constitution – what to do with your military-minded consulars; indeed he reasserted the ten-year gap before a second consulship. Had a province been made a less lucrative and desirable job, it might have been possible to confine commands without danger to the most suitable hands, and thus give them continual work (a system of rotation, to prevent a governor building up too much support in a single province, might still have been necessary). This in practice was what Augustus did, though he had the advantage that he was theoretical commander-in-chief of nearly all the legions, so that the man on the spot, as a mere subordinate, was less able to gain influence over the troops. Or, as happened later, provinces could have been subdivided, to create more, and less dangerously powerful, posts. The frantic competition for office was also eased when Augustus began the custom of having two sets of consuls in the course of a year; but this, it is true, might have been awkward without the continuity he provided in his own person. Furthermore, Cicero has nothing about the fatal tendency, which grew from fundamental social institutions, as well as from the checks and vetoes that he has actually proposed to reinforce, for the oligarchy to block all reform for fear of the support that its promoter would gain. Here the all-powerful Caesar and Augustus were at an immense advantage – but found a formidable task confronting them. Cicero also has nothing about that badly needed police force; Augustus created it, created also a strong city governor or prefect – and moved the army, in the shape of his praetorian guards, in as well. He also did something about the *plebs* and their grievances, and by taking 'tribunicial power' and thus focusing on himself the People's loyalty to their tribunes managed to reduce these last to insignificance.

But when we talk of the 'solutions' produced by Augustus it

is as well to remember that the state he founded was a progressively less veiled military autocracy, only slightly less corrupt
and oppressive to the poor and the provincials than its predecessor, and usually on uneasy terms with the upper classes on which
it depended; while the loss of political liberty was a factor in the
intellectual decline of an age that had an excessive regard for
authority in the arts and sciences as well as in society, and which
developed a radical pessimism about man and his social and moral
potentialities. This pessimism pervaded the political atmosphere,
and contributed in varying degrees to the new religions in which
so many of the best, as well as the most wretched, took refuge,
and which in the end burst the old forms and created a new
civilization.

But to return to Cicero. He does not think it is for him to tell
us how to go about creating his reformed and purified Rome.
Having commented on the law (hardly a law in our sense, but we
remember his definition of the term) that the Senate must be
'without fault' and an example to the rest of the community,
he lets Atticus remark cuttingly, 'You must allow me to say that
not only the censors but every juror in the city will be exhausted
in bringing that to pass.' Never mind, Cicero replies; we are talking of an ideal future.

It is true that we must not ask every theorist to be also a
practical reformer. Maps of Utopia are not valueless because
charts for the voyage are not appended. But we may perhaps regard this particular Utopia as an unsatisfactory compromise between, to use Cicero's words in a different context, Plato's Republic and the dung-heap of Romulus. We tend to import, into
his very Roman framework, real Romans – and then it begins to
look like a semi-totalitarian oligarchy busy bullying and deceiving its subjects. But of course it is meant to be nothing of the
sort. Its senators are mild and gentle, always able to see what
perfect justice requires, and swift to follow it; they have been
chosen by a loving and respectful People. Before we call Cicero
blind to human nature let us remember that the same criticism,
that the ideal state would not in practice work like that, could
be levelled at his great master Plato and many of the master's
disciples down to recent times; as Cicero, like Plato, knew.

Whatever the shortcomings of Cicero's political works, there
is no evidence that any of his contemporaries understood the
problems of the time as clearly or indeed produced nearly so
positive a contribution towards solving them as he did. Cato prob-

ably did not get beyond the usual condemnation of the morals of the ruling class – always a tempting solution for conservatives who do not want to criticize an inherited framework – and the waging of an admittedly gallant struggle to make it behave itself; though we should perhaps beware of underestimating one who was a serious student of philosophy (the Stoics did produce a few political theorists) but unlike so many of his contemporaries no littérateur. What we badly want is a *popularis* or Caesarian view of the crisis. Caesar's own writings, interesting as they are, do not fill the gap, for apart from setting his military achievements, on which his claim to *dignitas* was based, in the best possible light, they are engaged in very *ad hoc* self-defence. In Book I of the *Gallic War* he is warding off a possible charge of treason (for attacking the German King Ariovistus without authorization); while in the *Civil War* he is appealing, probably while the war is still in progress, to respectable, especially Italian, opinion, and attempting to show that it is he, not his opponents, who represents constitutional propriety and the rights of property, while those opponents threaten to unleash Sullan proscriptions and have historical links with Sulla and his worst adherents. What solutions, if any, he produced as Dictator we shall see in due course.

Sallust's analysis, as he looked back on the period in the *Catilinarian War*, when he had lost faith in all politicians, is exclusively moralistic; and unfortunately the two *Letters to Caesar*, ascribed to his younger days, are of very dubious authenticity. The second letter in particular, which *prima facie* dates from 51 or 50, is nonetheless an interesting document, even if it is only a later rhetorical exercise 'in the matter of' an earlier writer; and it may be based on ideas really put forward at that time by some of Caesar's more radical supporters. It is a bitter attack on Cato and his 'faction', who are said to be responsible for a Sullan reign of terror (i.e. they have got a number of Clodius' supporters condemned) and keep an unscrupulous grip on the magistracies and other offices. The People, it complains, is sunk in slavery; but extensive enfranchizement will help to remedy this, and colonies of old and new citizens together will provide more resources of manpower for the army to draw on. In Rome the Centuriate Assembly must be reformed, as Gaius Gracchus intended to reform it, in an egalitarian manner – this means perhaps only the moderate step of calling the centuries to vote in an order determined by lot rather than mainly by wealth, which had already been advocated by the highly respectable jurist Servius

Sulpicius in 63 on the grounds that it would make bribery harder. Juries should be drawn from a somewhat wider class, and the Senate should be enlarged, made more open to merit, and allowed to vote by secret ballot. Like all reformers at Rome, the author represents his proposals as at least in part a reaction to the good old days when the People was free and the Senate authoritative. It is clear that he is by no means a democrat, something inconceivable in the social, economic, intellectual and educational circumstances of his place and time. His proposals would however weaken the power of the old families and base the running of the state on a broader section of the propertied classes. That might have been to the good. But one may doubt whether a larger Senate would have been manageable; Augustus tried hard to keep numbers down and still had to bypass it in many matters for smaller councils; it is possible that Cicero in the *De Legibus* had actually intended to reduce it by excluding those under the rank of aedile, though he is not at all clear on this point. And generous enfranchizement, however welcome to its beneficiaries, would make the voters in Rome less representative than ever of the Roman People as a whole, and therefore less respected by the politicians. This again is made clear by developments under Caesar and Augustus. In this sense at least the often loosely used statement that Rome had outgrown the institutions of the city state is true. That, too, Cicero had failed to realize, though Caesar may have seen it. But monarchy as such was not inevitable, even if it had some undeniable advantages; had certain reforms been put through, senatorial rule might have been prolonged indefinitely. Cicero, in a sense, never 'despaired of the Republic'; and for this, in the darkest days of the Hannibalic War, Rome had publicly thanked one of her generals. Or does the fact that he never published, perhaps never finished, the *De Legibus* suggest that indeed he did despair?

There was another work that, if we may take the preface to the *De Legibus* to have been written in the late 50s, Cicero was then considering, though in fact he never produced it. This was a history of Rome. The intellectuals of Rome were well aware of her inferiority in art and science to Greece – and that the gap was narrowing. (The Greeks were probably aware of that too, though we need not perhaps believe Plutarch's story that Molon, on hearing Cicero declaim in Rhodes, had said he grieved for Greece, since the only glories left her were passing to Rome.) At any rate it was widely felt that there was nothing in Latin to compare with the work of the great Greek historians, and some people at least thought that Cicero was the man to fill the gap. He was tempted by the project. In the *De Oratore* he had discussed the writing of history, which was regarded as a branch of oratory, often with disastrous results, for the search for truth and understanding might be neglected for dramatic narrative tricked out with plausible but invented detail and equally invented speeches – speeches that did not, as with Thucydides, carry the weight of serious analysis but simply showed the writer's familiarity with the rhetorical rule-book; while the only form of historical interpretation might be simple-minded moralizing. But Cicero saw history as a task eminently worthy of the true orator, with his wide background knowledge and his deep under-standing of politics. It is possible that in the digression on L. Crassus' death he gave something of a sample of his work in the genre. The passage, though it rises to lofty eloquence at the end, is notably precise on places and, dates, and clearly indicates the sources it is based on. Cicero does not conceal his own political views, but he describes his hero's opponent without rancour (and when he did, later, in the *Brutus*, produce a fascinating work of literary history, he showed that his artistic assessment even of those whose politics he deplored was on the whole generous and unbiassed). In the *De Republica* he got involved, as we saw, in earlier history; and the *De Legibus* has several interesting pass-ages of antiquarian investigation, especially one concerned with burial customs, which almost certainly rests on Cicero's own researches – less extensive than Varro's, but perhaps controlled by considerably sounder judgement.

In the preface to this work Cicero makes Quintus suggest that his brother should write a history from the foundation of Rome, 'from Remus and Romulus', since the existing annals are quite unreadable; while Atticus is represented as wishing him to treat more recent times – and this indeed was the period with which he was best qualified to deal. But if the obscure history of early Rome was, Cicero may have felt, scarcely a possible subject for one who was not a professional scholar willing to devote his life to research, nonetheless recent history was for different reasons also to be approached warily, and the military side of the subject may have daunted him. But he does not refuse the demand out-right; he only proposes to defer the task till his old age, when he can no longer speak in the courts and has leisure enough for the vast amount of work involved. In fact that time never came;

though unoccupied through much of the 40s, he found in philosophy a greater emotional consolation and in some ways an easier task, especially as much of his writing was done in the country, away from archives. Nonetheless, in the last year of his life Cicero seriously thought of beginning his history, with the aid of Atticus, who had recently revealed himself as a historian, and had also shown himself on several occasions an admirable research assistant when Cicero wanted information for his dialogues set in the past. We may, with Cornelius Nepos, regret that this history was never written; for that of Livy, with all its honesty and eloquence, lacks the critical judgement of the sources and above all the feel for political life that Cicero could have brought to the task, as his account of the debate in the Senate in the digression in the *De Oratore* shows; though, like all ancient historians, he would doubtless have overstressed, to our eyes, moral examples and moral and political causation as well as the role of individuals, while his own limitations of understanding would have been in evidence. In the event, Rome had to wait for Tacitus to give her a historical work which, idiosyncratic as it is, unites a fair measure of careful scholarship with political insight and memorable eloquence, and thus lives up to the best standards of ancient historiography. But Cicero has after all left us the letters, and, as Cornelius Nepos said (very remarkably for his date) these come near to being a substitute for the history that was never written.

IO

THE GOVERNOR OF CILICIA
51-50 B.C.

Cilicia at this time (probably owing to Clodius' desire to provide a plum job for Gabinius in 58, though other arrangements had ultimately been made for him) was the largest Roman province in the East, made up of various awkwardly united parts. Cilicia proper was the highly strategic area in the farthest eastern corner of the Mediterranean, between the passes over the rugged Taurus mountains from Anatolia, and those over the Amanus range into northern Syria and Mesopotamia, and thus a vital link between East and West. To it was attached 'Rough Cilicia' and almost all the rest of the wild coast of southern Asia Minor, long a haunt of pirates; large areas of the plateau inland, with much of the main route to the Aegean coast; and, in addition, the island of Cyprus. It was not, in fact, a combination that was to prove long viable. Most of the province was dotted with cities, Greek in language and institutions though scarcely in race, to which much of the administration was delegated; their territories covered most of the countryside, where native languages were still spoken, but some of the wilder parts were tribal in organization. Defence and general oversight, particularly of Roman citizens in the area, devolved upon the Roman governor.

He was allowed very considerable freedom of action, partly because of difficulties of communication with Rome. But there were certain laws regulating governors' behaviour in general; each province had its basic rights and obligations fixed in its original charter, drawn up by a senatorial commission on annexation, and there were certain traditional guidelines that a governor was expected to follow in announcing, in his official edict, the principles that he intended to abide by in his administration. But great latitude remained, even supposing that a governor respected the laws and followed his own edict; and it was very difficult to ensure that he did either.

There was at this period virtually no permanent staff in the provinces, except for members of the garrison, some of whom might be seconded to primarily administrative jobs. Each governor

brought out with him most of the men he needed – an arrange-
ment that was, one would assume, expensive as well as lacking
in continuity. There was his quaestor, who was a regular magistrate, and his lieutenants or 'legates', who could act as his deputies
in all spheres, and were senators whose commission came from
the Senate, though their names were suggested by the governor;
there were, at a lower level, clerks, lictors, messengers and other
minor officials, often, except perhaps for the clerks, freedmen.
All these last drew a salary from the state. Some of these official
attendants would in fact be the governor's own freedmen; and
he would also be accompanied by numbers of his own slaves
and freedmen in a personal capacity. In addition he would choose
responsible men, chiefly of equestrian status, for administrative
and military duty as 'prefects'; and he was often accompanied by
young friends of good family, who might sit on his council in
the law courts or otherwise assist him, but were primarily there
to get experience and education themselves.

Cicero's task, then, would be partly military and partly administrative and judicial. He was under no illusions as to his military
capacity, and so he chose his legates carefully. One was his brother
Quintus, trained in Gaul under the greatest soldier of the day,
and himself an ex-governor; another was C. Pomptinus, who as
praetor in 63 had been one of Cicero's mainstays; he had since
then governed Gaul and actually triumphed, if against considerable opposition, for his deeds there. And at least one of the other
two legates is also known to have been an experienced soldier.
Among Cicero's other assistants, relations and Arpinate friends
bulked large, as was considered perfectly proper. His household
included Tiro, who acted as his secretary; and, though they were
neither of them old enough for any responsibility, both his own
son and young Quintus, with their Greek tutor, accompanied the
party. A governor was regarded as being on active service, and was
not accompanied by his womenfolk.

Cicero left Rome in the spring of 51, having arranged that
Caelius should send him reports of all that was going on, since
Atticus expected to be out of Italy for much of the time.
But he was in close touch with Atticus nonetheless. A new
series of letters opens as Cicero moves south from Rome. In
the first he described the ungracious way in which Atticus'
sister Pomponia parted from her husband Quintus near Arpinum
('so that you may see lessons and advice are needed from you
as well as from me'); stopping at Cumae he was gratified by a

farewell call from Hortensius ('a man in ill-health, a long way to come, and Hortensius at that'); at Tarentum he stayed with Pompey, from whom he hoped to get advice about the East, but being uncertain if Atticus was still in Rome did not fulfil his promise to 'write you a complete account of my Dialogues on the State with Pompey', though he did send Caelius an unusual eulogy of Pompey's soundness of views as revealed in them. He waited for some time at Brundisium for his legate Pomptinus to join him, and because he was himself unwell; Pomptinus was clearly as unwilling as Cicero himself to leave Rome, perhaps partly, as is later hinted, because of a love-affair there. Finally Cicero sailed on ahead, and towards the end of June was writing from Athens that there was still no news of Pomptinus, and that he was enjoying Athens and his friendly reception there, but that philosophy was in a state of confusion, the scholar in whose house he was staying representing the best of it. In many of his letters to Atticus he discusses the question of a new marriage for Tullia, who had recently parted from her second husband (there was little function for unmarried women in Roman society and apparently they were rare). And in almost all of them he begs Atticus, like everyone else he writes to, to see that his term of office, 'this enormous bore', is not extended beyond the single year specified, apparently, in Pompey's law and a subsequent senatorial decree: 'I cannot tell you how I burn with longing for Rome, how hardly I endure the insipidity of my present situation.' It was perhaps already apparent, and Caelius was certainly soon warning him, that all appointments to provinces would be held up by Caesarian tribunes anxious to avoid a successor being sent to Gaul, where Caesar's extra term would soon be running out.

Cicero employed some of his time in Athens in writing, mainly for Atticus' sake, to an exiled Roman noble, Memmius, who owned a piece of property that had once belonged to Epicurus and that his School was very anxious to recover; a letter that allows us to see that Memmius, the dedicatee of Lucretius' passionately Epicurean poem, was not particularly sympathetic to its thesis. At last Pomptinus appeared; the quaestor had also arrived; and the party set off, almost complete, across the Aegean in a small fleet of open boats. 'Travelling by sea is a great business even in July,' declared Cicero; the winds were either adverse or too strong. But 'we arrived at Ephesus on 22 July, on the six hundredth day after the battle of Bovillae [Clodius' death]', to another extremely gratifying welcome from native Greeks and

Roman businessmen alike; and Cicero was soon in his carriage on the 'hot and dusty' road across the Roman province of Asia, to reach Laodicea in his own province on the last day of July – from this day, he wrote, his year's tenure must be exactly reckoned. At Laodicea he drew the money granted him for expenses, but did not linger.

Summer was of course the campaigning season; and it was less advanced than appears, owing to the retardation of the calendar. Cicero moved East to join his troops, giving brief audience to delegations and administering justice in the towns on his route. The province was garrisoned by two legions, theoretically of 6,000 men each but much under strength; some of the men had been mutinous, and though Appius Claudius was believed recently to have subdued them and settled their arrears of pay, with some of the best troops he had retired to the farthest part of the province and 'where they are I do not know'. Others, recently discontented, were camping apart without any officers. The Senate did not like entrusting governors with large armies – the good side to this was that the provinces were not on the whole overburdened with Roman troops – but it had realized that the East was in a dangerous state and had tried to authorize levying in Italy for Cilicia and Syria, only to be met with a tribunicial veto. Crassus' defeat had been a severe shock, and except for Pompey's faithful friend Deiotarus, King of the Galatians (Celts who had invaded and settled in Asia Minor in the third century B.C.) none of the allied kings and princes who acted as buffer states for the Roman provinces were, thought Cicero, really loyal, any more than the provincials themselves. This was understandable; the Mithridatic Wars had ended only just over ten years previously, Syria and most of Cilicia were recently annexed areas, and they had not been wholly fortunate in their governors; but it was especially serious in that the Romans depended for most of their cavalry and light-armed troops at least on local levies, to support the legionaries, who were heavy infantry using first iron throwing weapons, followed up with swords. Cicero complained that his provincials were not worth enlisting, such poor material and so untrustworthy were they.

At first there was nothing to be heard of the Parthians. But in late August there was news from an allied monarch that they had crossed the Euphrates into Syria near the Cilician border in force; while the king of Armenia intended to invade Cappadocia, which was subordinate to Rome, in support of them. Since the said allied monarch was reporting to the Senate, and Bibulus should by now be in Syria and able to do the same, Cicero contented himself with a brief letter to Cato, remarking pointedly that he would try by his behaviour to ensure the loyalty of the allies and thus make up for his lack of troops. He marched into the Kingdom of Cappadocia, getting more reliable news of the Parthians as he did so, and took up a strong and easily provisioned position near the passes into Cilicia proper but conveniently placed also to counter an invasion from Armenia further north. He wrote to Atticus that his troops and the provincials were both in better heart, a levy of Roman citizens was being made, and that Deiotarus of Galatia was on his way with troops that would double his strength. In fact, Deiotarus had armed his men on the Roman model, and Cicero found that the Galatians, and some of the provincial auxiliaries, were in fact his best troops. It is interesting that Augustus was to incorporate a Galatian legion into the Roman army-list, and that parts of southern Asia Minor were to prove great recruiting-grounds under the Empire.

Cicero added that the boys had been sent to safety at Deiotarus' court, and would go to Rhodes if necessary; and he hoped that next year the Senate would not prevent Pompey coming out. He got a letter from Atticus that had been only forty-six days *en route*, which he regarded as quick; in his reply he remarks, 'I am glad that your little daughter is now a pleasure to you in Rome, and though I have never seen her I am very fond of her and sure she deserves it'.

He now sent a report to the Senate, which is an interesting example of this type of official document. In it he gave a full account of his dealings with the young king of Cappadocia, Ariobarzanes 'the Pious and Pro-Roman', as he styled himself, who had been specially entrusted to his care by senatorial decree. The king, whose father had recently been murdered, had come to meet him, and revealed that there were plots in favour of his brother, the Queen Mother had procured the exile of pro-Roman advisers, and the High Priest of Comana, almost an independent principality, was on the point of armed revolt. By a mixture of firmness and conciliation Cicero seems to have mastered the situation, though he felt unable to lend troops as requested. He was, perhaps not unjustifiably, pleased with his efforts, and it is likely that there were few Romans willing to be as gracious and tactful as he with foreign potentates. (Probably in about 61 he had entertained, and, so he prided himself, made a very favourable impression on, a distinguished Druid from Gaul, Divitiacus, who was on an unsuccessful embassy to Rome to get help for his tribe. Divitiacus will have had to converse through an interpreter, as he did with Caesar in Gaul; but one wishes Cicero had recorded more of their conversation, as it seems they discussed Druidic beliefs and practices.)

Cicero's strategic policy in Cilicia, one would assume, owed something to Quintus and Pomptinus, though he does not admit it even to Atticus; but it would certainly seem to have been sound. In another letter of almost the same time to the Senate he urged that a more adequate army be sent out as soon as possible, if the provinces on which the Roman economy depended (Asia, and Pompey's new ones) were to be kept safe. He sent his cavalry across the Taurus to get news and stiffen the loyalty of the Cilicians; while there they and the small force of Roman infantry in the area cut up some Parthian cavalry who had entered the province. Soon he followed with his main forces, hearing that the Parthian army was outside Antioch, the capital of Syria. He reached Tarsus, the chief town of his own province, on 5 October, and the foot of Mount Amanus a few days later; almost at the same time the Parthians in Syria retreated. Cicero is soon to be found describing his surprise attack on the hostile tribes of Mount Amanus, which separated Cilicia from Syria. It is clear that Pomptinus bore the brunt of the fighting, though it was Cicero as commander-in-chief who received the acclamation of *imperator*, usual on a victory, from his army. He wrote deprecatingly to Atticus that 'for a few days we camped at Issus, on the same spot as Alexander . . . a considerably better general than you or I'. Less modestly, he adds that it was the panic inspired by his approach that had caused the Parthians outside Antioch to retreat and emboldened Cassius to pursue and attack them successfully: 'my name was great in Syria'. For this version of affairs Cicero has been, perhaps rightly, laughed at; but he cannot actually be proved in error. He felt able to send to Deiotarus to say that his coming was not for the moment necessary.

At this point Bibulus belatedly arrived in Syria, and, says Cicero, somewhat complacently, 'I suppose he wanted to equal me in this empty title [of *imperator*] and began looking in this same Amanus for a laurel sprig in the cake.' As a result he lost a cohort (about 600 men), a serious blow, while Cicero successfully be-

169

sieged the stronghold of Pindenissus with all the resources of Roman military art, ramps, towers, artillery and so on ('but "what the devil," you will say, "who are these Pindenissites? I never heard of them" ').*

The town fell in December, and by usual Roman custom the booty was given to the soldiers ('the Saturnalia was certainly a merry time for them too'), except for the captives, who were sold for the profit of the treasury. Cicero's campaign was possibly justifiable from a military point of view; but there can be no doubt that he was also in search of a formal senatorial vote of thanksgiving to the gods at Rome, with a triumph to follow it up on his return. Caelius for one had openly been wishing him 'just enough fighting for a triumph', and Cicero, desperately anxious in the newly fluid state of politics to recover his old *auctoritas*, felt that this was a way to do so. He wrote a long letter to Cato detailing all his recent activities and asking him to support a 'supplication' (and shorter notes to other influential men; in fact he claimed to have written to every senator but two).

When the Senate debated Cicero's thanksgiving next May, however, Cato voted against it, though it was nevertheless finally carried. Cato wrote 'at greater length than I am accustomed to use' to say that he was glad of this outcome, but that Cicero ought to have preferred the attestation of upright and conciliatory behaviour that he had himself put through the Senate. But this, complained Cicero to Atticus, he had not asked for; he had specifically begged Cato to support the thanksgiving. Cato went on to say that Cicero ought not to hope too much for a triumph. Cicero wrote a polite answer to Cato's somewhat priggish and crabbed missive – the only direct utterance of his that we possess – indicating that he would find it easier to agree with his views if more of their fellow citizens were as little impressed by votes of thanksgiving to the gods. Caesar adroitly wrote to sympathize about Cato's unfriendly behaviour: base spite, Cicero called it. Cato, unfortunately, had as tribune renewed an old law against undeserved triumphs; but what made his behaviour now intolerable was that he subsequently proposed a thanksgiving of twenty days to Bibulus, who after avoiding the Parthians entirely and losing his cohort had sent, according to Cicero, a most misleading account of his actions. But Bibulus

* They will also be sought in vain on our map.

was Cato's son-in-law. As Cicero was not wholly unaware, Cato's principles, after creating maximum discomfort, sometimes collapsed in the end.

By the time that Pindenissus fell the campaigning season had ended. 'I am handing over the army to my brother Quintus to take into winter quarters in unsettled country.' Cicero himself wrote another report to the Senate, 'by two sets of couriers on account of the danger of the sea-voyage' (the ancients feared winter navigation greatly), stayed for a few days in Tarsus, dispatched a delegate to Cyprus to represent him there, and then re-crossed the Taurus for Laodicea and judicial business. From here, later in the winter, he told Atticus that Cassius' report had exaggerated his success, but when Bibulus sent one it was likely to show great nervousness; the Parthian army was wintering in Syria and according to Deiotarus, who had good information, the Parthian king himself would cross the Euphrates with all his force in the summer. Cicero was in terror that owing to the political situation in the West Pompey would be kept at home and the Senate would decide that the governors of Syria and Cilicia should continue to hold their provinces in person. Anyway, 'the excellent Pomptinus' was already off home, as he had arranged, and Quintus was not the ideal deputy, owing to his tactlessness and irritability, and his son's conceited nature (Quintus was isolated for the moment beyond the snowed-up passes, and unable to be present at young Quintus' coming-of-age). Cicero became progressively more worried. June and July would be his anxious time, as far as the enemy was concerned. Bibulus however could probably hold the Parthians till the year of office was up; but what then? Sometimes he thought Pompey would come, sometimes not. By May there seemed to be no question either of Pompey or any other legitimately appointed successor, though it had not been forbidden to leave a delegate (all provincial business had been held up in Caesar's interest). Pomptinus had gone, Quintus was not anxious to stay, and Cicero agreed with him that 'nothing could be more disagreeable and tiresome'; he also felt that his own ostentatious desire to leave the province after a bare year would look less sincere, if he left his brother, and was worried about the danger he might be exposing him to. But the quaestor, the only other possible deputy in rank, was quite unsuitable in character.

Early in June he arrived back in Tarsus. 'There I found much to alarm me – a great war in Syria, much brigandage in Cilicia, and difficulty in administration since I have only a few days left.' Bibulus' legates, quaestor and friends were all begging him to come to Syria; to his immense relief Bibulus himself (in terrible grief, poor man, over the murder of two of his sons in Egypt) did not join in this request; but certainly the Cilician forces must stay near the border. What was to be done? Suddenly Cicero's hope that some god would solve the problem was fulfilled. The new quaestor, whose appointment had not been impeded, but of whose coming there had been no news, appeared. And the Parthians disappeared — recalled by their king who feared a revolt. In the circumstances it was all right, or Cicero persuaded himself it was all right, to hand over to the young man, unknown as he was and untried as he obviously must be. Certainly, apart from the ex-praetor Quintus, there was no one who could be set over the head of a quaestor, and a noble at that. At last Cicero was off; after a journey along the sea-coast, he embarked at Side. 'My friends' letters are summoning me to a triumph, something that on account of this "second birth" of mine I think I should not pass over. So you too, my dear Atticus, must begin to want it, or I shall look too foolish.' Perhaps he thought Atticus would agree with the words that he had once put in the mouth of an opponent: 'what, you will say, is the value of that chariot, of the general walking in chains before it, the models of towns, the gold and silver, the lieutenants and officers on horseback, the entire procession?'

Cicero was even more satisfied with himself over the administrative and judicial side of his work. It seems that Cato was keeping a close eye on provincial government at this time; and Cicero was probably also made selfconscious by what he had said about the subject in many of his speeches, and in the essay addressed to Quintus as governor of Asia in the year 60; certainly by the recent publication of his political dialogues, and because he was known as a friend of the *equites*, whose activities as tax-gatherers and men of affairs it would be his duty to oversee and perhaps check. 'I am sure you understand that my professions over many years are now put to the test,' he wrote to Atticus, who was clearly urging him all the time to caution. One reason why he wanted only to stay a year was to avoid difficult situations and also the appearance of greed.

He was not interested in his province for its own sake; indeed his letters mention no remarkable facts, historic, social, economic or artistic about Cilicia or Cappadocia, areas with rich and varied traditions. But he was of course very preoccupied, both with his own business and with affairs at home, and it is not surprising if he took little account of the remains and usages of the pre-Greek peoples he later described as uncivilized (though a few of his contemporaries were beginning to be influenced by oriental religion and ideas, and Cicero does in a later treatise say that he and Deiotarus had questioned each other about the very different Roman and Galatian systems of augury). He was also bored by the details of administration, though diligent in carrying them out, and thought them quite unworthy of his abilities. But in the theory of provincial government he was to some extent interested.

It is sometimes said that the Romans, having acquired an Empire almost without design, exploited it without any attempt at justification. This is not wholly true. Already in the second century B.C. the idea was about that Rome had benefited the areas under her influence by doing away with kings, giving the cities, or rather their upper classes, a specious freedom, and imposing peace and order. Occasionally she even lowered taxes. It is pretty clear that the principle enunciated so casually in 60 to Quintus, that the governor's object is the welfare of the provincials, had been accepted by the more responsible Romans, such as Scipio Aemilianus and his friends, from this time on. It was, after all, what Greek philosophers had always taught about rulers. It is interesting that Cicero attributes Quintus' upright government not only to his character but to his philosophic education; indeed the genuine belief that morality depends on the study of philosophy is relevant to Cicero's, and to so many of his contempories', contempt for the lower classes.

But what was the justification for conquest in the first place? This was a pressing question, for the Romans were, at first for religious and then for philosophic reasons, much concerned with the definition of the just war. The *De Republica* insists that a state should only go to war in self-defence or to protect allies and dependants; and adds that it was by helping her allies that Rome acquired her Empire. This belief required a good deal of hypocrisy both from politicians and historians, who sometimes resorted to outright invention to show that Rome's wars had all been undertaken in such a spirit.

Another useful idea was a Greek one: some races were unworthy of freedom. Classical Greece had tended to think that barbarians wanted and needed monarchy. This was now applied to the Greeks themselves: they are used to servitude and have

long been ruled by kings. Even an exceptional philhellene like
Cicero despised most contemporary Greeks, especially the so-
called Greeks of the East. He warned Quintus in 60 against con-
tracting intimacies carelessly in his province, though admitting
that 'men worthy of ancient Greece' did exist. We are reminded,
again, of the eighteenth-century Englishman – who held that the
contemporary inhabitants of Italy were decadent, corrupt and
unwarlike, though they could paint and write music very well.
The Roman attitude was not perhaps entirely inspired by prejudice. In the second century one intelligent Greek, at least, the
historian Polybius, had thought Roman public morality much
higher than Greek, and Cicero himself was shocked by the
corruption and muddle of city affairs in Cilicia; while the history
of the Eastern provinces' climb to self-respect, and an economic
and cultural renaissance, under the Empire, implies a certain
demoralization now – for which, admittedly, the Roman conquest was in part responsible. In spite of their faults, however,
Cicero reminded Quintus, the Greeks are of course civilized and
must be treated as such; besides, we owe them a debt of gratitude. In fact the Roman record was probably worst in the West,
where the natives could less easily organize protest and affect
public opinion.

Cicero's opinions on more practical problems are displayed in
his letter to Quintus, upon which his own governorship provides
an illuminating commentary. It is clear that in his view the great
question is the regulating of disagreements between the provincials and Roman tax-gatherers and men of affairs: 'this is a great
business and requires the deepest consideration.' But if you are
sufficiently self-restrained yourself, he writes, you should be able
to control a dishonest businessman or a greedy tax-farmer,
especially as we have interest with both these classes. Quintus
must also remind the Greeks that there always have been taxes,
that after Sulla an attempt to cut down the powers of the tax-
farmers proved a failure, and that the Greek variety is worse
than the Roman, as the subjects of Rhodes show by wanting
to be transferred to our direct control; and that the money is
largely spent on defence and internal security. This last was
hardly true of Quintus' province of Asia, at any rate. We may
add however that there was something to be said for a situation
where judicial and fiscal authority were strictly separated; under
the Empire, the imperial financial officers came to have judicial
power as well. But of course during the Republic, especially when

the *equites* controlled the courts at Rome, governors might be undesirably under the thumb of the great tax-companies, which maintained vast organizations (and much the best postal service to Rome) in the provinces.

In 51, Cicero hoped to succeed in what he called Atticus' policy – pleasing both sides; for to his great relief the subcontracting of the year's tithes, on corn and other produce, was over before he reached Cilicia. This was the chief direct tax imposed by Rome in part and perhaps all of the province; grazing and customs dues were also exacted. On the whole, he seems to have succeeded in his aims. He had little real sympathy for debt, the scourge of the provinces as well as of Rome itself. But he claimed that he had been able to get the cities financially on their feet again, and thus better able to pay their debts and taxes, including arrears, on which they were offered lower rates of interest. He did this, he says, partly by persuading ex-magistrates quietly to pay back what they had embezzled, and partly by not even requisitioning the limited supplies and billeting permitted under Caesar's reforming law of 59. 'We refuse to accept not only fodder and the other things usually provided in accordance with the Julian Law, but even firewood, and no one takes anything beyond four beds and a roof – indeed often enough not even that, for we usually stay in our tents.' He complained that he was spending a fortune, but since even so he was able to put by a large sum from his expense grant, one can only conclude that such grants were far too high.

It is sometimes assumed that in other respects he favoured the Roman business community too far. He was, it is true, popular with most of them, but he maintained that this was largely because he was excessively polite to them and asked them to dinner, while arranging that they harmed nobody. He firmly refused to give any businessman the official position of prefect, which might carry the control of troops, a common custom that was the source of many abuses. He gave some of them letters of recommendation to other governors; but we know he thought the governors concerned responsible men (indeed he thought all those at present in the East were behaving well, a fact that may provide us less with reliable statistics for the average incidence of corruption than with evidence for the influence of Cato) and once or twice in these notes the recipient is reminded that of course he is not being asked to do anything unworthy of his fame. And if the businessmen were having difficulty in exacting the moneys due to them, the fault, in Cicero's eyes at least, will not always have been theirs.

The second great problem, according to the letter to Quintus, was controlling one's own subordinates. First, the superior officials appointed by the Senate – the quaestor and legates. In these lax and undisciplined days it is impossible to oversee them too rigorously, but they can be prevented at least from misusing the governor's authority. It should be added that, since the governor in practice chose his legates, they were under obligation to him, a very important fact, and the quaestor was supposed to regard his governor as a father. Next, the subordinate officials. Cicero is especially anxious that the lictor shall not be allowed to take bribes to release prisoners and that the low-grade attendants shall be kept in their place. And lastly, the personal friends and servants. Cicero has much to say about not letting slaves and freedmen get above themselves; even when slaves are faithful and reliable it is better, to avoid trouble and scandal, not to delegate business to them in the provinces. Wise advice, ancient feeling in these matters being what it was; and, in Quintus' case, badly needed.

In 51 all these worries recur. With his slaves and freedmen Cicero does not seem to have had trouble – except that Tiro's health was poor. Apart from a single occasion of the requisitioning Cicero had abjured, the legates behaved well – so did the prefects: one was 'a wonder' for his 'abstinence'. The quaestor was not quite so satisfactory: light-minded and light-fingered. But some of the misery Cicero suffered was apparently due to the way this upright suite of his nonetheless treated the provincials; he wrote even on the way out, 'They say, or omit to say, so much, every day in a way that is irritable, insolent or entirely stupid, tactless, arrogant'. It cut him to the heart, he said; why had he not got out of the job? How unsuited he was to it! How true it is that one should 'stick to one's last'! It is easy to imagine that the average Roman was intolerably rude to provincials. And in the end he was bitterly disappointed. All that show of rectitude was only a veneer.

When I decided that it was right and proper to leave for my quaestor a year's money from the annual expenditure voted to me, and pay back a million sesterces to the treasury, my staff complained that all that should have been distributed to them . . . I held my ground, since I valued my good name above everything. Yet there was no honour that I had not conferred on any of them.

1. Cicero from the Vatican Museum

2. The famous portrait of Pompey from the Copenhagen Glyptothek

3. A bust traditionally supposed to be Hortensius

4. A recently discovered head of Cato from Volubilis in North Africa

5. Cicero from Apsley House, London Other busts of Cicero have been identified from this, the only named one.

6. A possibly contemporary portrait of Caesar

7. A recently identified head, probably of Antony

8. A perhaps somewhat idealized portrait of the young Octavian

The last piece of advice pressed on Quintus in 60 was for Cicero's usual specific – mildness: to be combined of course with firmness, especially against those who give as well as those who take bribes. But mildness is specially necessary in the provinces, where there is no appeal from the governor to a jury. This is a point well taken. And for all his insistence that the governor must support the optimates, in other words the upper class, everywhere, as the Romans had regularly done in all provinces, Cicero's feeling for legal equality comes out in his praise for Quintus' accessibility to the complaints of the humblest.

In 51 Cicero was continually congratulating himself and Atticus on his mildness and justice. He allowed the cities to decide cases not involving Roman citizens in their own courts, a favour they welcomed as tantamount to the gift of autonomy. In the same letter he reports that 'access to me has been much freer than is usual for provincials: nothing is done through a chamberlain. I have been up and about in the house before daybreak, just as when I was a candidate for office. This has been popular and a great thing for them, while for me it has been no trouble so far, for I am an old campaigner.' It may however be that in calling all judicial business from the other districts north of the Taurus to Laodicea he was consulting his own convenience rather than that of the litigants.

His only recorded pieces of compromise with his conscience were occasioned by great men. The notorious affair of the city of Salamis in Cyprus shows Marcus Brutus, that honourable man, in a strange light. Brutus, who had gone out to Cyprus with his uncle Cato and subsequently served Appius as quaestor in Cilicia, naturally had interests in the province, and had given Cicero a memorandum about them. He had also recommended two men who had, he said, lent money to the people of Salamis. Cicero saw one, and promised to see that he got his money, but refused to continue the title of prefect, which Appius Claudius had granted him, and ordered some horsemen, whom Appius had given him, out of Cyprus. Soon after, a deputation from Salamis met Cicero at Tarsus and revealed that their creditor was claiming at the rate, exorbitant even by ancient standards, of 48 per cent compound interest, four times what Cicero had laid down in his edict and the Senate had recently endorsed: 'it meant ruin for the city'. Nonetheless he allowed the matter to stand over, rather than enforce payment at the lower rate. To his great surprise he then discovered that the real creditor was Brutus himself, who had obtained two senatorial decrees in order to get round the law against lending to provincials in Rome; but if Brutus was going to complain about him, 'I shall be sorry that he is angry with me, but much sorrier that he is not the man I thought him'. He pointed out, scandalized, that the troop of horse had been used to besiege the Salaminian senate in their council house and five of the senators had starved to death. And he even reproached Atticus strongly for begging him to do what Brutus wished. 'Shall I ever dare to read or even touch those books of mine you praise so much if I do anything of the kind? My dearest Atticus, you have really shown too much concern for Brutus in this affair, and not enough, I am afraid, for me.' Brutus' uncle, Cato, at any rate would approve of his actions. But he refused to let the envoys deposit the sum in a temple, to prevent further interest accruing, and he left the affair over for the next governor, though much afraid that he would be Brutus' brother-in-law. And he bombarded the King of Cappadocia, who was also in debt to Brutus, with letters, though the King was unable even to pay the interest on what he owed to Pompey (a flock of whose agents were harrying him) and Cicero believed that he was an absolute pauper; while he gave Brutus' agents in Cappadocia the rank of prefect, since they had no business dealings in his own province to disqualify them. It turned out that the next governor of Cilicia, though not Brutus' brother-in-law, was accompanied by the persistent Brutus himself as legate; how this affected King Ariobarzanes and the Salaminians we are left to wonder.

The problems bequeathed to Cicero by his predecessor were even more tricky. Before leaving Rome Cicero had written in friendly terms to Appius to make contact, and was in touch during his journey in order to try and fix a meeting. But Appius kept changing his mind about his route home, and when Cicero arrived in the province he found that his predecessor was still holding assizes at Tarsus, quite improperly after the arrival of the next governor, and there was no news from him or of the best legionary troops. Though in the end they passed each other very closely, and Cicero tried to see him, Appius apparently succeeded in avoiding the new governor, and then complained of his rudeness.

To Atticus Cicero wrote openly of all he discovered of his predecessor's abominable treatment of the provincials; he was 'not a human being but some sort of terrible wild beast'; he had imposed special taxes, and extorted large sums from towns wanting to avoid troops being billeted on them. 'Appius sent me two or three rather complaining letters on his way home, because I rescinded some of his decisions . . . having kept the province under a lowering régime, bleeding it and reducing it all he could and handing it over to me exhausted, he does not like to see me feeding it up.' But he tried to cover up for Appius as much as possible, and even permitted the laudatory embassies that Appius had demanded and that he had at first forbidden, to the relief of the cities concerned; though he rightly thought the practice an iniquitous one, and perfectly useless, as the Senate usually had no time to listen to them. And the ingratiating, if sometimes covertly barbed tone of his letters to Appius is not very impressive (a 'certain dissimilarity of policy' ought not to interrupt their friendship and all difficulties are the work of trouble-makers; though at one point he was provoked into explaining his less than total respect for noble birth alone).

But in both these cases Cicero was in a difficult position. It was very ticklish to interfere between a patron and his clients. Brutus is known to have been patron of Salamis; and Appius, who was not only a member of the Claudian family but had been in these parts himself as a young man, undoubtedly had extensive *clientelae* in the area too. Sometimes a strong patron could defend provincials against an oppressive governor; but the system was not working that way here.

Also, both Brutus and Appius were supremely aristocratic. And Brutus, now in his thirties, whom Cicero had recently grown to know better, looked to be the coming young optimate – nephew to Cato, intelligent and cultivated with an inclination to philosophy, a strong character – even a headstrong one: Caesar was to say of him that 'whatever he wants, he wants badly', and this obstinate streak may explain his behaviour over Salamis, though one need not assume that he authorized his agent's worst iniquities. Cicero found his letters, even when expressing requests, 'brusque, arrogant and insensitive' (his correspondence with Brutus for this period is unfortunately lost). Atticus, who was naturally a close friend of this important figure, in spite of the disparity of their ages, was anxious to bring him and Cicero together, and had written to say that if Cicero brought nothing back from his province but Brutus' goodwill, he might be satisfied; and indeed Cicero was very desirous later at least of good relations with and if possible influence over Brutus. As for Appius, he had been reconciled with Cicero by Pompey, and as we saw was a vital link in the alliance of Pompey and the optimates. Both Brutus and Pompey were urging the interests of Appius, both being now connected with him by marriage, and at this time Cicero felt a renewed loyalty to Pompey. Thus it was very difficult for him to antagonize either Brutus or Appius. The latter, in particular, remained a problem: Cicero soon learnt that Tullia and Terentia had displayed the comparative independence of Roman women by picking on Dolabella, a wild and ambitious young noble of great charm, as his new son-in-law – and that Dolabella was prosecuting Appius for treason; and somewhat later he also discovered that relations between Appius and Caelius, previously good, had degenerated into reciprocal prosecutions for unnatural vice.

There was one subject however on which Cicero was ready to offend useful, if less prepotent, friends. This was the 'aedile's tax' and related demands. Apparently any governor could be, or at least often was, asked by any friend about to be aedile to impose a tax to pay for his games, or to get a community to vote money for the purpose. In 60 Cicero had congratulated Quintus on relieving his province from what he calls 'this heavy and unjust tax', even at the price of involving both brothers in serious enmities with nobles. Now Caelius, who was elected aedile in summer 51 and proposed to give very fine games, was pursuing him with demands for panthers – Curio had recently got some from Cilicia for a friend. Cicero thought it would be too bad to drag the provincials from their livelihoods to hunt panthers, though he said that the professional hunters might be employed for the purpose; but, with a sting in the jest, he wrote that the panthers seemed to have decided to emigrate, since they were the only creatures in the province for whom traps were laid. Caelius also hoped for hard cash, but he got none – and a warning that those who prosecuted others should walk carefully themselves. A colleague of his also approached Atticus about obtaining panthers. 'I am glad you said you did not think I would. But in future, to any improper request, always say no firmly.'

What Cicero never does say is that (apart from the need to bring transgressors more successfully to book) the laws must be drastically tightened up and the powers of the governor more strictly delimited. Indeed, it was, no doubt, by staying voluntarily so far within the laws' boundaries that he was able to gain his reputation for 'abstinence'. Not only did he avoid much permissible requisitioning, he accepted only personal honours that did not run the provincials into expense, refusing the statues, the temples to him as a saviour god, and other honours that were perfectly legal. In his province, as at Rome, he failed to initiate lasting and thoroughgoing reforms. But he made some tentative efforts towards change. As consul in 63 he had tried to abolish 'free embassies', by which a senator on private business could claim official privileges in the provinces. The proposal was vetoed, and he only succeeded in limiting their duration, but the *De Legibus* recurs to the idea, which could only be intended to protect the provincials. And he might hope to have some permanent effect through his edict. It was usual to follow one's predecessors closely here, but it was possible to add and adapt, and indeed this is largely how Roman law did develop under the Republic. Though basing himself on the best earlier models, in particular the edict of his old teacher Scaevola, famous for his model government of Asia, Cicero had some new provisions encouraging the cities to cut down expense, which he was very proud of; and we may be sure that he formally forbade the 'aedile's tax', since Quintus had done so. It would be legitimate to hope that such provisions might become regular.

It may also be objected against Cicero that, throughout his governorship, he was simply moved by the thought of his own reputation for *abstinentia*, and for *elegantia* or good taste. Even a failure of harvest and consequent famine is blandly described as 'actually desirable for me', since by persuading dealers not to hoard grain he was able to reinforce his popularity. But it has been rightly pointed out that the ancients did tend to speak of their fame or glory almost as something objective and outside themselves. And once, towards the end, he protested, as if surprised, to Atticus that 'in all my life I have never felt so much pleasure as I do in this upright conduct of mine: and it is not my reputation, which is immense, but the thing itself that delights me. In short, it was worth it; I did not know myself, nor understand what I could do in this way. I am right to be puffed up; nothing could be more glorious.'

Even this is hardly innocent of self; and it was not, perhaps, Cicero's final verdict. To Caelius, as his year in the East drew to an end, he wrote, 'Rome, my dear Caelius, Rome! Stick to it and live in its light! All service in the provinces, as I realized long ago when I was young, is dull and sordid for one who is able to shine in the city.' In practice if not in theory, provincials, armies, independent states could all expect to be sacrificed to the ambitions of Roman politicians; and in this respect no one was more guilty than Caesar, even if he would not have agreed with Cicero about the sordid nature of reputation acquired abroad. For he had conquered Gaul, and tried to conquer Britain, almost entirely to gain glory, wealth and power, and to rival Pompey.

II

THE UNCERTAINTIES OF CIVIL
WAR 49-48 B.C.

Cicero told Caelius that he knew no one with a greater flair for politics; let others write to him of what had happened or was happening – Caelius could tell him what would happen. In spite of being 'very busy and as you know very lazy about writing letters' Caelius did manage to keep his promise to send his comments on events in Rome out to Cilicia – starting with a rumour that Cicero himself had been murdered on his way thither. His racy letters tell us much of the scandals and manœuvres of the uneasy period during which civil war between Caesar and Pompey drifted nearer, but they do not, unfortunately, make clear some of the most important legal and political elements in the situation; upon these scholars have expended an immense amount of ingenuity but reached no agreement. It is probable that, as later sources state, Cato and his friends had announced their intention of prosecuting Caesar (either for illegal acts as consul in 59 or for treasonable behaviour in Gaul) as soon as it became legal to do so, that is to say on his laying down his proconsulship. Caesar intended therefore to pass straight to a second consulship (and doubtless thereafter a new command); in 52 the tribunes had passed a bill allowing him to stand *in absentia*, though subsequent legislation had confused the position. At one point he seems to have considered standing in 50 for 49; but he soon fell back on the idea of standing in 49, the proper ten years after his first consulship, even though his command would probably run out in March of that year (if it did not do so earlier) and he would thus have by hook or by crook, or rather by using a tribune to veto the appointment of a successor, to stay on in Gaul till the elections or even the end of the year. He himself did not speak of the danger of a trial, but of the insult to his *dignitas* if he should be recalled or prevented from standing in absence; and at any rate by the end of 50 the optimates were determined that he should not hold the consulship again at all. Opinion in general soon saw the affair as a struggle between Pompey and Caesar, neither of whom could contemplate a position in which he would be at the mercy of the other.

In the summer of 51 it was not yet quite clear how closely Pompey would cooperate with Cato's friends, or the 'Faction' as Caesar and his propaganda called them. But the results of the elections seemed fairly favourable to the group; till one of the tribunes designate succumbed to prosecution, and young Curio decided to stand for his place. Caelius wrote, 'this has thoroughly frightened a lot of people who don't know his easy nature, but as I hope and wish, and as he proclaims himself, he will support the *boni* and the Senate'; Curio was thought to feel that Caesar had recently insulted him by rebuffing an approach. Meanwhile there appears to have been an attempt to recall Caesar before his command finished – though it had to be put off while Pompey went north, perhaps for a conference with Caesarian representatives. Caelius warned Cicero about his own situation in Cilicia. 'You know the usual pattern: a decision will be made on the Gauls; someone will veto it; then someone else will get up who will prevent the Senate deciding about any provinces since it can't decide about them all.' The affair dragged on, a quorum was unavailable; but Pompey agreed that the matter should be decided on 1 March of the next year, 50, and when the Senate voted that he and Caesar should each give up a legion to be sent against the Parthians, he decided for his part to give one that he had previously lent Caesar, who was thus to be deprived of two. And in the event the troops were not sent East at all, but kept in Italy.

Rome waited. In February Caelius, now aedile, wrote that the new consuls had been inactive, 'Curio's tribunate is a frost . . . and if it were not that I am fighting shop-keepers and officials of the water-supply the city would be asleep'; but he had to add in a postscript that Curio's tribunate had hotted up suddenly: 'he has frivolously gone over to the People and started speaking for Caesar'. Caelius thought it was due to a quarrel with the *pontifices*; later sources all state that Caesar had bought him. It may be added that his optimate father was now dead, he had married Fulvia, the widow of his friend Clodius, and that many of the younger generation were admirers of Caesar, and may well also have been in reaction against the Faction. 'He is absolutely bubbling over with all this,' wrote Caelius. His next letter does not unfortunately tell us what happened on 1 March; it does tell us that no one would have believed that a certain senator 'went in for adultery unless he'd been caught twice in two days. Where? you say. The last place I should have wished. I leave you to ask others – I like the idea of an *imperator* asking around who a man has been caught with.'

The next letter shows Caelius piloting Cicero's thanksgiving, of which we have already heard so much, through the Senate by arranging a compromise with Curio. Pompey was now saying that Caesar should leave Gaul in November, and Curio was preparing to resist. 'I tell you this: if they take extreme measures against Curio, Caesar will defend him and his veto. If, as seems likely, they get cold feet, Caesar will stay as long as he wishes.' It appears that in the summer Curio vetoed a proposal that Caesar should give up his province and said that Pompey (who had renewed his Spanish command in 52) should do so too; most of the Senate agreed, though not the Faction. It is not clear whether Caesar was serious in this suggestion – Caelius did not think so. As the summer advanced, Pompey fell seriously ill; all over Italy prayers for his recovery were offered, and the later sources suggest that this caused him badly to misjudge the support that he could count on in a possible war with Caesar; modern scholars have wondered indeed whether he ever really recovered his energy, and though Cicero does not speak of finding him noticeably altered on his return, he was soon to lament his lack of spirit and be doubtful of his health. About the same time as Pompey fell ill the officers sent to fetch the two legions from Gaul reported most misleadingly that Caesar's soldiers had no loyalty to him and would not fight for him in a civil war; it may also have been known or suspected by some that if the worst came to the worst Caesar's chief lieutenant, Labienus, whom we remember from his tribunate in the year 63, would revert to his earlier loyalty to Pompey. If so, that was the only one of the optimates' expectations to be fulfilled.

In August 50 the irresponsible Caelius was writing pityingly that capturing the Parthian king and his capital could not make up for missing the spectacle in Rome. He did not think peace could last a year. He was not sure what to do, and expected Cicero also to be wondering: 'I have ties and influence on one side, I hate the men – but not the cause – on the other.' In ordinary matters, he opined, one ought to follow the more honest course; but in war, the safer. Pompey would have the Senate and political opinion with him: Caesar would be supported by all those who feared justice or hoped for plunder, but he had the better army. 'Anyway there is time to estimate the forces of each side and make a choice.' Cynically but intelligently, he was to opt for Caesar.

Meanwhile Cicero and his suite, his lictors now carrying their axes wreathed with laurel in honour of his title of *imperator*, were making their way home, in spite of adverse winds. They heard somewhere *en route* of the death of Hortensius; possibly they touched at Rhodes, which Cicero had wanted the boys to see. Tiro, who had been in uncertain health for some time, had to be left in Greece, where he was the recipient of a number of really kind and affectionate letters, taking thought for his comfort and amusement and begging him not to move till he was properly recovered and not to spare money on his treatment. But Caelius was right that Cicero was anxious as to what his course of action should be. Already from Athens, where he stayed, enjoyably, on the Acropolis, apparently with the head of the Academy, he was writing to Atticus demanding advice. After all, he pointed out, it was Atticus who had urged him into close relations with both principals to the struggle.

Each counts me as his – unless one of them is pretending. Pompey has no doubts, he rightly judges that I greatly approve of his present political views. But I got letters from both of them at the same time as yours, seeming to make more of me than of anyone else. What am I to do? I'm not asking about the final decision – if it comes to fighting, I feel sure it would be better to be defeated with Pompey than victorious with Caesar – but about what will be happening when I arrive, about his standing in absence and dismissing his army. After all, when the consul says 'Speak, Marcus Tullius', am I to say, 'Please just wait till I see Atticus?'

Cicero thought that one advantage in his own attempt to get a triumph, largely as he admits from jealousy of Bibulus, would be that he would have to stay outside the walls and so could not attend the Senate. 'But they will try to get my opinion out of me. You will laugh at this perhaps: how I wish I were still in my province!'

From Cilicia Cicero had written covertly to Atticus about his suspicions that a freedman of Terentia was swindling him out of money; but now he managed an affectionate letter to his wife, asking her to come to meet him if her health allowed, so that they could concert plans. In the event they entered Brundisium at the same moment and met in the main square. As Cicero journeyed through Italy messengers were easier to come by, and he wrote to Atticus more and more frequently. (Poor Atticus, who was plagued with tertian and quartan fevers, doubtless malarial, all autumn and winter, may have needed all his patience, as almost every letter demanded an answer with advice in it.) Cicero was now defending himself for leaving Cilicia and saying that he was glad to be on the spot in case he could help in a peaceful solution or the victory of the *boni*; he would model himself on the ideal independent politician of the *De Republica*, and if this conflicted with canvassing for a triumph, the triumph could go hang; though probably it would be useful to keep his *imperium* (his official status and right of military command) by staying outside the city. Atticus told him, and he told himself, that Caesar had not really treated him as handsomely as he should have done. But it was embarrassing that Caesar and his agent Balbus went on sending polite letters, and there was that wretched debt of his to Caesar tying his hands; could he pay it off?

He announced to Atticus that openly he would support Pompey, 'but privately I shall urge him to peace'. He was increasingly unenthusiastic about his cause, for he thought the dangers in a war very great; Caesar had the support of all the disreputable elements, and he saw that everyone in Italy was desperately averse from fighting. Surely it was ridiculous to oppose Caesar at this stage: 'now we have to deal with eleven legions, as much cavalry as he may want, the Gauls beyond the Po, all these tribunes, the city rabble, our irresponsible younger folk, and a leader of great influence and boldness'.

Events were now hastening to a crisis. On 1 December Curio got the Senate to vote 370 to 22 in favour of both dynasts laying down their arms. The point was presumably to show how small the Faction was; it is unlikely that Caesar really intended to disarm. But the consul C. Marcellus, unauthorized by the Senate though accompanied by the consuls designate, on the strength of rumours that Caesar was marching on Italy, went to Pompey to give him the command of the two legions now in Italy and urged him to further recruitment. This naturally gave Caesar's propaganda a great opportunity. On 10 December – the day on which Mark Antony, the nephew of Cicero's disreputable colleague of 63, and son of a Julia, succeeded to his friend Curio's office and policy – Cicero, who had reached Campania, found Pompey there raising troops. He was friendly, and encouraging about Cicero's triumph. 'As for politics, he talked as though there was no doubt we should have war'; and he said that Caesar was now wholly alienated from him. Soon Cicero wrote, 'The political situation frightens me more every day; for the supposed *boni* are not united. How many *equites* and senators have I seen who are violently blaming the present conduct of affairs and Pompey's journey [to Campania] in particular! We must have peace. Victory will bring many evils, and certainly a despot.' This implies that even Pompey would be a tyrant; Caesar, Cicero felt sure, would be Cinna and Sulla rolled into one for savagery and greed. (How factitious the enthusiasm of the mid-50s had been!) It is clear that some of Caesar's supporters were talking rashly about abolishing debts and dividing property, though it was to appear that their patron would disavow their policy. For all his doubts about Pompey Cicero still intended to support him in public: 'it is another great evil for the country that I in particular cannot honourably dissent from Pompey in such great matters.' Soon he was saying that he would follow the herd like a stray ox – not a comparison very flattering to the aristocracy.

On 25 December he had a long talk with Pompey that almost persuaded him that Caesar's consulship was not to be endured under any circumstances, and that if Caesar lost his senses and had recourse to violence he could easily be suppressed. Pompey pointed out how wildly Antony was threatening, and 'talked like a statesman' about the danger of a mock peace. And Cicero was still taking a strong line two days later when he wrote to Atticus intelligently detailing all the alternative possibilities – including that which occurred: that on the pretext that a tribune was being obstructed Caesar would come down on Pompey and the Senate before they were prepared. But he appears soon to have swung back to advocating conciliation.

He does not seem to have been in a great hurry to get to Rome, and stayed some time in his villa at Formiae. He proposed to reach the city on 4 January 49 – he delayed his arrival by one day, out of consideration for Pompey's servants, at his villa at Alba, where he would stop on his way, as they would be celebrating a festival. His coming was awaited at Rome, he was assured, with great interest. He reached it according to plan, to a distinguished welcome, and remained outside the walls at Pompey's house. The Senate seemed willing to give him his triumph, but according to Plutarch he said that he would rather walk himself in Caesar's if a peaceful settlement could be made. He was busy in private conferences. But, as he wrote later, 'I could get nowhere; I had come too late, I was isolated, I was thought out of touch with the facts, I was among madmen wild for war.' Plutarch suggests that he supported a new offer by Caesar to give up Transalpine Gaul and keep the provinces of Cisalpine Gaul and Illyricum with two legions – or even only one; much as, in theory, as a letter to Tiro shows, he deprecated even this demand. Plutarch says that Pompey would have agreed to such a compromise (and doubtless gone to his province of Spain, as he had earlier told Cicero he would do if Caesar became consul); but that Cato – who had been very much in the background of late – helped to get it rejected. It is understandable that the Faction believed that to let Caesar get away with overstaying his time and to leave him unpunished for his undeniable irregularities meant confessing that their re-established Republic was pointless and powerless; and believed also, by now, that they would be in personal danger if he held a second consulship under any circumstances. It is also understandable that Cicero, who had no real stake in the Cato-Pompey régime, was well accustomed to compromise, and perfectly safe from Caesar, should have felt differently. It is clear also that Pompey and the Faction thought they would win in a war, and that Cicero was not sure of it. A few others, notably Piso, Caesar's father-in-law and Cicero's old enemy, also tried to mediate. But 'there are people on both sides who want to fight'. The Senate seems to have stiffened by now, and passed several votes hostile to Caesar. On the 7th Antony and a fellow tribune were advised to leave the Senate. They fled from Rome, though, says Cicero, no actual violence had been used to them. The Last Decree was passed, underwriting Pompey's activities; commands in various parts of Italy were assigned (Cicero was given charge of Capua). Governors to provinces were appointed, Domitius at last receiving Transalpine Gaul. When he heard the news, Caesar crossed the now unidentifiable stream that divided his province of Cisalpine Gaul from Italy – the Rubicon; 'let the die be cast', he proclaimed. On reaching Ariminum (Rimini) he found the two tribunes, with Curio and Caelius.

Caesar's speed had long been famous. There was no question of his troops – though he had only one legion to hand – refusing to follow him. There was none either of the Italian towns resisting, even in Pompey's own home country of Picenum. 'Swept along by madness, forgetful of the name he bears and the honours he has held, Caesar has occupied Ariminum, Pisaurum, Ancona and

Arretium.* So we have abandoned Rome – whether wisely or or courageously it is vain to argue.' Pompey, the consuls, and many senators left on the 17th – without even taking the money in the Treasury with them. Next day Cicero scribbled a note to Atticus: 'I have suddenly decided to leave before dawn, so as to avoid looks and talk, especially with these lictors and their laurel-wreaths. As for the next move, I really don't know what I am doing or shall do, I am so alarmed by this rash and insane proceeding of ours.'

Back in Campania he wrote to Atticus every day, apologizing with the reflection, 'I feel calmer when writing to you or reading your letters'. He was appalled by Caesar's behaviour: 'he says he is doing all this to protect his *dignitas* – but where is standing if there is no honour?' And he was little less appalled by Pompey's decision to leave Rome, though the shock to opinion in Italy might be salutary, he supposed. 'As to your request to tell you what Pompey is doing I don't think even he knows; none of us do.' Pompey was off to collect the legions removed from Gaul the year before, which were in the south: 'then, whether he wants to make a stand or cross the sea no one knows . . . if he does, I don't know where he will go or by what route or what I should do.' Over this last problem Cicero was to agonize day and night for months; the letters can talk of practically nothing else, and it would be impossible to follow here every shift of intention, or record every demand for advice, with which Atticus, still struggling with malaria in Rome, was besieged.

The first question was whether Terentia and Tullia (whose husband Dolabella – possibly younger than herself, charming and clever, but not very satisfactory to Cicero – was an ardent Caesarian) should stay in Rome: might it not seem disloyal? In the event they came to the villa at Formiae, and it appears that Quintus and his son were there too, though the boys' tutor, Atticus' freedman Dionysius, proved unwilling to throw in his lot with the family ('nothing in all these terrible troubles has grieved me more', Cicero was to write, in a fit of anger that passed in the end, as his anger usually did). Cicero toyed with the idea of sending the boys to safety in Greece – at this point he thought that if Pompey went abroad it would be to Spain, and that he would go too. Meanwhile he still took some part in optimate counsels: on 26 January he and Quintus met the con-

* Rimini, Pesaro, Ancona, Arezzo.

suls and many senators at Capua. These were now much readier
to negotiate with Caesar, who was offering terms. 'Even Cato now
prefers slavery to war, but he says he wants to be in the Senate
when terms are considered, if Caesar is persuaded to withdraw
his forces.' Cicero was afraid that Cato in this case might prove
an obstruction. 'There is much disagreement in our debates. Most
deny that Caesar will keep to his terms, and say that he has
only put forward these demands to prevent us making the necessary preparations for war. But I think he will withdraw his garri-
sons.' Later he wrote, 'It will be insane of Caesar not to accept',
and indeed the terms were easy ones (Caesar was to get his consulship and a triumph, and Pompey to disarm and go to Spain);
but he now showed less confidence that they would be agreed
to. And they were not, whether because there were inadequate
guarantees or because Caesar had really only wanted to gain
time and credit.

Cicero had given up his command at Capua, telling Pompey that
he had neither the troops nor the money to carry it out, for another one on the coast, which enabled him to live comfortably
in one or other of his villas. He was still not very active in his
duties, partly because levying seems to have proved unpopular to
the point of impracticability, and partly because he felt even now
that if uncompromised he might be able to assist negotiations. He
heard from Dolabella and Caelius that Caesar approved of this in-
action, but he was anxious not to be identified with that side
either – better not send Terentia and Tullia back to Rome. But
should he himself leave Campania and join Pompey, who seemed
to have 'no spirit, no plan, no resources, no energy'? Where was
he now, anyway – perhaps in a part of Italy that could only be
safely reached by sea?

But soon Cicero got a letter from Pompey advising him to come
to Luceria in south-eastern Italy, where he himself was. Cicero
recorded a protest at the abandonment of the Campanian coast,
where the corn-ships for Rome put in, but prepared to set off.
He was more distraught than ever: 'if I could sleep, I wouldn't
batter you with such long letters.' At one point he was so
disgusted with Pompey's behaviour – 'I consider that no statesman
or general of any nation has ever behaved more disgracefully' – so
uncertain whether Pompey's health could be relied on, so contemptuous of the consuls, so angry at his own exclusion from their
counsels (perhaps not very surprising) and so struck with the
number of people still in or near Rome, 'while we wander about

in poverty with our wives and children' (he was still in his villa at Formiae), that he almost decided to stay where he was and resisted Atticus' advice even to follow Pompey abroad. At other times Atticus' advice seems to have been on the other side; he was clearly as unable to make up his mind as was his friend. Nevertheless on 17 February Cicero set out for Luceria; but on hearing that Caesar had blocked the road turned thankfully back again. He also persuaded himself that at this season of the year he could not go to Eastern Italy by sea, and indeed in ancient times shipping was almost wholly suspended in winter. Later he admitted that he had not tried very hard to get through to Pompey.

Rumours, true or false, continued to agitate Campania. On 20 February it was learnt that Domitius Ahenobarbus was resolved to make a stand in Central Italy. Pompey would have to support him, thought Cicero, temporarily much encouraged. But, as Pompey himself wrote in letters, copies of which reached Cicero and were sent on by him to Atticus, it was impossible for him to use the once Caesarian legions against Caesar. It was also impossible for him to order Domitius, an independent proconsul, to retire. The result was that Domitius was forced to surrender, only to be generously dismissed by Caesar, who thus had a dramatic opportunity to show that he was far from planning the proscriptions of which everyone was so terrified. The episode was a great propaganda victory for him.

Cicero, unfairly no doubt, took Pompey's failure to support Domitius as the final dishonour. Not that it reconciled him to Caesar ('I have someone to flee, but no one to follow'), who was now trying very hard to win both Cicero and one of the consuls to his side. But Cicero was, he said, spending his time meditating on the ideal statesman whom he had described in the *De Republica* whose object was the happiness of his countrymen: neither Pompey nor Caesar, he said, had been thinking of that, and 'Pompey's plan from the start was to stir up land and sea, rouse the barbarian kings, bring savage races to Italy in arms and raise the largest possible forces. He has long wanted a tyranny on Sulla's model, and many with him want it too.' If they only wished, Caesar and Pompey could make peace; but 'both want to rule'.

Cicero was not the only person disillusioned with Pompey, and for a moment he thought that this might give him a chance to initiate negotiations. He had been too excited and anxious to work or read, spending his days instead with a boring elderly ex-consul who lived nearby, but now he asked Atticus to send him a certain book in Greek on Concord. Caesar's policy of strict respect for lives and property was winning round much opinion: 'the people of the town and countryside talk to me a great deal: they care for absolutely nothing but their land, their little farm-houses and bits of capital.' And 'see how upside-down things are: they fear the man in whom they formerly trusted and love the man they used to dread'. But Cicero was still not wholly won over. When Atticus wrote to him of senators who seem to have decided to stay in Rome, he wrote that he did not think them adequate precedents for himself, being men without any claim to courage or distinction. Indeed he was wavering back to thinking that he ought to join Pompey – even those who stayed themselves were attacking him for not following his benefactor. And on receiving a letter from Balbus begging him to reconcile Pompey and Caesar, he simply remarked sourly to Atticus that he sent him a copy so that it could be seen how he was mocked. It was likely that Caesar would be coming to Campania, and this would probably mean an interview, the prospect of which was worrying: would it be better to go to Arpinum, perhaps? And he was anxious about Quintus, too, feeling it unfair that he should be involved in his brother's course, while Caesar would be very angry at the lack of support from his old lieutenant. Quintus seems to have said that he would abide by his brother's decisions. To judge by the letters, he perhaps even refused to discuss politics: Cicero never mentions what Quintus thinks, or anybody else inquiring what he thinks either. He had, clearly, no importance apart from his brother.

Atticus was now advising Cicero to remain in Italy, declaring that Caesar would allow him to stay out of politics. But Cicero was not wholly convinced, and his family was at this point on the other side. And a rumour that Pompey had actually embarked at Brundisium for foreign parts brought on an access of grief: it was shameful not to be with him. 'Re-reading your letters [advising him to stay] makes me feel less ashamed, but only while I am actually reading.' But he certainly could not set off at once; and he took Atticus' advice about Caesar's visit to Campania: 'I shall follow your advice and stay here at Formiae so I shall not attract notice welcoming him to Rome, nor deliberately avoid him either.'

Caesar's agents Oppius and Balbus were stepping up the pressure on Cicero as preparation for the possible meeting. They sent him a copy of a letter from Caesar expressing mild sentiments and 'sane, so far as sanity is possible in this madness', as he granted. And they promised that Caesar would not ask him to fight against Pompey. It is easy to understand why Caesar was so anxious for Cicero's support; he was at this time attempting to represent himself, as we see from his account of the Civil War, as the most constitutionally proper of the leaders (had he not gone to war to protect tribunes in the exercise of their rights, and for a perfectly legal second consulship?), and hoped that enough of the Senate could be collected in Rome for his position to be regularized. The adherence of Cicero, ex-consul, lawyer, augur, author of the *De Republica* and old associate of Pompey, would be of immense value; Caesar had many nobles in his train, but they were mostly young or disreputable. Cicero would be a great prize. But Cicero was writing dispiritedly that he would go to Pompey, dreadful as the excesses brought about by his victory would be. 'It is what I owe him that moves me, not the cause, just as in Milo's case.' (We must never forget the importance of private obligations in Roman politics.) He held that the departure of the consuls with Pompey ruled out negotiations; and so he sent back the book on Concord. Soon after he got a renewed message that Caesar wanted him to help make peace; this time he wrote imploring to be allowed to start negotiations. However, on 20 or 21 March he heard that in fact Caesar was blockading Pompey who was still in Brundisium: 'tears prevent me from thinking or writing the rest . . . why did we not all follow his fate?' Should he perhaps try to raise the country towns? No, it would be useless. He theatrically declared that he wished Caesar would murder him as his old teacher Scaevola had been murdered. But only two days later he was wondering whether the news from Brundisium was true and feeling that he could take no decision yet. Nonetheless, from this point his intention was hardening to join Pompey 'not in a fight, but in a flight'.

Pompey in fact had embarked his forces and crossed the Adriatic. Caesar had entered Brundisium and was now on his way back to Rome. The meeting that Cicero had been dreading took place.

In both points I took your advice: I spoke so as to earn his good opinion rather than his thanks, and remained firm that I would not go to Rome. But we were wrong to think him easy to sway; I never found anyone less so. He said that my decision was a condemnation of him, and the rest would be less eager to come if I did not. I replied that their case was different. After a long conversation he said, 'Come then and work for peace'. 'On my own terms?' I asked. 'Who am I to give you orders?' he answered. 'I shall take the line,' I said, 'that the Senate does not approve of your going to Spain or taking an army to Greece and,' I added, 'I shall deplore Pompey's position at length.' At that he remarked, 'I don't want such things as that said.' 'So I imagined,' I replied, 'but that is why I don't want to be there – I must either speak in this way or not come; and there is much else that I could not be silent about if I were present.' The end of it was that he asked me to think it over, as a way of bringing the conversation to an end; which I could not refuse. So we parted. Thus I think Caesar is not pleased with me. But I was pleased with myself, which is more than I have been for a long time. For the rest, what a train he had with him – the 'army of the damned' as you call it . . . But I nearly forgot his disagreeable climax: if he could not get my advice, he'd take that of anyone he could, and would stop at nothing.

Cicero told Atticus that he was now going to Arpinum, and a decision could be put off no longer. Atticus must (of course) write with advice. After Arpinum, he intended 'to take a tour round my beloved villas, which I don't expect to see again'.

The visit to Arpinum, where he held the ceremony of his son's coming-of-age, was not very cheerful; everyone there was gloomy, and levying in Caesar's interest was going on. Cicero was now (usually) clear that he could not stay in Italy, and felt that he had made grievous mistakes: 'my present course is dishonour-able without being safe.' But he was not very decided where to go, at least in the first instance, as he did not know where Pompey was. Should he make for Athens or some other quiet place in Greece? Or for Malta, well out of the way? Back at Formiae, he was shocked to hear a story that Quintus' son had written to Caesar, and even seen him in Rome, telling him that his uncle was thoroughly disaffected and planning to leave Italy. Cicero felt the treachery deeply: 'nothing in all my life has been so bitter', and the young man's father was 'crushed'. But there was some hope that the story was exaggerated, and indeed it seems that this was the case – even that young Quintus had not actually seen Caesar, but only his officer Hirtius. Cicero continued however to write anxiously to Atticus, his co-uncle, about the young man's remarkable gifts and unsatisfactory character. 'I wish you had taken the young man in hand. His father spoils him and makes all my firmness useless. If I had the boy to myself, I could man-age him.' One wonders; all Cicero's protégés felt the need for emancipation.

At Formiae Cicero received visitors, and the usual rumours. Among the latter was a wild story that Pompey was marching to Italy from Greece round the head of the Adriatic. Among the former was Curio, on his way to Sicily for Caesar, 'you know what he's like, he was totally frank'; he spoke of Caesar having recalled exiles (the rehabilitation of criminals according to Cicero) and of his plans for the war; and also of how, before leaving Rome to deal with Pompey's lieutenants in Spain, he had clashed with a tribune, thus displeasing the People, who had been his supporters, and had also offended even the rump Senate he had collected in the city. Curio added that Caesar's clemency was mere policy. This is doubtless more or less true: it may be remembered that in Gaul Caesar had been responsible for a fearful massacre of German tribesmen, for which Cato proposed that he should be handed over to the enemy; and it is recorded that he took great delight in the gladiatorial games. He may well have felt differently about members of his own class; but it is understandable that Cicero continued to distrust him. 'Let the outcome in Spain be what it may, I am off.' Curio had promised him assistance in Sicily and said that Caesar would accept his departure from Italy.

But this was premature. Soon Tullia was begging her father to wait and see what would happen in Spain, and claiming that Atticus agreed with her. 'But I don't agree'; he thought it wiser to leave before Caesar were either defeated, in which case 'even Curio' would abandon him, or victorious, in which case he would come back and initiate a massacre. He also thought Pompey bound to return with a fleet to starve and ravage Italy. His comfort was the thought that, like all tyrants, Caesar would fall rapidly; but he admitted in the same breath that all prophecy was uncertain. He went on to say to Atticus,

I have commended to you all my concerns, though your affection for me makes such commendation unnecessary. Nor indeed can I find anything to write about – I am sitting waiting to sail. And yet nothing ever needed writing so much as this, that out of all your good offices to me nothing is so welcome to me as your kind and careful attention to my Tullia. It has pleased her very much, and me no less. Her courage is wonderful; with what patience she endures public disaster and private difficulties [she was pregnant, and Dolabella was a bad husband]. How brave she was at our parting! There is affection, there is deep sympathy in her nature, yet she wishes me to do right and be well spoken of. But enough on this subject, or I shall fall into self-pity.

Cicero's praise for Tullia now comes a second time when he is in personal distress, and it grows stronger and more frequent from this time on. She must have had great patience with her father, as well as the understanding that her similarity to him gave and that Terentia clearly lacked. She herself, by now, had had sorrows and disappointments enough; she probably also had intellectual interests, for earlier Cicero had claimed that she was like him in mind as well as appearance, and after her death, admittedly in a eulogistic work, he called her learned or accomplished. We know nothing of her education, but Atticus' daughter was certainly later given a good literary training. It is sad that not a word from her pen (or Terentia's either) has been preserved; and perhaps it is to put too much stress on a single anecdote of paternal protest to visualize her always with an impetuous and even unfeminine step. By comparison with her, young Marcus seems to have inherited his mother's practical outlook and abilities.

Cicero was still not off, however; the epistle just quoted encloses notes from Antony, who had been left as Caesar's somewhat hasty and careless deputy in Italy, and from Caesar himself (of whom such letters sent on to Atticus are the only ones to survive). They both warned Cicero not to go abroad. In his next letter however he is still thinking of going to Malta, right out of the way of the struggle. But

the tears of my family, begging me to wait for news from Spain, sometimes weaken me. Our boys wept grievously on reading a pathetic letter from Caelius, also imploring me to wait and not recklessly to sacrifice my fortune, my only son, and all my family; though my son is the braver of the two (and for that reason influences me more strongly) and worries about nothing but my good name.

Caelius wrote that he was just off to Spain; he warned Cicero that Caesar's policy of mildness would not last, and begged him not to damage Dolabella and Caelius himself, who would be involved in Caesar's wrath at Cicero's departure.

Nonetheless, Cicero asked Antony for permission to go to a neutral area – and was refused, though told that Caesar would probably give him leave. But Cicero had now been roused, and was proposing to slip away – though anxious, he said, about risking the boys' lives in a small boat. There could be no question of going without them, even though Cicero was by now convinced that the younger Quintus had no affection for his family. His resolution was strengthened by all he heard and saw of Caesar's followers. 'Good gods, is even Balbus thinking of getting into the Senate?' And as for Antony,

he is carrying Cytheris [the actress] around with him in an open litter as if she were his second wife. And there are seven other litters accompanying them, for his mistresses, and some for his *male* friends. See how shameful is the death we are dying and doubt if you can that Caesar, whether he returns victor or vanquished, will institute a massacre. I shall snatch myself from the grasp of these criminals in a rowing boat if I can't get a ship.

He had to admit that some of Caesar's supporters, like the lawyer Trebatius, were more respectable.

On 5 May he wrote in distraction, 'What is to become of me, or who is in not only a more wretched but by now a more disgraceful situation than I?' Antony now said that he had specific orders not to let Cicero go and 'I am watched on all sides'. This did not make him change his mind. He received a last visit from his old friend Servius Sulpicius, whose lamentable state of terror and uncertainty made Cicero feel resolute, but prevented him from confiding his plans.

He said Pompey was angry with him, Caesar not his friend: the victory of either would be terrible, for one was cruel and the other reckless, and both in straits for money, which could only be squeezed out of private property. He spoke all this with so many tears that I wonder such long-drawn misery had not dried them up. As for me, even this opthalmia which prevents me writing to you myself does not bring tears, but it irritates me, the more because I sleep so little. So please collect anything you can to comfort me, and send it – not from philosophy and books, for I have that at home, but somehow the medicine is too weak for the disease.

It was news of Caesar's defeat in Spain that he wanted.

There was one final dilemma, a mysterious possibility that Cicero should join in a 'Caelian' plan and put himself at the head of a Pompeian force – what or where is uncertain, possibly in Africa. (The reference may not be to his friend Caelius, presumably now in Spain with Caesar.) But this soon came to nothing. And when he went to his house at Pompeii, to disarm suspicions that he was intending to slip away from the coast, and was told that the centurions of the troops there wished to put the town in his hands, he fled precipitately and before dawn back to Cumae. What could he do with a mere three cohorts, he asked? Besides, it could have been a trap. Now it was bad weather holding him up, and then calms. He wrote to Atticus of Tullia's premature delivery of a weakly child, and remarked that he would say no more about his plans for fear of spies. On 7 June, however, he was writing from on board ship a farewell letter to Terentia; it was not quite as late in the sailing season as it sounds, owing to the error in the calendar.

All the miseries and difficulties with which I worried you to death (and I am very sorry for it) and little Tullia too, who is dearer to me than life, are dismissed and ejected. I realized what caused them the day after we parted. I threw up bile in the night, and felt immediate relief, as though a god had cured me. You will thank that god in piety and purity as is your custom. I hope we have a very good ship – I write this immediately on coming aboard. Then I shall write numerous letters to our friends, commending you and our little Tullia most earnestly to them. I should urge you both to be brave, if I had not found you braver than any man . . . First of all, you must look after your health. Second, if you agree, use the villas which are farthest from detachments of soldiers. The farm at Arpinum, with the servants from town, will be convenient if food prices go up. Dear Marcus sends his love. Look after yourself and good-bye.

In spite of his previous idea of going to Malta he seems to have made straight for Macedonia, where Pompey was encamped. He had taken, in the end, if not necessarily the bravest, at least the most uncomfortable course. He had with him his brother and the boys, not to mention those embarrassing lictors with their laurel-wreaths, but he was almost entirely cut off from Atticus, Tullia, his 'beloved villas' and everything that he loved in Italy. We have very few letters from the next period, and this may be because he did not write many. 'You may ask why I do not write; I am deterred by lack of worthwhile matter, finding no satisfaction in what is going on here.' And messengers probably rarely came his way.

It is clear that he was very unhappy in Pompey's camp. 'The rest of Pompey's supporters were glad to see him,' says Plutarch, 'but when Cato met him he privately blamed him greatly for following Pompey.' Cato declared that though he himself could not abandon his old policy, Cicero would have been more use to his country and friends by staying in Italy – and safer too. It is interesting to find this subsequent justification of Cicero's sluggish course in the winter, which some modern scholars have stigmatized as treason to the state.

These words disturbed Cicero's resolution, as did the fact that

Pompey made no great use of him. But this was his own fault, since he did not deny that he was sorry that he had come, disparaged Pompey's preparations, showed suppressed disapproval of his plans, and did not refrain from jokes and cracks about the foreign contingents; while he himself went darkly round the camp without a smile, he made others laugh in spite of themselves.

Plutarch appends some of the jokes in question. The best was made after Pompey's first defeat by Caesar (who had returned victorious from Spain, been elected consul at last, and transported his army to Macedonia); an officer of Pompey's drew hopeful attention to the fact that he still had the eagles of seven legions. 'That would be splendid,' said Cicero, 'if we were fighting jackdaws.' He mocked at the faith in oracles and prophecies with which Pompey, Labienus and many others were now supporting themselves; while he hated as much in practice as he had done in prospect Pompey's use of Eastern troops – the employment of barbarians against citizens as he saw it. A couple of years later he summed up to a friend his experience in Pompey's camp.

In the first place, his forces were not large enough, and they were low in morale; then, apart from the commander-in-chief and a few others (I mean among the leaders) the rest were extortionate and greedy in their conduct of the war and their talk was so bloodthirsty that I shuddered at the thought of victory itself. And these great men were deep in debt too. Why go on? The only good thing was the cause itself. Seeing all this, and despairing of victory, I first pressed for peace, which I had always urged; then, when Pompey violently rejected the suggestion, I tried to persuade him to draw the war out. He was convinced for a time and seemed likely to agree, and perhaps he would have done it had he not gained confidence in his troops in an engagement; from then on this great man ceased to be a general.

Cicero's military judgement was perhaps pretty poor, but Caesar too thought that Pompey had been misled by his success in breaking out of his position near Dyrrhachium, on the Adriatic coast, in July 48.

On his return to Italy Cicero also told Atticus how everyone who had stayed in the peninsula – 'yes, even you, Atticus' – had been marked down for proscription or confiscation. This was worse than Caesar's army of the damned. In short, there was no place for Cicero in this war; whichever side he was in contact with disgusted him. Later letters, to Pompey's friend Varro and others, suggest that he was not alone in his distress, though he was more outspoken than the rest, being as usual quite unable to bridle his tongue. He claimed in a later speech to have remained personally on good terms with Pompey, though he did not spare him the lash; when asked pointedly where his son-in-law Dolabella was he replied 'with your father-in-law', and Pompey is said finally to have complained that Cicero might at least have feared him if he had been on the opposite side. He does seem to have renewed his intimacy with Cato, who was wearing mourning and declaring that nothing was so bad as civil war; too late, as usual.

In the winter of 48 Cicero received a frank letter from Caelius, who was now praetor in Rome, but had quarrelled with Caesar's deputies there, largely, it appears, about Caesar's continued moderation over the problem of debt. 'I have not lost confidence in Caesar's victory,' Caelius wrote, 'but I assure you death is better than the sight of these people. If it were not for fear of the cruelty of your side, we should have been thrown out of here long ago. Except for a few money-lenders there is not a class or a man in the place who is not for Pompey.' It was doubtless the last letter that Cicero was to get from the friend whom a later historian described as 'brilliantly worthless'. Caelius was about to raise an open insurrection against Caesar in southern Italy; he summoned to his aid Milo, whom Caesar had not recalled with the other exiles. The revolt was easily put down, and both Caelius and Milo met their deaths.

Cicero's son-in-law Dolabella also wrote to him, a few months later, from Caesar's camp and at Caesar's instance, advising him not to follow Pompey if he escaped from his position (this was before Pompey's success mentioned above), but at least to retire to some peaceful place like Athens and trust in Caesar's generosity. Probably news of Cicero's unenthusiastic attitude to the Pompeians had got out; at any rate another attempt was being made to detach him.

It is clear that Cicero was not present at the final battle of Pharsalus, in which Pompey, who had chased Caesar eastward, was in his turn overwhelmingly defeated, his army destroyed and himself driven into flight; though it is just conceivable that Quintus, who was certainly not with his brother, was there, and even the seventeen-year-old Marcus, who had been given command of a troop of horse and according to his father had done very well with it; he probably found such work easier than declamation. Instead Cicero remained with Cato at Dyrrhachium, in poor health according to Plutarch, but this may have been an excuse. Sizeable forces were still there, and the fleet was nearby. Here they were at the mercy of rumours – and prophecies. One episode can be recovered. In a later dialogue Quintus is represented as recounting a story he has heard from his brother:

C. Coponius, commander with praetorian rank of the Rhodian squadron, a very sensible and well-educated person, visited you at Dyrrhachium and told you of a prediction made by one of the rowers of a Rhodian vessel. In less than thirty days Greece would be drenched in blood, there would be devastation at Dyrrhachium, and the fleet would put out to sea in a panic; looking back the fugitives would see the tragic sight of the town on fire. But the Rhodian squadron would return home quickly and safely. You were somewhat disturbed, you told me, and M. Varro and M. Cato, both highly educated men, were greatly alarmed [one can believe this: Cato was a Stoic, and Stoics usually believed in prophecy, while Varro was a deeply religious man]. In fact Labienus arrived a few days later, fleeing from Pharsalia with news of the destruction of the army. The rest of the prediction was soon fulfilled.

The Pompeians crossed to Corcyra, the naval base, and Cato offered Cicero, as proconsul, the command of the surviving forces. 'But when Cicero refused the command and was altogether unwilling to take a share in further fighting, he was almost killed, for Pompey's son and his friends called him a traitor and drew their swords; however Cato intervened and with difficulty rescued him and got him out of the camp.' So Plutarch; of this undignified and inglorious scene Cicero himself tells us nothing, and it may have been exaggerated. He seems by now to have been joined by his brother, and we next hear of him at Patrae (Patras) in the Peloponnese, staying with the kindly Roman friend of Atticus who had looked after Tiro there. But here, a final disaster, Cicero quarrelled with the hitherto at least apparently devoted Quintus, perhaps over both money and politics. Quintus probably blamed Marcus savagely for the position they found themselves in, and he proposed to get in touch with Caesar, who was offering forgiveness to all who applied to him. Perhaps Quintus even hoped for a closer association such as Brutus and others agreed to accept; Caesar was still much in need of able lieutenants. For mere forgiveness Marcus was also ready to receive. On the arrival of a letter from Dolabella with Caesar's permission for him to return to Italy, Cicero made blindly homewards. In the middle of October 48 he landed, as he had landed on happier occasions, at Brundisium. This time there was no Terentia or Tullia to meet him.

12

PRIVATE AND POLITICAL GRIEFS
48-45 B.C.

Almost at once he admitted to Atticus, whose letters revealed astonishment at his arrival, that he had acted on impulse rather than reflection. At first he could receive some comfort in his 'mental and physical distress' from being told that Atticus and others approved his action; though he now thought that it would have caused less talk and trouble if he had stayed somewhere quietly abroad till things were more settled, as Servius Sulpicius and others were doing. It must be remembered that he was still proconsul.

> To be stuck in Brundisium is wretched all round . . . but how can I come nearer as you suggest without the lictors whom the People gave me and who cannot be taken from me while I retain the rights of a citizen? I made them mix with the crowd as I entered the town lest the soldiers should attack them, and ever since I've stayed indoors. I've written this to Oppius and Balbus.

Atticus' suggestion that he should travel by night did not attract him.

He wrote briefly to Terentia, telling her that there was no need for her to come to Brundisium, there was nothing she could do there. He was more shocked to hear of Tullia's ill-health than of the death of Pompey, murdered on landing as a fugitive in Egypt. 'I am not surprised at Pompey's end,' he wrote to Atticus. 'Every king and nation saw that his case was hopeless, and I expected this to happen wherever he went. I cannot but mourn his fate; for I knew him to be an honest, decent and serious man.' Such an eulogy on his domestic virtues was all that one of his oldest political associates could find to say for Pompey the Great.

Oppius and Balbus wrote telling Cicero to keep his lictors, and the Caesarian commander at Brundisium, Cicero's reconciled enemy Vatinius, did nothing to make life difficult for him; indeed the two are to be seen henceforth on surprisingly genial terms – a sign of the superficiality of some of Cicero's hatreds, as well as his enthusiasms, and of the amiability of Vatinius, a cheerful fellow always ready to laugh at himself and his grotesque appearance. But there was an awkward moment when Antony, who after leading Caesar's left wing at Pharsalus was again formally in charge of Italy, forwarded a letter from Caesar which stated that no Pompeians should return to Rome or Italy for fear of disturbances, and said he would have to enforce the principle. Cicero sent a friend to explain about Dolabella's letter, and Antony finally exempted him and another senator by name in his edict on the subject – publicity which Cicero did not welcome. He may also have felt that both going to Rome itself and leaving Italy again had been made impossible; and he stayed on in poor health and spirits in Brundisium (probably in a hired house, as we hear nothing of his kind host of former years).

By now (December 48) the Pompeian forces had rallied in the province of Africa, with Cato and other leaders, and Cicero realized that he was being blamed for not joining them. He had no desire at all to do so; they were still relying on barbarian monarchs, principally now the King of Mauretania, and there was no reason to suppose that they had changed for the better in other respects. But if they were after all to win, how would they punish Cicero's defection? Of course he regretted his action, he wrote, but Balbus and Oppius must not think so. At the end of December his relations with the other side gave him cause for anxiety too. He had been appalled to hear that Quintus had sent his son to Caesar to traduce his uncle as well as to make his own and his father's peace; and that Quintus claimed that Cicero was maligning him to Caesar, though Caesar himself denied it. And indeed, as he told Atticus, Cicero had written to Caesar to say that Quintus had always favoured the Caesarian side and had not advised Cicero to join Pompey – a generous act in the circumstances, if it may also be true that he did not wish Caesar to think him unable to make up his own mind. 'It is the most unbelievable thing that ever happened to me, and among all these evils the bitterest.' People had heard Quintus publicly abusing his brother in Greece. 'You know his style, you may even have experienced it; it has all been turned onto me.'

A few days later he had incontrovertible proof of Quintus' attitude. Letters from him to various people in Italy fell into his hands.

I should never have opened them, if it hadn't happened like this. A package was brought to me. I undid it to see if there was a letter for me. There was nothing; but a letter to Vatinius and another to

Ligurius.* I gave orders that they should be delivered. Both immediately arrived burning with indignation and crying out on Quintus'
villainy. They read me the letters, full of all sorts of slanders against
me. At this Ligurius began to rage; he said he knew that Caesar
detested the man, but had shown him favour and given him all that
money for my sake. After this painful scene I wanted to know what
he had written to others, for I thought it would damage him if this
abominable behaviour became generally known. I discovered the rest
were in the same style. I am sending them to you; if you think their
delivery will do him good, deliver them; it doesn't hurt me. As for the
broken seals, I think Pomponia has his seal. He showed me the same
bitterness at the start of our voyage, and so distressed me that I was
confined to bed afterwards; and now he is said to be working not so
much for himself as against me.

So I am beset from all directions, and I can hardly bear it; rather
I absolutely cannot bear it. Worse than all my other afflictions combined is the thought that I shall leave that poor girl deprived of
father, inheritance, everything. For that reason I would indeed like to
see you, as you promised. I have no one else to whom I can entrust
her, since I see the same fate has been prepared for her mother as
for me. But if you don't find me, consider this as commendation
enough, and soften her uncle towards her as much as you can.

I am writing this on my birthday. I wish that it had not then been
decided to rear me, or else that my mother had never borne a second
child. Tears prevent me from writing more.

Exactly what Quintus had been saying we do not know; but
among complaints made directly a little later in a letter that
Cicero found insulting was the charge that he had been kept short
of money. Among the things that worried Cicero about Tullia was
that Dolabella, now tribune, had taken up Caelius' agitation against
debt, and clashed with Antony. He might thus forfeit the influence with Caesar that had made the connection something of an
insurance, and his demagogic behaviour was shocking to Cicero.
He was an unsatisfactory husband to Tullia in every way, and the
idea of divorce was mooted again; but this would make Tullia's
fate entirely her parents' responsibility.

By May the news from abroad was that Caesar, who had pursued Pompey to Egypt and become involved there with local
politics, the young Queen Cleopatra, and a nasty little war, was
blocked up in Alexandria, incommunicado from the West; while
the *boni* in Africa were becoming powerful and it was thought

---

* A minor Caesarian officer.

they might invade Italy. Cicero heard that all the ex-Pompeians hitherto residing quietly in Greece or Asia were off to join them (at one point Quintus was supposed to be so too) and this of course made his own return to Italy even more conspicuous. Deep in despair, he was convinced that even if Caesar forgave him, the Caesarians would lose the war and he himself and Terentia with him would be proscribed by the victors. He tried to see that some provision should be made for the children, perhaps by conveying property to Atticus or another; but Terentia was acting 'wickedly' about her will, and Atticus must try to persuade her to change her mind; the details are obscure, but it was the children's interests that Cicero thought at stake. A number of very short notes were written to Terentia, but they do not take issue with her directly over this matter; they do reveal that outside financial questions Cicero still had some faith in her judgement – she is to decide whether Dolabella can safely be divorced or whether he is too powerful – and that old habit still had some sway; he wrote that though there was no news to give or receive he still liked to write to her and hear from her.

The months dragged on. Caesar delayed interminably in Egypt; then there were disturbances in Asia that required his presence. Italy was in a state of unrest. Cicero wrote despairingly that there was no hope of a quick peace, and that the Caesarians in Rome, led by Oppius and Balbus, seemed to be turning against him. What should have been a ray of pleasure came in the early summer: 'My Tullia joined me on 12 June and told me much of your attentiveness and kindness to her,' he told Atticus; she had taken a journey that Cicero had previously described to Terentia as long and unsafe, and Plutarch tells us (in a passage with some certain errors in it however) that Cicero did not think Terentia had made proper provision for her in it. But 'her own courage, sympathy and devotion, far from giving me the pleasure which I ought to have in such an incomparable daughter, grieve me terribly, when I think that the lot of so noble a creature is so wretched, and that through no blame of her own, but by great fault on my part'. Two days later he wrote of sending Marcus – who was presumably with him some or all of this time, though not otherwise mentioned – to Caesar, and Tullia back to Terentia as soon as she was willing, since she and her father were both of them so wretched. But in fact Cicero changed his mind about Marcus, though at some stage he did entrust a young friend with messages for Caesar, and Tullia stayed on, though the torrid

Apulian summer did neither her nor her father any good, and the latter thought that 'any punishment is better than staying here'. He was still distracted about Terentia's will; Tullia's lack of complaint was unexampled, he said, and touched him beyond bearing. He suggested to Atticus that some of his moveable property – silver, fabrics or furniture – might be hidden somewhere so that she could have that to fall back on if her parents' property were confiscated: of course it was impossible to sell land at present, for nobody would buy. And it was time to divorce Dolabella – it should have been done earlier, before he asked for the second instalment of the dowry: 'it would have been both cheaper and more manly.' There were plenty of grounds: either his disgraceful political behaviour (he was now trying to put up a statue to Clodius – Cicero was horrified to think of a son-in-law of his doing such a thing) or his adultery and riotous living. The divorce went through, though not till some months later.

As summer wore on Cicero received a 'sufficiently generous' letter from Caesar, saying that he would soon be in Brundisium, and he also heard that the younger Quintus had seen Caesar and both he and his father had been forgiven. Cicero could not but rejoice, though he still felt that there were 'other dangers from other sources' and that Caesar, regrettably, had the power to change his mind any time. Quintus himself had recently written in a more friendly manner, perhaps owing to Atticus' remonstrances; but Cicero, whose resentment had been dying down, was plunged back into bitterness by seeing a copy of a letter that Quintus had written to Caesar some time earlier; he half-wished that Atticus had not sent it on. We cannot doubt that Quintus' whole course of action had been ill-judged, and rooted in his violent temper; but the grudges of many years had probably come to the surface – grudges over the way his brother had used him as a tool, especially in Gaul and Cilicia, without giving him real gratitude or influence in return, grudges over his disastrous marriage, over Cicero's contempt for his trusted Statius, grudges, perhaps, going back still further, to his own small stature and inferior abilities.

Hearing that, against previous expectations, Caesar intended to go straight from Greece to Sicily, Cicero determined at last to leave Brundisium. But it soon became clear that the Dictator would have to make a detour by that town to deal with some mutinous troops. If so, Cicero wrote, he would have to wait and see him; would Atticus send advice? Could he not come himself?

Whether Atticus did indeed come south or not, the series of letters ceases for some six months. But we know from Plutarch that Caesar landed at Tarentum and that Cicero went to meet him outside Brundisium

not entirely without hope, but embarrassed at making trial, in front of many witnesses, of the attitude of a victorious enemy. But it was not necessary for him to do or say anything undignified, for Caesar, seeing him coming to meet him far in advance of any others, got down to greet him and continued his journey for a considerable way in private conversation with him.

Caesar clearly gave him permission to go to Rome or anywhere else he pleased; and he probably allowed him to dismiss his wretched lictors. Cicero was, one assumes, not in the mind to query his constitutional right to remove what the People had bestowed.

He set off homeward at once, after almost a year of boredom and inactivity. *En route* he sent Terentia the last, and curtest, of all his surviving letters to her. 'I imagine that I shall get to Tusculum either on the 7th or the day after. Please see that all is ready. I shall perhaps have a number of people with me, and shall probably stay for some time. If there is no bath in the bath-house, get one put in; also anything else necessary in the way of food or for our health. Goodbye. 1 October, near Venusia.'

The Rome to which Cicero returned was much altered. Many of his old friends and rivals were dead; so were many of the younger generation. Pompey was gone. Bibulus, obstinate to the last, had refused to yield to illness and died in command of Pompey's fleet. Appius Claudius had succumbed to a fatal disease in Greece, Domitius Ahenobarbus had fallen at Pharsalus, both of them in Pompey's service. Caelius and Milo had been killed in their ill-fated revolt; Curio while fighting dashingly for Caesar in Africa. Cato was soon to perish in Africa too; unable to persuade the city of Utica to continue the fight after the main republican forces had been defeated, he helped those who wished to do so to escape, but himself committed suicide, thus linking his name for ever with the town in which he died and cheating Caesar of the most dramatic of all possible displays of *clementia*.

There were other changes from the 50s too. There was no disorder in the Roman streets for one thing, now that Dolabella had been called to heel; but there was no opportunity for independent activity in courts or Senate either. There was less extravagance; many had lost wealth in the struggle, others perhaps dared not display the riches they had, and after a while Caesar's sumptuary laws, if a failure in the long run as sumptuary laws usually were, had a temporary effect on entertaining and dress. Tastes had changed too, at least in literature. In rhetoric there was a reaction against the ornate style, of which Cicero was the greatest if by no means the most extreme exponent, in favour of an 'Attic' sobriety, professedly based on the Athenian orators of the fourth century B.C.

Cicero was almost sixty – an old man by the standards of his time. It would not have been strange if he had failed to adapt to this new world, and had retired to dwell on memories of the past. But this would be to reckon without his extraordinary vitality. In fact his last five years were to be in many ways the richest and most remarkable of his life. He made a rapid recovery from his depression and ill-health at Brundisium; he picked up with old friends and made new ones; for a time at least he led a more active social life than ever before. He counter-attacked the Atticists, while taking some account of their criticisms, and partly as a result, partly owing to his age, to which a calmer manner was considered appropriate, produced what is perhaps to our eyes at least some of his finest prose, sparer and simpler than before. His renewed concern with style led him to write again, and most interestingly, on rhetoric; and turning back to his early love of philosophy he produced a body of work which, if not deeply original or of first-rate intellectual distinction, had many admirable features and greatly expanded the philosophical resources of the Latin language. And at the end, for six months, at a time of great crisis, he was the almost undisputed leader of Roman policy. It is true that he was often nostalgic for the past; that in some ways he was something of an anachronism; and his path was certainly not free from grief and disappointment. But nonetheless these last years are a remarkable achievement.

For these years, too, more letters survive, though we must not forget that, apart from that with Atticus, we have lost almost entirely his correspondence with leading figures and have only that addressed to a collection of persons less important to him. But at any rate we can see him, early in 46, picking up the threads of his old life; writing for example to Brutus, whom Caesar had put in charge of Cisalpine Gaul, to recommend friends, or to ask

him to protect the possessions and interests in his province of the
municipality of Arpinum – incidentally revealing that he had had
his son and nephew and a personal friend appointed to office
in the town to reorganize its affairs – this is the first sign that
things had been patched up in the family. He also gets in touch
with others; with a young Caesarian acquaintance (to whom he
says that it was the influence of others that led to his opposing
Caesar), and with his optimate ex-quaestor of 51 (to whom on
the contrary he claims that the Caesarian friends now thronging
his house are unwelcome to him). Above all there is an interesting series of letters to Varro, Pompeian and scholar, last seen at
Dyrrhachium at the time of the battle of Pharsalus, who was now
back in Italy and whose position Cicero thus found comfort-
ingly like his own – though he had never got on very easily
with Varro, and if he admired his learning, quite rightly thought
little of his prose style; but he now tried to draw closer to him,
and wrote,

I must tell you that on my return to the city I was reconciled with
my old friends, I mean my books; though I had not abandoned their
companionship because I was angry with them, but because I felt a
sense of shame. I thought that I had not obeyed their precepts by
plunging into turbulent events with such untrustworthy allies. They
forgive me, they call me back to my previous habits, and tell me that
you were wiser than I in never leaving them.

In the spring he was considering a visit to Varro on the coast;
but news of the decision in Africa was being awaited, and Cicero
was inclined to think it not the moment to be seen on the Campanian riviera. He was torn between wishing Caesar to be defeated, and his belief that he himself would now be safer if
Caesar won. Soon news of Caesar's successes reached Rome, and
Cicero wrote that he had not dared to leave the city lest he be
thought to have panicked, or to be slipping off abroad, or simply
unable to bear the behaviour in Rome of the Caesarians, to which
he claimed to be hardened. But it was not pleasant to be in
Rome; the victors, he complained, were triumphing over him and
his friends, while the defeated were angry with them for being
safe.

It was an awkward situation, and what would ultimately
happen was still not clear. Cicero wrote again to Varro,

Let this be agreed between us, that we will live together in our
studies, from which we formerly sought only pleasure, but now our

very being. We shall not be found wanting, supposing that anyone desires to make use of us in rebuilding the state, even if as workmen rather than architects, rather we shall hasten to offer ourselves. But if no one uses our assistance still we will read and write on political subjects; and if we cannot do so in the Senate House and the Forum, yet in writing and literature, like the wisest men of old, we will serve the state and enquire into manners and laws.

It may be that in saying this he was thinking of taking up the *De Legibus* again; but even the writings of this period not on strictly political subjects had some political aspects to them. The first and one of the most interesting results of his new-found energy was the *Brutus*, which we have already spoken of as an accomplished history of the development of oratory at Rome, with fascinating material about Cicero's own education and career. Cicero says that recent writings by Brutus and Atticus (the other figures, beside himself, in the dialogue) are what have inspired him to begin to write again. Brutus' work was possibly his treatise *On Virtue*; Atticus' was certainly his *Annals*, a brief handbook of Roman chronology. For the moment Cicero committed himself wholly to neither philosophy nor history; as well as a history of oratory, the *Brutus* was also a contribution to the debate with the Atticizers. Furthermore, it was a lament for the days when the *res publica* still stood, when oratory, which (he argues) can only flourish in a free state, found its proper rewards in courts and Senate. How happy Hortensius had been in dying on the eve of the Civil War! It seems likely, from the generous (if perhaps just) compliments on Caesar's style as a speaker, that the work was destined for his eye: and it almost sketches out a programme for him. The comparison with Sulla that had hitherto frightened everyone with the thought of proscriptions now takes on a new meaning: Sulla had in the end restored the Republic. And Cicero was perhaps also trying to associate Brutus, both participant in and dedicatee of the work, with himself in this demand; though he was certainly also trying to detach Brutus from the Atticists, with whom his style may have had some points of connection; we know that Brutus criticized Cicero's manner and his 'effeminate' rhythms.

The *Brutus* itself was not the only work that Cicero dedicated at this time to his important and able young friend, with whom he was anxious for so many reasons to be on close terms. He followed it up with 'a little work, the fruit of these shorter

nights', in which he tried what oratory could do to make acceptable to a fairly popular audience some of the ethical paradoxes
of the Stoics, who themselves disdained literary ornament. He
dissociates both himself and Brutus from Stoicism in the preface,
and his own language would suggest that he saw the work chiefly
as a *jeu d'esprit*; though with hindsight we can regard it as a
transitional work, a first step towards philosophy. But it is noteworthy that Cicero chooses the less extreme of the Stoic paradoxes
to treat, those which he considers were also held by Socrates
and are 'much the truest'. He has nothing to do with such extravagances as holding that the wise man alone is truly a king, truly
handsome, never feels pity, and so on; but to read that virtue
was enough to make a man happy, that the wise man could never
really be an exile from his city, or lose his freedom, or suffer
from poverty, was likely to be comforting reading for defeated
boni. And comforting writing too; Cicero could never reconcile
himself to the loss of political liberty by claiming that the true
freedom was moral freedom, and the general ancient love of glory,
the Roman preoccupation with standing or *dignitas*, and his own
temperament always made him over-sensitive to what people
thought of him, as the letter to Varro referred to above shows
for this very period. But in these last years he tried more and
more to satisfy himself with the approval of his own conscience.
The little treatise avoids contemporary references, perhaps wisely,
but sticks to recent Roman examples, best adapted to its popular
audience. The resulting preoccupation with Clodius and others
gives it a perhaps misleadingly backward-looking air.

The *Stoic Paradoxes* began with a compliment to Cato, whose
speeches had made Stoic philosophy acceptable to the Senate.
Perhaps this was one reason why, after the news of Cato's death
reached Italy, Brutus asked Cicero to write a laudatory memoir
of his uncle – a substitute for the funeral oration that had not
taken place. Cicero wrote to Atticus,

The question of the *Cato* is a problem for Archimedes. I cannot
contrive to write what your dinner companions will read calmly, let
alone with pleasure. Even if I were to avoid his speeches in the
Senate and all his political intention and policy, and laud simply
his firmness and strength of character, even this would be unpleasant for your friends to hear. But it is impossible to praise the
man properly without working up these topics: how he foresaw the
present and coming state of affairs, how he fought to prevent it, and
laid down his life that he might not have to see it.

In the end Cicero was pleased with his work: 'I like my *Cato*; but then Lucilius Bassus likes his works.'* Brutus however was perhaps not entirely satisfied; at any rate, he wrote a *Cato* himself, stiff and restrained in style beside Cicero's. Caesar praised the latter's for its eloquence in the warmest terms (it is, alas, lost except for insignificant fragments) but he was sufficiently displeased by the matter of the work, and doubtless of Brutus' too, to embark on an *Anticato*, apparently a conventional bit of invective accusing its subject of meanness and heavy drinking, that probably did his own reputation no good, since many even of the Caesarians had been under the impression of Cato's personality.

In spite of his comparatively outspoken writing Cicero was taking steps to safeguard his position. At one point he wrote to Varro in some alarm about a relation of Caesar's who had been put to death, whether with the Dictator's authority or not. 'And so I continue to go out to dinner with our present masters. Well, what should I do? One must take account of circumstances.' The chief of these precautionary dinner parties were with Hirtius, a loyal officer of Caesar in Gaul and a man of fairly humble background with modest literary pretensions; he was to write the last book of the *Gallic War* for Caesar, and appears to have had a great admiration for Cicero, who liked him well enough in return. Another precautionary move, perhaps, was to lend a large sum of money to a secretary of Caesar's – which it proved very difficult to recover.

In June Cicero and Varro were together for some days at Tusculum; this visit seems to have further stimulated Cicero's reawakening interest in philosophy – at any rate he wrote to Varro afterwards a letter full of philosophical jokes. A little later he was announcing Caesar's imminent return. He was now very confident about his position; he was in the counsels of Caesar's friends, he said, and there could be no doubt that he and Varro were better off under Caesar's victory than they would have been under that of his opponents.

He wrote about the same time to another friend, Papirius Paetus (about whom not a great deal is known save what can be inferred from these letters – that he was an Epicurean, a gourmet, and had lost money in the recent turmoils), in somewhat similar terms: he is amazingly cultivated by Caesar's friends and has

---

* A writer clearly deservedly unknown; possibly not Lucilius Bassus, but Lucilius' Bassus, i.e. mentioned by the well-known satiric poet of the late second century.

no reason to fear anything from the great man himself, though of course, he adds, where there is no law there can be no security. He claims to be controlling his tongue, but that he cannot help being saddled with responsibility for various sharp and witty remarks; indeed, he continues with some complacency, he gathers that Caesar considers himself a judge of their genuineness, and has given orders that they shall be brought to him with the other news of the day. We may assume that Caesar was content to keep Cicero on a light rein, and that he should to some extent lend his authority to, and to some extent act as a licensed jester against, the régime. As for Varro, he was to dedicate an anti-quarian work on religion to Caesar and accept a commission to establish a public library in Rome.

Cicero goes on to tell Paetus that Hirtius and Dolabella have become his pupils in oratory and his masters in dining: he hastens to reassure his friend that in spite of this he will not be an expensive guest to entertain when he comes to visit, though he would, please, like a hot bath. The present age may be less shocked and surprised than its predecessor at Cicero retaining the friendship of Dolabella after his divorce from Tullia, but there can be no doubt that there was political calculation in it. In another letter, written at leisure in Tusculum since his pupils have gone off to meet Caesar and, he hopes, put in a word for himself, he remarks that he has done as the Sicilian tyrant Diony-sius II did, who when driven into exile opened a school.

The plan pleases me too; it has many advantages. First of all, what is especially important now, I protect myself against the dangers of the time . . . Then I benefit, firstly in health, which suffered when I gave up my exercises. And secondly my oratorical capacity, if I had any, would have dried up if I had not gone back to practising in this way. There is a final matter which you might put first – I have finished off more peacocks than you have done young pigeons.

To another friend he wrote that Cassius (who had received a legateship from Caesar) was also practising declamation with him, and he proposed, if Caesar would allow it, to devote himself entirely to literature.

In fact, immediately after the *Cato* he had turned to a longish treatise, again dedicated to Brutus, on the ideal orator. Though he claims to be writing as a critic rather than a teacher, it clearly reflects his new activity. Why should not the teaching of oratory, he asks, be as honourable as that of law was in Roman eyes? 'Of course not if you teach like a schoolmaster, but if you do so by advising, exhorting, asking questions, sharing your knowledge, sometimes reading or listening with your pupil.' We may assume, from the preoccupations of the work, that Hirtius and the others (apart from being told not to beat time to their own rhythms, twiddle their fingers and make odd faces) heard a good deal of argument against the Atticists, as unable even to master the plain style properly, especially to salt it with humour, and quite unable to rise to the higher flights of the medium and grand styles when the subject demanded it; moreover, as being averse from occasional rhythmicality simply because they were incapable of it. Cicero agrees that there is nothing to be said for the ignorant Asian rhetoricians who are slaves to rhythm, which in the wrong place gives an impression of artificiality and insincerity, and who fall into a 'chant' or 'howl' when delivering their speeches; and he stresses that the grand manner in the wrong place is ludicrous and disgusting. He insists that style must be varied, and suited to the subject-matter; and points out that the real Attic model should be Demosthenes, who could be grand as well as simple. His arguments are mostly unanswerable, and history vindicated him; nothing of the Atticists survived.

There is much that is interesting in this work, the *Orator*, apart from the long technical discussion of rhythm, which has sparked off an immense amount of controversy, partly because Cicero's practice does not seem always to coincide with his theory; this is drawn largely from Aristotle and later Greeks, whose terminology is not very clearly reproduced in Latin. There is some consideration of alternative word-forms, between which he chooses on grounds of euphony, without attempting to be consistent. His criticism is on the whole sympathetic and sensitive, notable for illuminating parallels from the art of painting. It is worth observing that Cicero is still concerned with forensic and political oratory – show speeches and the writing of history take a lesser place; in fact, under the Empire, oratory moved into the declamation-room, and Tacitus for one knew well enough the connection that this development had with the loss of liberty. Cicero is still in reminiscent mood, though he speaks modestly of his abilities and also of his originality in the treatise: he is often thought to be original, he says, when he is only saying what is old and generally unknown. His renewed interest in philosophy is visible both in the preface, where he outlines a modern version of the 'ancient and obscure' Platonic doctrine of Ideas (less hostile to art than the original) in order to convey what he means by an ideal orator, and in the concluding paragraph in which he gracefully concedes to Brutus that this ideal of his may be mistaken, or he may himself change his mind about it; for probability, rather than truth, is all that he has ever thought attainable, even in matters not involving, as this does, popular approval and the pleasure of the ear.

This work summed up many of his final beliefs on style, though it was perhaps about the same time that he wrote a preface to some translations of Demosthenes and Aeschines, with a similar polemical purpose. Early in the following year he wrote to a friend, 'I am exceedingly glad that you think so well of my *Orator*. I do believe that I have put into that book any judgement I may possess on the art of public speaking. If it is what you say you think it, then I too am worth something. If not, I am ready for my reputation for good judgement to suffer in the same proportion as the book.' On the whole he and it pass the test; but Brutus was never to accept Cicero fully as the mentor, both in style and politics, that he was so anxious to become.

Meanwhile Cicero's social life went on. Some of his most amusing letters come from this period, though they are hard to date precisely. We have some sparkling ones to Papirius Paetus, in which he discusses the early history of the Papirii, considers the subject of indecent words, of which the Stoics deny the existence, or laments the decline of true Roman humour, diluted by Italian immigration, or worse, now even by trousered Gauls from beyond the Alps. He boasts that he has actually been brave enough to give Hirtius a return dinner

though without a peacock; my cook was able to imitate everything in the meal except the hot sauce. This then is my life now. In the morning I receive at home both large numbers of *boni*, who look gloomy, and also these joyful victors who treat me in the most respectful and affectionate manner possible. When the stream of visitors has dried up, I wrap myself up in my studies, either reading or writing. People even come to listen to me as a learned man, because I am a little more learned than they are. Then the rest of the day is given to bodily pleasures. I have already grieved for the state more deeply and longer than any mother for her only child.

One of the dinner parties was described in more detail to Paetus, the one at which Cicero found himself in company with the actress Cytheris, Antony's mistress.

I am writing the letter of which you are reading a copy on my tablets after taking my place at dinner at three in the afternoon.* Where? you ask. At Volumnius Eutrapelus' house. Your friends Atticus and Verrius are reclining† on either side of me . . . Listen to the rest. Cytheris lay down next to Eutrapelus. 'What?' you say, 'Cicero at such a party, Cicero

> Whom they all gazed at, to whose countenance
> The Greeks all turned their faces?'‡

I promise you I had no notion she would be there. But after all even Aristippus the Socratic did not blush when he was accused of keeping Lais as his mistress. 'I keep Lais', he said, 'but I'm not in her keeping' (it's better in Greek; make your own translation if you will). As for me, even as a young man I was never attracted by anything of this sort, much less now that I am old. What I enjoy is the company. I talk about whatever crops up, and change my sighs into loud laughter.

There were dangers after all in this course of life. As he wrote to another friend, perhaps about this time,

For the last ten days my stomach has been in a bad way, but as I had no fever I could not persuade people who wanted my assistance that I was really ill. So I have taken refuge here at Tusculum, after two days of complete fasting, without even a drop of water. Starved and exhausted, I was hoping for help from you rather than expecting you to ask it from me. I am frightened by all sorts of illness, including that for which your master Epicurus is roughly treated by the Stoics; he complains of trouble with his bowels and bladder; they think the one is a result of gluttony and the other of an even less respectable form of indulgence. I was really afraid of dysentery. But I think I am better for the change, or perhaps the rest as well; or possibly the disease is simply wearing itself out. But in case you wonder how it happened or how I deserved it, the sumptuary law, which is supposed to bring plain living, has done for me. Your gourmets, trying to bring into fashion vegetables exempted under the statute, make delicious dishes out of fungi, herbs and grasses of all kinds. Meeting with some of these at Lentulus' augural banquet I was seized with a violent diarrhoea which has only begun today, I think, to check itself. Thus I who used easily to go without oysters and eels, am now caught by beets and mallows. So I shall be more careful in future.

* The usual time.
† It will be recalled that men (usually not respectable women) reclined on couches to eat.
‡ From a Latin tragedy.

There were also many much more serious and formal epistles written in these months after Caesar's return. Apart from composing a large variety of letters of introduction and recommendation, Cicero made it his business to get in touch with a number of exiles, urging them to sue for pardon and promising to use his influence in their support. His motives were doubtless mixed; he wished to be kept in countenance by others who had also humbled themselves to accept forgiveness, he wished to show his power with the new régime, and to increase his influence by putting distinguished men under an obligation to him; but he also wished to bury old divisions, to make it possible for Caesar to restore the constitution, and to ensure that if he did so there would be suitable men at hand to assist him. Not that he was wholly optimistic on this point; he wrote to Paetus that even Caesar did not know what would happen: 'we are slaves to him, and he to the times', and in particular to associates who could not safely contemplate a restoration.

Among those he begged to make their peace was M. Marcellus, the optimate consul of 51, now living in Lesbos, a man of strong character and, as the *Brutus* attests, wide education, who might count as the leading optimate still extant; also Caecina, son of an old legal client and one of the most important men in Etruria, who had written on its religious traditions – and against Caesar. Cicero told Caecina that Caesar was showing special favour to intellectuals, and assured him also that the Dictator always spoke with respect of Pompey and had advanced numerous ex-Pompeians to important commands. To others he had to confess that Caesar was less forgiving to those who had fought in Africa; but he thought (at one point at least) that he was becoming more reasonable every day. And in September 46 there was an event which seemed infinitely promising. At a meeting of the Senate Caesar's father-in-law L. Piso mentioned the case of Marcellus; his cousin C. Marcellus fell at the Dictator's feet, and the senators rose in a body to implore mercy. Caesar, complaining of Marcellus' 'acerbity', unexpectedly, and not very enthusiastically, gave way. It was a real concession to the Senate. Cicero describes the scene in a letter to Servius Sulpicius, who had accepted from Caesar the governorship of Greece; he himself decided, when his name was called, to break his custom of not speaking in the House, and launched into a brief speech of thanks to Caesar, of which he subsequently published a version.

The *pro Marcello*, brilliant as it is, may look to us like a step on the road to the grovelling flattery of imperial times; but Cicero had surely struck the right note in appealing to Caesar's desire for glory. Military achievements, he says, may be astounding rather than glorious, and the credit is shared with the army and with fortune; true fame is of civic growth. Caesar had apparently spoken his fear of conspiracies, and, with the depression that haunted his last months, was repeating that he had lived long enough both for nature and for glory. Cicero maintains that everyone is, must be, passionately loyal to Caesar, since he alone can reconcile all parties and restore the Republic, and that he must therefore live on. There is no need to go back over the past. 'We must now compare not the two causes, but the two victories,' and all will agree that victory has fallen to the man most ready to use it generously. Let Caesar put the crown on his achievement by restoring the old institutions – the courts, the freedom of the Senate and so forth. It is surely clear that in all this Cicero is entirely sincere, however high-flown his language. His old policy of concord and unity has found a new content. But he was expressing a wish, rather than an expectation.

M. Marcellus, on hearing the news, was in no hurry to set off home, but he wrote a very polite letter to Cicero, such a letter as Cicero's heart must have swelled at receiving from so great a noble (whose closeness to him he greatly exaggerates in the speech). Others also wrote in the most grateful terms, or begging him to undertake their cause. Caecina's words may be quoted:

There is no need, my dear Cicero, to wait for my son. He is young. He is too eager, too inexperienced, too anxious to think of everything. You must run the whole campaign; all my hope is in you. You have the wisdom to know what pleases Caesar and wins him over: it must all start and end with you. You have much influence with him, and more with his associates . . . you are always so energetic on your friends' behalf that they have come not simply to hope for your help, but demand it as I am doing too.

Cicero continued to put forward his best efforts; only to one correspondent does he respond with asperity, refusing his assistance; we do not know what lay behind this. But he wrote to tell one suppliant, Q. Ligarius, that 'I called on Caesar this morning and went through all the indignity and trouble of meeting and having speech with him.' He had in fact launched into an appeal, while Ligarius' brothers fell at Caesar's feet. The Dictator had talked and looked encouragingly, though that was all that could be said at present. Later Cicero made a formal speech in the Forum for Ligarius. According to a not very likely story of Plutarch's, Caesar said beforehand, 'Why should we not hear a speech from Cicero again, since the verdict on Ligarius as a villain and an enemy is certain?'; but he was seen to change colour, shake, and drop his papers at Cicero's eloquence, and capitulated to the praise of his own clemency and generosity. Cicero did not abuse his old leader to compliment his new; the Civil War was a blow of Fate, the standing of the two leaders equal, that of Pompey's followers, he hinted, superior.

Either because there are so many gaps in our series of letters, or more probably because Cicero was to some extent averting his eyes from public affairs, and was blind to certain aspects of them, we hear remarkably little from him of Caesar's activities: first of the unprecedented honours that greeted his return – a thanksgiving of forty days, the dictatorship for ten years, seventy-two lictors, a three-year 'control of morals'; then of his four triumphs celebrated in late September, and the vast donations to his soldiers and those of the poor eligible for corn-distributions; there were also games (with a giraffe-hunt) in honour of his daughter Julia, now many years dead; the Forum Julium, which Cicero had once been involved in helping to build, was dedicated, and within it the temple to Venus Genetrix, the ancestress of the Julii, and a statue of the Dictator, riding a horse that had been taken from a monument to Alexander. Other gigantic buildings were planned. Cleopatra appeared in Rome with her court, to establish herself in one of the surburban villas or 'parks' across the Tiber. With her Cicero did have some dealings, of a purely literary kind, as he claims, and came to dislike her and her courtiers' arrogance intensely.

Nor was he apparently interested in or impressed by the important and long-overdue programme of social and political reform that Caesar began to put in hand. The great plans to settle soldiers on the land, particularly that of political opponents, necessarily impinged on all landowners; but even here Cicero was extraordinarily off-hand. He laughed at Paetus for asking him where lands were going to be divided: he knew nothing these days save from Balbus, who had better be asked direct. There was threatening activity not far from Tusculum, but Cicero did not propose to worry. He would enjoy his property as long as he could; even his life, these last four years, had been on borrowed time, he said.

Caesar also took a census of the city population, and cut down the numbers eligible for free corn, though he made concessions to fathers of families. He banned *collegia* again in the cause of order, and proposed to settle many of the poor in colonies overseas; on the other hand he tried to attract doctors and teachers to Rome. He also attempted to limit the proportion of slave labour employed in the countryside, to reduce the danger of slave revolts. He probably drafted a moderate law about debt; he altered the composition of the juries, though not dramatically. These measures showed that he was not the social revolutionary that had been feared, and even amounted to some extent to a denial of his *popularis* past, though equally they were not designed to please the rich. For the most part they were thoroughly statesmanlike. Only on the reform of the calendar (which made 46 an exceedingly long year with three intercalary months) do we have a comment of Cicero's: when someone mentioned that the constellation Lyra would rise next day, 'Yes,' he said, 'by edict'. If true (and we must regret that we have not Caesar at hand to pronounce on its genuineness) this saying sums up Cicero's attitude: for him nothing could counterbalance the fact that Rome was being ruled 'by edict'; directly and autocratically.

Let us listen to him excusing himself to Paetus for political inactivity.

Do you imagine there will be fewer senatorial decrees if I am in Naples? When I am in Rome and frequenting the Forum, senatorial decrees are drawn up in the house of my admirer and your friend [Balbus?]. If my name comes into his head, I am put down as a witness and I learn that a decree supposedly proposed by me has reached Syria and Armenia before ever I have heard anything about it at all. And don't think I'm joking. I assure you, I have had letters from distant monarchs thanking me for voting that their titles should be recognized, when, far from knowing they had been recognized as kings, I had no notion that they even existed.

Scholars differ as to whether Caesar was still thinking of restoring the old constitution, or whether, with whatever degree of willingness, he saw a kind of monarchy, perhaps partly on the oriental model, as the only solution. Did he really say that Sulla's resignation showed that he did not know his alphabet? At any rate, before decisive steps in any direction could be taken, he had to leave Rome again, at the end of 46, to deal with Pompey's sons, who had escaped from Africa to Spain and succeeded in raising large forces there. The Dictator took Hirtius and others of

Cicero's recent habitués with him, leaving Rome to his deputy, the Master of Horse, and to some City Prefects, a powerful office with dubious antiquarian precedent; the ordinary magistrates were not elected. Even so, this time Cicero had not the faintest hankering for Caesar's defeat. He owed nothing to Pompey's sons – quite the reverse, indeed, if the elder had really tried to kill him at Corcyra – and he had no respect for them. There can be no doubt that he will have agreed with Cassius who, early in 45, in a very friendly and frank letter from Brundisium, which made philosophical jokes and asked for news from Spain, wrote 'Damn me if I am not anxious. I prefer our old, forgiving master to trying out a new and cruel one. You know what a fool Gnaeus Pompeius is, you know how he imagines cruelty a virtue, you know how he is always thinking we are laughing at him. I am afraid he might answer our teasing like a boor – with the sword.'

But Cicero was soon in no frame of mind to follow the news from Spain closely. It is time to turn back to his family life.

The letters to Atticus are usually mere notes at this time, elliptic and colloquial, and doubtless written in the illegible hand that Cicero once apologized to Quintus for, admitting that he would seize any pen or other materials that came to hand (Atticus by contrast had regular and elegant writing). They strike a very different note from the carefully composed missives that often fall, or complain that in the circumstances it is not easy to fall, into recognized epistolary genres, such as recommendation, consolation and so on; even in the amusing letters to Paetus and others we feel at the back of Cicero's mind a consciousness that letters full of jokes form one of these accepted classes. From this year, 46, there are only two series of letters to Atticus, from the spring and autumn, and this makes it difficult to follow the affairs of the family in a period in which traumatic events followed on each other. Some time after Cicero's return to Rome Tullia and Dolabella were finally divorced, though Tullia was again pregnant; extracting her dowry from Dolabella's grasp proved a problem, but as we saw Cicero remained on good terms with his still powerful son-in-law. And there was a second divorce, that of Cicero himself and Terentia. The rights and wrongs of this unhappy business are irrecoverable; Terentia naturally defended her various financial dealings. On the other hand there was a superficial reconciliation with Quintus. But almost the only mention of him in the year's letters is a sour one; what a fool he makes of himself by being so proud of a minor priesthood that his son has been given, and how impudent of him to ask Atticus to contribute to the expenses of it! The passage also makes a not very clear, but clearly contemptuous, reference to the freedman Statius, to whom Quintus was obviously still clinging.

With the failure of these old ties Cicero turned the more to Atticus and Tullia. It was probably in the summer that he wrote, 'On my life, my dear Atticus, I don't think – I won't say Tusculum, though for the rest I am happy enough there, but even the Islands of the Blest would be worth being without you all day long. Well, for these three days we must harden ourselves to it – to assume that you feel as I do, which of course you do.' A new pleasure in his life was Atticus' little daughter, affectionately known as Attica after her father and now probably about five years old – a lively child, but liable to alarming bouts of fever. As for his own son, young Marcus seems to have been unable to inspire his father to any continuous interest, but it may be around this time that he wrote for him a short treatise on certain aspects of rhetoric in the form of a catechism. But Marcus was not thinking of study; he approached his father in the autumn cautiously, via Atticus: could he go to Spain with Caesar, and could he have a decent allowance? As for the latter, Cicero was willing to give him what certain of his acquaintance gave their sons; 'on Spain I brought up two considerations. The first I had mentioned to you, that I was afraid of malicious tongues; "was abandoning one side not enough? Did we have to join the other?" And second, that he would find it mortifying to be put in the shade by his cousin's favour and influence.' However, he did not at once refuse his permission, though the plan clearly fell through in the end.

In the autumn Cicero went on a tour of his country properties. A little later he was to write that he was not so eager to leave Rome as he used to be, since there was no longer business to distract him from his own work when he was in his town house, which was as pleasant as any of his villas; perhaps old age was beginning to tell on him, or perhaps this was only a mood. For he had recently considered buying a property at Naples, then a quiet place and still delightfully Greek in atmosphere as in origin; and now on his way down the coast he stopped at a new acquisition near the little town of Astura and wrote in delight with the solitude and 'everything about the villa, the shore and the view of the sea'; the house stood on a promontory, positively 'in the water', with views along the coast to Antium and Circei, and wooded grounds behind it. It was perhaps now that he went on to Cumae, whence he wrote to Paetus and another friend whom he wished to visit; both were suffering from gout, a common affliction among the Romans. And from Campania he finally came to Arpinum. Hence he wrote detailing plans for his journey home by short stages.

> How I wish I could hasten directly to my Tullia's embrace and Attica's kiss! Do pray write to me of her, so that while I am at Tusculum I shall know what she is chattering of, or if she is in the country how she writes to you. Meanwhile give her my love, by letter or by word of mouth, and to Pilia too. And though we shall be meeting immediately, write to me if you've any news.

> Just as I was folding up this letter a courier who had been benighted arrived with yours. Having read it I am of course very sorry about Attica's slight fever. Your letter gave me information about all the other matters I expected. But when you write that 'a little fire in the morning suggests old age', well, to have a little lapse of memory suggests it more – I had assigned the 1st of December to Axius, the 2nd to you, and the day of my arrival, the 30th, to Quintus. This is all I have for you, nothing new. 'What need for a letter, then?' Well, what about our meetings when we chatter about whatever comes into our heads?

Nonetheless Cicero, or his friends, were looking out for another wife for him. Possibly before this, Hirtius had proposed his sister as a possible bride; Cicero had refused, on the grounds that it was impossible to devote oneself both to a wife and to philosophy. A few days later he wrote, 'As for Pompey's daughter I wrote back to you that I had no such idea at present. The other lady you mention, I think you know. I never saw anyone more hideous. But I am nearly home, so – when we meet.' Doubtless they discussed this, and at some time before the end of the year it became known that he proposed to marry his rich young ward, one Publilia. Plutarch says that Terentia declared that he was infatuated, but that really he acted on the advice of his friends and relations and entirely from financial motives: these, by Roman standards, were far more proper considerations. A modern scholar has convincingly suggested that Publilia's family also stood usefully high in Caesar's favour. The only surviving comment of Cicero's own is a cryptic one; in answer to a letter of congratulation he wrote,

> I should not have taken any new decision at so unhappy a time had I not on my return found my household affairs in as bad a way as those of the state. In my own house I knew no safety, had no refuge from intrigue, because of the villainy of those to whom my safety

and property should have been most precious from my undying kindness to them. So I thought it wise to fortify myself by the loyalty of new connections against the treachery of old ones.

What this culminating treachery of Terentia and her freedman had been we cannot say.

We may assume Atticus' approval of the new departure; it is perhaps relevant that when almost as old as Cicero now was he had contracted a marriage that had apparently brought him a very happy family life. But not everyone was so favourable; at the wedding a comment was made on a man of Cicero's age marrying a young girl: 'She will be a woman tomorrow' was the bridegroom's swift reply.

But the ill-assorted marriage lasted only a few weeks. Early in January 45 Tullia gave birth to a son in Rome. She seemed at first to be regaining strength, but a few weeks later she died in her father's house at Tusculum. We are spared the report of her illness and her father's agonizing anxiety, but we can imagine easily enough that he had few thoughts left for his bride. According to Plutarch he even thought that Publilia was pleased at Tullia's death. He told her that he wanted to be alone and sent her back to her mother.

He could not bear either Tusculum or his house in the centre of Rome, and found refuge for the first weeks with Atticus, where he sat in the library reading the Greek philosophers on Grief. But our first direct view of him is in early March, at his new house in lonely Astura, where he had gone to avoid all company, though he wrote every day to Atticus. For once at least he was making heroic efforts to master his feelings, or at least to hide them. He asked Atticus to make his excuses for all engagements on grounds of ill-health rather than grief. It seems that it was not expected or approved that men should go into mourning for women, and as so often Cicero ran the risk of being considered emotional and extravagant.

He had turned now, in his search for comfort, to writing rather than reading.

You are my witness that I have not been remiss on my own behalf. At your house I read everything that anybody has written on overcoming grief; but my sorrow defeats all consolation. I have even done something, which I am sure no one did before. I have written a Consolation to myself. I shall send the work to you, if the copyists have written it out. I can assure you no consolation is so effective. I write all day, not that I do any good, but it distracts me for the moment –

not enough, for my grief bears me down, but it gives me a respite, and I try everything I know to compose not my mind but my face, if I can – and sometimes it seems to be a sin to do so, and sometimes that it will be a sin not to. Solitude helps to some extent, but it would be more effective if you were there nonetheless. That is the only reason I have for leaving the place, for given the circumstances it is well enough. And yet this very thing hurts me – you will not be able to feel the same towards me; all you liked in me has gone.

It must have been a mild and sunny spring; on 9 March he wrote, 'In this lonely place I speak to no one; in the morning I hide myself in a thick wood, and do not come out till evening. Next to yourself I have no better friend than solitude. In it all my converse is with books. It is interrupted by weeping, against which I struggle as much as I can, but so far it is an unequal battle . . .' Next day he continued, 'I don't want you to leave your own business to come to me. I will rather come to you if you are kept for some time. Though I would not have left your sight unless I had been beyond absolutely any aid at all. If any relief were possible it would be in you alone, and as soon as I can find it in anyone it will be in you. And even now I cannot do without you.' He was as dependent on daily letters as ever, while the only other person whom he could imagine welcoming the sight of was Brutus, who had written 'wisely, but uselessly' from Gaul. There is, significantly, no mention of Quintus – or of Marcus.

Others, including in time Caesar, wrote the obligatory letters of consolation; one survives, though it cannot have reached Cicero till considerably later. This is the famous piece by his old friend Servius Sulpicius who wrote from Greece in terms remarkable for one in Caesar's employment, and one so timid as he was. Should not men who had lost what ought to be as dear to them as their children, namely their country, position, rank and honour, be hardened to all else? Could Tullia have found a trustworthy husband of suitable rank, could she have seen her children doing well, when all was so chaotic? And then

On my way home from Asia, as I sailed from Aegina to Megara, I began to look at the shores around me: behind me was Aegina, before me Megara, to the right Piraeus, to the left Corinth: cities which had once flourished above all others, but now lie fallen and destroyed before our eyes. I began to think to myself thus – ah, do we little men rebel if one of us die or is killed, we whose lives must be short, when in one region so many dead cities lie overthrown? Will you not control yourself, Servius, and remember that you were born a man?

While at Astura, Cicero recurred to a suggestion that, it seems, he and Atticus had already discussed. He wanted to build a shrine to Tullia, something, he said, that several of the authors whom he spent so much time reading had approved. He had decided on the sort of building he wanted, and on the architect, but was not certain about a site.

I feel myself almost as though bound by a vow and promise, and the long space of time after my death is more important to me than this short one, which yet seems to me too long. I have tried everything, and I find no peace. For while I was busy on the work I mentioned to you earlier I was bathing my wounds: now I reject everything, and find nothing so easy to endure as solitude.

The *Self-Consolation*, which was famous in antiquity, is lost, but a fragment quoted by a Christian author helps us to understand what was in Cicero's mind in forming the plan of a shrine. The Greeks believed that many divine beings had originally been humans of outstanding qualities or achievements; the primitive cult of such 'heroes' and 'heroines' had been complicated by more sophisticated and philosophical theories of the nature of the divine and its relation to the human soul. Even in Rome, in the previous hundred years or so, a few great men had received worship for a time at least after their deaths. Cicero doubtless did not envisage future generations praying to Tullia's spirit; he was not even a firm believer in a future life, and certainly he never mentions its possibility in the letters of this time. Nor, to do him justice, did he wish to erect a monument to his own grief – that grief of which, as we have seen, his society did not approve. Rather he wished to give Tullia the only immortality he was certain of, the immortality of glory, and to pay the highest honour he could to her transcendent qualities, to assert in all seriousness that they were transcendent.

If it was right that the children of Cadmus or Amphitryon or Tyndareus* should be raised by glory to heaven, surely she also deserves the same honour and dedication, and I shall give it to her. Best and most accomplished of women, with the blessing of the immortal gods I shall set you in your consecrated place among them, for all mortals to approve.

Cicero considered putting the shrine on his own land at Astura, Arpinum, or Tusculum; but he wanted a more frequented spot

* All heroes of Greek legend.

and soon proposed buying a property in the Vatican suburb of Rome. Atticus, who was not very enthusiastic about the project, was deputed to carry out negotiations, which proved complicated and finally unsuccessful, though things got so far that he was told to look out for columns for the building; while Cicero even tried to mobilize Oppius and Balbus to provide financial backing. After a time he came to think that the property would also do for him to live in in his old age; he could not, for many reasons, bear the neighbourhood of the Forum, but nor did he wish to be far from Atticus and his family.

Meanwhile, even from the first the outside world had been breaking in on the solitude of Astura, and the letters show Cicero capable of directions and comments. Terentia made a fuss about Cicero's new will, providing for his little grandson (who cannot have lived long). Brutus, as we saw earlier, revealed shocking ignorance in his *Cato* about the course of the great senatorial debate in December 63. Cicero asked Atticus for various items of historical information for use in the *Consolation*. It emerges that arrangements were being made for young Marcus to go to study in Athens, a plan he probably liked less than his own of going to fight in Spain, or the alternative he had mooted of taking a house in Rome; but he was always docile, and perhaps especially unwilling now to upset his father. There were a great many business affairs that Cicero had to give instructions about; and he was still 'concerned about our dear Attica's health'. And on 28 March

I write you this in my own hand. Please see what you can do. Publilia writes to me that her mother has talked to Publilius,* and would come with him to talk to me, and she would accompany them if I allowed. She begs me imploringly and at length to let her come and to answer her. You see what a tiresome affair it is. I wrote back that I was in an even more wretched state than when I told her I wanted to be alone; and therefore did not wish her to come to me at present. I thought that if I did not answer she would come with her mother. I don't now; it was clear that the letter wasn't her own. But I want to avoid what I see will happen, the visit of the others. The only way to avoid it is to leave; I'd rather not, but it is inevitable. Now what I'm asking you is to find out how long I can stay here without getting caught. You will do it, to use your phrase, 'with moderation'.

In fact, Cicero left Astura a few days later to stay near Rome on a farm belonging to Atticus. He returned to Astura at the be-

* Probably Publilia's uncle, or perhaps brother.

ginning of May in a calmer frame of mind, though he was still obsessed with the shrine: 'I want it to be a shrine and I can't be dissuaded. I am eager to avoid anything like a tomb.' Some months later, however, it was found that Caesar proposed a big development scheme in the Vatican area, and the plan lapsed for ever.

Cicero's long retirement was clearly exciting comment, and indeed we have a letter from a friend reproaching him with it. Writing to Atticus, Cicero called him to witness that in these last weeks he had been meeting and talking easily to people, and pointing out how much, and what difficult stuff, he had succeeded in writing. On 5 May he heard that Pompey's sons were on the run in Spain. 'Hirtius writes to me that Sextus Pompeius has left Corduba* and fled to Hither Spain, Gnaeus has fled I don't know where; nor indeed do I care.' He turned back to his philosophical writings.

* Cordova.

13

THE CONSOLATIONS OF
PHILOSOPHY
45-44 B.C.

It was probably in the autumn of 46, or even earlier, that Cicero
formed the plan of giving Rome its own philosophical literature;
several works seem to have been begun before Tullia's death. He
was not absolutely the first in the field. There had been frequent
reference to philosophers and philosophic doctrines in Roman
literature for a hundred years at least; but of actual treatises there
were (apart from Lucretius' poem and another piece of philosophical verse of which we hear, since Cicero found it unreadable)
primarily a few prose works on Epicureanism; these he deprecated
as much for style as for subject—indeed, he did not really bother
to read them—they said nothing new, for the Epicureans were
bound to the *ipse dixit* of their founder; another reason why
Cicero despised them. But there was also, as we saw, at least one
treatise on ethics by Brutus – the book *On Virtue*, dedicated to
Cicero himself, and briefly referred to by him more than once. It is
possible in fact that he does not give his friend his full due. The
later critic, Quintilian, thought that Brutus' philosophic treatises
were impressive, much better than his speeches: 'you can see that
he means what he says' (how this echoes Caesar's judgement of
Brutus!); but his work *On Duties*, or *De Officiis*, possibly later
than Cicero's work on the same subject, is criticized for dealing
with particular cases without referring them to general principles. It
is reasonable to suppose that Cicero was in part inspired by a desire
to outdo Brutus. He stood, at this point, between two paths,
down which the examples of his two chief friends beckoned him.
Atticus, who was to follow up his *Annals* with works on biography
and family history, was pretty clearly still wishing that Cicero would
write history: in several of the philosophic works Cicero continues to justify his refusal. The letters do not discuss philosophic
problems with Atticus, as they do historical ones; and if Cicero
introduces Atticus as a character in a couple of his dialogues, it
is as an almost silent one; even the defence of Epicureanism is put
into other mouths. However, Atticus was perfectly willing to see

to the copying and dissemination of Cicero's new works, as we can for the first time observe him doing.

There were some who thought the task that Cicero had undertaken a pointless one. In the *Academic Treatises* Varro is made to object that anyone likely to be interested in philosophy can read it in Greek. But Cicero claims that both those who could not understand that language and those who could should find philosophy in Latin worthwhile; after all, he says, Roman poetry and oratory are worth reading, heavily influenced as they are by Greek models. We must not suppose, however, from his envisaging a readership among those without Greek, that Cicero wanted to make his subject available to a really wide audience; he thought it 'entirely unsuitable for the multitude', and his works, most of them significantly dedicated to those serious students Brutus and Varro, cannot really be called popularization, though Cicero plumed himself on making some things clearer than they had ever been made in Greek. (The *Stoic Paradoxes*, by contrast, had borrowed something from the 'Cynic diatribe', the popular moralizing literature of the Cynic philosophers, who addressed themselves to the people.)

Primarily Cicero intended his works for the young: 'I do not think it possible, or even to be desired, that all shall turn to these studies; I trust a few may, whose influence may yet spread widely in the republic'. It does not appear that Cicero in fact found many readers among the new generation – as we shall see, his kind of philosophy was fact going out of fashion; but he was surprised, he tells us, by the number of older men who read his work and found themselves helped by it; and it has been remarked that his undramatic conclusions, and his obvious experience of many of the problems in life about which he writes, are likelier to appeal to the mature reader. ·

His account of his aims shows that there was a strongly political aspect to his writings; after all, ethics was to him the crown of philosophy, and what but the decline of ethical standards had led to the downfall of the Republic? His action was political in another sense too: since he was excluded from public life 'it was in my books that I was speaking to the Senate and Assembly. I considered philosophy a substitute for political activity.' Amidst all the vigorous justification of the new occupation however there is one note of self-depreciation: in his last philosophic work – long after the crisis of Tullia's death, be it noted – he says that in his opinion Scipio Aemilianus, who proclaimed his hours of leisure to be busy and profitable, but who wrote nothing, deserved the higher praise: 'for from this we may understand that, in the activity of his mind and the study of those questions to which he devoted his consideration, he was never unoccupied and never lonely. I, however, have not strength of mind to forget my solitude in silent thought, and so have turned all my intentions and efforts to this work of writing.'

But he did also think that it redounded to the glory of Rome to have a literature dealing with such an important and serious subject. And the linguistic challenge of putting Greek philosophy into Latin dress attracted him. He would not admit that Latin was a less rich language than Greek, and thought that its potential for subjects not yet treated ought to be exploited (this aspect of the philosophical programme clearly did interest Atticus). Cicero often complains, as Lucretius had done, of the difficulties he has to face, and in the treatises themselves, as in the letters, he lets us see him at work, finding Latin equivalents for Greek technical terms. In fact the chief problems did not lie in the vocabulary, but in the syntax, of which he speaks much less. And he did not entirely overcome them. Latin, which can be so forcible and majestic, is much less supple, and much more concrete, than Greek, which had also by this time been the vehicle of philosophic thought for 400 years (Plato in his day had had difficulties not wholly unlike Cicero's). Even so simple a matter as the absence in Latin of the definite article was a serious drawback, like the fact that the language has few, but always vivid, metaphors, so that it was not easy to use words in new metaphorical senses. And Latin is much less hospitable than Greek to compound words and neologisms. In fact Cicero's extreme sensibility to the genius of the language, and his respect for usage, have been seen as drawbacks; he would not force the language into new patterns if they seemed harsh to his ear. Of course he was right not to attempt a word-for-word translation from the Greek; but though he sometimes acclimatizes a word on a Greek model, he often feels it necessary to use a descriptive paraphrase, or to translate the same Greek phrase differently in different contexts, thus spoiling the clarity and concision of the argument. Nonetheless he did expand the boundaries of Latin to some degree, and a number of his coinages have come down to us. We do not often remember, when we use the words 'quality', 'essence', or 'moral', that *qualitas, essentia,* and *moralis* are words, directly modelled on Greek originals, that are first found in Cicero and were taken up again later.

We can see Cicero's linguistic achievements and limitations most clearly when he is undertaking a strict translation from the Greek. For the most part this is only done for short passages of Plato or Epicurus. But though he did not, as he said in one of his first treatises, rule out the possibility of simply translating works of Plato and Aristotle, which would be a gift of great value to his countrymen, in fact what he embarked on was an attempt 'to expound the famous old system of philosophy in Latin' for himself. The form he chose was, very naturally, the dialogue, which had been used, in part to sweeten the intellectual pill and in part to reflect the play of argument and counter-argument, since Plato's time. Several of Cicero's philosophical works are set in charming frames, as the rhetorical and political dialogues of the 50s had been; though these courteous, formal discussions in the libraries and gardens of the great villas belonging to Roman nobles differ greatly from Plato's more casual and incomparably vivid encounters in the streets and shops, even the prison, of Athens, in which everyday conversation glides insensibly into philosophic argument. In the end however Cicero seems to have lost interest in the dialogue form; it plays a minimal part in the *Tusculan Disputations* and is given up altogether in his last work the *De Officiis*.

He wrote his philosophic works very quickly; almost all of them in less than two years from 46 to 44. 'They are mere transcriptions; they cost me very little labour; all I provide is words, of which I have plenty,' he wrote, almost certainly of some of his treatises, to Atticus. But though there are admittedly signs of speed and careless revision, this modest remark has misled scholars; it has proved impossible to show that Cicero was merely copying out large chunks from the lost Greek philosophers of the third to first centuries B.C. He doubtless drew on memories of the wide reading of his youth (and possibly lecture notes?); he certainly looked up various sources as he wrote – we see him in the letters sending to friends for works that can have been only marginally relevant. And he insists indeed that he had never in the interim given up *reading* philosophy. He acknowledged his sources generously by ancient standards (the footnote had not yet been invented). He had at his disposal the libraries of his friends, some of them famous (too often the fruits of booty from the East. The first public library in Rome was yet to be founded, though there were such facilities in some Greek cities; nor were there in Rome any scholarly institutions, like the Schools at Athens, with collections built up over the years.) It is true of course that he was not attempting philosophic originality: 'I yield to many in my knowledge of philosophy; but as to what is the business of the orator, to write in an appropriate, clear and elegant style, since it is a study I have spent my life on, I think that in arrogating it to myself I am in a way claiming my own'. It was with the presentation of other men's ideas that Cicero was concerned; and indeed the school to which he belonged, the sceptical New Academy, put as much weight on the knowledge and criticism of established views as on the development of its own.

This to Cicero is 'the ancient system of philosophy', which he regarded (not wholly justly) as the creation of Socrates, Plato and Aristotle. More properly, it had developed from them through the 'Middle Academy', of which perhaps the greatest, though not the most extreme, representative had been in the second century the brilliant Carneades, who argued that nothing can be certainly known, and scandalized Rome, when he visited it as an ambassador from Athens, with his lectures, in which he argued one day for and the next against Justice as the foundation of the State. He refused to do anything so dogmatic as write a book, but his arguments were preserved by his disciples. The New Academy was a method rather than a doctrine. It was far from nihilistic or pessimistic: it shared the urge of all Hellenistic philosophy to reassure mankind – the Sceptics' suspension of belief was an intellectual form of the tranquillity and detachment with which Stoics and Epicureans alike tried to endow human life. One who refused to believe or disbelieve any statement would eschew the emotions, desires and ambitions that disturbed the soul. But Cicero was well aware that Scepticism was no longer fashionable in Greece.*
His own first master Philo had accepted and developed Carneades' admission that even if no statement could be called true or untrue one could at least form probable views; and Antiochus, Philo's successor as head of the School, had gone further, introducing Stoic and other more dogmatic elements and claiming that he was restoring the old Academy of Plato. But Antiochus himself had died in the early 60s and of what happened after him Cicero took little account. As we saw, he was not much impressed by developments in Athens when he passed through in 51, at which time Antiochus' brother was head of the Academy. And when young

---

* There were, in this great age of revivalism, to be some revivals of certain forms of Scepticism after Cicero's death; but they are a minor phenomenon in the intellectual history of late antiquity.

Marcus went to Athens he was put under the care not of an Academic, but a distinguished Peripatetic, or follower of Aristotle.

It would be unfair to say that Cicero was entirely ignorant of recent trends in philosophy. The most dramatic event of the first century was the rediscovery of Aristotle's so-called esoteric works, the technical treatises and lecture notes, as opposed to the semi-popular dialogues, or 'exoteric' writings. Today we have lost these latter, and possess only the esoteric works. But some time after Aristotle's death his own books and manuscripts had passed into the hands of persons ignorant of philosophy and had been forgotten. Sulla however carried off to Italy the library of which they had finally become a part, and it was in Italy that scholars catalogued and edited them.* It is likely that Cicero, who knew at least one of the scholars concerned, had read some of these works; the delightful introduction to Book II of the *De Finibus* shows him going to the great library in Lucullus' villa at Tusculum to borrow them (and finding Cato there 'wallowing' in books on Stoicism); but he never sets out to convey Aristotle's doctrines in Latin. Perhaps he found them largely above his head.

The second great development of the period was the rise of Neo-Pythagoreanism, and influenced by it the 'Middle' Platonism that concentrated on the metaphysical and itself partly Pythagorean side of the master's work. Pythagoras' ascetic creed, with its curious mathematical and musical mysticism, had originally grown up in the Greek cities of southern Italy, and had had some influence in Rome from early times. Cicero was interested in this influence as a historical phenomenon, and he used some Pythagorean colouring (such as the doctrine of the music of the spheres) in the *Dream of Scipio*; elsewhere too he plays with some of its ideas, as for example that of reincarnation. He says in one of the treatises that he may one day write on the subject; and in fact, for a dialogue which is otherwise lost, or was never written at all, he translated a great mystical passage from Plato's *Timaeus*, a dialogue which he confessed he did not wholly understand; one of the interlocutors in this projected work was to be his friend Nigidius Figulus, remembered after his death as a magician and a Pythagorean (the scene was set in Greece, and what is also unparalleled in Cicero's works, one of the speakers was a Greek and a professional philosopher – this was a graceful compliment to the man,

---

* It is sometimes thought that this famous story overdramatizes the revival of Aristotelian studies.

who was young Marcus' teacher). But on the whole the outlook of the Pythagoreans was alien to Cicero. Nor was the unusually religious attitude of Posidonius, the leading Stoic of the day, some at least of whose voluminous works Cicero read and used, capable of dominating him, though according to many scholars Posidonius was the greatest intellectual influence of his day.

Cicero remained loyal to the outlook of the New Academy as represented by Philo, with certain eclectic, mainly Stoic, modifications. We have seen that not only Philo himself, but Scepticism in general, had points of contact with rhetoric, which was also ready to argue both sides of a case and had long been thought to aim at probability rather than truth. Thus it is not wholly fair to say that Cicero was an eclectic Sceptic because he was as congenitally incapable of making up his mind in philosophy as in life. In political action he had not always been indecisive; nor had he been notably good at seeing the point of view of opponents of the *boni*. And in political theory he had never had any doubt as to what he believed. In both the *De Republica* and the *De Legibus* he had explicitly rejected Carneades and his Scepticism, insisting that it is possible to know what justice is, and how the State should be based on it. Whether he worried very much about this fundamental inconsistency in his position is doubtful. He certainly did not mind about inconsistencies between the strictly philosophical works; once he makes one of the other characters (who are more usually employed in paying him compliments) point out such a contradiction, only to sweep it aside in his own person: the Academics 'live from day to day' and need not care about such things. He also had a rather dubious tendency, picked up from Antiochus, to claim that different theories came to the same thing at bottom.

It is clear that Cicero's sceptical and eclectic position carried certain advantages for his educational mission. The Sceptic had to be able to expound and criticize rival views; and Cicero believed strongly that it was too common for the young prematurely to adopt a closed system on the authority of a master. At times he even concealed his own opinions, his readers complained. He retorted that he was trying to persuade rationally, not to browbeat by his own authority. Conversely, they objected that as an Academic he ought never to put forward views as his own; but he could reply that he was only indicating what was probable. There is something in Cicero's freedom of spirit, in spite of his logical lapses, that his own civilization was to lose much by abandoning, but which was greatly to profit the distant future. The *Academic Treatises*, or

Academica, the first of the works in the cycle, starts from a modest admission of ignorance and insists that the New Academy searches for the truth without contentiousness, though 'somehow most men prefer to go wrong and to defend tooth and nail the opinions they are besotted with, rather than lay their obstinacy aside and seek for the most consistent views'. Nowhere in his philosophic works is there any equivalent to the invective of political life; Cicero treats even the despised Epicureans with politeness, while he insists that he is reproducing their views as accurately as he can. Personally, he maintains, Epicurus and his followers were excellent men; it is only that they are rather stupid. (This insistence on amenity is drawn from Plato.)

The gateway, the grand Propylaeum, through which Cicero's readers were to approach philosophy, was the *Hortensius*, a dialogue based on Aristotle's *Protrepticus*, by which as its title indicates readers were to be *turned towards* philosophy. The *Hortensius* was set in the late 60s; in it Catulus was made to praise poetry, Lucullus (in fact the author of a historical work) history, and Hortensius oratory; the last also made a lively attack on philosophy, dilating on the unworthy behaviour of many philosophers and on the more extravagant theories of the Stoics and Epicureans. Finally Cicero in his own person undertook the defence of philosophy. It is strange that a work so widely read in late antiquity should have been lost. It is not only its electric effect on St Augustine, but its remaining fragments as well, that suggests it was extremely eloquent in its advocacy of detachment from ambition and pleasure, its assurance that the mere search for truth – for Cicero cannot promise its attainment – is enough to make man happy here below, and its culminating suggestion – again, it is only a suggestion—that if the soul is divine and immortal, then the greater its purity and intellectuality in this life, the more likely it is to escape from the cycle of further incarnations and return to its home in the heavens above.

After the *Hortensius* Cicero got down to technical questions. The *Academica* or *Academic Treatises* are concerned with epistemology: what, if anything can we know? The work is said by Pliny to have been written in Cicero's villa at Puteoli, on the Bay of Naples, which was famous for its colonnade and woods, and which its owner actually called the Academy; true, such evocative names were fashionable. If Pliny is right, it was perhaps in the autumn of 46 that Cicero was working at Puteoli, and planned the final scene in which the speakers leave Hortensius' seaside villa by boat for their own homes. But he was still busy on the dialogue at Astura and elsewhere in summer 45. It was originally set among the same interlocutors as the *Hortensius*, and Cicero defended the propriety of these great political figures concerning themselves with philosophy; but, as we see from his letters to Atticus, he finally became convinced that he had made them implausibly learned. He decided to bring the date down some years, and first he considered making Brutus and Cato the main characters (obviously there was no plethora of qualified Romans). But Atticus told him that Varro, who had promised to dedicate to Cicero the work on rare and archaic Latin words that he was – very slowly – producing, wanted to be given a part in something. Cicero rather reluctantly acceded; he wished as usual to take on himself the advocacy of the views he preferred, and he was afraid that the prickly Varro would not at all like being given a secondary role; he could, he said, imagine all too well Varro's face as he read. 'But the arguments of Antiochus are very persuasive', he comforted himself, though he proposed for his own part to defend a more strictly Sceptical position.

Curiously enough, we possess the second of the two books into which the earlier version was divided (often known as the *Lucullus*) and a fragment only of the second version which was in four books and was, its author thought, 'more brilliant, more concise, and better'. Cicero probably agreed with Antiochus at least in his belief that epistemology and ethics were the two most important subjects in philosophy: 'no one can be wise who does not know that there is an origin of knowledge and an end to be desired, and is thus ignorant of whence he came and where he should be going'. But he later wrote that what he wanted to do in this work was to show 'what philosophic method I thought least arrogant and most consistent and tasteful'; presumably he felt that the arguments between Stoics and Sceptics as to what could be known or 'comprehended' (*comprehensio* was his word for the Greek technical term) gave him special scope for his method of expounding and weighing up rival views. It is indeed the subject on which he is most purely the Sceptic, least influenced by Stoicism or even the semi-Stoicism of Antiochus. He also takes the opportunity to give a brief account of the development of the philosophic schools descended from Socrates, who as he elsewhere says 'was the first to bring philosophy down to earth' and whose preoccupation with ethics left its stamp on all the philosophies of the Hellenistic period – the Academy, founded by Plato, the nearly allied Peripatos of Aristotle and his successors, and Stoicism; he sketches their doctrines in ethics and science as well as epistemology, the subject in hand. This account could well serve as an introduction to a reader new to philosophy. (Handbooks giving such material on the history of the Schools were common in Greek.)

On the whole in the *Academica* Cicero moves through the complicated arguments with impressive clarity, though there is some fairly tough going. He was distinctly proud of his achievements; he told Atticus that there was nothing like his work even in Greek. 'My very clever books', he called them, and spoke of his care to be accurate as well as stylish. It is fairly plain that no Greek sources are being slavishly followed.

It seems to have been more or less simultaneously that Cicero was at work on the *De Finibus Boni et Mali,* or *On Supreme Good and Evil,* which he dedicated to Brutus. Ethics had been from the start his ultimate objective: 'the most essential part of philosophy', as he called it in the *Academica.* Again, he was primarily concerned to show 'what each philosopher has said and what has been said against him'. He began with the doctrine that to his mind was the easiest both to understand and refute – Epicureanism. He introduced the School, which he had not discussed in the *Academica*, and declared his opposition to its scientific and logical, as well as its ethical doctrines. Its atomic theory, he objects, is unoriginal, and the uncaused swerving of some of the falling atoms which is meant to allow for free will is ludicrous; the ideas that there are innumerable identical worlds, and that the sun is only about a foot across, are incredible; and Epicurean logic is amateurish and lacking in rigour. Cicero insists that he is not biassed against Epicurus by his lack of style: 'he expresses his meaning, and is clearly understandable'; and he establishes his right to expound the doctrine, having studied it in youth. He lets a character describe at length and reasonably fairly Epicurus' view that the most naturally desirable thing in life is pleasure, but that this does not involve crude hedonism, rather a régime of simplicity, virtue and (of course) detachment. But in the second book, in his own person (in a passage carefully marked as exemplifying the Socratic method of cross-examination), he complains that this ought not really to be called pleasure at all. Epicurus was better than his doctrine. And he refuses to allow that virtue is to be sought only for its practical advantages. This indeed was the aspect of Epicureanism that really stuck in Cicero's throat; he even called it disgraceful.

In Book II Cato is given the opportunity to develop the Stoic belief that what we naturally desire is virtue, and this is enough to make men happy. But again Cicero has objections. Stoic ethics may start their argument from Nature, but they end with the unnatural Stoic paradoxes, the wise man eschewing all emotion and totally denying the power of everything disagreeable. In the last book the eclectic and partly Peripatetic views of Antiochus, which Brutus is said to approve, are put forward. Desire for knowledge and action are said to be among man's natural instincts as well as desire for virtue; and though material goods and bodily advantages are less important than virtue for the happy life, they cannot be totally ignored. Though Cicero in his own person again strikes a Sceptical note, these views of Antiochus are not refuted at length. It might have been as well to question the presupposition of the whole argument, that following Nature will lead us to the happy life; but the slippery concept of Nature was not something that Cicero ever examined critically; nor, unlike Plato, did he ever struggle with the problem of the fundamental nature of virtue.

Next in the cycle came the *Tusculan Disputations* or *Conversations at Tusculum*. These are slightly different in character from the preceding works. After the end, the means: the five books teach their readers to despise death, endure pain, moderate sorrow, avoid other disturbances of mind, and believe that virtue is sufficient for happiness – a doctrine that the *De Finibus* had in fact doubted, but that is here described as the glory of philosophy. The style is frankly rhetorical; this is the sort of 'declamation', or rhetorical practice, Cicero says, that he makes use of in old age with his friends and pupils. It is made agreeable by frequent quotation from the poets (often translations from the Greek made by Cicero himself) and by vivid anecdotes. Atticus found all this easier going, and re-read the first book at least for comfort. It is indeed the most attractive part of the work. Cicero wastes no words on the fables of punishment in hell; no one now believes in them, and the Epicureans are losing their time in combating them. The only real alternatives are that the souls, at least of the wise, are divine and will rise to heaven; or that there is no life after death at all. The former is what Cicero argues, and hopes; he does not assert it. He speaks 'not as Delphic Apollo . . . but as one petty man out of many'. In either case, what is there to fear? And Cicero dwells on the peaceful and contented ends of Socrates and Cato.

Of all his philosophical works the *Tusculan Disputations* is, one feels, the one Cicero wrote most for himself; the most sensitive and emotional of beings is trying to persuade himself into the serenity of the Sage, into independence of the fears and hopes, the pain and grief, that had racked him for so long. The death of his daughter, he admits, showed him as less than such a Sage; and he reminisces about his other vicissitudes. But philosophy is 'the medicine of the soul', and its haven of refuge. He still rejects the extravagances of the Stoics, but it is clear how greatly their ideal impresses him: 'I fear that they alone will turn out to be true philosophers'. He dismisses the view of Aristotle that the passions, properly harnessed, are useful; no – anger, grief, sexual love, fear, all are despicable. And he adheres to the old theory of Plato, taken further by the Stoics, that reason, the intellectual part of the soul, can subdue the passions, which, since they are irrational, are also unnatural for man. Such a strongly intellectualist ethical theory could only commend itself to an élite: 'virtue does not easily accompany tardy minds'; but even of that élite it demanded too much, and many found themselves betrayed in the last resort by the philosophy on which they had placed their dependence. It was no wonder that religion was to be summoned increasingly to the aid of mankind.

With the work *On the Nature of the Gods* (*De Natura Deorum*), Cicero moves on to theology, which he treats, as was usual in his time, as a branch of 'physics', or study of the natural world. It is quite independent of epistemology or ethics; there is no divine revelation to tell us either what is, or what we ought to do; rather theology is closely linked to astronomy and cosmology. And this is partly because, however fine the substance of which the gods were made was thought to be, there was little attempt to conceive of them as immaterial.

Do the gods exist? If so, how and where? And do they care for mankind? These are the questions that the interlocutors – the dialogue is again set in Cicero's youth – take up. This time too the Epicurean begins, expounding 'with confidence, as that school always does' his happy gods, with no interest in man, who live in the interstices of the innumerable worlds and can be adored without fear. The speaker weaves in a lively if often prejudiced account of early systems from Thales on, with their bewilderingly inconsistent theological beliefs, and attacks Plato and the Stoics. Why should God suddenly create the world, as Plato held? How could He actually *be* the world, as the Stoics declared? The divinities of both schools, he argues, are too far from what we ordinarily mean by the word 'god', which he supposes to reflect an innate human conception. Cotta (who had been suggested by Atticus as a suitable person for the Academic role) has little difficulty in showing, with a welcome breadth of reference to Egyptians who worship animals, and other peculiar races, that such an innate idea does not exist. It is ridiculous to suppose that the gods are in any way anthropomorphic: not having human functions, how can they need human organs? And how, pray, can Epicurus' gods be happy if they are idle (it was a belief of Aristotle's that happiness is activity) or good if they are not beneficent (Roman morality, as we know, was based on reciprocal obligations)? If they are made of atoms, of however special a type, how can they be immortal? Cotta concludes that Epicurus was really an atheist, but did not dare to admit it, and maintains that his views have proved a destructive force in society.

Next comes the Stoic, Lucilius Balbus (no relation of Caesar's friend Cornelius Balbus), who reasserts the existence of the gods. Belief in these has grown, rather than declined, with advancing civilization; and they have intervened in history, by prophecy and other means (the Stoics believed in divination). Fundamentally the Stoic view is pantheistic; the world, the universe itself, since fire or heat is the principle of life in all nature, is divine, and it exercises a providence over mankind. Balbus reaches this conclusion by some sophistic arguments designed to prove, for example, that the world as a whole must be rational, since parts of it are so. But there are other gods as well; the motion of the heavenly bodies must be voluntary, and themselves therefore conscious. Cotta also discusses the other forces, ideas and persons that men have called divine, rejecting the myths but attempting to find the gods' true nature from the meaning of their names, an unconvincing but typically Stoic practice. He makes much of the argument from design in propounding the divinity of the world. Nature, he claims, works so reasonably and perfectly that it must be sentient; and Cicero here writes some passages of great splendour, if excessive length, on the beauty and rationality of the universe as it was conceived in his day, when the earth was the centre around which all else revolved. How could the Epicureans' fortuitously colliding atoms produce such a pattern?

And let us first behold the earth as a whole, placed in the centre of the universe, a solid mass formed into a globe by its own pressure on all sides, clothed with flowers and plants, trees and crops, their innumerable multitudes marked with inexhaustible diversity. Add to these the ever-flowing coolness of springs, the watery transparency of rivers, the deep green that robes their banks, the hollow depth of caves, the ruggedness of rocks, the overhanging loftiness of the mountains and the illimitable expanse of the plains; add too the hidden veins of gold and silver, and the unending strength and abundance of marble. Think of all the different species of animals, both wild and tame! Think of the birds, of their flight and their song! Of the pasturing cattle, of the life of woodland creatures! What then need I say of mankind? Who have been as it were appointed the tillers of the soil, and do not suffer it to be laid waste by monstrous beasts nor made barren by rough brambles, and by whose industry the plains, the islands and the shores shine bejewelled with houses and cities. Could we see these things with our eyes, as we do in our minds, no one viewing the whole earth could doubt of the divine reason.

And from the earth Cicero moves out to the moon and the stars that encircle it, and moves too from heightened prose into verse – his own verse, the translation of the astronomical poem of Aratus made in earlier years and now, in the age of the 'new poets', Catullus and the rest, probably as unfashionable as his philosophy. But there can be no doubt, for those who can read this passage in the original, that it is in prose that Cicero comes nearest to true poetry.

Cotta, to whom the Sceptic's role falls again, declares that 'as a Cotta and a priest' he accepts the religion of his forefathers; he certainly speaks also for his author, consular and augur as he was. But Cotta is ready to argue that the Stoic arguments are, as arguments, unconvincing. Much of his case is lost, whether by chance or the design of pious scribes, and it seems that his (or his source's) arguments do not correspond perfectly with those of Balbus. It is clear that he stressed the wickedness and confusion also to be found in the world, as well as making hay of the Stoic attempt to derive knowledge of the gods from wild etymologies of their traditional names (if you try to derive Neptune from *natare*, to swim, you are more at sea than he is). Finally the participants disperse; to the Epicurean, Cicero says, Cotta's arguments appeared convincing, but to me those of Balbus 'seemed closer to resembling the truth'.

The works *On Divination* and *On Fate* are supplements to *On the Nature of the Gods*, dealing with questions that Cotta had there passed over rapidly. In these subsidiary areas Cicero firmly rejects the Stoics' case. In the first of the two, in spite of one or two merely agnostic remarks, he comes out firmly and perhaps courageously against all forms of divination. 'I thought I should be doing myself and my countrymen a great service if I could root out superstition'. This is not, he insists, the destruction of religion; he appeals again to the beauty of the world and the order of the heavens as proving the existence of some kind of divine reason, and insists that religion and science, which help us to understand that world, are closely linked (science, to him, as to nearly all the ancients, is little more than the contemplation of nature).* Superstition, which prevents all tranquillity of mind, besieging us every instant with apparent hopes and fears, is something very different (and ancestral practices, which should be allowed to persist, are different again).

Cicero is not arguing, it must be understood, against the old wives' beliefs that he held unworthy of his steel, but against the Stoics, most of whom accepted many, or all, forms of divination – as above all his own contemporary Posidonius did. These forms can be divided into artificial, based on the pseudo-scientific systems of interpretation such as haruspicy (the study of entrails), augury or astrology, and on the other hand natural, i.e. direct prophesying by dreams and visions. Quintus Cicero is this time his brother's victim; he begins by supporting the Stoics, but later relapses into the Peripatetic position, that natural divination, in which the soul is in direct contact with the divine, is alone true. Many of Cicero's arguments – drawn from Carneades, who, he says, saved the honour of philosophy on this issue, and from the eclectic Stoic Panaetius – are directly anti-Stoic: for example, Cicero claims that the Stoics' views on divination are incompatible with their belief in predestination. If all is pre-determined, how can they define divination as foreknowledge of what happens by chance? Cicero is a bit cavalier with predestination, but he is to come back to it in the book *On Fate*. He fastens next onto Quintus' refusal to explain *how* artificial divination is possible: it is true that there are some inexplicable connections in nature – that of the moon with the tides, the magnet with the iron – but how can a beast's heart possibly have anything to do with finding a treasure? How can the position of the stars at the instant of one's birth have more influence on one's whole life than heredity and local climatic conditions? Quintus had

* Compare Arthur Young in the eighteenth century: 'the *undevout* astronomer is *mad*'.

listed numbers of successful prophecies. As well as complaining that he wants arguments, not examples, Cicero insists that most of these are or may be fictional. Of course a few will come true by chance, but few do; the astrologers all prophesied that Crassus, Pompey and Caesar would die in their beds (Cicero was writing shortly after the Ides of March). He also points out that no one learns useful things like the answers to scientific or artistic problems, or how to read, or what course of action is morally right, from divination (the gift of tongues would not seem to be a claim he had met). And he insists that it is unworthy of the gods to imagine them as communicating with men in such ridiculous and obscure ways: as so often his moral and aesthetic sense strongly influences his intellectual beliefs. He also points out from his experience of Asia in particular how contradictory the various forms of augury and haruspicy are; and that it is particularly ludicrous to say either that we choose a beast with entrails relevant to our case by some special sympathy, or that at the moment of the beast's death the gods dispose the innards suitably, making a heart, for example, disappear altogether. His chief contempt, however, is reserved for astrology, in his time an exotic, un-Roman and newish doctrine: 'what incredible madness – for not all errors should be described as mere folly.' Natural divination is treated with less contempt, but no less decisiveness; possibly physicians can tell something about a man's health from his dreams; any other significance is most unlikely. But Cicero's spirited struggle against his countrymen's superstition was doomed to failure; it was as vain to try to drive back the rising tide of belief in the occult as it was to rebuild the Republic.

The work On Fate, or De Fato, is now very fragmentary; it is a dialogue between Cicero and Hirtius, and examines the problems of free will and determinism that have exercised philosophers in many periods. Hirtius will have been flattered at the dedication, but it is hard to suppose him able to cope with predestination. Here, using Carneades once more, Cicero attacks the Stoic belief in Fate, often in a singularly modern way, as for example when he argues that to insist on the truth of a future event is not to assert the necessity of determinism but simply to explain the meaning of words. He holds that the Stoics have confused different meanings of 'cause', and that while environment and so on may influence our propensities, they cannot bind our will.

Just before and after Caesar's death Cicero wrote the two sympathetic essays *Cato on Old Age* (this is the elder Cato, the famous Censor) and *Laelius on Friendship*, which he dedicated to Atticus, who shared his experience of both. Cicero was not unaware of what the philosophers had written on these questions; but these little works are very much his own. In both he evokes with pleasure, and for the last time, his beloved second century and the age of Scipio Aemilianus. In the first, using Cato's own works for details, he shows, like a true Roman aristocrat, how the old may find occupation and duty in books and agriculture, in teaching the young and advising the state, and are recompensed for the pleasures of youth by the enjoyment of *auctoritas* – a wistful note, here, perhaps. They will not lose their mental powers if they exercise them; but they must accept the course of nature. In the second, he rejects the view that friendship is based on utility, insisting rather on the community of opinions (ancient intellectualism again?) and desires – necessarily virtuous ones – that unite its true practitioners. He describes affection and goodwill as the one true joy of life. The philosophers might approve this; but Cicero had also found it to be true.

The summer of 44 also saw the lost work *On Glory* and the start of the work *On Duties* or *De Officiis*, which he addressed to his son, now struggling with philosophy at Athens. His father wished him, he said, to know Academic doctrine as well as that of his Peripatetic master, while by studying philosophy in Latin as well as Greek he would improve his command of the language. As it turned out, Marcus was to be spared the series of further works with which his father threatened him.

The *De Officiis* professes to draw on the Stoics, especially Panaetius, but not to follow them too closely. Indeed, much of the discussion is concerned with practical questions, as a complement to the theoretical ethics of the *De Finibus* perhaps. Roman conditions, and Cicero's own experiences, clearly underlie it. Panaetius gives Cicero his framework: duty is, of course, seen as action in accordance with Nature, here a man's particular nature as well as human nature in general, for the moderate Panaetius had not concerned himself with the Ideal Sage. But Panaetius is cricitized for omissions; above all, he never fulfilled his promise to discuss the apparent conflicts of the right and the expedient, and his successors' treatment of the matter did not satisfy Cicero, who therefore embarked 'with his own forces' on filling the gap. This he does in the not very well argued, but perhaps unrevised, third book, which maintains – quite dogmatically! – with a mass of illustrations from Roman history and the rhetorical schools, that since virtue is the only desirable thing, as the Stoics held, or at least far the most desirable, as the Peripatetics believed, the right and the expedient can never conflict, though sometimes it may not be clear what is really right. The culminating example is that of Regulus, who returned to torture and death at the hands of the Carthaginians rather than save himself by advising what would be against Rome's good. Cicero consistently agrees with those Stoics who favoured a high, even a quixotic, level of generosity, even where others of the school had been more legalistic.

The *De Officiis* also gives us Cicero's last word on various politicians – the greedy Crassus, Caesar the destroyer of liberty – and on various aspects of political life at Rome, such as the corrupting expenditure on games, the need for the politician to care for all classes, and the State's conservative role in protecting property. Throughout the work, his belief is that the first of all duties is that to the State. This is based on the conviction that all men are naturally linked by social feeling, the highest of the four cardinal virtues to which human nature is naturally drawn; as a result we have some duties even to foreigners and slaves. Here again is the classical view that the virtues are natural to man. It was to weaken, among the writers on politics, as well as those on ethics and metaphysics, in the more pessimistic centuries that followed – centuries in some ways psychologically subtler, but often credulous, repressive and morbid.

14

CAESAR'S LAST MONTHS
45-44 B.C.

The letters of the months before Caesar's death show that Cicero's attention was not only directed towards philosophy. In May 45 he was reading Hirtius' answer to his own *Cato*, which he thought gave him some inkling of the way Caesar would treat the subject. Since Hirtius' work praised the literary skill of Cicero's, he told Atticus to publish it widely. Atticus was a little doubtful; and Cicero defended himself rather weakly by arguing that these people's abuse would win Cato greater glory, and that he himself would be glad to see Hirtius' talent recognized, but his thesis laughed at. Later on came news that Caesar said he had learnt eloquence from Cicero's work, but Brutus' *Cato* made him think, by comparison, that he possessed it; and his own violent attack on his dead enemy reached Rome.

Atticus meanwhile tried to persuade his friend to write an essay of political advice to Caesar, as a mark of respect and co-operation. Cicero obediently got out the approved literary models, the letters of Aristotle and others to Alexander. 'But where is the similarity? They were writing what was honourable for themselves and acceptable to Alexander. Can you think of anything of that sort? Nothing occurs to me.' However, he produced a draft, which Atticus was all for sending off, and Cicero thought for a while it would do. 'There is nothing in it unworthy of a loyal citizen – loyal as the time allows – and all political theorists say we should bow to *that*.' But he insisted on putting it up to Oppius and Balbus first, and they turned it down. 'They were frank, and I am grateful that they did not conceal their opinion, and especially for wanting so many changes that there is no point in my rewriting it'; it was all flattery even as it was, he said: had he been giving genuine advice there would have been no problem. The whole thing was unnecessary, and Caesar might have thought it a sop for the *Cato*. The trouble seems to have been Cicero's demand that Caesar should reorganize the constitution before leaving on the Parthian campaign he was planning;

though it was in fact what he was said at this time to be proposing to do.

Atticus wanted a revision; but 'about the letter to Caesar, upon my oath I cannot do it; it isn't the disgrace that deters me, though it emphatically ought . . . but I cannot think of anything'. Let us hold our tongues and be at least half free, he said. After this Atticus gave up; but Cicero toyed for a while with the idea of a political dialogue set well in the past, in Greece at the time of the destruction of Corinth in 146. He bombarded his friend with requests for historical information. 'Please dig out for me, from somewhere, who were Mummius' Ten Commissioners: Polybius doesn't name them. I remember the consular Albinus, and Spurius Mummius; I think I have heard Hortensius mention Tuditanus. But in Libo's *Annals* Tuditanus became praetor fourteen years after Mummius was consul; it doesn't fit at all.' There was a good deal of discussion, with a looking-up of old senatorial decrees, which illustrates the historical scrupulosity of both men, in certain contexts at least. 'How hard you work! You look after these matters, you arrange my affairs, and are almost as diligent about your own business as about mine!' But the dialogue too fell through. Atticus also urged that something should be written for Dolabella, who was on very friendly terms with his ex-father-in-law at this time; something general and political would be suitable, thought Cicero. A little later he did write a eulogy of Cato's sister,* recently deceased, as several other friends did, and he seems to have considered publishing a collection of his letters, of which he kept copies, now in Tiro's charge. Such a carefully selected and polished anthology as he clearly envisaged would have been of far less value to us than what we actually have.

By mid-May Cicero had, by a great effort, resolved to return to Tusculum, where Tullia had died.

I shall, I think, conquer my feeling and go on from Lanuvium to Tusculum; for either I must go without my place there forever (for my grief will be the same, only less visible) or else I don't know what difference it makes whether I go there now or ten years hence. Nor will the reminders be stronger than those which torment me perpetually day and night. 'What,' you will say, 'does learning do you no good?' In this matter I am afraid it does the opposite: I should perhaps have harder nerves without it.

---

* Not his half-sister Servilia, alive and well.

A little later he wrote, 'I shall find Tusculum more convenient since I shall receive your letters more often and sometimes actually see you: otherwise it was more bearable at Astura, and it is very true that the things that chafe me do hurt me more here; but wherever I am, they are with me'. Soon Atticus visited him, and this was a comfort, but Cicero was depressed again when he left. By the end of the month, however, he was writing more in his old style and reproaching Atticus for going ahead alone with the reading of a new book on the rarefied subject of Greek accentuation.

The letters of this time deal mostly, and elliptically, with private and business affairs; Cicero complains repeatedly that he has only trifles to occupy himself with (in this class he includes his philosophic works: if he had not thought of writing these, he says, he would not know what to do with himself). We may quote some paragraphs of a letter of early June as a sample.

You have done right about the aqueduct. You may find I do not owe any column tax; although I think I heard from Camillus that the law has been altered.

What better reply can we make to Piso than Cato's desolate condition? And not only for Herennius' co-heirs, but also, as you know (for you discussed it with me) for young Lucullus: the money was borrowed by Cato as guardian – for that is relevant too – in Greece. But he is acting like a gentleman in saying he will do nothing against our will. So as you say, we shall decide when we meet how to arrange the thing. You were very right to meet the other co-heirs.*

You ask for my letter to Brutus, but I haven't the copy. However it is safe and Tiro says you should have it; and I remember, when sending you his letter blaming me I enclosed my answer to him. You will see that I get off the nuisance of jury service.

News of young Marcus, now on his way to Athens with a considerable retinue, was not very satisfactory; or rather there was little news – he seems to have omitted opportunities to write. News of young Quintus was worse. 'Asinius Pollio has written to me about our villainous nephew; he says quite openly what the younger Balbus recently made pretty clear, and Dolabella hinted at. I should be upset if there were room for new grief.' Quintus was trying to turn Caesar, with whom he was in favour,

---

* Atticus and Cicero may have been guardians to Cato's son, who appears to have owed money to Lucullus' son and to one Herennius, whose estate had now passed to Piso (the consul of 58?) and others.

against his uncle and, to a lesser degree, against his father too; this last fact may have assisted a certain *rapprochement* between the brothers. If we are tempted to feel a sneaking sympathy with a clever young man trying to escape the smothering influence of his distinguished relative, we ought also to remember that disloyalty to the elders of one's family, though by no means unheard of, was very seriously regarded among the ancients, and that Dolabella soon reported something so bad that 'if the whole army did not know about it I would not dare to write it myself, let alone dictate it to Tiro' – and it has in fact been cut out, perhaps by Atticus.

More cheering news was that of a large legacy from a rich businessman of Puteoli. Cicero proposed however, it seems, to turn over much of the property to Quintus, who was in straits for money again; he cared nothing himself for wealth now, he said, since he had no one to leave it to (so much for poor Marcus!). This consideration facilitated the divorce from Publilia, which Atticus arranged this summer. 'Let me know what people say about it. "As if the public cared for that!" No, I don't imagine they do; that farce is finished.'

The outside world sometimes broke in. Cicero noted distastefully that a statue of Caesar had been set up in the temple of the deified Romulus, and with pleasure that another, carried in procession with those of the other gods, had evoked no applause. An impostor claiming to be Marius' grandson, who had amassed a following, wrote asking Cicero, as a relation, to defend him. Cicero politely declined, pointing out that Caesar was a relation too. But on hearing that the brother of the King of Cappadocia was coming to Rome, he felt it necessary, owing to his previous connection with the court, to ask him to stay. 'I suppose he wants to buy some kingdom from Caesar, for as things are he he has not a foot of ground of his own.' But the prince had made other arrangements for his visit, doubtless to Cicero's relief. Others were gathering in preparation for Caesar's return. One who never reached Rome was the recently pardoned Marcus Marcellus; instead, there came news that he had been murdered at the Piraeus by an associate in a fit of madness. Servius Sulpicius, who happened to be at hand, wrote Cicero a vivid account of how he had found the party's camp in disorder, most of the slaves fled in terror, and how he had arranged the funeral at the Academy and ordered a marble monument.

Brutus however returned from his governorship in Gaul, causing Cicero a good deal of flurry. One reason seems to have been that he had divorced his wife, the daughter of Appius Claudius, and a new marriage would inevitably be a political step. Cicero took a sudden interest in the movements of Brutus' mother Servilia, and was probably pleased when he chose his cousin Porcia, the daughter of Cato and widow of Bibulus. But in the circumstances he and Brutus were not attuned in mind, and Cicero left Tusculum towards the end of June partly to escape the frequent visits that Brutus, who was staying in his own house there, felt it proper to make, and partly to arrange new leases for his farms at Arpinum. At Arpinum he felt cut off from Atticus and 'while I am pursuing streams and solitudes to make life more bearable, I have not yet put a foot outside the house; such heavy and unceasing rain are we having'. Still, he found the place soothing, and could work there. He was gratified by the success of his speech for Ligarius, which Atticus had given a great send-off, probably by having it read aloud at a dinner party of important persons; Oppius and Balbus 'like it amazingly' and had sent it to Caesar. But he promptly decided that such triumph was unphilosophical, and tried to disclaim it. He was frankly annoyed, however, when Balbus took a copy of part of the *De Finibus*, and Caerellia one of the whole, from Atticus' scribes, before it had been revised or had reached Brutus, its dedicatee. (Caerellia was an elderly lady whose correspondence with Cicero, said to be gossipy and undignified, we would wish to have survived.)

Young Quintus was also on his way home. To Cicero, now back in Tusculum, there came a letter which began 'most insultingly, but perhaps he didn't stop to think', with the words, 'I myself, whatever ugly things can be said against you . . .' (though intimating that its writer did not agree with them) and complaining that no notice had been taken of his desire to hire a house in Rome – because, so his father explained, he could not stand his mother. To her however he wrote in most dutiful terms. 'What incredible frivolity.' Quintus' machinations were the more alarming, in that Cicero had also incurred the hatred of one of Caesar's hangers-on, the musician Tigellius. But too much anxiety was unnecessary, for most of the Caesarians were friendly enough: 'for that matter, as you know, these people are more my slaves that I am theirs, if politeness is servility.' Ultimately Quintus' relatives consulted together and decided to overlook his aberrations if he would marry and settle down. But his father went to meet him in so angry a state of mind that Cicero himself tried to pour oil on the waters. In Rome however the young man continued on his course.

The younger Balbus is here. Absolutely no news, except that Hirtius has been defending me fiercely against Quintus, who is at it everywhere, especially at dinner parties, and when he is done with me comes back to his father. His most convincing charge is that we are thoroughly disaffected from Caesar, we are not to be trusted, indeed I am even to be feared; it would be alarming if our monarch did not know I have no courage. Also that my son is being bullied, but he can say that as much as he likes.

Brutus, who had gone north again to meet Caesar on his return from Spain, had tried to intervene with Quintus. He himself was affectionately received by Caesar, who promised him the praetorship for next year and the consulship thereafter, and presumably approved of his marriage. Brutus wrote that Caesar 'had joined the *boni*'. Cicero commented sourly that he did not know where Caesar would find them, unless he first hanged himself, and that such credulity was unworthy of Brutus' descent (the fact that Brutus could count among his ancestors Lucius Brutus, who led the overthrow of Tarquin the Proud, the last King of Rome, and also a later tyrannicide, was soon to become a matter of some moment).

Cicero finally succeeded, again on Atticus' urging, in writing to Caesar, if only about his *Anticato*. 'I sent a copy to Oppius and Balbus, and wrote to them to send it on to Dolabella if they themselves approved of the work.' It passed these censors, and Cicero assured Atticus that he had been able to write 'without flattery, but what I think he will read with the greatest pleasure'. He really had admired the book, he said; but after Caesar's death he called it an impudent work.

Caesar's advent was now apparently imminent, and Cicero was worrying about how far he should go to meet him, and with whom he could stay. But here the series of letters to Atticus breaks off. Caesar did not actually enter Rome till his triumph in early October, a triumph that caused much bitterness, since however veiled in name it had been won in fact over citizens. There was a demonstration by a tribune that angered Caesar greatly. Cicero was more dispirited than ever about politics; he wrote that things were being done that even Caesar disapproved of. But he himself was not entirely inactive in public affairs, being summoned more than once by Lepidus, the Dictator's Master of Horse, to take part in senatorial or augural duties ('I suppose he wants augurs for the consecration of the temple'). Vatinius, old enemy and recent friend, wrote from Illyricum to ask for support in getting a thanksgiving for his victories (in return he would look for a slave who had absconded after stealing valuable books from Cicero's library). Cicero also made a short formal speech on behalf of his and Pompey's old ally King Deiotarus of Galatia, who was accused of having attempted to assassinate Caesar in the East. In spite of compliments to Caesar, Cicero had the courage to animadvert on the irregular circumstances of the investigation, with the accused absent and Caesar, both judge and intended victim, hearing the case in his own house; and he also praised Pompey openly. Not that this last could be thought foolhardy; a few months later Caesar allowed his old enemy's statues to be restored, one of the few acts of the period which Cicero rose in the Senate to praise. He sent a copy of the speech for Deiotarus to Dolabella, calling it deprecatingly a minor work.

Cicero had, too, to do his duties as a patron, and there are a number of letters from this year recommending provincial, especially Sicilian, acquaintances to their governors, or intervening with officials responsible for the division of land to Caesar's veterans and colonists. He took particular trouble for the town of Buthrotum, near Atticus' estate in Epirus, which was in danger of losing its lands. Cicero delivered a petition to Caesar, with whom he was dining, and received a promise to exempt the Buthrotans if they paid their arrears of tax; Atticus advanced the money, but it was worrying that Caesar intended to put off telling the assembled colonists that they would have to go elsewhere until they had left Italy. His death was to leave Atticus and Cicero still much exercised over the affair. Such episodes show that Caesar was still gracious to Cicero; indeed, after his death Cicero admitted that the Dictator had been amazingly patient with him. And it is probably in these last years that Caesar paid him the most splendid of compliments, writing that it was a greater thing to have advanced the frontiers of the Roman genius than to have done the same with the frontiers of Rome's Empire.

In December both men were in Campania, Caesar perhaps visiting the veteran colonies, and Cicero wrote, it is not certain from which of his villas, the famous letter about having Caesar to dinner, which it is impossible not to quote in full:

What a troublesome guest! I don't regret it though, for it was very pleasant. But when he arrived at Philippus'* place in the evening of the second day of the Saturnalia, the villa was so full of soldiers that there was scarcely a room free for Caesar himself to dine in. Two thousand men, in fact; and I was very anxious about what would happen next day. But Cassius Barba came to my aid, and posted sentries; the camp was in the grounds, the villa was set with guards. *He* stayed with Philippus on the third day of the Saturnalia till one o'clock, admitting no one – accounts, I think, with Balbus. Then he went for a walk on the shore; after that he had a bath. That was when he heard about Mamurra;† his face did not change. After anointing he lay down to dinner. He was on a course of emetics, so he ate and drank freely and with enjoyment. It was a splendid meal, elegantly served, and not only that but

cooked and flavoured well,
And with good talk – why, most enjoyable.‡

His entourage were generously entertained in three other dining rooms. The humbler freedmen and slaves had everything they wanted – the grander I entertained in excellent taste. In short, it was clear I knew how to do things. But my guest was not the sort to whom one says, 'Do pray come again when you are back'. Once is enough. We did not talk of serious matters, but a great deal about literature. In fact, he enjoyed himself and was pleased. He said he would spend a day at Puteoli, another at Baiae.

Now you know about a visit, or a billeting, which as I said was troublesome but not disagreeable. I shall stay here for a short time, then go to Tusculum. When he was passing Dolabella's villa, and nowhere else, the whole armed force rode on either side of him. This comes from Nicias.§

By this time, preparations for the coming Parthian campaign were beginning to dominate the horizon. Young Quintus said gloomily that he must go on it. ' "Why must you?" I said, "Debt," he said, "and yet I haven't even got my travelling expenses." Here I borrowed some of your eloquence: I held my tongue.' Quintus went on to say that he was sorry his uncle Atticus was angry with him; he would put things right by doing what he and his mother wanted – marry. ' "I think you should do it before

* The husband of Caesar's niece, who was the mother by an earlier marriage of C. Octavius, later known as Octavian and then the Emperor Augustus.
† Complaints about this follower of his?
‡ A quotation from the satirist Lucilius.
§ A Greek scholar, a friend of Cicero and Atticus; what he reports was meant perhaps an honour to Dolabella.

you leave; then you will please your father too." "I will do as you advise," says he. So ended our dialogue,' concludes Cicero drily.

But there were more important reactions to the prospect facing Rome than those of Quintus. Caesar had tied up the magistracies for years ahead in preparation for his absence; he had enlarged the Senate, including in it a few partisans who claimed, but whom conservative Romans thought unworthy of, the honour — sons of freedmen, centurions, Gauls. And on the last day of December a dramatic event showed how little concern he had for the forms of government compared with a desire to reward his adherents. In the morning it was learnt that one of the consuls was dead; Caesar promptly had a successor elected for a single afternoon.

So in the consulship of Caninius nobody had breakfast. However, no crime was committed in that period; the consul's vigilance was so great that during his entire term of office he never closed an eye. You may laugh, for you are not on the spot; if you were here to see it, you could not help weeping. And if I were to tell you the rest? There are countless things like this.

Cicero was credited with other jokes on the same occasion: Caninius' consulship was like Epicurus' atoms, too small for the naked eye; could Caninius remember in whose consulship he was consul? But he also wrote, 'You cannot conceive the shame I feel at living in Rome now.'

It is understandable; he did not dare, or think it worth while, to vote against the increasingly extravagant honours pressed on Caesar by a Senate largely consisting of his creatures; only Cassius and a few others did that. Some of those heaping privileges on Caesar may have been wanting to make him unpopular; others may have believed that the loyalty of a by now heavily Hellenized populace could best be focused on a figure royal and divine, like the rulers of the East (in fact the People does not seem to have been wholeheartedly for Caesar at this time). What Caesar himself ultimately intended is not clear;* had he, at least, in adopting in his will his great-nephew Octavius, been dreaming of leaving his position to a successor? He rejected a few of the wilder honours, and disclaimed the name of king, when some of the

---

* If we accept the account of the imperial historian, Dio, Caesar was possibly aiming at becoming an Eastern-style king. But Cicero, who is our only contemporary source, while making it clear that he had accepted divinization, pretty plainly did not think that he intended to take the title 'king', which he can ascribe to him only by extension or metaphor.

people greeted him with it. But he clamped down on the tribunes who arrested those responsible, caused offence by failing to rise when the Senate as a body waited on him, and showed that he was determined to have the substance of permanent power. In the new year we find him not only consul but *dictator perpetuus*: Dictator for life. The very essence of the traditional Roman dictatorship had been its brief term. His portrait appeared on the coins, the first time that of a living Roman had done so. There could be no illusions now; the matter of a royal title could only be a further irritant. At the ancient festival of the Lupercalia on 15 February Caesar was sitting on the Rostra, in the wreath, the purple toga and the golden chair recently voted him, when Antony, his colleague as consul, thrice offered him a diadem, the white headband of Persian and Hellenistic kings. Caesar refused it, ordering it to be taken to Jupiter on the Capitol. It may be that he had staged the entire scene to drive home his refusal of the title; if so, it was a miscalculation – some insisted on believing that Caesar would have accepted if the crowd had applauded, and Cicero, who had probably watched the scene, could even say later that Antony's action made him the real murderer of Caesar. Wild rumours circulated; that there was an oracle saying that only a king could defeat the Parthians, and that a proposal to give Caesar the name would be moved in the Senate; also, probably, that Caesar had met evil portents when sacrificing. It seems that Caesar's megalomania – his belief in his own Fortune, to put it in Roman terms – and his undoubted contempt for the Roman political system had led him too far, and that events then got out of his control. He knew he was hated. One day Cicero went to his house with a petition, and was kept waiting a long time; not the treatment a Roman consular was used to. Caesar noticed it, and said to a friend, 'Can I doubt that I am detested, when Marcus Cicero has to sit waiting instead of having access to me at his convenience? And if anyone is easy-going it is he. But I have no doubt that he hates me bitterly.' This story was told to Cicero after Caesar's death.

The pressure on Brutus to emulate his ancestors was apparently becoming intense; there is no reason to think that Cicero joined in it, but Plutarch speaks of anonymous messages, and the austere and forceful Cassius, abandoning his Epicurean detachment and his belief that Caesar was a tolerable master, is said to have urged on his brother-in-law. But if Brutus had been slow to become disillusioned with Caesar, his fundamental beliefs were not in doubt. He had said, in Pompey's time, that it was possible to live honourably without ruling others; without liberty for oneself one could not live at all. The Empire, then, was nothing to him; the Republic all. Tyrannicide was generally applauded in the ancient world; what honours and rites, what hymns and invocations to the famous tyrant-slayers of the past he had seen in Greece, Cicero once remarked; and the Romans had their own parallel tradition. The closer the tyrant was, by blood or friendship, to the assassin, the greater the latter's merit. In comparison with his destruction of the aristocracy's liberties, the great reforms, especially the public works, that Caesar planned or was credited with planning – the draining of the Pomptine marshes, the digging of the Corinth canal – weighed as nothing; or rather they were signs of the tyrant's *hubris*; and did not Aristotle maintain that it was the very mark of a tyrant to embark on such works to keep the people busy and enslaved?

The conspiracy was headed by Marcus Brutus and Cassius, who were both praetors; and by Decimus Brutus (a distant cousin of Marcus, much favoured by Caesar, in whose will he figured), Trebonius and others holding office under Caesar. It included men from both sides in the Civil War. Marcus Brutus refused to allow anyone to be touched except Caesar himself; a decision which might prove that philosophic tyrannicide is not a practical doctrine. The meeting of the Senate on 15 March – the Ides of March – three days before Caesar was to leave Rome, was to be the place. It is possible that the setting was partly chosen to reflect the story that the senators tore Romulus to pieces when he became an oppressive ruler. Cicero was not invited to join the plot; he was clearly too old, too nervous. But he had had a great part in keeping alive the sentiment which inspired the conspirators. He was in his place in the Senate on the Ides.

The scene he witnessed is familiar to us all from Plutarch's account, which Shakespeare follows closely. Caesar nearly did not come; he was unwell, his wife begged him to stay at home (perhaps Calpurnia really did have bad dreams; there were rumours and suspicions all about). But the greatly trusted Decimus Brutus persuaded him to appear. The consul Antony, whose loyalty to Caesar was as undoubted as his physical strength and courage, was detained outside by Trebonius. A body of gladiators had been posted near by. The rest of the conspirators surrounded Caesar on the excuse of begging for a friend's pardon; on his refusal a sign was given, daggers were drawn, and Caesar was repeatedly stabbed till he fell. Did he really exclaim at Marcus Brutus' part, or is this one of the ironies of the rhetorical historian, no more to be believed in than the prodigies that we are assured foretold the event, the apparitions that squeaked and gibbered in the Roman streets? But Cicero himself noted that the Senate was assembled in an annexe of Pompey's theatre, and even that Caesar fell at the base of Pompey's statue.* And it may be true, since both Cicero and Antony later asserted it, even if in a rhetorical context, that Brutus raised his dagger and called on Cicero's name, congratulating him on the restoration of liberty. Indeed, his prompt endorsement would be well worth having. But it may be that he fled, as most of the other senators disastrously did, before Brutus was able to address them at any length. Caesar's body, as Cicero again attests, lay long in the hall, where no one dared to approach it. The Liberators, as they were to call themselves, then tried to calm the People in the Forum, and one source tells us that they continued to call on Cicero's name. There could be no doubt of his reaction, even if a brief surviving note of congratulation to one of the conspirators was not written on this occasion, as some scholars believe; and before night he went up to take counsel with Brutus and the others, who had occupied the Capitol.

A personal friend of Caesar's was to say to Cicero a little later, 'If Caesar with all his genius could not find a way out, who will do so now?'

---

* A brief account of the scene at *De Divinatione* II 23, perhaps written only a few weeks after the event, is in fact our earliest source.

15

THE ATTACK ON ANTONY
44 B.C.

The fifteen months or so from the Ides of March to the summer of 43 are far and away the best documented in all Roman history; the correspondence here numbers over 200 letters and includes communications from, as well as to, many leading actors in the drama. In addition, Cicero's public utterances are represented by the thirteen *Philippics*, all delivered either to the Senate or the People between autumn 44 and spring 33 (except the famous second, perhaps published in pamphlet form). They mark most of the important stages in the struggle against Antony. Furthermore, Cicero's preoccupations in late 44 are reflected to some extent in the theoretical works on which he was then engaged. Finally, the imperial historians treat the supreme crisis, and the entry on stage of Octavian, the future Emperor Augustus, in considerable detail; and they had much evidence to go on, though of varying quality and all too often partisan or apologetic tendency. Two of the works they used, now lost, were by men active in the events they wrote of, and, it is worth noting, not sympathetic to Cicero. One is the autobiography of Augustus himself, and the other the famous history, praised in an ode of Horace, by Asinius Pollio. Pollio we have already met, giving Cicero news of young Quintus in Spain; a Caesarian, later notorious for his provocative and outspoken behaviour under Augustus, he governed Further Spain in 44–3.

On the Capitol, Cicero advised the Liberators to summon the Senate, presumably to the temple of Jupiter Capitolinus. Since Brutus and Cassius were praetors, Brutus indeed the senior or 'urban' praetor, on whom constitutional initiative devolved in the absence of the consuls, and since Antony the surviving consul had fled, this proceeding would have been legal enough. And of course it was of the utmost importance to get an immediate declaration that Caesar had been a tyrant, perhaps a public enemy. Cicero never doubted that his advice had been right; though Antony might have countermanded a meeting if it were not to take place at once – and meetings after nightfall were not legal. The conspirators however, whether from timidity, scruple, or because too much time had passed, decided instead to negotiate with Antony, an act with which Cicero said later that he had refused to have anything to do. It is not certain whether he was already declaring that Antony should have been killed too—he undeniably thought so later. It is also not certain whether he was right: there was some reason to think Antony might be approachable, and killing a consul, even one irregularly appointed, was not at all the same thing as killing a *dictator perpetuus*; it would be unlikely to conciliate respectable opinion.

But the Liberators' omission, or inability, to take any real action at all was fatal. During what must have been for many a sleepless night, Lepidus, Caesar's Master of Horse, brought his troops into the Forum, directly below the Capitol, and probably declared himself at the consul's orders; and Antony seized Caesar's papers and private treasury. On the 16th he, as consul, summoned the Senate to meet on the following day. The temple in which it met was well surrounded by veterans. Initiative had passed into Antony's hands. But he used it for a compromise. All Caesar's laws and decrees were to be approved – and thus Antony's own office confirmed – but the assassins were to be spared. The Liberators were still on the Capitol; but Cicero spoke in support, recalling the famous Athenian amnesty after the restoration of the democracy in 403 B.C. He told Atticus subsequently that he only did so because the cause was already lost.

It is not easy to be sure what Antony's intentions really were. The man was a natural soldier, skilled and daring. According to Plutarch he was at his best in a crisis and extremely popular with his troops, whose hardships and whose jokes he shared, whose love-affairs he furthered, and whom he inspired by his flamboyant Asianic oratory. He was flamboyant also in his generosity and in his way of life. His pleasures – drink, women and the company of actors – never ruined his splendid constitution, and indeed in his recently discovered portrait he looks 'as strong as a gladiator', as Cicero called him, but they did at times distract him from his ambitions. Some historians, in a praiseworthy attempt to get away from seeing the period after Caesar's death solely through the eyes of first Cicero and then Augustus and his propagandists, have tried to rehabilitate Antony as a genuine moderate, later driven into violent courses by the Liberators' intention to seek armed support in the provinces. They point out that to confirm Caesar's arrangements *en bloc* was the only way to keep Italy, the veterans and the provinces quiet, and that the supremacy of the Liberators would have alienated many of the Caesarian party and probably ensured civil war. But it is possible to see Antony's moderation as only a means – a means of keeping both Liberators and Caesarians quiet while he set about laying the foundations of a military and popular dictatorship (without the name). After all, violence on 16 March could only have benefited Lepidus – it was his troops who would have had to apply it. Soon Lepidus (with the acquisition of the high priesthood) had gone off to his provinces of Nearer Spain and Gaul. Meanwhile Antony, having insisted on a public funeral for Caesar and the public reading of his will which made generous benefactions to the People, worked these up to a frenzy of regret and abstained from restoring order until Brutus and Cassius had been forced to flee from Rome and their duties there. And so Antony was left in control – unchallenged except by young Dolabella, who had been promised Caesar's consulship when Caesar left for Parthia, and who calmly assumed the vacant office on the Ides of March. Some of the Liberators, notably D. Brutus and Trebonius, went off to their assigned provinces too; and Cleopatra, to Cicero's joy, soon 'fled' home to Egypt.

Cicero himself, clearly feeling impotent, left Rome for the country and the coast, at the usual season. We now begin to know more of his reactions, for he wrote as usual almost every day to Atticus, even if this meant dictating during a dinner party or writing in a boat. Among the instructions and queries about business affairs there are complaints of the continuing unsatisfactory behaviour, both public and private, of his nephew Quintus, who was disrespectful alternately to his father and mother and who proclaimed that for the future he looked to Antony (later there was a total volte-face, which did not impress his uncle at all). There are also frequent, touchingly affectionate messages to little Attica. And there are numerous inquiries and comments on politics.

Cicero reported that the country towns were delighted by the death of Caesar. He was fearful of the unrest in Gaul which the late Dictator's friends were gloomily prophesying, and which wild rumours attested; but this did not materialize, and at first Cicero was inclined to think that Antony cared more for his dinner parties than public affairs. But soon he revealed himself as bitterly discontented with the course of events and much alarmed by the consul's behaviour. The tyranny has survived the tyrant, he writes repeatedly: Caesar's arrangements are all in operation, his partisans in possession of the country villas of old Pompeians – and are we even to have the magistrates that he appointed for the next two years?

O my dear Atticus, I am afraid that the Ides have given us nothing but joy, and satisfaction for our hatred and grief. The reports that are brought me from Rome! and the things I see taking place here! . . . you know I love the Sicilians, and think it an honour to be their patron . . . but here is Antony taking a vast sum of money to stick up a law 'carried by the Dictator in the Assembly' which makes the Sicilians Roman citizens. There was nothing about this in Caesar's lifetime. And what about our friend Deiotarus, is that case not similar? He deserves indeed to have any kingdom you like – but not to get it through Fulvia.

(Fulvia, the widow of Clodius and Curio, was now Antony's wife; she was one of the forceful ladies with whom he was surprisingly prone to get involved.)

Antony was in fact collecting money assiduously, and not only from the bribes of oriental potentates and others; as well as Caesar's private treasury he had appropriated the cash reserved for the Parthian War, which was stored in the Temple of Ops or Wealth. His control of Caesar's papers gave him immense powers of patronage; the gift of citizenship to Sicily looks like vote-catching on the grandest scale (and Cicero's conservative conviction that a non-Italian, mainly Greek-speaking area should not be enfranchized will have been widely shared; in fact the measure did not come into operation). And towards the end of April Antony was touring the veteran colonies and drumming up support from them. Cicero found that these things also alarmed his old Caesarian friends Hirtius and Pansa, who now, as consuls designate for the next year, had gained an adventitious importance. (They had also taken up again their lessons in oratory with him 'so I get no rest even at the seaside; it's my fault for being too easy-going'.) But he was not very optimistic when, a little later, Brutus and Cassius, who had provided themselves with a bodyguard of young men from the country towns and were staying on their estates south of Rome, begged him to win Hirtius over. Was he to make Hirtius sound by dining with him? he grumbled; nonsense – all that lot want war. He reported after one such dinner that 'the text they repeat is that a very great man has been killed, the whole state thereby thrown into confusion, that we would undo his *acta* as soon as we dared, and that his mercifulness had been his undoing'. We may doubt if they wanted war, but they had no love for the Liberators. Hirtius said that he 'feared violence from our side as much as from Antony; both had good reason to keep a force to protect them, but he feared both'. Later he wrote begging Cicero to see that Brutus and Cassius took no action and did not leave Italy, but waited quietly till Antony's year of office had run out. Cicero thought that these two, with whom he was in fairly close touch, had no plans at all, and like himself only wanted peace. He believed, for one thing, that 'no one, or only such as might be easily defeated' would follow Brutus, who had little military experience and no pull with Caesar's veterans, in a new civil war. Nonetheless there is no doubt that he and his friends had their eye on Decimus Brutus, the one Liberator with an important army and province, who was busy strengthening his position in Cisalpine Gaul, and also on Pompey's younger son Sextus Pompeius, who was reported to be again at the head of a force in Spain. So Antony could give some plausibility to a claim that he was acting in self-defence.

During this period Antony was conspicuously polite to Cicero. He wrote effusively to ask his permission before recalling from exile a henchman of P. Clodius. Cicero wrote back, equally effusively and entirely insincerely, that he had no objection in the world. And Antony was also polite to Brutus and Cassius, though they communicated with each other by means of public edicts. What everyone needed was time. For one thing, what would be the policy of Caesar's heir? During his lifetime Caesar had brought forward his young great-nephew Octavius, and in his will he adopted him as his son. The eighteen-year-old Caesar Octavianus (as he was called by those accepting the adoption) had just returned to Italy from Macedonia. His intellectual ability and delicate health were doubtless apparent to all; Caesar had perhaps seen signs of the extraordinary patience, political skill and ruthlessness with which, in spite of never becoming much of a soldier, he was to make himself gradually master of the Roman world. Cicero met him, perhaps not for the first time, in April: 'Octavius is here with me; he is most polite, most friendly. His own people call him Caesar; Philippus [his stepfather] does not, so I do not either. I do not believe that he can be a good citizen: so many surround him who threaten death to our friends and say the situation is not to be borne'. But even if Octavian was not going to approve the Liberators, he was likely to appear as a rival to Antony, especially as the latter was sitting on all the money left by Caesar. What, also, of Dolabella? In Antony's absence from Rome at the end of April Dolabella came forward as a champion of the republicans by throwing down a column erected to Caesar's memory in the Forum which was the focus of a cult in his honour. Cicero was delighted, and thought that here was a possible leader at last and Rome would soon be safe for Brutus again, especially as the poorer classes did not resent Dolabella's act. Cicero wrote off enthusiastically to encourage his ex-son-in-law and establish his own position as adviser, or 'Nestor to his Agamemnon'. Atticus was more cautious and reminded his friend that Dolabella still owed him money; and the affair fizzled out.

Cicero intended to come back to Rome for the meeting of the Senate on 1 June, because he had business to do there for Atticus (the Buthrotum affair was pressing). But he was now playing with the idea of going right away afterwards. 'From the preparations I see being made, I judge that the Ides achieved little. And so I think more and more every day of Greece. For I don't see how I can help dear Brutus, who as he writes himself is thinking of exile.' He wanted primarily to see how his son was getting on in Athens. He several times asked Atticus to see that the boy was generously provided for, for the sake of his father's rank as well as his own convenience. But Marcus' news was not wholly satisfactory; one of his tutors wrote cautiously that he was doing well 'at present', and one for a long time did not write at all. However there did come several encouragingly lengthy and stylish letters from Marcus himself. The latter point was an important one to his father, whose letters to his son seem frequently to have taken him up on his use of language. None of these survive, and from Marcus only one to that tactful intermediary, 'dearest Tiro', not only congratulating him on acquiring a small property, but expressing regret for 'the errors of my age' and implicit obedience to his 'kindest and dearest father' and to his command to dismiss a Greek teacher of rhetoric who had been regarded as leading him astray; with a reassuring account of his present blameless way of life, and a request for a secretary to copy out his lecture notes. Friends passing through Athens also reported back reassuringly to Cicero, among them Trebonius, on his way to his province of Asia but apparently thinking of literature rather than war. And 'on this subject I am easily cheated and willingly show myself credulous', wrote Cicero. But he still wanted to go to Greece. Sometimes he half hoped thereby to get right out of the way of the civil war that might come. He knew that this time he would not be allowed to remain neutral – he was too compromised with Brutus and the Liberators, and the temper of the times was bitterer than it had been five years earlier; he knew too that life in camp suited his temperament as little as ever, and his present age even less.

In fact he was hopelessly undecided as to what he should do. The political situation, he thought, changed every hour. At this point there was some idea that Brutus should return to Rome and address the People. Atticus wanted Cicero to write him a speech, but Cicero, doubtless correctly, thought Brutus would be offended. However, Brutus did want advice, which Cicero felt he could not give. Nor, he found, could he improve the elegant but chilly oration which Brutus had made to the People on the Capitol, and now sent to be criticized before publication. 'He has achieved in this speech with perfect taste the manner he prefers and the style he thinks best for oratory. I, rightly or wrongly, have aimed at something else. You will tell me what you think yourself,' he went on to Atticus, echoing his arguments in the *Orator*, '. . . but if you recall the thunders of Demosthenes you will see that it is possible to be at once thoroughly Attic *and* impressive'. Atticus thereupon suggested that he should write a version of the speech as he would himself have given it – another suggestion vetoed on grounds of tact.

Cicero now began to be anxious about coming back to Rome, since the city was full of soldiers. Hirtius for one decided not to go to the Senate on 1 June, and advised Cicero not to do so either; Varro sent on a letter, the signature erased, warning all opponents of Caesar that the veterans would be dangerous. Cicero decided that, as he would clearly not be free to oppose Antony, he had better keep out of Rome; it is to be remembered that so distinguished and senior a consular would have to speak at worst in second or third place in the Senate, and his position was thus very exposed. He now took the step of asking both consuls for a legateship, under which he could conveniently go abroad (a senator may have needed such special permission), and accepted that offered by Dolabella.

On, probably, 2 June, by legislation that was irregular because due notice had not been given, violence was used, and a thunderstorm made the assembly ill-omened, Antony passed not only an agrarian law, calculated to please the veterans and the poor, but a bill exchanging his prospective province of Macedonia for Cisalpine Gaul, leaving him however the troops now in Macedonia, which consisted of the legions Caesar had made ready for the Parthian War. His intention was clearly to dispossess Decimus

Brutus. Cicero had earlier said that this would mean war; but nothing seemed likely to happen immediately – Antony had to get the legions to Italy, for one thing, and might not try to take over Gaul till his consulship ran out. Marcus Brutus and Cassius were still acting cautiously; they had dispersed their bodyguard of young men from the country towns on Antony's advice. Shortly after this the Senate, under Antony's influence, commissioned them to purchase corn in, respectively, Asia and Sicily. What a humiliation to have to accept anything from such a quarter, thought Cicero, and especially such paltry posts; but perhaps it was better than sitting idly on their country estates. He still did not think he had any suggestions to make. 'Brutus follows his mother's advice, and entreaties too; why should I intervene? But I will consider what kind of letter to write to him.' He was prudent to fear to tangle with the redoubtable Servilia, who was still a power in the political world, as a visit which he paid to Brutus a few days later, and described in a well-known letter, showed.

I arrived at Antium before mid-day. Brutus was glad to see me. Then in front of various people, Servilia, dear Tertia [Brutus' sister and Cassius' wife] and Porcia [Brutus' new wife], he asked what I thought. Favonius was present too [the old ally and imitator of Cato's, sometimes known as Cato's Ape]. I argued, as I had been planning to do on the way, that he should take the Asian corn commission, as there was nothing now left to us to do but to see that he was safe; for in this lay the protection of the state itself. When I had embarked on this speech, Cassius came in. I repeated my views. Hereupon with a determined look – you would say he was breathing battle – Cassius said he was not going to Sicily. 'Was I to accept an insult as a favour?' 'What are you going to do then?' I asked. He replied that he would go to Greece. 'What about you, Brutus?' I said. 'To Rome,' he replied, 'if you agree.' 'Indeed I don't; you would not be safe.' 'If I were, would you advise it?' 'Yes, and that you should not go to a province either now or after your praetorship; but I will not be responsible for your entrusting yourself to the city.' I mentioned the reasons, which will no doubt come to your mind, why he would not be safe. After this they complained at great length, especially Cassius, that opportunities had been lost, and blamed Decimus severely. I said that they should not go over the past, but I agreed. When I began to speak of what should have been done (I said nothing new, but what everyone says every day) without entering on the question whether anyone else should have been touched, but saying that the Senate should have been called, the People which was burning with zeal stirred up more vigorously, the whole state taken over, your friend Servilia burst out, 'Well, I never heard anything like this!' I checked myself. But it seemed to me that Cassius would go abroad – for Servilia promised to see that the mention of a corn commision should be removed from the decree of the senate – and our friend Brutus quickly dropped his foolish talk of wishing to be in Rome. He decided therefore that his Games should be held in his name without him. He seemed to me to be intending to set out for Asia from Antium. In short, nothing pleased me in this journey of mine except the feeling that I had done my duty. It would not have been right that he should leave Italy without my seeing him.

One notes Cicero's sublime unconsciousness of doing exactly what he had just told his friends not to do in talking of the past; no wonder Servilia was annoyed. One also notes that, Antony or no Antony, the Republic was working much as usual, if a great lady could get a senatorial decree altered after the event.

By now there were fears that Sextus Pompeius might invade Italy from Spain, and Cicero had become sufficiently decided on going to Greece – decided at moments, that is, and provided his financial affairs could be straightened out first, and provided people didn't disapprove too much – to start worrying about his journey. If the Macedonian legions were going to land at Brundisium, he had better avoid the place. But what about pirates, if he took the longer sea-route from Western Italy? Travelling with Brutus might be a protection. What were the dates of the Olympic Games, and of the Eleusinian Mysteries, at which he hoped to be present? Would Atticus be coming over in the autumn? Should Cicero himself be back for 1 January, when new political initiatives might be expected? Atticus seems to have been as undecided as Cicero and even more nervous for him. Cicero wrote to Tiro that 'my dear Atticus, because he knows that I used to be liable to sudden terrors, thinks it is still the same, and does not see that I am walled about with the protection of philosophy; and indeed, being timid himself, he falls into a panic'. He added that he had no intention of quarrelling with Antony. A little later he and Atticus met briefly and Cicero wrote afterwards, 'I am sorry that, as you tell me, you shed tears when you had left me . . . but I am glad that the thought that we shall meet shortly consoled you. It is indeed what chiefly supports me. My letters will not fail you.' It is very clear that there were only two ties that now bound Cicero to Italy, Atticus' affection and his own delight in 'those jewels of Italy, my little country houses'.

Nonetheless he was still not happy about leaving; he protracted his departure in order to keep the question open as long as possible. He moved gradually south, hearing and commenting on news as he went and especially anxious about others' reactions to his plans. Sextus Pompeius in Spain appeared to be disbanding; what were the latest developments in the Buthrotum affair? How shocking that the games to be given in Brutus' name were advertised for July – the new-fangled name given to the month Quintilis in honour of Caesar; it had much distressed Brutus. Young Quintus came as far as Campania with his uncle, in order to be personally reconciled with Brutus. Cicero had no faith whatsoever in this reformation, and wrote to Atticus to take no notice of the laudatory letter that he would entrust to the young man himself. But Quintus did give enough evidence of a change of political heart to catch it from Antony (whose financial irregularities he perhaps proposed investigating) in a manifesto. He next seems to have tried to attach himself to Octavian, but he was to be proscribed with the other members of his family a year later. A late source suggests that he made amends for his volatile career by refusing under torture to betray his father's whereabouts; one would like to believe it.

As for Brutus, Cicero wrote, 'he is not so eager to have me as his fellow traveller to Greece as I thought'. He decided that he must be home by the new year. He was writing, and planning writing, as he travelled; and discovered when coasting down south-west Italy that he had sent *On Glory* to Atticus (to be read aloud at his dinner parties) with a preface that he had used elsewhere; he composed a new one on ship-board and sent it off: 'please cut that one off, and stick this one on'.

At the very last minute he turned back. He had indeed actually reached Syracuse, but adverse winds drove his ship back to Italy. He then heard that there had been a meeting of the Senate on 1 August, that Brutus and Cassius had asked consulars and ex-praetors to be present and said that there was hope of an agreement with Antony, and that his own absence was being criticized. Atticus too had changed his mind and wrote that Cato would not have approved of Cicero's departure – an argument likely to move him. It emerged further that Caesar's father-in-law Lucius Piso had attacked Antony in the Senate, which suggested that there was hope of detaching some of the Caesarians, though Cicero, over-pessimistic as often as over-optimistic, had never believed in the possibility; and it must have been bitter to him to find his old

enemy taking up a struggle that he himself seemed to be avoiding. On his way home Cicero again met Brutus, who showed himself delighted at this new decision; he had been respectfully con-
cealing from his senior a conviction that it was wrong to visit the
Olympic Games at this juncture. He openly praised L. Piso. But
Cicero insisted to Atticus that he was not going home to take part
in politics, as Brutus hoped. 'For what can be done? Did anyone
support Piso? Did he even return to the Senate next day?'

In this Cicero was a bad prophet of his own actions; and perhaps he knew it, and was writing primarily to reassure Atticus.
Must he not have felt as though fate had intervened to bring to
nothing his desperate efforts to escape so that he must perforce
play his part in the crisis that all summer had been threatening
to break?

In order to understand the situation that faced him, we must
recall the different forces in the political world that autumn. There
was Antony, with his consulship and four splendid legions, on the
point of arriving in Italy. There were the Liberators, who could
only count, for immediate support, on D. Brutus' two legions in
Cisalpine Gaul, though several minor provinces were in the hands
of members of the group or sympathizers; while Pompeian remnants, especially Sextus Pompeius and his troops, might be
expected to join them, and M. Brutus and Cassius, if they decided
to take bold steps, were likely to achieve striking results. For
Cassius might well be able to win over the army in Syria, where
he had once commanded with success, while Brutus had political
influence and connections in the East. Then there was Octavian,
aged only eighteen but the legal heir to Caesar's name and fortune (heir also to some of Caesar's closest advisers, including the
inseparable Oppius and Balbus) and rapidly gaining favour with
plebs and veterans. Next, Lepidus with an army in Nearer Spain,
and Dolabella now on his way to Syria, two of the few surviving
great *nobiles*, were independent politicians, though Lepidus had
cooperated with Antony after the Ides, and Dolabella, as Cicero
believed, had now been bribed into doing so. Finally, the consuls-
designate Hirtius and Pansa, and also L. Piso and many others,
were reasonably respectable ex-Caesarians who had no sympathy
with the Liberators, but had come to distrust Antony and were not
particularly close to Octavian. They numbered no heroes among
their ranks (and Hirtius was seriously ill all autumn). Most of the
Senate, as it was to turn out, sympathized with them or with the
Liberators, but it naturally included some Antonians.

In this situation coalitions would have to be made. Cicero's importance lay not only in his seniority and prestige but in the fact that he was on fairly close terms with several of the groups, all of which had taken care to be scrupulously polite to him of late. He must have seen from the first that any opposition to Antony in Rome would have to be based on the dissident Caesarians, who might include the coming consuls. It must be for this reason that, having just got back to a great welcome in Rome, he refused to be present in the Senate on 1 September, on the pretext of exhaustion. Antony was to propose honours to the memory of Caesar. Clearly Cicero could not support these, but to oppose them might alienate the Caesarians. Antony was furious at Cicero's absence; so furious that it is possible that he had thought of the occasion as a trap. Next day, however, in Antony's own absence, Cicero delivered the speech later known as the first of his *Philippics*, in reference to Demosthenes' orations rousing Athens against Philip of Macedon. It was a very clever piece of work; personally mild in tone, it took up Piso's criticism of 1 August, and represented Antony's actions as not only unconstitutional, but also unpopular with the People and in disaccord with Caesar's intentions. It is clear to whom all this was addressed. Only one consular dared to speak in Cicero's support; but Antony's violent reaction shows the significance he laid on the speech.

Cicero wrote a little later that it was impossible to attend the Senate safely, and that there was no kind of law or freedom in the State. But that he was readier than he had been throughout the summer to take some kind of action is suggested by this and other letters, which however despondent are aimed at stiffening the fibre of republican provincial governors, some of whom were having to deal with emissaries from Antony who attempted to displace them. Soon there was news of Pompeian or pro-Liberator movements in the East, and Cicero's hopes were raised. On 19 September Antony, having according to Cicero taken lengthy counsel with his wine-pots, attacked him in the Senate with a violence no doubt well within the Roman tradition, but which necessarily meant that they were henceforth *inimici*, formal enemies. Cicero was again not present. The charges that Antony made can be reconstructed from the *Second Philippic*, that masterpiece of invective which could not be delivered, or even published at once. It appears from this that Antony blamed Cicero for all the political disasters of the last twenty years. He accused him of instigating the murder of Clodius, the quarrel of Pompey and Caesar, above

271

all the assassination of the latter; he claimed that he had irritated and alienated Pompeians, Caesarians, everybody. He was clearly trying to isolate Cicero, especially from the Caesarians. In the Senate he still spoke respectfully of the Liberators, particularly of Brutus; in a speech to the People a little later he represented himself as implacably hostile to them.

Cicero, much alarmed, wrote to Cassius, who was still in southern Italy, that Antony was seeking an opportunity for slaughter and had made the allegation of responsibility for Caesar's murder in order to stir up the veterans. All he, L. Piso and the third outspoken consular could now do, he went on, was to make it obvious that Antony would not let them speak freely. The only other consulars with any authority were ill or absent; and so all hope lay in Brutus and Cassius. It should be noticed that Cicero now seems to be assuming that they will be taking active measures in the provinces. Later he wrote that Antony was going from bad to worse, and certainly intended to avenge Caesar's death. He was much upset that measures had been taken to impede a legate of Cassius' on the grounds that he was leaving to assist a public enemy.

Meanwhile he must have been working on the *Second Philippic*, which rebuts Antony's charges and paints an unforgettable, if unreliable, picture of their author's violence and dissipation. The famous peroration strikes a more solemn note; it is worth quoting even in the pale reflection of a translation.

Remember for once, I beg you, Mark Antony, the State; think of your ancestors, not your associates; do with me as you please, but with the State make your peace. But that is your affair; I shall speak for myself. I fought for the Republic when I was young, I shall not abandon her in my old age. I scorned the daggers of Catiline; I shall not tremble before yours. Rather I would willingly expose my body to them, if by my death the liberty of the nation could be recovered and the agony of the Roman People could at last bring to birth that with which it has been so long in labour. Almost twenty years ago in this very temple I said that death could not be premature for one who had reached the rank of consul; how much more truly must I say it now that I am an old man. For me indeed, fathers, death is even desirable, after all I have attained and accomplished. I have only two wishes, one that at my death I may leave the Roman People free – the immortal gods can grant me no greater boon than that; and secondly that each citizen may prosper according to his deserts towards the Republic.

Cicero himself, still unharmed but still uncertain what to do, was back by late October in his seaside villa at Puteoli, consoling himself with the *De Officiis* or *On Duties*. Its insistence on the necessity of putting private friendship and enmity below duty to the State is perhaps significant of present tensions. For the main objection to any alliance of Caesarians and Liberators was the Roman stress on personal loyalties. Was it not the Caesarians' duty to take vengeance on the Liberators? Was it not, above all, Octavian's?

Indeed only a few weeks before Cicero had read a moving statement of the supremacy of personal ties. C. Matius was a friend of Caesar's whom Cicero had always respected; but he had raged through the spring and summer at Matius' grief for Caesar's death and his prophecies of disaster, and only recently been persuaded into a grudging epistolary reconciliation. To him Matius replied in a famous letter:

I know the charges people have been piling up against me since Caesar's death. They blame me for lamenting the death of a friend and being angry at the fate suffered by a man I loved; for they say country should come before friendship – as though they had already established that his death had been to the public advantage. But I will not make clever points; I confess I have not reached that level of philosophy. It was not Caesar I followed in the Civil War, but a friend; I did not like his acts, but I would not desert him.

He pointed out that he had gained neither wealth nor office from Caesar's victory – unlike others; and he had done his best to save lives – as Caesar had used his power to do. 'What unheard-of arrogance, to let some glory in their deed, but others not even grieve freely! even slaves have always been allowed to fear, rejoice and feel grief at their own choice, not another's; and this freedom those "authors of liberty" as they call themselves are trying to deprive us of by terror.'

These quiet words deserve to be set beside Cicero's peroration; and they may well make us feel unease at Cicero's triumph in the death of a man he had long known, whom he had praised so highly and from whom he had received such benefits; while it is right to be reminded that admirable men could feel very differently from him. But when Matius went on to say that his political views had always been proper ones, and that his recent assistance to Octavian in giving games in Caesar's memory, and his familiarity with and support of Antony, had had no political aspect, Cicero might have had a case for calling him irresponsible; for these actions had political effect.

K   273

During the autumn came exciting rumours, via Servilia, of Brutus' and Cassius' welcome in the East. It was also the period of Antony's brief reconciliation with Octavian, forced on them, significantly, by the veterans; when it collapsed, with Antony accusing Octavian of an attempt on his life, Cicero, who was now, sad to say, hardened to the idea of political assassination, regretted, and said that all the *boni* regretted, that it had not succeeded. Octavian, he thought, was a promising youth; but there was nothing to be hoped for in politics, for Antony was off to Brundisium to fetch the legions from Macedon, which he intended, Cicero feared, to win over with gifts of money and bring to Rome 'as a yoke for our necks' (more probably they were intended for use against D. Brutus). He reassured Atticus that he would be cautious, he would not take the lead; and he went on to write of his literary plans. He was thinking of leaving busy Puteoli for Pompeii, 'not that anything is more beautiful than this place, but there would be fewer tiresome interruptions there'. But on 1 November, before he could move, there arrived an astonishing epistle from Octavian, who had won over many of the veterans settled in Campania by a huge donative and seemed to be preparing to fight Antony; he wanted Cicero's support and proposed a secret meeting. 'That at least is childish, to think it could take place secretly. I showed him in a letter that it was unnecessary and impossible.' Octavian's emissary told Cicero that Antony was marching on Rome with one legion, exacting money from the towns he passed,

and he asked if Octavian should go to Rome with 3,000 veterans or hold Capua and block Antony, or go to the other Macedonian legions, now marching up the Adriatic coast, which he hopes will be his; for according to him they refused a bounty from Antony, insulted him, and left him standing when he tried to address them. In short he offers himself as a leader and thinks I should support him . . . In fact, I advised him to go to Rome; I think he will have the city rabble on his side, and if he can make them believe in him, the *boni* too. Oh Brutus, where are you? What an opportunity you are missing! I didn't prophesy this, but I thought something of the sort would happen.

And then the usual problem. 'Shall I come to Rome or stay here? Or flee to Arpinum – the place is a safe refuge? I think of Rome, in case I'm missed there, if it appears that anything has been achieved. Tell me the answer. I was never in a greater quandary.'

Octavian wrote again and again, begging Cicero to go to Rome and saying that he wanted to act through the Senate. Cicero replied that the Senate would dare to do nothing before the new year.

I don't trust his years; I don't know what he's up to; I don't want to act without your friend Pansa. I'm afraid that Antony is in a strong position, and I don't want to leave the coast, and I fear something great may be done in Rome with me away. Varro disapproves of the boy's project; I don't. He has a strong force. He can have D. Brutus on his side . . . I see war is on us. Please answer this.

In spite of his anxieties, Cicero was still able to discuss his literary work with Atticus; and after a while he seemed to have 'taken his own advice' and made up his mind to go to Rome. 'I had rather be there and useless than not there when I am needed, and I was afraid of being cut off from the city. I had rather be with you than away from you, worrying about us both.' However, having started on his journey he fell into a panic that Antony would catch him on the Appian Way, and turning off it he bolted to Arpinum – alas, forgetting the great peroration to the *Second Philippic*, which he had doubtless written with total sincerity, and forgetting also the philosophy that he had optimistically told Tiro now walled him round. He stayed at Arpinum for some time, still anxiously demanding advice by every letter-carrier. He was alarmed by reports of Octavian's thoroughly Caesarian speech to the People in Rome, and uncertain whether his power would really be preferable to Antony's. He wrote that he had

told Oppius, who urged me to embrace the youth, his whole cause, and his band of veterans, that I could not possibly do so unless I was convinced Octavian would show himself not only no enemy, but actually a friend to the tyrannicides. When he replied that he would do so, I said, 'What then is the hurry?' He doesn't need my aid before 1 January, and we shall see what his intentions are before the Ides of December, over the question of Casca [the tyrannicide who would, unless prevented, have entered on his tribunate by that date].

Meanwhile, Cicero distracted himself with the *De Amicitia*, as a present for Atticus, who had recently written that the little book on old age was a comfort to him. Cicero also wrote that he was now eager to undertake, with Atticus' aid, the history that he had so often been urged to embark on. But the book on friendship was to prove the last of his works, apart from letters and speeches. It is suitable that this swan-song, charming if not very profound, should be dedicated to Atticus, and that it should be set once again in the period that had so often proved Cicero's inspiration, that of the younger Scipio, and in the mouth of the perfect friend, Scipio's devoted Laelius.

At last, on 9 December, Cicero got himself to Rome, largely, he said in the last surviving letter to Atticus, owing to the urgency of his own financial affairs (as in 48, the expectation of war had made money tight, and he was finding it difficult both to pay his debts and get paid what he was owed). As for the Republic, 'even Hippocrates forbids medical treatment in hopeless cases'. By this time Octavian had been forced by his army's unwillingness to face other Caesarian veterans to retire to Etruria, where he reinforced his troops. To his joy, two of the Macedonian legions declared for him (and he also captured the army's elephants). When Antony marched north, after extracting expressions of loyalty in Rome, it was not to deal with Octavian, since his remaining troops were also unwilling to fight him, but to take over Cisalpine Gaul from Decimus Brutus, before the year should end and the new magistrates intervene by denying the legality of the law granting him this province. Cicero wrote more than once to Decimus, urging him in only slightly veiled language to resist Antony in spite of the lack of orders from the intimidated Senate, and to welcome the support of Octavian and his forces. He pointed out that Decimus was committed twice over, once by his part in the Ides of March and again by having already raised fresh troops. What effect these letters had we cannot know. But on 20 December the tribunes, since both the consuls were away, summoned the Senate, which filled up, so Cicero claimed, with expectant *patres* once he was known to be there. For an edict of D. Brutus had arrived, declaring that he would keep his province and putting himself and his men at the disposal of the Senate and People. Thus it was impossible to wait for January. The *Third Philippic* persuaded the Senate – perhaps a less crowded and representative body than Cicero claimed – that Antony's act was one of civil war and that Octavian and his army must be recognized: D. Brutus and all other governors were told to keep their provinces till further notice (which incidentally confirmed the dubiously loyal Lepidus in Nearer Spain and Southern Gaul). The Senate would not go so far as Cicero wanted and declare Antony a public enemy, though in the *Fourth Philippic*, his report to the People, Cicero argues that what it had done came to the same thing. But he was exhilarated by his achievement: 'I have laid the basis for a constitution.' After his long months of hesitation he was at last wound up for decisive action.

A modern historian has called this treason to the legal head of the government. But this is to oversimplify. Cicero believed that a consul should cooperate with the Senate; and the law giving Antony Gaul was irregular – though most laws were that, these days. He believed also that Antony was a tyrant rather than a consul, and that right is more important than law, or rather is law – that slippery doctrine that the *Philippics* explicitly repeat. We know that this was a belief that Cicero had long held; but we may admit that it was a dubious 'basis for a constitution'.

16

VICTORY AND DISASTER
43 B.C.

The next six months were the heroic period of Cicero's career, his *aristeia* as the Greeks would term it. Perhaps they seem the more consistently heroic because we have much semi-official correspondence to and from him, but no intimate letters, and because the later *Philippics* are mostly brief and at their best achieve a concentrated eloquence that does indeed recall the force and urgency of Demosthenes.

On 1 January 43, with Hirtius and Pansa at last consuls, the Senate met in the Temple of Jupiter Capitolinus, with an armed guard to protect it. Pansa began, from Cicero's point of view, unpropitiously, by calling first on his own father-in-law, Fufius Calenus, who had been a commander and consul under Caesar and was a man whom Cicero thoroughly disliked, but to whom he had perhaps been recently – and grudgingly – reconciled. Calenus was a friend of Antony and duly proposed negotiating. Cicero replied in a speech that he worked up into the *Fifth Philippic*, pouring scorn on the idea as inconsistent with the decisions of 20 December and fatal to morale and preparations in Rome and Italy. He insisted again on the irregularity of Antony's behaviour and especially of his June legislation, and on the greed for money and land of his disreputable followers; the suggestion that he might be given Transalpine Gaul was insane; rather the ultimate decree should be passed at once and an amnesty given to those abandoning Antony's camp. The question of rewards for the loyal commanders and soldiers was also on the agenda. Cicero praised Decimus Brutus, but probably for the moment dared do no more for one of Caesar's assassins; Lepidus was to be given a statue as a reward for making peace with Sextus Pompeius; Octavian, 'this heaven-sent youth', was to be recognized as holding a command of praetorian rank, given a seat in the Senate, and allowed to stand for office early. Some of these favours were not wholly unprecedented, though for the Senate simply to co-opt a member was very odd, and indeed Cicero's comparatively modest proposals were outbidden by others.

At the end of his speech Cicero gave, rashly, a personal guarantee that Octavian had sacrificed personal ties to patriotism. 'I promise, I undertake, I engage, conscript fathers, that C. Caesar will always be such a citizen as he is today, and as we should particularly wish and pray him to be.'

The honours were passed without difficulty, but over the declaration of war and the embassy the debate raged for three days. Pansa and L. Piso seem to have supported Calenus; Fulvia and the rest of Antony's family probably entreated for approval; and on the fourth day, apparently on the motion of Servius Sulpicius, the Senate agreed to send to Antony, though with demands resembling an ultimatum. The three envoys, all senior consulars, were to be L. Piso, L. Philippus (Octavian's stepfather) and, much against his will and in spite of his poor health, Sulpicius himself, who took Cicero and his own son aside to say that having proposed the embassy he could not refuse to serve on it. Possibly as a *quid pro quo* for the fire-eaters and the Senate in general, Antony's agrarian law was declared invalid. Immediately after the house rose Cicero was summoned by a tribune to address the People; the *Sixth Philippic* insists that the embassy is doomed to failure. As ever, Cicero is ingratiating, recalling his own comparatively humble background, his devotion to the People to whom he owes his rank and for whose welfare he has often fought; he is now facing the greatest public meeting he has ever seen – united, like all Italy, in this last fight for liberty. 'Other races can endure slavery: liberty is the Roman People's birthright.' If we may trust his own accounts, the People supported him warmly throughout this period.

The Senate might drag its feet and Pansa have his moments of unreliability. But to a remarkable degree Cicero was now the real ruler of Rome. He could call Hirtius and Pansa 'my consuls'; they might procrastinate (Quintus Cicero had abused them as useless in a recent letter to Tiro, in his usual intemperate language) but they were basically under his spell; less accurately, Cicero also spoke of Octavian as 'my Caesar', accepting the adoption that he had originally refused to recognize. His energy was amazing; we have only a part of the vast number of letters that he dispatched to every corner of the Roman world – in particular, most of the letters to M. Brutus are lost, as are all those to Octavian and the consuls. To these, to Asinius Pollio in Further Spain, to Plancus and Lepidus in Gaul, to D. Brutus at Mutina, to the governor of Africa, to the various Liberators in the

East, the letters were borne, often too slowly (and Pollio complained that Lepidus intercepted his mail); they offered news, encouragement, honours. To each he adapted his language with the necessary tact – one could not write to the ex-Caesarians Pollio or Plancus as one did to the Liberators. Plancus in particular, son of an old friend but with a brother in Antony's camp, who commanded five legions in Further Gaul, was bombarded by Cicero with flattery and appeals, and promised his support to the Senate in elegantly written replies. Masses of correspondence indeed were directed to Cicero. It was to him, as much as to the Senate, that the commanders reported, complained, justified themselves. His claim to be working day and night in the service of the State must have been largely true. He was at last, he will have felt, the heir and equal of the great consulars of his youth, Scaurus, who had 'ruled the world with his nod', or later Catulus; he stood where, after 63, he had felt he had the right to stand. He was revealed as the *rector reipublicae* on whose duties and qualifications he had since that time written and meditated; and he put all he had into playing the part.

Soon Hirtius, though still unwell, went north to join the army; Pansa was intermittently busy levying troops and cash. The treasury was so poor that religious festivals had to be omitted, and the rich tried to evade the new taxes; they had been milked pretty severely in the last years, and it is not surprising that there was much longing for peace. The Antonians' cry was indeed peace and the saving of citizens' lives; as Cicero's influence grew, the watchword of liberty was also turned against him.

Offers from Antony were rumoured to have been received by consulars in Rome – presumably Fufius Calenus – and at the end of the month Cicero spoke again in the Senate,* explaining why he, 'the nursling of peace', was now so urgent for war: the differences were too deep for peace to be possible – Antony was the opponent of all the *boni*, the leader of the greedy *improbi*, urged on especially by his brother Lucius (who added insult to injury by describing himself as patron of the *equites*): 'I do not fear peace: but I fear war clothed with the name of peace.'

In fact the famous embassy did achieve nothing except, shortly before it reached Antony, the death of Servius Sulpicius. Antony refused to give up the siege of Mutina where Decimus Brutus was at bay, and made some concessions and various counter-con-

---

* The *Seventh Philippic*.

ditions, including, though perhaps only if Brutus and Cassius were to be in office, five years in Further Gaul with six legions. Cicero pronounced the demands intolerable, of course. The Senate refused to declare war, but on the motion of Antony's uncle, L. Caesar, supported by Calenus and Pansa, it did declare a *tumultus*, or state of emergency, which Cicero was to argue meant the same thing; and it probably passed the Last Decree. Hard on the meeting came news of a first clash between the forces of Hirtius and Antony, and next day the Senate met again, to hear Cicero deliver the *Eighth Philippic*. He pointed out that it was ludicrous not to admit there was a war on, or to suggest another embassy; declared Antony a common criminal, a danger to all men of property, against whom every class was united; denied that he had lost his temper with Calenus, though he admitted to 'vehemence' in dealing with him; and announced that in spite of his rank, which excused him, he would put on military dress (especially the military cloak, or *sagum*) in obedience to the declaration of emergency. A chance fragment of a letter to Octavian, preserved in a late grammarian, shows that he did 'go down to the Forum in a *sagum*, when the other consulars meant to wear togas'.

He took every opportunity to push the Senate into marks of enmity towards Antony, including that offered by the death of Servius Sulpicius; who might be represented as a martyr of the Republic, though in life Cicero had often thought him timid and indecisive. He pronounced a noble funeral tribute in the *Ninth Philippic*. Servius' legal publications were a sufficient monument of his life; but his death should be commemorated not only by the proposed public funeral, but by a statue, as ancestral custom demanded for an envoy killed in performance of his duties. Such had been Servius' old-fashioned simplicity that the statue should be of plain bronze, and show him on foot (Lepidus and Octavian had recently been granted gilt equestrian statues; Lepidus omitted to thank the Senate). Cicero overrode all objections that Servius had died, not been killed; and the statue of the great lawyer stood in the centre of Rome for hundreds of years, a memorial, as Cicero had hoped, though not to such a posterity as he had hoped, of the solemnity of the struggle against Antony.

Cicero had written to tell Cassius, who was somewhere, it was not yet clear where, in the East, of recent events.

How I wish you had invited me to the feast on the Ides of March! There would have been no left-overs. As it is, your leavings keep me busy – yes, me particularly. It is true that we have two admirable consuls, but the consulars are a disgraceful lot. The Senate is firm, but firmest in the lowest ranks. Nothing could be firmer and better than the people, and the whole of Italy, but nothing more shocking and criminal than the envoys Philippus and Piso; they were sent to give certain instructions to Antony according to the decision of the Senate. When he refused to obey any of them they proved ready to bring back a series of intolerable demands from him to us. So there has been a reaction towards me and I have great popular support in a salutary cause.

It is not wholly surprising that many senior members of the Senate, who had reached their position as compliant followers of Caesar, were to reduce Cicero to sighing for the consulars of the years after 63, whom at the time he had excoriated; but who had at least believed in the rule of the *boni*. Nor is it surprising that, as in those years, Cicero was himself again the object of jealousy and irritation. But he had enough support to suggest that there was genuine fear of Antony, whose measures in general the Senate was persuaded to declare invalid. Cicero no doubt exaggerates the unity, like the importance of Italian support. The country towns had shown that they cared little either for the quarrels of Roman nobles or their constitutional convictions. Cicero made much of the recruits levied in Italy; but apart from the fact that Antony's officers could also raise forces, if Cicero believed that raw recruits could counter-balance the Caesarian veterans under Antony (and Octavian) he was woefully mistaken; nothing could counter-balance veterans, as he was to discover.

Some time early in February came welcome but ticklish news from the East. Marcus Brutus had been in Athens in the autumn, attending lectures on philosophy and – as events moved towards war – collecting support among the students. Cicero's son undoubtedly dropped his books with delight; a more talented student, also given an officer's post though his father was only a freedman, was the future poet Horace. Brutus succeeded in peacefully taking over the government of Macedonia from the son of Hortensius, and also the forces in the neighbouring province of Illyricum on the Adriatic. He further besieged Antony's brother Gaius, who had come to take over Macedonia; young Cicero received the surrender of some of his troops. Brutus wrote that he had eight legions including local levies and was at the disposal of Senate and People. What would the Senate feel about this? In fact, Pansa proved ready to propose Brutus' legitimization, and, swayed perhaps by Cicero's eloquence, the Senate passed it in the teeth of Fufius Calenus and the carefully prepared speech he read out. Brutus was to be given far-reaching powers to raise money and supplies and urged to keep his army near Italy. Cicero sent his speech, with that of 1 January, to Brutus, calling them half-jokingly his 'Philippics'; Brutus replied that they deserved the name, and as a result was sent the rest too.

The situation further East was less easily resolved. There were rumours, but still no certain news, of Cassius, who had in fact succeeded in taking over all the troops in Syria, plus those left in Egypt by Caesar – eleven legions in all. But it was now learned that Dolabella, stopping in Asia on his way to Syria, had seized, tortured and killed its governor, the Liberator Trebonius. For once the whole Senate was united: Fufius Calenus, perhaps glad to show his abhorrence of Cicero's recently much-prized son-in-law, who had now sunk in his estimation to being one of the two 'foulest and filthiest beings since the creation of man', led it in declaring Dolabella a public enemy. Who then was to govern Syria? Fufius proposed that the consuls, once Mutina was relieved, should draw lots; others suggested a special command. Cicero, in the *Eleventh Philippic*, argued against both suggestions in favour of recognizing Cassius, who (he asserted) held command there by the law of Nature, and of giving him supreme power over the whole East. It is clear that Cicero had to meet hostile reactions to his praise of Cassius, even though he did not actually eulogize the murder of Caesar; and also warnings, previously offered in the case of Brutus, that the veterans would be angry at such power going to a Liberator. Should the Senate be swayed by their wishes? he replied; their day is over; the new recruits matter more. Pansa was angry at the speech, and the proposal to assign Asia to one of the consuls was in fact passed. Cicero promptly took the matter to the People, an action that should have been against all his principles; but Pansa again intervened, claiming that Cassius' own family were opposed to Cicero's proposal – it seems his mother-in-law Servilia in particular did not wish to offend the consul.

This was a defeat for Cicero, reflected in another attempt to treat with Antony, which was inspired by Piso and Calenus and furthered by Pansa. They represented Antony as despairing of success and willing to make concessions, and Cicero agreed to be one of the five consulars to go to him. It then became clear that there was no basis for supposing that Antony had had a change of heart and Pansa was forced to reopen the question. One of the envoys resigned and Cicero complained that he had been tricked and also that he was so hated by Antony's followers (many of whom he had abused in scurrilous detail) and by the veterans, who had been worked up against him, that his life would not be safe in their vicinity. The lawless state of Italy is also revealed by the fact that he did not even dare to go to the suburbs. But his job was in Rome: 'here is my place, here I keep watch, here I stand guard'. He urged that the embassy should be reconsidered; it was soon dropped.

About 19 March Pansa left Rome finally to join Hirtius and Octavian, intending that they should advance on Mutina, which Antony was anxious to take before they got there, Decimus Brutus being almost at the end of his tether. The campaigning season was about to open, and the time for negotiations was past. In Rome, where a personally insignificant urban praetor was now senior magistrate, Cicero's influence was stronger than ever. His next speech was directed against two belated letters to the Senate urging peace from Plancus and Lepidus in Gaul (privately he wrote Plancus a firm, and Lepidus a distinctly curt, rebuke). He had also to deal with a letter that Antony had sent to Hirtius and Octavian, attempting to disengage them from the alliance. This lamented that Caesar's friends should be on different sides: 'let not fortune see two armies, sprung from one body, fighting with Cicero as the trainer of gladiators'; and also that some of these friends should be cooperating with Pompeians and with Caesar's assassins – and, worse, condemning Dolabella for executing one of these. He also hinted that he could rely on the support not only of Lepidus but of Plancus. Cicero tore the argument to shreds; such divisions, he argued, were dead and done with; but it will have been a relief when another letter from Plancus to the Senate expressed his devotion and excused his inactivity. Cicero replied with a vote of thanks and honours, against some opposition. In the middle of the debate he received, and read aloud, a letter giving at last official news of Cassius' success; the impression made was enormous.

On 1 April Marcus Brutus wrote to Cicero – it is probably the first of his surviving letters – announcing that he had captured Antony's brother and asking for reinforcements, money and advice. He had learnt of Cassius' stroke, but was afraid of its effect on public opinion. And he praised young Marcus Cicero's energy and devotion in his service.

Both the military and political positions were delicately balanced. But for a time it looked as if Cicero had walked the tightrope successfully. On 14 April, as an officer of Pansa's recounted in a vivid letter, Antony attempted to prevent Pansa's four newly raised legions joining Hirtius and Octavian, simultaneously attacking the camp of the two latter to prevent aid being brought. But Hirtius was after all not only a gourmet and the author of Book VIII of the *Gallic War*. He had foreseen the move, told Pansa to hurry, and detached a strong veteran force to meet and assist the new arrivals. If we may believe a late source, in the ensuing battle the grim and silent efficiency of the veterans on both sides, and their immense superiority to the new recruits, were made frighteningly obvious. Though Pansa's troops and their assistants had to retreat to his camp, Hirtius himself came up in time to catch Antony's forces retiring and handled them very roughly. Octavian had successfully guarded his and Hirtius' camp with a handful of men. A week later Hirtius, with the aid of a sortie by Decimus Brutus, was again to defeat Antony, who raised the siege of Mutina and retired West. But would even Lepidus support a beaten man?

In Rome rumour first told of an Antonian victory, and it was put about that Cicero intended to seize power, and its symbol the *fasces*; possibly this was to serve as an excuse for an Antonian *coup*. But a friendly tribune reassured the People 'who with one voice declared I had never had a thought but for the welfare of the State'. In a few hours the truth about the first battle emerged. Cicero wrote to M. Brutus:

The consuls have proved what I often told you they were. As for the boy Caesar, his natural courage is extraordinary. I only hope we may be able to guide and restrain him as easily as we have done till now. That will be more difficult, certainly, but I do not give up hope. The young man is convinced (chiefly by me) that our survival is due to to himself; and it is certain that if he had not turned Antony back from Rome, all would have been lost.

Three or four days before the great victory the whole community fell into panic and streamed out with wives and children to join you; but on 20 April it came to itself and would now like you to come here instead. That day I reaped the supreme reward for my great labours and many wakeful nights – if real and true glory be a reward. The whole population of Rome pressed to my house and escorted me up to the Capitol, then set me on the Rostrum amid huge noise and applause. I am not vain – nor ought I to be; but the union of all classes in thanks and congratulations does move me, for that I should be loved by the People for serving its welfare is a great thing. I would rather, however, that you heard all this from others.

The poets of antiquity, above all the tragic poets, had reiterated time and again that mutability is the law of the world; lightning strikes the peaks, and great men are laid low at the height of their prosperity. Cicero was as blind to coming disaster, was to fall almost as suddenly, as Agamemnon or Oedipus.

His last surviving speech, the *Fourteenth Philippic*, warns that the war is not over and rejects suggestions that the toga should be resumed; but it makes a solemn proposal for a long thanksgiving, the title of *imperator* to all three generals, and honours and rewards for their men. He praises the dead in lofty, traditional language, evoking the famous public Funeral Orations of Athens, and proposes that one or other of the consuls shall contract for a great monument to those who had fallen 'for the life, liberty and prosperity of the Roman People, for the city of Rome and the temples of the immortal gods'.

He did not yet know that in the first battle Pansa had been mortally wounded; and that in the second, in an assault on Antony's camp, Hirtius had been killed. Personally undistinguished as the two men might be, their disappearance was disastrous: militarily, because it helped to prevent the effective pursuit of Antony; politically, because government was to be paralyzed by the vacancies and by the prospect of elections with their attendant intrigues; and because there was now no buffer, among the army leaders, between Octavian and the Liberators.

The reasons that I could not follow Antony at once, Cicero [wrote Decimus Brutus] were these: I had no cavalry or pack-animals; I did not know Hirtius had fallen . . . I was unwilling to trust Caesar until I had met and spoken with him. So the day passed. Next morning I was summoned by Pansa to Bononia [Bologna], but on my way I was told of his death. I hurried back to my wretched little forces; for so I may really call them. They are badly reduced and in a terrible way through every kind of shortage. Antony had two days start of me.

Octavian almost immediately showed himself recalcitrant. He would not hand over Pansa's troops or the veterans. 'I cannot give orders to Caesar or he to his troops – two bad things,' Decimus was soon writing (Cicero found him a laconic and businesslike correspondent). It may be pointed out that in December

Octavian had not scrupled to negotiate closely with this most hated of all the Liberators; but now Octavian was in danger not from Antony, but from his own recent allies.

The friends of the Liberators were so overjoyed at 'the disappearance of Caesarian leaders and veterans alike', as Pollio wrote, that they acted somewhat prematurely. Antony and his followers were at last declared enemies of the state; a triumph and other honours were voted to D. Brutus – Cicero also proposed that his name should be entered in the calendar on his birthday, which was also the day on which news of his victory had reached Rome, but the Senate was 'grudging, not grateful'. On the other hand the Senate was distinctly chilly to Octavian. Cicero did at least propose for him an ovation, the minor form of triumph, but it is uncertain whether this was passed. Next day D. Brutus was formally given command of the consuls' troops and ordered to pursue Antony; there was an attempt also to put under Decimus the legions that had originally revolted to Octavian, but Cicero showed that this was folly. Lepidus and Plancus were summoned to help him. Cassius was given his command in the East and ordered to deal with Dolabella – Cicero added a suggestion that M. Brutus should support him if possible; and, most provocative of all, Sextus Pompeius was given command at sea. Whether Cicero concurred in this is not clear. But unfortunately, as Decimus Brutus reported, busybodies had repeated to Octavian a *mot* of Cicero's which its author was not, it seems, able to deny: that the young man should be praised, rewarded and exalted – *tollendum*, which means not only 'taken up', but 'taken off'. Octavian remarked coolly that he had no intention of letting this happen. Later, a further slight was offered him in that he was omitted from the board settling veterans with land allotments, though Cicero, who was on it, tried to get him and Decimus included; and his troops, owing to the financial stringency, were only given part of their promised reward. The men were furious with Cicero, wrote Decimus (their correspondence is extremely interesting, but unfortunately the most confidential matters were not committed to writing but communicated via trustworthy messengers).

Meanwhile Decimus was making slow progress after Antony, who collected men, including slaves, as he fled, and he could not get Octavian to prevent Antony's juncture with Caesar's old officer Ventidius, who had been raising troops in Central Italy. On 6 May Decimus wrote that he knew from captured papers that

Antony was writing to Lepidus, Plancus and even Pollio. Shortly afterwards, Antony shook off Decimus' pursuit by a feint and got across the border into Lepidus' province of Southern Gaul. As these pieces of news reached Rome, Cicero was in consternation. 'It seems that the war is not stamped out after all, but further inflamed.' Decimus however still hoped for Lepidus' loyalty (and Lepidus himself wrote an extremely proper letter to Cicero) and certainly he thought that in the last resort Octavian as well as Plancus could be trusted.

Plancus had written repeatedly to Cicero assuring him of support, and also answering for Lepidus, with whom he was proposing to unite in order to block Antony's path. But he was warned that Lepidus was untrustworthy, and soon he learnt that on 29 May Antony and Lepidus had joined forces; he fell back and implored Cicero to send someone to his aid. Was all this disingenuous? Possibly not, for he did in fact join Decimus Brutus. Lepidus meanwhile wrote to the Senate to put all the blame on his troops:

I call gods and men to witness, fathers, that I have always been loyal to the Republic in heart and mind, and thought nothing more important than the general welfare and freedom, and I should have shortly given you proof of this if fortune had not taken the decision from my hands. For my whole army, faithful to its old wish to preserve Roman lives, and the general peace, has mutinied . . .

Lepidus' legate fell on his sword.

Antony was now again a force to be reckoned with. Decimus Brutus wrote tersely to Cicero in early June: he *must* be sent money; troops must be recalled from Africa and Sardinia; Marcus Brutus must be summoned. In Rome, there was another conference with Servilia, and the Senate urgently recalled both Brutus and Cassius. But Brutus was already on his way East to put down Dolabella, who in fact was in flight and soon to commit suicide; and it seems possible, though it was not Cicero's belief, that his arrival in Italy would simply have precipitated the Caesarians into each others' arms. Cicero was also trying to have the elections put off till January, and attempted to prevent friends leaving their place at the front to canvas in Rome. As for the financing of the enormously swollen armies spoiled by recent donatives, this was, he said, the worst problem of all.

Relations between Cicero and M. Brutus had not been wholly happy in these last months. Cicero had been unable to send the money and troops Brutus asked for; Brutus had always hated the use of Octavian, or Octavius as he insisted on still calling him (or else, ironically, 'your Caesar'); he seems even to have preferred Antony, unless his gentle treatment of Antony's brother Gaius was merely a sign of his strictly correct attitude: to Cicero's hints he replied stiffly about proper trial by the Senate or People, since Gaius was still a citizen. And he remarked that Cicero should not shortsightedly allow immense powers to those he thought on the right side. It is sad, indeed, to see Cicero, the peaceful and civilized, in so savage a role. He had learnt, it seems, the lessons of the last years all too well; above all, he had been impressed by the failure of Caesar's policy of *clementia*.

I utterly disagree with you, Brutus, and do not allow your mercy; rather a salutary severity is better than the empty show of clemency. If we are to be merciful, civil wars will never cease . . . You will be overwhelmed, believe me, Brutus, unless you show forethought; for the people you have to deal with will not always be the same, nor the Senate, nor the leader of the Senate. Think that this advice is given you by Apollo of Delphi; nothing can be more true.

So he wrote when Lepidus had been declared a public enemy, and Brutus hoped that his property would be spared for the sake of the children, who were also his own nephews.

Brutus was appalled by the news that Octavian was now aiming at the consulship. In June Cicero wrote that

Caesar, who has so far been guided by my advice and is a fine young man, of remarkable firmness, has been stirred up by certain persons with villainous letters and dubious intermediaries and messengers confidently to expect the consulship. As soon as I heard of it, I wrote to him again and again, blaming to their faces the friends who seem to be supporting his ambition; and I did not hesitate to expose the origin of these wicked plans in full Senate.

But Brutus reproached Cicero deeply for what happened. Perhaps now, or possibly already much earlier, he wrote a very forceful and formal protest after Atticus had sent him a copy of a letter from Cicero to 'the boy':

By the way in which you thank him for his services to the Republic, so humbly and humiliatingly – what am I to say? I am ashamed of our position and fate, but I must say it – *commending* our safety to him, you make it quite plain that the tyranny has not been got rid of, that we only have a new tyrant in place of the old. Read what you say, and dare to deny that these appeals are those of a subject to his king.

And he openly accused Cicero of too great a desire to 'live and be rich and be called a consular'. What, above all, his pride could not swallow was Cicero's begging Octavian to forgive the Liberators. We also happen to have an isolated letter from Brutus to Atticus, about Cicero,

I know that he has always acted with the best of intentions. But he seems to me to have done some things – how shall I put it? – unskilfully, though the most experienced of men; or not disinterestedly, though he did not hesitate for his country's sake to incur the enmity of Antony in all his power. I do not know what to say to you, except this: Cicero has stimulated rather than stifled the boy's greed and desire for power . . . let Octavius call Cicero father, seek his advice in all things, praise him and thank him; Cicero will find his deeds opposed to his words . . . Long life to him, if he can endure it in cringing subservience, if he is not ashamed to think of his age, his rank and his achievements. As for myself, I shall fight against realities: against autocracy and extraordinary commands, tyranny and power which places itself above the laws.

If Cicero saw this letter he must also have been hurt by Brutus' charge that there was a gap between his writings about liberty and his actions, and complaint of his continual reference to the Nones of December 63 ('*we* are not always dwelling on the Ides of March').

But there was no breach; Cicero had always taken a good deal from Brutus. He wrote a letter of condolence on the death from illness of Porcia – her suicide is a later embellishment. And in July he wrote a long letter of self-defence. He pointed out that it was not only for Octavian that he had proposed rewards, and that the great Athenian legislator Solon, one of the Seven Sages, had said that a country was held together by two things – rewards and punishments; though no doubt there was a proper mean in both. Through the Liberators' omissions a terrible storm still threatened Italy after Caesar's death; and they themselves had prudently retired, for the Stoics say that the wise man never runs away, leaving Cicero to make use of the strong feeling in Italy. (As usual, Cicero has somewhat rearranged his own share in events.) As to Octavian, 'I secured him honours – none of them, Brutus, undeserved, none of them unnecessary. When we began to recover our freedom, when the heroism even of D. Brutus had not yet stirred itself and become visible, when our whole protection lay in the boy who had torn Antony from our throats, what honour should not have been decreed him?'

In this Cicero had a case; and it was appallingly bad luck that Antony should have escaped from Mutina and that both consuls should have been killed there. It was also appallingly bad luck that Cicero, who had often been genuinely looked up to by young men, should now have had on his hands perhaps the most formidable nineteen-year-old in history. He had not been unaware of the difficulty of holding his coalition together; he had tried in the face of financial difficulties to see that the troops were rewarded promptly and by the Senate, and from the clamorous demands for honours that reached him from their generals he might well think that these would suffice to secure their loyalty. But he underestimated the magic of Caesar's memory and Caesar's name; and he, who so desired glory, perhaps never understood the thirst for power that drove many politicians. Was it, anyway, so surprising that many now felt that law and constitutional propriety had become meaningless, and that power, or peace, were the only things worth aiming at?

Now everything had gone wrong. Already at the end of April Cicero had been writing of his exhaustion: 'I shall, as usual, serve the State, though I am very tired; but no weariness should stand in the way of duty and loyalty.' He knew that the Senate was now divided and powerless.

Believe me, Brutus,* as one who is not vain, I am totally ineffective. The Senate was my weapon, and it has fallen to pieces. Your magnificent break-out from Mutina and Antony's flight with his army cut about brought such great hopes of certain victory that there has been a general relaxation of energy, and those forceful speeches of mine look like shadow-boxing . . . I can do no more than I have done.

But there was a more basic trouble: 'We are the playthings, my dear Brutus,† of the whims of the troops and the arrogance of their generals; everyone demands political influence in the state to correspond with his military power.' And Cicero's last datable letter, to M. Brutus on 27 July, explicitly admits his fear that, owing to the evil councillors around the boy, he will not be able to fulfil his pledge of 1 January as to Octavian's loyalty.

Octavian indeed made no move to join D. Brutus and Plancus, whose last letter complains of him bitterly for this. Henceforth we are left to the tender mercies of the imperial historians, who are often inaccurate. They indicate that at one point Octavian

* Decimus Brutus this time.
† Marcus Brutus.

proposed that he and Cicero should be consuls together, the real power remaining in Cicero's hands; and that Cicero was tempted. But if so the Senate was recalcitrant, and put off the elections, though it may have promised that Octavian should stand for praetor. Octavian then sent 400 soldiers to Rome with his demands: the consulship, money for the troops, and the cancellation of the decree declaring Antony a public enemy. One of them is said to have shown his sword: 'if you do not give Caesar the consulship, this will give it him.' Cicero is supposed to have observed sardonically that one could not say no to that sort of request; but the Senate stood firm. Thereupon Octavian's army demanded, or was said to have demanded, to march on Rome; and like his adoptive father Octavian crossed the Rubicon – but this time with eight legions. As far as we can tell from the confused accounts in our sources, Cicero was trying to organize the defence of Rome, trying to raise money to bribe Octavian's troops. In a panic the Senate allowed Octavian to stand for the consulship; Cicero is said not to have been present. But he was active again when two veteran legions, which had fought for Caesar, at last landed from Africa; there was also one of new recruits. All three went over to Octavian. The citizens streamed out to meet him on his approach; in the end, Cicero went too, 'the last of my friends to greet me', as Octavian said. Soon after, a rumour of mutiny among the troops lit a last flicker of hope; the senators met; Cicero welcomed them at the door. But the rumour proved false and Cicero was smuggled away in a litter.

The urban praetor committed suicide. Cicero did not. On 18 August 43 Octavian, still aged only nineteen, became consul together with a cousin. A special court was set up to punish Caesar's murderers. After a few weeks, Octavian returned to the north, ostensibly against Antony; but in Rome, with his approval the sentences on Antony and Lepidus were rescinded.

Somewhere around the same time Pollio left his province in Spain to join Antony. He was probably moved by opportunism, though in the spring he had been writing about his desire for peace and the preservation of citizens' lives (which has in fact an Antonian ring). Plancus followed Pollio's example. Decimus Brutus' men deserted him and he fled in disguise, only to be captured by brigands and killed on Antony's orders.

Cicero had been able to leave Rome for Tusculum. His last surviving words – they are in truth not heroic ones – are from a fragment of a letter thanking Octavian for the permission: 'your giving leave of absence to Philippus and myself gives me double pleasure, implying as it does forgiveness for the past and indulgence for the future.' At Tusculum he must have spent a number of weeks. We know nothing of his mental state, but if, after the elation and tension of the last months, he collapsed with exhaustion and despair it would be no wonder, and it would explain the silence of his biographers. Possibly he dared not write to Atticus; but more probably the latter, who was later a friend of Octavian's, cautiously destroyed these last letters for their reproaches of or revelations about him.

Meanwhile Octavian met Antony and Lepidus in northern Italy. Their armies were unwilling to fight one another; none of the three were working for anything but power – unless Octavian at least genuinely desired to avenge Caesar. So why not (temporarily) join forces and eliminate the Liberators? Not but what one source tells us that Antony threatened that he would ally himself with them if Octavian did not join him – and this is not inconceivable. They set themselves up as Triumvirs for the Restoration of the Republic for five years, and parcelled out the western provinces among themselves. Land and money were essential requisites for their followers; they could be secured, and enemies eliminated, by proscriptions. The fears of the *boni*, and the warnings of Cicero, about Antony's victory were thus far justified. A few men were first to be killed informally; then a list was got out, with a declaration that Caesar's *clementia* had proved a failure, and the promise of reward to anyone producing the head of one of the men named. Antony saw to it that all the Cicerones had a place on the list. It was later represented that Octavian had taken much persuasion to agree to the death of the man he had called father; but his usual cold ruthlessness must have been reinforced by the knowledge that at this stage, if not earlier, Cicero would have been ready to do the same by him.

For the rest, let us turn to Plutarch:

Meanwhile Cicero was at his country property at Tusculum, with his brother; but when they learnt of the proscriptions they decided to move to Astura, a place of Cicero's on the coast, and thence to sail to Brutus in Macedonia, for there was already a report that he was in control there. Worn out with grief, they made the journey in litters; and on the way they would halt, and with their litters placed side by side would lament to each other. But Quintus was the more dejected, and he began to consider his desperate position; he said that he had taken nothing from home, while Cicero too had small resources for the journey; it was better therefore that Cicero should press on in his flight, but that he should provide himself from home and then hasten after him. Thus they decided, and after embracing each other and weeping aloud they parted.

Quintus, then, not many days later was betrayed by his slaves to those in search of him, and killed together with his son. But Cicero was brought to Astura and finding a ship he embarked at once and sailed along the coast as far as Circei, with a fair wind. From there the pilots wished to put out to sea at once, but whether he feared the sea, or had not yet entirely lost his trust in Caesar, he went ashore and travelled on foot fifteen miles in the direction of Rome. But again losing resolution and changing his mind he went down to the coast at Astura. And there he spent the night in terrible and desperate calculations; he even decided to make his way secretly to Caesar's house and kill himself on the hearth so as to haunt him as a vengeful spirit. But fear of tortures deterred him from this course too; and revolving in his mind many confused and contradictory plans he put himself into the hands of his servants to be taken by sea to Caieta, where he had a property and a pleasant retreat for hot weather, when the summer winds blow most sweetly.

The place has also a temple of Apollo, a little above the sea. From it, as the vessel was rowed to land, a flock of crows approached with loud clamour, and alighting on both ends of the sail-yard cawed, or pecked at the ends of the ropes, and everyone thought the omen a bad one. Nonetheless Cicero disembarked and going to his house lay down to rest. Then most of the crows perched on the window cawing tumultuously, but one flew down to the couch where Cicero lay with muffled head and tried to remove the clothes from his face with its beak. The servants, seeing this, blamed themselves for waiting to be spectators of their master's death, while wild things came to his aid and cared for him in his undeserved misfortune, and they themselves did nothing. So partly by entreaty and partly by force they got him into his litter and carried him towards the shore.

Meanwhile the assassins reached the house, led by Herennius, a centurion, and Popillius, a military tribune, who had once been defended by Cicero on a charge of parricide. When they had broken down the doors, which they found closed, Cicero was not to be seen and those in the house disclaimed all knowledge. Then, it is said, a young man to whom Cicero had given a liberal education, a freedman of his brother Quintus, Philologus by name, told the tribune that the litter was being carried through the shady paths in the wood towards the sea. The tribune then took a few men with him and ran round towards the exit, while Herennius hurried along the paths. Cicero, perceiving him, ordered the servants to put the litter down. He himself, with his left hand on his chin, as was a habit of his, looked calmly at his murderers. His neck and hair were unkempt and his face was worn with anxiety; so that most of those present covered their faces while Herennius was dispatching him as he stretched his neck out of the litter to the stroke. He was in his sixty-fourth year.

It was 7 December.

Even in this, the fullest and least embroidered account of Cicero's death, there are implausible rhetorical touches; the story of the crows has probably been improved, and it is hard to suppose that Cicero had much faith in avenging spirits, even his own. And Plutarch adds that 'Cicero's own freedman Tiro makes no mention at all of Philologus' treachery'. But though Tiro was clearly not present, he was well placed to receive the testimony of the slaves who were eye-witnesses, and Plutarch would probably have told us if his own version differed in other significant respects from Tiro's. If Cicero lamented and vacillated in advance, and then met the end bravely, that accords with what we know of him; so does the loyalty which, unlike Quintus, he inspired in all, or most, of his slaves.

An imperial rhetorician, as it happens, collected and discussed the verdicts of various writers on Cicero's death. Livy was to declare that 'he met nothing like a man except his death, which might seem the less undeserved, because he suffered nothing worse from his victorious enemy than he would, in the same place, have inflicted on him'. The only historian who did not admit that Cicero perished bravely was Asinius Pollio; whose account is also the only one to reflect, with a vivid immediacy, its author's personal knowledge of his subject. But even Pollio's final verdict was not too harsh:

It is unnecessary to praise the ability and industry of a man whose many great works will remain immortal . . . Could he only have borne prosperity more calmly and misfortune more boldly! In either case he was convinced that things would never change. Hence great gusts of jealousy arose against him, and his enemies were the bolder in attacking him, as he was readier to provoke enemies than to resist them. But since no man possesses perfect virtue, it is by the best in his life and talents that he must be judged. And I at least would not even lament his death, had he not thought death such a lamentable thing.

It does not appear that Brutus either was deeply grieved by Cicero's death. According to Plutarch, though he finally executed Antony's brother Gaius in revenge for Cicero and D.

295

Brutus, he said that he felt more shame than pity for the former, and that those who could endure tyranny bore most responsibility for it.

A Roman who had received official honours could expect that after his death his body would be carried to the Forum, together with the images of all members of his family who had held high magistracies. Here a relative or friend would recite his eulogy, and a lament be sung to the flute, before the body was borne outside the city to the funeral pyre and the monument in which the ashes were to rest. Such rites were not for the proscribed. Their heads were taken to the Triumvirs; and Antony, or his wife Fulvia, had that of Cicero, together with the hand that had written the *Philippics*, nailed up on the Rostra. By a curious irony, Cicero had once written of Antony's grandfather, murdered in 87, words that could have been (and indeed with variations were, by generations of declaimers) used of himself: 'the head of the man, who had preserved the lives of so many citizens, was now placed on the same Rostra from which, as consul, he had with so much constancy defended the Republic.' Popillius, his murderer, is said to have set up a statue of himself with the head of his victim beside him.

There is some suggestion that Cicero's mutilated body was given decent disposal by a loyal friend, that very Aelius Lamia who in 58 as a leader of the *equites* had been banished from Rome for Cicero's sake, and who was probably a native of Formiae, close to the villa where Cicero was killed. His own property was doubtless sold up; we know that some of his beloved villas found their way into the hands of prominent partisans of Antony and Octavian.

What fate awaited his friends and family? Brutus and Cassius, of course, were to fall at Philippi. According to one source, Brutus died comforting himself that he left a reputation for virtue behind him; according to another, lamenting in the words of a tragic poet that the virtue he had practised had proved only an empty word. Young Marcus Cicero was to fight at Philippi, and then at sea under Sextus Pompeius, but he was ultimately pardoned by the victorious Triumvirs, and even, some years later, given a consulship by Octavian – during the course of which it fell to him to announce Antony's death to Rome. Contemporaries observed the poetic justice. Marcus twice governed a province, and must have had practical ability, but he was remembered chiefly as a heavy drinker. He remained loyal to his father's memory. He showed both these last characteristics in giving a beating to a rhetorician who had, at table, deprecated Cicero's style. As far as we know, he had no descendants.

Terentia is said to have survived to the age of 103 and re-married twice, one of her husbands being the historian Sallust; but this has been doubted. Quintus' widow Pomponia, in spite of her bad relations with her husband and the recent divorce, is said to have taken cruel vengeance on his and his brother's betrayers. Atticus, in spite of his wealth, was not proscribed; com-bining prudence with humanity as ever, he had been protecting Antony's family in Rome. Though he went into hiding for a while, we know that he succeeded in saving several friends; it is unlikely that he did, or could have done, anything to save Cicero. He lived on for fifteen years. It is perhaps hard for us to forgive him for being, as usual, on excellent terms with all the leading men of the time. His biographer tells us that he was soon a close correspondent of both Octavian and Antony, and his daughter Attica, heiress to his wealth, was by Antony's good offices married to Octavian's right-hand man, Agrippa; while their daughter was, by Octavian's desire, betrothed as a baby to his own stepson, the future Emperor Tiberius. Atticus himself was at the age of seventy-seven attacked by an incurable disease; quiet and calm as ever, he determined to commit suicide by star-vation. He was buried in his uncle's monument by the Appian Way.

Tiro devoted himself to his master's memory, writing a biography, publishing Cicero's notes for his speeches to set beside the finished versions, and possibly being responsible for an un-critical collection of his *bons mots*. He seems to have been a careful but uninspired scholar. Like Terentia he is said to have lived till extreme old age (but this may rest on an error), on a little property in Campania, probably the same that young Marcus had congratulated him on acquiring.

He will have seen Cicero's literary fame to some extent surviv-ing changes of fashion. But the heroes of those who looked nostalgically back to the Republic were the more single-minded Cato and Brutus; and though parts at least of Cicero's political doctrine – the alliance of Senate and *equites*, the influence of Italy – came to fruition under Augustus, his works do not seem to have been appealed to in this connection. Indeed his was not a wholly tactful name to mention, though he could be referred to as the enemy of the now execrated Antony, and it was thought worthwhile to claim that he had foreseen Octavian's rule in a dream. When many years had passed, however, the Emperor, or so Plutarch ends the *Life* we have so often quoted by telling us, came one day upon one of his grandsons reading; it was a volume of Cicero, and the boy hid the book nervously under his clothes. But Augustus saw him doing so, took it, and stood reading it for a long time. At last he handed it back, saying 'an eloquent man, my child, an eloquent man, and a lover of his country'.

17

THE ONE SURE IMMORTALITY

But Augustus' verdict was far from being a final one; and even Cicero might have been satisfied, could he have known the influence he was to exert and the love he was to inspire, at certain times at any rate, after his death. He was a man of so many aspects that his posthumous fortunes cannot be easily traced especially in brief compass. In the first couple of centuries after his death his reputation stood less high than it was to do later. He was regularly read in schools for his style, certainly. Livy advised his son to study 'Demosthenes and Cicero, and then whoever most resembles Demosthenes and Cicero'; he himself, and some later writers, notably Tacitus in his early but admirable dialogue on oratory, show his influence, while to Quintilian, the distinguished writer on education and rhetoric in the late first century A.D., Cicero was 'the name not of a man, but of eloquence itself'. But his broad and balanced views of rhetorical education had little influence, save on Tacitus and Quintilian; and, on the whole, formal Latin prose style for long followed very different paths, searching for the striking and epigrammatic, and avoiding Ciceronian balance and fullness, and the supposedly tedious and repetitive Ciceronian cadences. There was an explicit complaint in the second century – by an admirer, it is true – that he did not use enough strange, archaic or poetic words.

His correspondence was published, probably in the later first century A.D., but it does not seem to have created great excitement, and as a man and a politician he was often ignored or misunderstood, though Plutarch's *Life* was fairly sympathetic in intention. The early-third-century historian, Dio Cassius, whom we have often quoted, was a loyal subject of the Emperor and tended to regard Cicero as a weak and vacillating turn-coat; he reads him a long lecture on constancy by the mouth of a philosopher whom he is imagined as meeting during his exile at Thessalonica, and he gives great space to the traditional reproaches in a speech attributed to his opponent Fufius Calenus.

Seneca praises Cicero's philosophical works as the chief Roman contribution to the subject; but he is chiefly concerned with their elevating style. Indeed, what else there was, like Seneca's own contribution, was mostly semi-Stoic moralizing, and though philosophers nowadays complain that Cicero lacks intellectual rigour, he was too sceptical and argumentative for that increasingly pious and obedient age, while educated men could still approach philosophy in Greek if they so desired. But the early Christians were struggling with real philosophic and theological issues, and with the need to explain their beliefs in terms acceptable to a pagan audience, and not necessarily one that could read Greek. So it is not surprising that many of them found inspiration not only in Cicero's language and technique, but even in some of his arguments. The North African writer Minucius Felix led the way in the early third century with an apologetic dialogue closely based on the De Natura Deorum – that work of which the ideas were to resound down the centuries, and of which the very ambiguity has increased the influence. But the writer most famous for his 'Ciceronian eloquence' was Lactantius: like other Christians he claimed that Cicero's arguments had entirely destroyed pagan religion, adding of course that this does but show the powerlessness of reason without Revelation. He takes up however the arguments for divine providence and claims that Cicero in his ignorance nonetheless shared some Christian beliefs, such as the identity of moral law with the law of God. He builds on Cicero's ethical teaching, too, praising his care for mildness, though pointing out that he lays too little stress on pity, forgiveness and repentance. And later St Ambrose took the De Officiis as a rough basis for his discussion of the duties of a Christian.

More dramatic were the cases of St Jerome and St Augustine. Jerome, who was above all a writer and rhetorician, was unable to leave his books behind him on retiring to Jerusalem. But once, as he tells us in a letter, when he lay ill with a fever, it seemed to him that he came before the Judgement Seat and on claiming to be a Christian was told, 'You lie; you are a Ciceronian, not a Christian; "where your treasure is, there will your heart be also".' For a time thereafter he foreswore all pagan literature; but he was unable to keep up this renunciation, and had to defend himself, with scant success, against accusations of perjury.

As for Augustine, his Confessions shall speak for themselves. His education naturally involved the reading of Cicero. At the age of nineteen

I came in the usual course of study to a work of one Cicero, whose style is admired by almost all, not so his message. This book however contains his exhortation to philosophy; it is called the *Hortensius*. This book indeed changed my whole way of feeling. It changed my prayers to thee, O Lord, it gave me different plans and desires. Suddenly all vain aspirations lost their value; and I was left with an unbelievable fire in my heart, desiring the deathless qualities of wisdom.

Throughout his long and varied mental development Cicero stood by Augustine, who never succeeded in learning Greek. If the wisdom that he first found after reading the *Hortensius* was Manicheism, he later discovered arguments in Cicero's scepticism against that doctrine; and if ultimately he rejected Cicero's beliefs on such fundamental subjects as the naturalness of virtue, the freedom of the will and the value of good works, he still used his writings extensively, as the *City of God* shows, for information on pagan religion and other matters, while his style never entirely rid itself of a Ciceronian impress.

Many of Cicero's works were lost or little known in the early Middle Ages, but he was not wholly forgotten, though it was sometimes supposed that Tullius and Cicero were two persons. He was regarded as an authority on rhetoric, and the youthful and jejune *De Inventione* was an essential handbook – something that would have distressed its author. (So was an even drier rhetorical work addressed to one Herennius, which was not even by Cicero at all, though medieval opinion assigned it to him as the rhetorician *par excellence*.) At times however he was primarily identified with philosophy; the *Dream of Scipio*, detached from the *De Republica* (which was ultimately lost) and misinterpreted as a defence of the contemplative life, was much read. Neither of these works, of course, was at all typical of their author. But some of the easier philosophic treatises, especially the *Tusculan Disputations*, *De Officiis* and the *Topica*, with the two essays on friendship and old age, were also widely known. Even to Dante Cicero was still a philosopher.

In the later Middle Ages social and economic developments began to lead to a new interest in republican Rome. A prosperous and educated class of laymen came into being in the city-states of Italy and elsewhere; republican ideals, a greater hope in this world, the need to express oneself fluently on practical and personal matters – all these things sprang to new life. The consequences begin to be seen in Petrarch. As a child he had been spellbound by the mere sound of Cicero's language; as an unwilling law student he studied him surreptitiously. His love for him never failed: 'you are the living source with whose flood we water our meadows, you are the leader whose advice we follow, whose applause is our joy, whose name is our ornament'. It was not merely a question of style; Petrarch found Cicero's work a comfort in the face of old age, pain and death, an almost Christian source of wisdom to be set against and above the dry learning of contemporary Aristotelian scholars. He sought eagerly for Ciceronian manuscripts and re-discovered some of the speeches, and the letters to Atticus. Here was no wise contemplative. The shock of contact with Cicero's personality was great; so great that Petrarch composed the famous letter to the shade of Cicero, in which he reproached him above all for his return to politics after the death of Caesar. 'Why did you involve yourself in so many contentions and useless quarrels, and forsake the calm so becoming to your age, your position and the vicissitudes of your life? What vain splendour of fame drove you . . . into a death unworthy of a sage?' The speeches too, he felt, showed Cicero's inconstancy; it was the *pro Archia*, with its praise of poetry, that attracted him most. But though Petrarch remained convinced that Cicero should have accepted Caesar's clemency and the establishment of the Empire, he thought of him as teaching how to live, as well as to write, and his freedom of mind and love of his country, his ideals of glory, friendship, literature and love of natural beauty, all met a receptive soul.

Fifty years later Cicero's *Letters to his Friends* were found. But this time they were greeted very differently, at least by the Florentine statesman Coluccio Salutati: he held that they shed valuable light on the fall of a free state and that it was the duty of every citizen to defend his country; their author had acted as a true philosopher and a true Roman. Salutati's friend Vergerio, writing in Padua where traditions of republican liberty survived even under a line of princes, produced an answer in Cicero's name to Petrarch's letter, claiming that during his lifetime there had always been hope for the Republic, so that her battles were worth fighting, and that Caesar's clemency was hateful, implying as it did autocratic power. Caesar or Cicero, Brutus and Cato? The question continued to be canvassed, and even when Caesar and monarchy were justified, it was with a new feeling for the claims of public life and patriotism. To many men Cicero came to represent, as has been said, 'the ideal union of political action and literary creation'. The *De Oratore*, dealing with the education and eloquence of the public man, replaced the barren *De Inventione*. The philosophic works kept their place; 'Tully's Offices', as our ancestors in this country knew the *De Officiis*, (*On Duties*) formed the basis of a gentleman's moral outlook. His praise of Plato contributed to the Platonic revival, distant as that was from the outlook of Cicero's New Academy, and though scholars in Greek were apt to attack his ascendancy jealously. Even to science, in a newly inquiring age, Cicero could give assistance; Copernicus was partly inspired to his revolutionary discoveries by a casual reference in Cicero to the theories of an Alexandrian astronomer. A refreshingly tart note is struck among the chorus of adulation by Montaigne, who objected to the *longueurs* of the treatises; he said of these, not quite falsely, that one could drop off for a quarter of an hour and pick up the thread without trouble.

Cicero's style and language were the object of even more admiration and discussion. It was not only that humanists from Petrarch on had learnt from him to write political rhetoric, personal letters and graceful dialogues suited to a lay audience (and also, regrettably, invective); there was after a time a thoroughgoing attempt to purge Latin of all medieval barbarisms. A movement developed to take Cicero and Cicero alone as a model; to some, no word, even no case or tense of a word was allowable if it was not to be found in his works, and even the language of religion might be entirely paganized. Such excesses were ridiculed by the greatest of the humanists, who refused to be 'Cicero's apes', and claimed to be following his spirit rather than his letter in expressing themselves and their own concerns more freely; thus above all Erasmus, who loved and admired the ethical works. But the controversy raged till nearly the end of the sixteenth century, when the dawning baroque turned rather to Seneca and Tacitus; and soon the question of the right Latin style became less urgent, as the various vernaculars, themselves, it must be remembered, much influenced by the Latin revival and by Cicero himself, established their dominating position.

To the seventeenth century, the age, in most parts of Europe, of monarchy and the baroque, Cicero had not very much to say; though in England, where opposition to monarchy was a lively issue, an unknown writer saw the tragedy of Cicero's career and embodied it in a play. More importantly, the English writers who from this time were attempting to establish a basis for religion and morality in Nature as opposed to Revelation found themselves relying on, or having to reject, many of Cicero's arguments, especially those of Balbus in the *De Natura Deorum*. The second path was taken by Locke, but under the banner of a quotation from that work. There was an increasingly bold progression towards mere deism. At last Hume, in the most consciously Ciceronian of all these works, as well as the most brilliant and influential, the *Dialogues concerning Natural Religion*, returned with new and more powerful arguments to Cotta's wholly sceptical position, if cautiously veiled. Above all, he exploded the argument from design. In his ethical works too Hume confessed a deep debt, primarily to the *De Officiis*; while the clear, elegant and unpretentious literary style that he adopted for philosophy surely betrays the same inspiration.

We have seen that eighteenth-century England had certain affinities with Ciceronian Rome. It is not surprising that on a less philosophical level too this was Cicero's great age. Middleton's detailed, eulogistic and highly successful biography was published, and translations of the speeches and letters appeared. But many read him in the original too, in youth at least; Locke, immensely influential on education, had insisted on his value for developing rhetorical ability, epistolary skill and sound morality. His dignified but often easy style was highly sympathetic to the age; the sensible, moderate tone of the treatises was to the taste of a period that feared 'enthusiasm'; while his political views, liberal but not democratic, accorded excellently with those of most of his readers – and indeed on the supposedly pressing questions of faction and corruption he had much to tell them. The great orators of the House of Commons knew him well, if they did not imitate him slavishly: Burke was entirely aware of the parallels between his own attack on Warren Hastings and Cicero's on Verres. But let Gibbon sum up for us: in reading Cicero 'I tasted the beauties of language, I breathed the spirit of freedom, and I imbibed from his precepts and examples the public and private sense of a man'.

In France his reputation stood equally high. To the *philosophes* true philosophy was concerned with men and society, not with high-flown metaphysical systems or logical conundrums; a free and inquiring mind like Cicero's was their admiration, and many were bitterly opposed to the despotism under which they saw the French living. Montesquieu thought him '*un des plus grands esprits qui aient jamais été*', but his greatest devotee was Voltaire, who maintained that, with other writers of antiquity, he had 'taught us how to think'. He held the *Tusculan Disputations* and the *De Natura Deorum* to be the finest works of human wisdom, the *De Officiis* to be the best guide for mankind in action (in which his friend and enemy Frederick the Great agreed); he defended Cicero for the sincerity with which he had opened his heart to his family and friends in lamenting his griefs, and even undertook the cause of his poetry (which was probably as good as his own); while his not very interesting tragedy *Catilina, ou Rome Sauvée* was, he claimed, written to introduce Cicero and his virtues to the theatre-going public – he took the part himself at its first, amateur, performance. He also wrote a more amusing fable, in which the Emperor of China, about to reject a Roman embassy because of its disgustingly superstitious views on augury, is converted to an admiration of the Roman Republic by hearing a translation of the treatise *De Divinatione*. More seriously, his *Letters of Memmius to Cicero* present his deistic views in the form of an open tribute.

For many aspiring members of the revolutionary generation Cicero was of even more immediate significance. For a long time there had been in France no tradition of public or forensic eloquence; now both were required. Many of the leading revolutionaries were lawyers; most were non-noble, eager to make their way by talent; little wonder that Cicero was a hero to almost all of them, from Mirabeau through the Girondins to Desmoulins and even Robespierre, and that his speeches were imitated more closely than had been usual on the English side of the Channel.

The eighteenth century would have admired the *De Republica*. Its partial rediscovery in 1820 came too late; its views on the mixed constitution and even on Natural Law now seemed out of date and naïve. The reaction was about to set in; above all, and disastrously, in the estimation of the philosophic works. An age that valued originality highly showed that these drew heavily on Greek sources; their only interest, it would seem, lay in enabling scholars to reconstruct certain aspects of Hellenistic thought. It was an age, too, of great metaphysical systems, above all in Germany; Cicero's philosophy did not appear serious. In a rapidly changing world antiquity was less authoritative, less relevant, and where it was still admired, Greece tended to take place above Rome. In literature, both romanticism and realism challenged formal rhetoric. Furthermore, Cicero's political character was almost irreparably damaged by the attacks made on it by some of the finest Roman historians of the period, especially the great

L 305

Mommsen, who joined passion and eloquence to his unparalleled learning and force of mind. He was under the spell of Caesar's efficiency and success, and he abused Cicero as an unsuccessful turn-coat. But the charge that Cicero in 63 abandoned a 'democratic' for a conservative party betrays nineteenth-century ideas of party politics as well as failing to do justice to the nuances of Cicero's words and actions both before and after that year.

Such a picture of Roman political life has now been given up (and we have grown disillusioned with military dictatorships). But what replaced it with many scholars was investigation into the network of ties and relationships that formed the basis of the great dynasts' power, and an insistence that labels such as optimate and *popularis* meant little. It is an attitude that in England at least was related to and influenced by the work of Sir Lewis Namier on the eighteenth century, with its conclusion that the party labels of Whig and Tory had little practical significance. To such a viewpoint Cicero, so often isolated and ineffective, offered little interest; while his emphasis on political principles (whether he lived up to them or not) seemed either unrealistic or hypocritical; and his lack of genuine sympathy for the troubles of the poor, and of really profound understanding of the problems of his day, has alienated those who approach the period from a social or economic angle. But the most notorious of his denigrators in recent years has been the French historian Carcopino, whose *Secrets de la Corréspondance de Cicéron* has accused him, without much regard for the evidence or for Roman conditions, of almost every pettiness under the sun.

There have always been those more sympathetic to him as well. Controversy is still rife in many areas, and no portrait of Cicero is likely to achieve unquestioning adherence. But recently it has seemed that the pendulum has been swinging back. Not, certainly, to an exaggerated and uncritical estimate of Cicero's political importance, intellectual achievement, or personal virtues; but to the admission that this importance, these achievements, even these virtues were not entirely the figments of his own fertile imagination; that, in short, Cicero is to be taken seriously. If his treatises are mainly of historical interest today, and his oratory too is out of fashion, surely his efforts to control an unstable temperament, and still more his struggle to preserve political liberty, however inadequately understood that liberty might be, should evoke an answering echo in our own time. We may feel that in his early years Cicero united amazing application with, by

Roman standards, exceptional brilliance, breadth of knowledge, honesty and humanity, but that he was to some extent intellectually superficial and emotionally facile. The successes of his consulship damaged his judgement, and his defects of vision and character became clear; on the other hand, it seemed at first as if his political rejection and exile were only to make him more egocentric, more insecure and more repetitive – forever regurgitating well-edited versions of his past career; though even the unhappy 50s show him thinking more deeply than Romans had ever done about the function and qualities of the orator and statesman, and the nature of and possible remedies for the political disasters of the time. But what is most impressive about Cicero is the sensitivity and energy that enabled him to go on growing into old age. His style was reconsidered, and developed; if his relationships with some of his oldest intimates broke down in recriminations (for which it is not easy to apportion the blame, though Cicero will not have been faultless), those with others deepened and matured. There can be little doubt that he felt more sorrow over the condition of Rome than for the loss of his own position of influence, connected as the two things were; and he tried honestly to attain to an emotional independence, in which popular acclaim should not affect him, and personal griefs, and fear for his own safety, should be under his control. To some extent he was still self-deceiving; he remained prone to emotional extremes, and inconsistencies of judgement and mood still follow hard upon each other in his letters; nor can we quite forget that if he was ready to provoke Antony, he was not able to face him, and that he begged mercy from Octavian, though in the end he died bravely. But one must honour his attempt to live up to standards which are, on the whole, so fine. For some the most turgid *longueurs* and the most shameless disingenuities of his speeches are counterbalanced not only by the passages that still seem amusing, elegant or grand, but also by his ability to criticize, and to laugh at, himself, the generosity of his judgements of others, and the kindness and charm with which, when at ease, he could meet his friends. He has seemed to many a tragic figure, and surely rightly – though he is often a petty, and an irresistibly comic, one as well. Tragic, too, are many of the other figures of the time: the brilliant Caesar, trapped at last by megalomania and a partly justified contempt for a tradition that others still revered; Cato, high-minded and courageous as well as narrow and stiff-necked in his defence of the old order, but repeatedly driven to compromise, when it was too late for compromise to do any good; the proud and passionate Brutus; perhaps even Pompey, ambitious and lacking in candour, yet not ill-intentioned. But we know none of them as we know Cicero. And in one way, as his great rival said, he out-distanced them all: he 'extended the frontiers of the Roman spirit'.

REFERENCES

A = letters to Atticus; f = letters *ad familiares*; Qf = letters to Quintus; MB = letters to M. Brutus; App. = Appian, Civil Wars; Plut. = Plutarch, *Cicero*; Sall. = Sallust, *Bellum Catilinarium*; Suet. = Suetonius, *Divus Julius*. Other abbreviations are standard.

1. ARPINUM AND ROME 106–90 B.C.

Description of Arpinum, *de leg.* II 1–3; interrelated families, *ib.* III 36; Marius in politics at Arpinum, Val. Max. VI 9.14; old Cicero's politics, *de leg.* III 36; Marius' rise, Plut. *Marius* 4–7; M. Gratidius, *Brutus* 168; L. Cicero, *de or.* II 2; his daughter, *pro. Lig.* 21, Schol. Gronov. 292 Stangl; culture outside Rome, *de or.* III 43; Valerius Soranus, *Brutus* 169, *de or.* III 43; bathes, *Tusc. Disp.* V 74; C and agriculture, Qf III 1.2, *de sen.* 15–16; house in Rome, Plut. 8.6, Qf III 1.2; rels. w. Antonius, *de or.* II 3; Visellius Aculeo, *de or,* I 191, II 2; C's mother, f XVI 26.2, Plut. 1; Q's stature, Macrob. II 3.4; C in L. Crassus' house, *de or.* II 2; his wife's Latin, *Brut.* 211; rhetoric taught in Greek, *de or.* I 13; school of Latin rhetoric, *de or.* III 93; Suet. *de rhet.* 26; C studies Crassus' speeches, *Brut.* 169; rhetorical exercises, *de inv.* I 17–18, II 153; C's promise as student, Plut. 2.2; desire for glory, Qf III 5.4; Phaedrus, f XIII 1.2, *de n.d.* I 93; 'position, authority', *pro Clu.* 154.

2. AT THE FOOT OF THE LADDER 90–77 B.C.

Scaurus' influence, *pro Scauro* frag., *de off.* I 76; L. Crassus' great speech, *Brut.* 164, *de or.* I 225; 'wisely *popularis*', *de rep.* II 54; Crassus' death, *de or.* III 1ff; C on Roman law, *de or.* I 197; on XII Tables, *de leg.* III 59; C and Q. Scaevola, Plut. 3.1, *de amic.* 1; C and Stilo, *Brut.* 207; Atticus' youth, Nepos *Att.* 1, *de leg.* I 13; younger Marius, Nepos *ib.*; C knows Caesar, Qf II 14.1, *de prov. cons.* 40; the two fatherlands, *de leg.* II 5; C on Strabo's staff, ILLRP 515 (ILS 8888), *Phil.* XII 27; with Sulla, Plut. 3.1, *de div.* I 72; C hears Marius' speech, *post red. ad Quir.* 19–20; C and Scaevola Pontifex, *de amic.* 1; attempted murder of Scaevola, Val. Max. IX 11.2; C on these years, *Brut.* 227; Scaevola's attitude, A VIII 3.6; his death, App. I 88; Gratidianus, *de or.* I 178, II 262, *de off.* III 80–81; 'I came to the Forum', *Brut.* 311; listens to orators, *Brut.* 305; declaims, *ib.* 310; and Philo, Plut. 3.1, *Brut.* 306; Plato C's god, A IV 16.3; and Diodotus, *Brut.* 309, A II 20.6; on Greek lyric, Seneca, *Ep. Mor.* 49.5; C's verse, Plut. 2.3, Tacitus, *Dial.* 21; why orators are rare, *pro Cael.* 46; delicate digestion, Plut. 3–2; fast party, f IX 26; on love, *Tusc. Disp.* IV 68–76, cf. Seneca, *Ep. Mor.* 96; looks and elegance, Pollio *ap.* Elder Seneca, *Suas.* 6.14; physical exercises, *pro Cael.* 11; necessary for orator, *de or.* III 220; gladiators, *Tusc. Disp.* II 41; Roscius, Plut. 5.3; acting and oratory, *de or.* I 128, III 213–27; gesture of amazement, Quintil. *Inst. Or.* XI 3. 100; C's distinct

309

speech, Seneca *Ep. Mor.* 40 II; music in tragedy, *Ac.* II 20; Diodotus and music, *Tusc. Disp.* V 113; Molon, *Brut.* 312; 1st surviving speech, *pro Quinctio*; nervous, *Ac.* II 64; speaking out of doors, Quintil. *Inst. Or.* XI 3.27; success of *pro Roscio, Brut.* 312, *Or.* 108; speech for Arretine woman, *pro Caec.* 97; Terentia's sister, Ascon. *in Tog. Cand.* 70 Stangl, Plut. *Cato* 19.3; her wealth, Plut. 8.2; strongminded, *ib.* 20.2; pious, f XIV 7.1; C leaves Rome, Plut. 3.4, *Brut.* 313–15; Ser. Sulpicius, *Brut.* 151; C in Athens, *de leg.* II 1.4; at Academy, *de fin.* V 1–2; studies with Antiochus, Plut. 4.1, *Brut.* 315; with Epicureans, *de fin.* VI 1.3; and oratory, *Brut.* 315; Eleusinian mysteries, *de leg.* II 36; at Delphi, Plut. 5.4; at Corinth, *Tusc. Disp.* III 53; regrets its destruction, *de off.* I 35; at Sparta, *Tusc. Disp.* II 34, V 77; at Smyrna with Rutilius, *de rep.* I 13; Asian rhetors, *Brut.* 315; at Rhodes with Molon, *Brut.* 316; and Posidonius, *de n.d.* I 6, Plut. 4.4; C's health, Plut. 8.2–3; no siesta, *de div.* II 142.

3. POLITICAL APPRENTICESHIP 76–70 B.C.

New men's industry, *Verr.* II 3.7–8; C's important cases, *Brut.* 318; Hortensius' style, *ib.* 301–3, Quintil. *Inst. Or.* XI 3.8; Cato as quaestor, Plut. *Cato* 16–18; Romans at Eryx, Diod. Sic. IV 83.6; tomb of Archimedes, *Tusc. Disp.* V 64–6; dedic. of silver, Plut. 1.4; devotion to duty, *id.* 6.1; at Puteoli, *pro Planc.* 64–6; C on his maturity, *Brut.* 318–19; speech on S. Italy, *pro Tullio*; C on Committee, Syll. ³ 747.12, *de n.d.* III 4.9; patron of Sparta, f XIII 28a; avoids tribunate, Dio 36.43; scandals in courts, esp. *Div. in Q. Caec.* 8, *Verr.* I 38–9, *pro Clu.* 61, 79; Lucullus' intrigues, Plut. *Luc.* 5–6; Pompey's speech, *Verr.* I 45; 'boy executioner', Val. Max. VI 2.8; Varro's handbook, Aul. Gell. XIV 7.2; P's blushes, Seneca *Ep. Moral.* XI 4; M. Crassus' youth, Plut. *Crass.* 1 and 4–5; his greed, *de off.* III 73–5, cf. I 25; fire-brigade, Plut. *Crass.* 2; lack of convictions, *id. ib.* 7; Caesar's prosecutions, Plut. *Caes.* 4.1–2; Hortensius' sphinx, Plut. 7.6; Verres' case a challenge, *Brut.* 319; C not seeking 'spoils', *Verr.* II 1.21; Catulus, *Verr.* I 44; preliminaries to trial, *Div. in Q. Caec., Verr.* I 6. 19, 21, 30–31, II 1.16, *pro Scaur.* 25–6; Cotta's law, Ascon. *In Pis.* 21 Stangl.

4. THE BID FOR THE CONSULSHIP 69–64 B.C.

C's games, *de off.* II 58; Sicilians' aid, Plut. 8.1; on orators, *de or.* II 10; speech for Etruscan, *pro Caecina*; for Gallic governor, *pro Fonteio*; Hortensius' decline, *Brut.* 320, C's unparalleled talents, *ib.* 322; atmosphere at trial, *ib.* 290; C's perorations, *Or.* 131–2; M. Caelius, *pro Cael.* 9; C known as philhellene, A I 15.1; pretends to forget Greek artist, *Verr.* II 4.5; reputation for malice, Plut. 5.4; irritates with puns, *pro Planc.* 85; family affairs, A I 5, I 6, I 8; Tullia's engagement, A I 3.3; C. Piso, *Brut.* 242; d. of Lucius, A I 5.1; of Visellius Varro, *Brut.* 264; of C's father, A I 6. 2, Ascon. *In Tog. Cand.* 64 Stangl; A in Epirus, A I 5.7, Varro *Res Rust.* II 2ff; C at Tusculum, A I 5.7 etc.; at Formiae, A I 4.3; his Academy, A I 8.2 etc.; Lyceum, *de div.* 1.8; letter on works of art, f VII 23; painting of Sulla, Pliny *NH* XXII 12; table, *id. ib.* XIII 92; expenses of Tusculum, A I 4.3; Terentia's property, e.g. A II 4.5; Atticus' slaves, Nepos *Att.* 13.3, books, e.g. A XII 6a; gladiators, A IV 2a; C stands for praetor, A I 10.6, I 11 2–3; election, *de lege Man.* 2; Cornelius, Ascon. *In Corn.* 47–9 Stangl; decay of political life, A I 11.3; deserting the optimate cause, Dio 36.44; 'concord of the orders', *pro Clu.* 152–4; 'wrapping the jury in darkness', Quintil. *Inst. Or.* II 17.21; C as praetor, A I 4.3, Plus, 9; speech for Cornelius, Ascon. *In Corn.*; blame for taking case, *In Vat.* 5; '1st Catilinarian Conspiracy', Sall. 18–19, *pro Sulla* 67, 81; Egypt, Ascon. *de rege Alexandrino*; C stands for consul, A I 1.1–4; Domitius, A VIII 1, *Brut.* 267; Q's letter, *Comm. Petit.*; how to become consul, *pro Mur.* 43ff; C's wide acquaintance, Plut. 7.2; support from nobles, Sall. 23.6; triumphant election, Ascon. *In Tog. Cand.* 72 Stangl.

5. THE FATHER OF HIS COUNTRY 63 B.C.

Sullan veterans, Sall. 16–1; shortage of money, *In Vat.* 12, *pro Flacco* 67; Spartacus, Plut. *Crass.* 8–11, App. I 116; hostages, Plut. 18; pub. of C's speeches, A II 1.3; Catiline's trial for murder, Dio 37.10; his character, Sall. 5, 15–6, *pro Caelio* 12–14, *Cat.* I 46; tried for seducing Vestal, Sall. 15; Rullus' bill, *de leg agr.* I–III; honours to P, Dio 37.21; C's speeches, *id. ib.* 25; trial of Rabirius, *pro Rab. perd. reo*, Dio 37.26–8; style of C's speech, *Or.* 102; Caesar *pontifex maximus*, Plut. *Caes.* 7; consular elections, *pro Mur.* 43–53; Fulvia and Curius, Sall. 23. Diod. Sic. 40.5; Cato and Nepos stand for trib., Plut. *Cato* 20; imitation of ancestors, *de off.* I 116; Cato's mind, Plut. *Cato* 1; his youth, *id. ib.* 2–4; talks philosophy in Senate, *Parad. Stoic.* 1; as quaestor, Plut. *Cato* 16–18; debate on 22 Sept., Suet. *Div. Aug.* 94; Crassus' information, Dio 37.21; meeting of 21 Oct., Sall. 29; news from Etruria, *id.* 30; Catiline under house arrest, Dio 37.32; conference of 6 Nov., Sall. 27, *pro Sulla* 52; meeting on 8 Nov. Sall. 31, *Cat.* I; Catiline's letter, Sall. 35; C reports to People, *Cat.* II; Lentulus, *Cat.* III 9, 16, *Brut.* 235; Cassius, *Cat.* III 16, Ascon. 59–60 and 82 Stangl; Cethegus, Sall. 43; recovery of Hortensius, *Brut.* 323; trial of Murena, *pro Mur.*, Plut. *Comp. of Demosth. and Cic.* 1.5; unfair on Stoics, *de fin.* IV 74; Allobroges etc., *Cat.* III, Sall. 40–45; *pater patriae*, *In Pis.* 6, Plut. 23; civic crown, Aul. Gell. V 6 15; People's reaction, Sall. 48.1; night of Bona Dea, Plut. 19–20; meeting on 4 Dec., Sall. 48.2–3; attempt to implicate Caesar, *ib.* 49.1; C's memoir, Ascon. *In Tog. Cand.* 83 Stangl; quaestors' clerks, *Phil.* II 16; Atticus' role, A II 1.7; debate on 5 Dec., Sall. 50–54, A XII 21.1, *Cat.* IV; by-play, Plut. *Cato* 24.1–2; evening of 5th, Plut. 22; last day of Dec., f V 2.7; Pistoria, Sall. 59–61.

6. POMPEY'S RETURN TO ROME 62–60 B.C.

C called on in 1st place, A I 13.2; Caesar and Nepos back down, Plut. 23; trials, *pro Sulla* 5–6; Cato's corn law, Plut. *Cato* 26.1; Senate frustrates Pompey, Plut. *Cato* 30; C on debts, *de off.* II 84; attacks on C, *pro Sulla* 21–3, 30–31; letters to and from Celer, f V 1 and 2; long letter to Pompey, Schol. Bob. 167 Stangl; brief reply to Pompey, f V 7; C's new house, f V 6.2; 'built of marble', *Parad. Stoic.* 13; C in debt, f V 6.2; consul buys house, A I 13.6; Antonius in Macedonia, A I 12.2; unreliable messengers, A I 13.1; Mucia's divorce, A I 12.3; Pompey's approach to Cato, Plut. *Cato* 30.2–4; 'as you said', A I 13.4; Clodius affair, A I 12.3, 13.3; 'Caesar's wife', Plut. *Caes.* 10.6; Pompey's speeches to People, A I 14.1–2; in Senate, A I 14.2; 'of me he only said', A I 14.5; trial of Clodius, A I 16.1–6; jealousy of Terentia, Plut. 29.2; C's reaction to result, A I 16.6–11; Clodius and Lucullus, Plut. *Luc.* 34, *pro Milone* 73; incest with Tullia, Dio 46.18.6; Clodius seeks tribunate, A I 18.4, 19.5, II 1.5; 'the Clodian drama', A I 18.2; C's tribute to A, A I 17.5; remembered as C's friend,

Seneca *Ep.* 21.4; Q in Asia, A I 15.1, 16.14, 17.1–7, Qf I 1; Afranius as consul, A I 16.12–13; P's triumph, Pliny NH XXXVII 12–14; alienation of *equites*, A I 17.8–9; C's policy, A I 17.10; his isolation, A I 18.1; studies, A I 20.7; 'fish-pond fanciers', A II 1.7, Varro RR III 17; Lucullus' luxury, Plut. *Luc.* 39–40; Pompey and C at dinner, *id. ib.* 41.2–6; C on d. of Catulus, A I 20.3; C on Cato, A I 18.7, II 1.8; agrarian bill, A I 18.6, 19.4, II 1.6; embassy to Gaul, A I 19.2–3; unworthy joke, A II 1.5; publication of speeches, A II 1.3; of memoirs and poem, A I 19.10, 20.6, II 1.1–2; Pompey's arrangements in East, Plut. *Pomp.* 46; C on his influence with Pompey, A I 19.7; and with Caesar, A II 1.6; Cato's opposition to Caesar, Plut. *Caes.* 13.1–2; Cato and bribery, Suet. 19.1.

7. FROM OPPOSITION TO EXILE   59–57 B.C.

C's plans, A II 3.3; reads political philosophy, A II 2, 12.4; laws not mentioned, Dio 38.7.6; events of spring, Dio 38.1–8, 9–10, Plut. *Caes.* 14; C on Cato's role, A II 9.1 and 2; working on geography, A II 4.1 etc.; C on Egypt, Cato, posterity and the augurate, A II 5.1–2; Antium the place for politics, A II 6.1; news of Clodius via Clodia, A II 9.1; the Egyptian embassy, A II 7.3; the augurate, *ib.*; Curio calls, A II 8.1; Clodius' adoption queried, A II 12.1; uncertain political situation, A II 15.1; callers, A II 14.2, 15.3; new agrarian law, A II 16.1–2; Pompey's prevarication, A II 16.2; Pompey ready for tyranny, A II 17.1; 'the foolish streak', A II 17.2; A invited to Arpinum, A II 16.4; Caesar gets Transalpine Gaul, A VIII 3.3; opposition to Three 'causes me not hope', A II 18.1; Bibulus' edicts, A II 19.2, 20.4, 21.5; Caesar offers C a post, A II 18.3; C refuses seat on board, *ib.*; summons A, A II 19.5; his fears, A II 20.3; C on Pompey, A II 21.3–4, 23.2; on the situation, II 19.3, 20.3–5, 21.1–2; busy in courts, A II 22.3; A gets letter not in C's hand, A II 23.1; C summons A again, A II 22.4; informer and plot, A II 24.2; speech for Flaccus, A II 25, *pro Flacco*; 'all Italy', Qf I 2.5; new magistrates favour, Dio 38.15.6; Clodius' laws, *id. ib.* 13; organizes *collegia*, *In Pis.* 9; Piso treats C with respect, *ib.* 11; Clodius' new bills, *ib.* 14.1–4; C in mourning, *ib.* 14.7; demonstration by *equites*, Senate forbidden to wear mourning, *pro Sest.* 26–9; C visits L. Piso, *In Pis.* 13; Clodius to the assembly, *pro Sest.* 39–40; Pompey's actions, Plut. 31, *In Pis.* 77; Cato's advice, A III 15.2, Plut. *Cato* 35; Cato in Cyprus, Plut. *Cato* 35–8; C's departure, Plut. 31.5; Clodius' further bills, *de dom.* 4–7; C's property damaged, Plut. 33.1; where to go? A III 3 and 4; dream of Marius, *de div.* I 59, II 137; letter from Brundisium, f XIV 4; Plancius, *pro Planc.* 98–101; 'My brother', Qf I 3.1; at Thessalonica, A III 9–15; Clodius quarrels with Pompey, *de har. resp.* 49; tribunicial moves, *pro Sest.* 68; letters to A, A III 15–21; situation in Rome, Plut. *Pomp.* 49; C in Dyrrhachium, A II 22.4; apologizes to A, A III 20; A's new wealth, *ib.*; letters to Terentia, f XIV 1; and to Q, Qf 1.4; attempt of the 8 tribunes, A III 23; Sestius in Gaul, *pro Sest.* 71; vote on 1 Jan., *de dom.* 68–9; battle in Forum, *pro Sest.* 76–7; letter to Nepos, f V 4; Senate summons Italians, *de dom.* 30; bill proposed by all magistrates, *In Pis.* 35.

8. RETURN AND RECANTATION   57–52 B.C.

C's return, *pro Sest.* 131, A IV 1; his house, A IV 1.7; calls A home, A IV 1.8; speech to priests, A IV 2.2; 'all the prestige of the state', *de dom.* 1;

priests' decision, A IV 2.3; compensation, A IV 2.5; troubles at home, A IV 2.7; post on Pompey's staff, A IV 2.6; censorship, *ib.*; gangs attack house, A IV 3.2; fighting in Rome, A IV 3.3–4; C on Milo, A IV 3.5; oracle on Egypt, Qf II 2.3; 'As for Pompey', f I 1.2; 'when I listen', f I 2.3; Clodius attacks Pompey, Qf II 3.2; 'and so he is preparing', Qf II 3.4; Gabinius, *in Pis.* 49; trial of Sestius, Qf II 3.5, 4.1; C and agrarian law, f I 9.8; 'after dinner', Qf II 6.3; Luca, f I 9.9; 'you're the man', *ib.*; Domitius, Suet. 24; the palinode, A IV 5; C speaks for Caesar in Senate, *de prov. cons.*; Clodius and prodigy, *de harusp. resp.*; C's letter to Lucceius, f V 12; to Spinther, f I 7.10; hesitates to attack Hortensius, A IV 6.3; open letter to Spinther, f I 9; 'what is more shameful', A IV 6.1–2; defends Balbus, *pro Balb.*; 'for what can be more wretched', A IV 8a; elections, Plut. *Cato* 41–2; consular legislation, Plut. *Pomp.* 52; C hopes for quiet and blames Cato, f I 8.4; friendly with Pompey, A IV 9; argument with Cato, Dio 39.21–2; attack on Piso, *In Pis.*; quarrel and reconciliation with Crassus, f V 8; to A on Crassus, A IV 13; d. of Julia, Plut. *Pomp.* 53; Q's villas, Qf II 1; Q unhappy in Gaul, Qf II 15; Nervii, Caesar BG V 38–40; tragedies, Qf III 5.7; Domitius and patronage, Qf II 4.18; loan from Caesar, A VII 3.11; to A on Caesar, A IV 19.2; 'my zeal', Qf II 14.2; on grammar, *Brut.* 252, *Or.* 155–60; Oppius, Aulus Gellius VI 1.1 etc.; C works with him, A IV 16.8; C speaks in Senate, Qf II 15a.5; 'I find no recreation', A IV 10; 'I am tortured', Qf III 5.4; hot summer, Qf III 1.1, Plut. *Cato* 44.1; speeches for defence, *pro Scaur.*, *pro Planc.*; Spinther disapproves, f I 9.19; C and Gabinius, A IV 18.1; Qf III 1.5; speech for financier, *pro Rabirio Postumo*; demoralization in Rome, A IV 17.2–5, 18.3; Cato's efforts, A IV 15.7–8; Pompey as Dictator, Qf II 6.4; C to Curio on Milo, f I 6.3; Clodius' d., *pro Milone*, Asconius *In Mil.*; Cato on Pompey's consulship, Plut. *Cato* 47; Crassus' death, Plut. *Crass.* 31; Milo's trial, Asconius *In Mil.*; Milo at Massilia, Dio 40.54; further trials, f VII 2.2; journey to Ravenna, A VII 1.4; C's augurate, *Brut.* 1; Appius on augury, f III 9.3; menu, Macrob. III 10–12; Pompey's marriage, Plut. *Pomp.* 55; reforms, *ib.* 55, Dio 40.56; Cato not consul, Plut. *Cato* 49; C blames him, *ib.* 50; Cato in the courts, *ib.* 48; at the games, *ib.* 46; at the theatre, Seneca *Ep. Mor.* XCVII 8; Pompey's law on provinces, Dio 40.56.1; A's marriage, Qf II 3.6; his house, Nepos *Att.* 13.2; simple dinners and dinner service, A V 12, VI 1.13, Nepos *ib.* 13.5–6; Cleopatra's service, Athenaeus VI 229c; reading aloud at dinner, Nepos *ib.* 14.1, A XVI 2.3; walks, A IV 10.1–2, *de Fato* 8; at Arpinum, *de leg.* preface; A's farms in Italy, Nepos 14.3; C's relations with Q, Qf II 9.1; Q's properties, Qf III 1; C's library, A IV 8; young Q, esp., Qf III 3.4; Caelius' trial, *pro Cael.*; 'a good right', Quintilian VI 3.69; Trebatius, f VII 5–18; P. Crassus, Qf II 8.2; verses to Tiro, Pliny *Letters* VII 4; Tiro's virtues, A VII 5.2; 'I am more upset', A I 12.4; 'I am so grateful', f XVI 16; Tiro's shorthand, Isidore *Orig.* I 21, cf. A XIII 25.3; Tullia, Qf II 4.2, 6.1, A IV 4a.2, 16.5, and the trial, A IV 5.4; Terentia and Pomponia, Qf II 6.2; C on Pompey's games, f VII 1.2–4; C's epic, f I 9.23, A IV 8a.3.

9. CICERO ON THE REPUBLIC 56–52 B.C.

Catullus on C, poem 49; C on Lucretius, Qf II 10.2, Jerome *Chron.* 94 B.C.; *otium cum dignitate*, esp. *pro Sest.* 98–100; to Spinther on it, f I 9.23; 'a heavy and laborious task', A IV 16.2; borrows Varro's works, A IV 14.1; to

Q on *de rep.*, Qf III 5.1; Lucretius on politics, Lucr. III 59–86; Scipio on astronomy, *de rep.* I 15–26; the three forms of state, *ib.* 42–71; history of Rome, *ib.* II 4–63; Justice and Law, *ib.* III; education, *ib.* IV; ideal citizen, *ib.* V–VI; dictatorship, *ib.* VI.12; aim of state, *ib.* V 8; *De legibus* on Natural Law, *de leg.* I 17–end, II 8–16; on religion, *ib.* II 19–end; on constitution, *ib.* III 6–11; writing history, *ib.* I 1; C's views on historiography, *de or.* II 51–64; death of L. Crassus, *ib.* III 1–12; ancient burial customs, *de leg.* II 56–7; hopes to begin history, A XVI 13a.2; Nepos frag. 18 (Peter HRR).

10. THE GOVERNOR OF CILICIA 51–50 B.C.

Pomptinus, Sall. 45, *de prov. cons.* 32, Dio 39–65; Pomponia, A V 1.3–4; Hortensius, A V 2 1–2; Pompey, A V 5.2, 6.1, 7, f II 8; Brundisium, A V 8.1; Athens, A V 10; Tullia's marriage, A V 4.1, 21.14, VI 1.10, 4.2, 6.1; 'this enormous bore', A V 2.3; longing for Rome, A V 11.1; letter to Memmius, A V 11.6, f XIII 1; C crosses Aegean, A V 11.4, 12.1; Ephesus, A V 13; on the road, A V 14.1; Laodicea, A V 15.1; skeleton legions, A V 15.1; mutiny and settlement, A V 14.1; troops mislaid, f III 6.5; Senate levies, f III 3.1; disloyalty, A V 18.1; news of Parthians, A V 18.1; C's strong position, etc., A V 17.2; Deiotarus, A V 18.2; boys sent to safety, A V 17.3; A's quick letter, and his daughter, A V 19; report to Senate, f XV 2; letter to Cato, f XV 3; other letter to Senate, f XV 1; arrival in Cilicia, course of fighting, A V 20, f II 10; Caelius wishes C a triumph, f VIII 8.1; letter to Cato, f XV 4; his answer, f XV 5; C's answer, f XV 6; comment to A, A VII 2.7; prospects for next year, A V 21; anxieties in May, A VI 3; on return to Cilicia, A VI 4.1, 5.3; drawbacks of Q, A VI 6.4; new quaestor unknown to C, A VI 2.10; not heard of, A VI 4.1; arrives, A VI 6.3; 'my friends' letters', A VI 6.4; triumph, *In Pis.* 60.

Rome's benefits, Polybius 36.17; governor's duty to provincials, Qf I 1.24; learnt from philosophy, *ib.* 29; justification of conquest, *de rep.* III 37–8; friendship with Greeks, Qf I 1.16; relations with Roman businessmen, *ib.* 6–7; fixing of tithes over, A V 16.2; financial recovery of cities, A VI 2.5; no requisitioning, A V 16.2; sum saved, f V 20.9; rule as to prefects, A V 21.10 etc., letters of recommendation, f XII 53–9, 61–5; other governors good, A VI 1.13; controlling staff, Qf I 1.10; Tiro's health, A VI 7.2; prefect a wonder, A V 17.2; quaestor poor, A VI 3.1; rudeness, A V 10.3; final demands of staff, A VII 1.6; need for mildness, Qf I 1.22; Greeks allowed to try own cases, A VI 1.15, 2.4; access to C, A VI 2.5; affairs of Brutus, A V 21.10–13, VI 1.3–7, 2.7–9, 5.3–5; Brutus as legate, Plut. *Brut.* 4.2; letters to Appius, f III; C tries to meet him, A V 16.4, f III 4.2, 5.3; Appius' complaints, A VI 1.2, f III 8.1; his abominable behaviour, A V 15.2, 16.2, 17.6; Pompey urges his interests, A VI 2.10; so does Brutus, A VI 3.7; Appius and Dolabella, f III 12.2–3; and Caelius, f VIII 12.3; aedile's tax, Qf I 1.26; Caelius' demands, A VI 1.21, f II 11.2; panthers for a colleague, A V 21.5; C refuses statues and temples, A V 21.7; free embassies, *de leg.* III 18; edict, A VI 1.15, f III 8.3–4; enjoyment of virtue, A V 20.6; to Caelius on Rome, f II 12.2.

11. THE UNCERTAINTIES OF CIVIL WAR 49–48 B.C.

C on Caelius as politician, f II 8.1; 'very busy' f VIII 1.1; rumour C murdered, f VIII 1.4; Cato threatens to prosecute Caesar, Suet. 30.3 and

4; bill of the tribunes, Caesar *BC* I 32.3; Curio's tribunate, f VIII 4.2; attempt to recall Caesar, App. II 27; 'you know the usual pattern', f VIII 5.2; legions for East, f VIII 4.4; Caelius as aedile, f VIII 6.4–5; gossip from Rome, f VIII 7.2; C's thanksgiving, f VIII 11.1–2; 'I tell you this', f VIII 11.3; Curio's veto, f VIII 13.2; Pompey ill, Plut. *Pomp.* 57, *TD* I 86; officers' reports, Plut. *Pomp.* 57; Caelius uncertain who to join, f VIII 14.1–3; C hears of d. of Hortensius, *Brut.* 1, A VI 6.2; Tiro in Greece, f XVI 9, 11, 12, A VII 2.3; C writes from Athens, A VI 9.1, cf. *TD.* V 22; to Terentia, f XIV 5; she meets C at Brundisium, f XVI 9.2; A's health, A VII 2 etc.; C defends his return, A VII 3.1–2; says Caesar not generous, *ib.* 3; the debt, *ib.* 11; lack of enthusiasm for war, *ib.* 5; 'now we have to deal', A VII 7.6; vote in Senate, App. II 30; consul gives Pompey command, *id. ib.* 31; C meets Pompey, A VII 4.1–2; 'the political situation', A VII 5.4; 'it is another great evil', A VII 6.2; following the herd, A VII 7.7; talk with Pompey, A VII 8.4; the alternatives, A VII 9.2; C at Alba, A VII 7.3; reaches Rome, f XVI 4; the triumph, Plut. 37; 'I could get nowhere', f IV 1.1; new offer by Caesar, Plut. *Caes.* 31; Cato's opposition, *id. Pomp.* 49; Piso mediates, Caesar *BC* I 3.6; 'there are people', f XVI 11.2; flight of the tribunes etc., Caesar *BC* I 5; 'swept along by madness', f XVI 12.2; 'I have suddenly decided', A VII 10; 'I feel calmer', A VII 11.5; 'he says he is doing', A VII 11.1; on Pompey, A VII 12.1; the women, A VII 12.6, 13.3, 14.3; Dionysius, A VII 18.3 etc.; sending boys to Greece, A VII 13.3, 17.1; meeting on 26 Jan., A VII 15; 'even Cato', A VII 15.2; 'it will be insane', A VII 17.2; C's command on coast, A VII 11.5, VIII 3.4; Caesar's attitude, A VII 21.3; 'no courage, no plan', A VII 21.1; letter from Pompey, A VIII 1.4; 'if I could sleep', A VIII 1.4; 'I consider that no statesman', A VIII 2.2; turns back, A VIII 3.5; Domitius' stand, A VIII 6.1–3 etc.; C's reaction, A VIII 8; 'I have someone to flee', A VIII 7.2; ideal statesman, A VIII 11.1; 'Pompey's plan', A VIII 11.2; unable to work, A VIII 9a; book on Concord, A VIII 11.7; 'the people of the town', A VIII 13.2; 'see how upside down', *ib.*; senators in Rome, A VIII 14.2, 15.2; letter of Balbus, A VIII 15a; prospect of meeting Caesar, A VIII 15.1; Quintus, A IX 1.4, 6.4; A advises remaining, A IX 2a 1; C unconvinced; rumour Pompey embarked, A IX 6.3; 're-reading your letters', A IX 6.5; 'I shall follow your advice', A IX 7.2; letter of Oppius and Balbus, A IX 7a; 'it is what I owe him', A IX 7.3; returns book, A IX 9.2; attempt at mediation A IX 11a; 'tears prevent me', A IX 12.1; shall C raise towns, A IX 12.3; 'not in a fight', A IX 15.3; meets Caesar, A IX 18; must go to Arpinum, A VIII 9.3; at Arpinum, A IX 19; 'my present course', A X 1a; where to go? A X 4.12, 7.1; young Q, A X 4.5–7 and 11, 6.2, 7.3; rumour, A X 9.1; Curio's visit, A X 4.8–11; 'let the outcome', A X 6.1; Tullia and A for staying, A X 8.1; 'I have commended', A X 8.1; Attica's education, Suet. *de gramm.* 16; Tullia's learning, Cic. ap. Lact. *Div. Inst.* I 15.18; her hasty step, Macrob. II 3.16; notes from Antony and Caesar, A X 8a and b; 'the tears of my family', A X 9.2; Caelius' warning, A X 9a; Antony refuses permission, A X 10.2; plan to slip away, A X 10.3; Quintus, A X 6.10; 'Good gods', A X 11.4; 'he is carrying Cytheris', A X 10.5; Trebatius, A X 1.3, 11.4; 'what is to become of me', A X 12.1; visit of Ser. Sulpicius, A X 13.2, 14.1–3; 'Caelian' plan, A X 14.3, 15.2, 16.4; C at Pompeii, A X 16.4; Tullia's delivery, A X 18.1; farewell letter to Terentia, f XIV 7.

'You may ask why', A XI 4.1; in Pompey's camp, Plut. 38; sums up experiences, f VII 3.2; plans for proscriptions, A XI 6.2; disillusion shared by Varro, f IX 6.3, and M. Marcellus, f. IV 7.2; letter from Caelius, f VIII 17; 'brilliantly worthless', Velleius Paterculus II 68; his revolt, Caesar *Bell. Civ.* III 20–22; letter from Dolabella, f IX 9; young Marcus, *de off.* II 13.6; C at Dyrrhachium, Plut. 39; prophecy, *de div.* I 68; C refuses command, Plut. 39; C at Patrae, A XI 5.4; receives permission to return to Italy, A XI 7.

12. PRIVATE AND POLITICAL GRIEFS   48–45 B.C.

C admits impulsiveness, A XI 5.1; his distress, *ib.* 3; others stay abroad, A XI 13.1, 14.2; 'to be stuck', A XI 6.2; letter to Terentia, f XIV 12; Tullia's troubles, A XI 6.4; death of Pompey, *ib.* 5; Oppius and Balbus, A XI 6; Vatinius, A XI 5.4; negotiations with Antony, A XI 7; attitude to Pompeians in Africa, A XI 7.3; regrets, *ib.* 5; Q and Caesar, A XI 12.2, 8.1; 'it is the most', A XI 8.2; 'you know his style', *ib.*; 'I should never have opened', A XI 9.2; letter of Q, A XI 13.2–4; Dolabella's actions, A XI 14.1, 15.3; Caesar in Alexandria, [Caesar] *Bell. Alex.*; Pompeians off to Africa, A XI 14.1, 15.1; Terentia's will, A XI 16.5, 24; notes to Terentia, f XIV 19, 21–4; Tullia's visit, A XI 17.1, 17a, Plut. 41; Marcus, A XI 17a, 18.1; secreting property, A XI 25.3; divorcing Dolabella, A XI 23.3; letter from Caesar; Q and son forgiven, A XI 20; C and Q A XI 21.1, 22.1; Caesar to return via Brundisium, A XI 22.2; does so, Plut. 39; letter to Terentia, f XIV 22.

d. of Bibulus, Caesar *BC* III 18; of Appius, Lucan *Phars.* V.1; of Domitius, Caesar *BC* III 99; of Curio, Caesar *ib.* II 42; of Cato, [*id.*] *Bell. Afr.* 88; Plut. *Cato* 59–70; C writes to Brutus, f XIII 10–14; to Caesarian friend, f XIII 29; to ex-quaestor, f V 21; to Varro, f IX 1; declines to visit him, f IX 2.4; 'let this be agreed', *ib.* 5; C on Hortensius' d., *Brut.* 1–5; on Caesar as speaker, *ib.* 251–62; on Cato, *Parad. Stoic.* 1; 'the question of the *Cato*', A XII 4.2; 'I like my *Cato*', A XII 5.2; Caesar on it, A XIII 46.2; C to Varro on dinner parties, f IX 7.1–2; loan to Caesar's secretary, A XII 21.2 etc.; C and Varro at Tusculum, f IX 6.4–5; C announces Caesar's return to Varro, f IX 7.2; to Paetus, f IX 16.3–4, 7–10; Varro dedicates work to Caesar, Augustine CD VII 35; in charge of public library, Suet. 44.2; 'the plan pleases me', f IX 18.2; Cassius a pupil, f VII 33.2; C on teaching, *Or.* 142–4; on Atticists, *ib.* 28–32, on Asians, 25–7, 230–31; on Demosthenes *ib.* 23–7, 104, 110ff; on rhythm, *ib.* 149ff; on Ideas, *ib.* 7–11, 101; on fallibility, *ib.* 237; preface on Demosth. and Aeschines, *de opt. gen. orat.*; letter about *Or.*, f VI 18.4; early history of Papirii, f IX 21.2–3; improper words, f IX 22; decline of Roman humour, f IX 15.2; C dines Hirtius, f IX 20.2–3; at dinner with Cytheris, f IX 26; dysentery, f VII 26.1; 'we are slaves to him', f IX 17.3; letter to Marcellus, f IV.7; to Caecina, f VI 5 and 6; Caesar angry with fighters in Africa, f VI 13.3; to Ser. Sulpicius, A IV 4.3–4; Caesar's glory, *pro Marc.* 4–10, 25–30; the two causes, *ib.* 16; let him restore republic, *ib.* 23; letter from Marcellus, f IV 11; 'there is no need', f VI 7.5–6; C refuses aid, f VII 27; writes to Ligarius, f VI 14.2; speech for him, Plut. 39, *pro Ligario*; praises Pompey in it, *ib.* 18–19; honours to Caesar, Dio 43.15; triumphs, *ib.* 19–21; games, *ib.* 22–4; dedication of Forum Julium etc., *ib.* 22; C and Cleopatra, A XV 15.2;

and division of land, f IX 17.1–2; Caesar's enactments, Dio 43.25–7; C
on reform of calendar, Plut. *Caes*. 59.3; 'will there be fewer', f IX 15.4;
Sulla and the alphabet, Suet. 77; Cassius' letter, f XV 19.4.

Tullia's divorce, and her dowry, f VI 18.5 etc.; divorce from Terentia,
Plut, 41.2; sour letter about Q, A XII 5.1; 'on my life', A XII 3.1; Attica, A
XII 3 etc.; treatise for Marcus, *Part. Orat.*; Marcus' wishes, A XII 7.1; C
not so eager to leave Rome, f VI 18.5; considers house at Naples, f IX
15.3, 15.4; Astura, A XII 9; writes from Cumae, f VII 4, IX 23; from
Arpinum, A XII 1.1; Hirtius' sister, Jerome *adv. Iovin.*, I 48; 'as for
Pompey's daughter', A XII 11.2; marriage to Publilia, Plut. 41.3; 'I should
not have taken', f IV 14.3; Tullia's illness, Plut. 41.5; C gets off engagements, A XII 13; 'you are my witness', A XII 14.3; 'in this lonely place', A
XII 15.1; 'I don't want you to leave', A XII 16.1; Brutus' letter, A XII 14.4;
Caesar's, A XIII 20.1; Sulpicius', f IV 5.4; 'I feel myself almost bound',
A XI 18.1; frag. of *Consol*. in Lactantius, *Div. Inst*. I 15.18; Terentia and
the will, A XII 18a; Brutus' ignorance, A XII 21.1; C asks for historical
advice, A XII 20.2 etc.; Marcus sent to Athens, A XII 27.2, 24.2; Attica's
health, A XII 33; threatened visit of Publilia, A XII 32; C leaves Astura, A
XII 34.1; 'I want it to be a shrine', A XII 36.1; urban development, A
XIII 33a; reproached for retirement, f V 15; defends self to A, A XII 38a;
'Hirtius writes to me', A XII 37a.

13. THE CONSOLATIONS OF PHILOSOPHY   45–44 B.C.

Philosophic poem, Qf II 10.2; Epicurean works, *fin*. I 8, *Ac*. I 5; Brutus'
de virtute, *fin*. I 8 etc.; his philosophic works, Quintil. XI 123; his *de off*.,
Seneca *Ep. Moral.*, 95.45; Atticus' works, Nepos *Att*. 18; Varro made to
object to philosophizing in Latin, *Ac*. I 4–8; 'I do not think it possible', *div*.
II 5; 'it was in my books', *div*. II 7; Scipio's use of leisure, *off*. III 4;
riches of Latin, *fin*. I 10 etc.; new words formed, Plut. 40; might translate Greek, *fin*. I 7; 'to expound the famous', *Ac*. I 3; 'they are mere transcriptions', A XII 52.3; sends for books, A XIII 31.2, 32.2 etc.; always *read*
philosophy, *Ac*. I 11; 'I yield to many', *off*. I 2; Carneades in Rome, *Ac*.
II 137; Pythagoreanism in early Italy, *TD* IV 2.5; finds *Timaeus* hard, *fin*.
II 15; rejects Carneades, *de rep*. II 8.9, *de leg*. I 39; 'live from day to
day', *TD* V 33; young take too much on trust, *Ac*. II 8, *de n.d*. I 10;
'somehow most men', *Ac*. II 9; Epicurus virtuous, *TD* III 30, 47; C ex-
pounds him accurately, *fin*. I 13; Augustine, *Confessions* 3.4; C writes at
Puteoli, Pliny NH XXXV 4; final scene, *Ac*. II 147–8; changes speakers, A
XIII 12.3, 16, 19.3–5; dedicates to Varro, f IX 8; 2nd ed. *'more brilliant'*, A
XIII 13.1; 'no one can be wise', *Ac*. II 29; 'what method of philosophy', *div*.
II 1; 'the most essential part', *Ac*. I 34; Epicurus 'expresses his meaning',
fin. I 15; declamation in old age, *TD* I 7; A re-reads *TD*, A XV 2.4; 'not as
Pythian Apollo', *TD* I 9; 'medicine of the soul', *ib*. III 1 etc.; 'virtue does
not easily', *ib*. V 68; confidence of Epicureans, *de n.d*. I 18; A suggests
Cotta, A XIII 19.3; 'and let us first behold', *de n.d*. II 98–100; 'I thought I
should be doing', *div*. II 148; prophecies about Crassus etc., *ib*. II 99;
divination not useful, *ib*. II 11–12; contradictory, *ib*. II 28; astrology, *ib*.
II 90; 'natural divination', *ib*. II 100ff; the old occupied with books, *de sen*.
38; agriculture, *ib*. 24.51–60; teaching, *ib*. 29; advising state, *ib*. 61–4;

will keep mental power, *ib.* 22; must accept course of nature, *ib.* 72; friendship not based on utility, *de amic.* 26–31; but community of mind, *ib.* 61; the true glory of life, *ib.* 20–23; Marcus to study Academics, *off.* I 2; will receive more works, *ib.* I 2, III 121; Panaetius' omissions, *ib.* I 7, 10; Regulus, *ib.* III 99ff; C follows more generous Stoics, *ib.* III 51, 63, 89, 91; on Crassus, *ib.* 73–5; on Caesar, *ib.* I 26, II 23, 28; III 82–3.

14. CAESAR'S LAST MONTHS 45–44 B.C.

Hirtius' *Anti-Cato*, A XII 40.1, 41.4, 44.1; Caesar on C's Cato, A XIII 46.2; C's proposed letter to Caesar, A XII 40.2, XIII 26, 27, 28.2; Caesar said to be restoring constitution, A XIII 31.3; proposed political dialogue, A XIII 30.2 etc.; 'how hard you work', A XIII 6.4; something for Dolabella, A XIII 13.2; Cato's sister, A XIII 48.2, 37.3; letters to be published, f XVI 17.1, cf. A XVI 5.5; C returns to Tusculum, A XII 46.1, 45.1; A visits him there, A XII 50, 49.1; book on Greek accents, A XII 6.2; 'you have done right', A XIII 6.1–3; news of Marcus, A XIII 1, 24.1; 'Asinius Pollio has written', A XII 38.2; 'if the whole army', A XIII 9; legacy, A XIII 45.3, 46.3, XIV 10.3; divorce from Publilia, A XIII 34; statues of Caesar, A XII 48, 45.2, XIII 44.1; false Marius, A XII 49.2; Cappadocian prince, A XIII 2a.2; death of Marcellus, f IV 12; Brutus' marriage, A XIII 16.2, 17.1; C at Arpinum: weather bad, A XIII 16.1; success of speech for Ligarius, A XIII 19.2; Balbus, Caerellia and *de fin.*, A XIII 21a, 22.3; correspondence with Caerellia, Dio 46.18; Tigellius, and 'for that matter', A XIII 49.1–2; younger Q, A XIII 40.2, 41; 'the younger Balbus', A XIII 37.2; Brutus and young Q, A XIII 41; C on Brutus, A XIII 40.1; C writes to Caesar, A XIII 50.1, 51.1; calls his *Cato* shameless, *Top.* 94; question of meeting him, A XIII 50.4; Caesar's triumph, Plut. *Caes.* 56; C active in Senate and as augur, A XIII 47a, 42.3; Vatinius' letter, f V 19; restoration of Pompey's statues, Plut. 40–44; C sends speech to Dolabella, f IX 12.2; letters of recommendation, f XIII 30–39; Buthrotum affair, A XII 6a.2 etc.; Caesar compliments C, Pliny NH VII 117; Caesar to dinner, A XIII 52; young Q and Parthia, A XIII 42.1; Caninius' election, f VII 30.1–2, Macr. II 3; Caesar's final months, Dio 43.44–51, 44.1–11, Plut. *Caes.* 56–61; Lupercalia, *Phil* II 85–6; C kept waiting, A XIV 1, 2.3; Brutus urged on, Plut. *Brut.* 9; his views, Quintilian IX 3.45; C on honours to tyrannicides, *pro Mil.* 80; the Ides, Plut. *Caes.* 62ff etc.; Brutus calls on C, *Phil.* II 28, 30; so do conspirators, Dio 44, 20.4; note of congratulation, f VI 15; 'if Caesar with all his genius', A XIV 1.1.

15. THE ATTACK ON ANTONY 44 B.C.

C advises calling Senate, A XIV 10.1; refuses to negotiate, *Phil.* II 89; thinks Antony should have been killed, A XV 11; *coup* of Antony and Lepidus, Dio 44.22; C's speech, *Phil.* I 2; 'strong as a gladiator', *Phil.* II 63; the funeral, A XIV 10.1; Dolabella assumes consulship, Dio 44.22; Cleopatra departs, A XIV 8.1; C writes at dinner, A XIV 6.2; in boat, A XIV 16; on young Q, A XIV 10.4, 17.3; reports country reactions, A XIV 6.2; fears unrest in Gaul, A XIV 4.1; on Antony, A XIV 3.2; Caesar's *acta* in operation, A XIV 6; 'O my dear Atticus', A XIV 12; temple of Ops, A XIV 14.5; Hirtius and Pansa alarmed, A XIV 19.2 etc.; Hirtius fears violence, A XV 1.3; their attitude, A XIV 22.1; Brutus' lack of attraction,

A XIV 20.3; Antony and C exchange letters, A XIV 13.6; C meets Octavian, A XIV 12.2; Dolabella's actions, A XIV 15, 16.2; C writes to him, A XIV 17a; A cautious, A XIV 19.5, 18.1; C plans to go to Greece, A XIV 7.2 etc.; 'from the preparations', A XIV 18.4; worries about Marcus, A XIV 7.2, 16.3; letter from him to Tiro, f XVI 25, 21; should C write speech for Brutus? A XIV 20.3; or give advice? A XV 1.5; or correct speech? A XV 1a, 2.2; danger at Rome, A XV 5.2; C accepts legateship, A XV 8, 11.4; laws of 2 June, *Phil.* I 6, V 7–8; Brutus and Cassius to buy corn, A XV 9.1, 10; 'I arrived at Antium', A XV 11; fears of Sex. Pompeius, A XV 21.3; C worries about journey, A XV 25, XVI 4.4 etc.; 'my dear Atticus', f XVI 23.1; 'I am sorry that', A XV 27.2; 'those jewels of Italy', A XVI 6.2; young Q's farewell, A XVI 1.6, 5.2; he turns to Liberators, A XV 19.2; his brave death, Dio 47.10; Brutus not keen to travel with C, A XVI 5.3; C hears of Senate meeting, A XVI 7.1 etc.; meets Brutus again, A XVI 7.1; 'for what can be done?' A XVI 7.7.

Oppius and Balbus close to Octavian, A XIV 10.3, XVI 15.3; Dolabella's collaboration with Antony, App. III 7–8; C absent on 1 Sept., *Phil.* I 12; Antony angry, *ib.* 11–12; one consular supports C, f XII 2.1; letters to governors, f X 1–3, XII 23; Antony's speech, *Phil.* II 3–40; C to Cassius, f XII 2; Antony going from bad to worse, f XII 3.1; peroration, *Phil.* II 118–19; C at Puteoli, A XV 13; on private ties, *off.* III 28; Matius' letter, f XI 28; rumours from Servilia, A XV 13.4; Antony and Octavian, Dio 45.8; C on these, f XII 23.2; C going to Pompeii, A XV 13a 2; letter from Octavian, A XVI 8; 'I don't trust his years', A XVI 9; C discusses his works, A XVI 11; decides to go to Rome, A XVI 12; bolts to Arpinum, A XVI 10; 'I told Oppius', A XVI 15.3; A comforted by *de Sen.*, A XVI 11.3; the history, A XVI 13a 2; C reaches Rome, A XVI 15.5–6; Octavian retires to Etruria, App. III 42; C writes to D. Brutus, f XI 5–7; Senate on 20 Dec., *Phil.* III, f X 28.2, XI 6.2, XII 22; 'I have laid', *Phil.* V 30, f XII 25.2.

16. VICTORY AND DISASTER 43 B.C.

Senate on 1 Jan., *Phil.* V; reconciled with Fufius, A XV 4.1; who proposes negotiations, *Phil.* V 1–2; C opposes, *ib.* 3; Antony's irregularities, *ib.* 8–25; rewards for Lepidus and Octavian, 1, *ib.* 38–44; pledge, *ib.* 50; three days' debate, *Phil.* VI 3; Pansa and Piso, App. III 54; Fulvia and family, *ib.* 51; Sulpicius, *Phil.* IX 9, VI 4; agrarian law invalid, *Phil.* VI 14; C on his origin, *ib.* 17; unanimity of Italy, *ib.* 18; 'other races', *ib.* 19; Q abuses consuls, f XVI 27; 'my Caesar', f XI 8.2; Pollio complains, f X 31.1; day and night, f IX 24.4; 'ruled the world', *pro Font.* 24; Hirtius and Pansa, *Phil.* VII 11, 13; financial troubles, Dio 46.31; 'nurseling of peace', *Phil.* VII 8; death of Sulpicius, *Phil.* IX 1–2; news of first clash, *Phil.* VIII 6; military dress, C *ap.* Nonius 48L; Lepidus omits thanks, f X 27; tribute to Sulpicius, *Phil.* IX; survival of statue, *Digest* I 2.2.43; C to Cassius, f XII 4; Antony's *acta* repealed, *Phil.* XII 12; C on recruits, *Phil.* XI 39; Brutus in Athens, Plut. *Brut.* 24.2; Horace, *Sat.* I 6.47; Marcus, MB II 4.6, 5, *Phil.* X 13, XI 26; Brutus writes to Senate, *Phil.* X 1; Pansa proposes his recognition, *ib.* 2; C supports it, *ib.* 2; Fufius opposes, *ib.* 4; C sends speech to Brutus, MB II 3.4, 4.2; rumours of Cassius, f XII 5.1; news of Dolabella, *Phil.* XI 4–6; he is declared public enemy, *ib.* 9; C urges recognition of Cassius, *ib.* 29; is opposed, f XII 7.1; new attempt to treat, *Phil.* XII; letters from Plancus and Lepidus, *Phil.* XIII, f X 6.1; C answers them, f X 6, 27; letter from Antony to Hirtius and Octavian, *Phil.* XIII 22–48; from Plancus, f X 5; news of Cassius, MB II 2.3; Brutus to C on 1 April, MB II 3; battle of Mutina, f X 30; veterans, App. III 68–9; 2nd battle, App. III 7, Dio 46.38; rumours at Rome, *Phil.* XIV 12–16; 'the consuls have proved', MB I 3.1–3; C proposes thanksgiving, *Phil.* XIV; 'the reasons that', f XI 13.1–2; 'I cannot give orders', f XI 10.4; Decimus as correspondent, f XI 24; Octavian's earlier negotiations with D. Brutus, Dio 45.14–5; 'the disappearance', f X 33.1; Senate's reaction, Dio 46.40, MB I 15.9, f X 33.1; 'grudging, not grateful', MB I 15.8; C's joke, f XI 20.1, 21.1; Octavian badly treated, App. III 86; Decimus' pursuit of Antony, f XI 10; reports Antony and Lepidus in touch, f XI 11; Antony in Southern Gaul, f XI 13; 'it seems that the war', f XI 12.1; Lepidus seems loyal, f X 34.3–4; Decimus still hopeful, f XI 23; Plancus' letters, f X 23; 'I call gods and men', f X 35; Lepidus' legate, f X 25.4; Decimus to C, f XI 26; conference with Servilia, MB I 18.1; Brutus and Cassius recalled, MB I 10; C and elections, f X 26; and finance, f XII 30.4; Brutus and C. Antonius, MB I 4.2; 'I utterly disagree', MB I 2a.2; 'Caesar who has so far', MB I 10.3; 'by the way in which', MB I 16.1; letter to Atticus, MB I 17; C on Porcia's death, MB I 9.1; defends himself, MB I 15; 'I shall, as usual', f XII 25a.1; 'believe me, Brutus', f XI 14; 'we are the playthings', MB I 10.3; last letter to Brutus, MB I 18 3–4; Plancus complains, f X 24; Octavian and C to be consuls, Dio 46.42; App. III 82; final collapse of government, App. III 89–98, Dio 46.43–7, Vell. Pat. II 65.1; C's letter to Octavian, *ap.* Nonius 702L; C's death, Plut. 47–8.

Other accounts, Elder Seneca, *Suas.* VI; Brutus' reaction, Plut. *Brut.* 28.1–2; C's hand on Rostra, Plut. 49.1, Dio 47.8; 'the head of the man', *de Or.* III 10; Popillius' statue, Dio 47.11; C's burial, *Anth. Lat.,* XII Sapientes; C's property, Pliny NH XXXI.6, cf. Vell. Pat. II 14.3; young Marcus, App. IV 51; as consul, Plut. 49.4; beats rhetorician, Quintil. X 5.20; Terentia, Jerome *Adv. Iovin.* 1.48, Pliny NH VII 158; Pomponia, Plut. 49.2; Atticus in the proscriptions, Nepos *Att.* 9–12; friendly with Triumvirs, *ib.* 19–20; daughter, *ib.* 12.1–2, 19.4; death, *ib.* 21–2; Tiro's death, Jerome *Euseb. Chron.* 01. 194.1; publishes C's notes, Quintil. X 7.31; collects jokes, Macr. II 1.12, Quintil. VI 3.5; C's supposed dream, Plut. 44 etc.; Augustus on C, Plut. 49.3.

17. THE ONE SURE IMMORTALITY

Livy on C, Quintil. X 1.39; Quintilian, X 1.112; complaints on style, Seneca *Epist. Moral.* CXIV 16; Fronto I 3; Dio 38.18–29, 46.1–28; Seneca on C's philosophy, *Epist. Moral.* C; Lactantius holds C destroyed paganism, *de ira Dei* II 4–10; Jerome, *Epist.* 22, 30; Augustine, *Conf.* 3.4; Petrarch, *Sen.* XVI 1, *Fam. Rer.* XII 8, XXI.10, XXIV 3, etc.; Copernicus, *de revolutionibus orbium caelestium,* dedic. epistle; Montaigne, *Essais* II 10; Erasmus, *Ciceronianus*; C. Middleton, *A History of the Life of Cicero*; Gibbon, *Autobiography* (p. 6 Everyman edn); Montesquieu, *Pensées Diverses: des Anciens*; Voltaire, *Remarques de l'esprit sur les Mœurs* IV; *Essais sur la poésie épique* III; Mommsen, *A History of Rome,* Bk V esp. ch. XII.

BIBLIOGRAPHY

It would be quite impossible to list the books and articles that I have used in writing this book or in making up my mind, over the years, about Cicero. It will be more useful to name some works that those interested in him or his period would find helpful.

Almost all his works are translated, by various hands, in the useful bilingual Loeb series; the old translations of the letters, by Shuckburgh and Jeans, are well known; the letters to Atticus can now be consulted in the splendid Latin and English edition, with commentary, of D. R. Shackleton Bailey (1965–8). L. P. Wilkinson's selection of the letters, in his own translation, is excellent, and now available in paperback. J. Carcopino's well-known work, translated as *The Secrets of Cicero's Correspondence* (1951), is ingenious but unreliable.

The older biographies, notably that of J. L. Strachan-Davidson (1894), excellent in its day, have to some extent been superseded by a better appreciation of many aspects of Roman life; so has G. Boissier's attractively written *Cicéron et ses amis*, translated as *Cicero and his friends* (1897). H. J. Haskell's *This Was Cicero* (1942) remains a spirited introduction, intelligent rather than scholarly. Of recent lives, D. Stockton, *Cicero, a Political Biography* (1971) is thoroughly recommendable as what it sets out to be; D. R. Shackleton Bailey's *Cicero* (1971) quotes very generously from the letters and is witty and perceptive about Cicero the man; both books are frankly one-sided. A very detailed account of Cicero's last year can be read in H. Frisch, *Cicero's Fight for the Republic* (1946; published in Denmark). There are essays on various aspects of the subject in *Cicero*, ed. T. A. Dorey (1965). An excellent brief summing up, in pamphlet form, of the state of play in international Ciceronian scholarship is A. E. Douglas, *Cicero* (*Greece and Rome, New Surveys in the Classics*, no. 2, 1968).

The most detailed biography, in fact, is in German, M. Gelzer's authoritative *Cicero: Ein Biographischer Versuch* (1969); so is the best introduction to Cicero's philosophic works, W. Süss, *Cicero: Eine Einführung in seine philosophischen Schriften* (1966). I am particularly indebted to this; also to K. Büchner, *Cicero: Bestand und Wandel seiner geistigen Welt* (1964) and, for Cicero's reputation in later centuries, Th. Zieliński, *Cicero im Wandel der Jahrhunderte* (1897) (though much later work has been done on this last subject).

Most of the other ancient sources are also to be found in the Loeb edition (but there is no translation yet of Asconius, and the other ancient commentators on Cicero's speeches). There are Penguin translations of Plutarch's most relevant lives. There is no wholly satisfactory general history of the period in English: the *Cambridge Ancient History* is not at its best here, and is becoming ancient itself. H. H. Scullard, *From the*

Gracchi to Nero (3rd edn., 1970) is an excellent, accurate, brief text-book. There is an English translation of M. Gelzer's detailed life of *Caesar* (1968); unfortunately not of his *Pompeius*. Shorter lives of Caesar, for the general public, by J. P. V. D. Balsdon and M. Grant are available. There are many books on particular aspects of the period; one that might be mentioned here is L. R. Taylor, *Party Politics in the Age of Caesar*, of which there is a recent reprint in paperback.

THE ROMAN POLITICAL SYSTEM

The following outline adds little to the information scattered through the text, but it may be convenient to have this collected for reference.

The People:
Under Sulla's basically conservative constitution, the People, i.e. the body of adult male citizens (slaves and foreigners, including the natives of the 'provinces' into which the area ruled by Rome outside Italy was divided, being naturally excluded) retained the ultimate legislative power in Rome. They exercised this directly, not through representatives. In their various forms of assembly they could not, as in democratic states in Greece, discuss proposals, but only vote on them after listening to speakers put up by the presiding magistrate. In the commonest type of assembly the People was divided into its thirty-five tribes (artificial territorial divisions, each, apart from the four city tribes, made up of various areas in Italy). A majority of individual votes determined the vote of the tribe; a majority of the thirty-five tribal votes carried a measure. For the election of most regular magistrates and some other purposes, the assembly voted not by tribes but, in the same way, by centuries. In this, originally military, organization, the People met on the Field of Mars outside the walls, and was divided on the basis of wealth into five classes, and within these into 'centuries'. There were more centuries in the top class than in any of the others, though there were clearly fewer rich men than poor ones; thus the rich had disproportionate weight in the assembly. This was because they had once been the only class that mattered in warfare, being alone able to provide themselves with good armour, before the State took over the task. Voting started with the top class, and in fact the lowest classes might not be called on to vote at all, for an over-all majority of the 193 centuries could be obtained from the first few classes. (This account is somewhat simplified.)

Voting at this time was by secret ballot. Only a small proportion of the electorate, scattered over Italy and indeed owing to emigration all over the provinces, would be on hand to vote. In the 1st century disorder and violence in the assemblies were common.

The Senate:
The Senate was in theory only the advisory council of the consuls, but in practice its authority was vast and its decrees valid in many spheres. It met sometimes in the Senate House by the Forum, at other times in various temples, under the presidency of a consul, or failing him a praetor. The presiding officer called on members to speak roughly in order of seniority. After Sulla the Senate was in practice elected by the People, as it con-

323

sisted exclusively of ex-magistrates; but tradition, the politician's need of wealth and experience, and pressure from above, including bribery meant that these almost all came from the upper class. This class included many families technically 'plebeian', as the stranglehold of the earliest aristocracy, the patricians, had been broken in the fourth century B.C., leaving these latter only minor privileges, mostly ceremonial and religious. What mattered now was to be 'noble', i.e. to have had a consul in the family; it was difficult at this time to break into the very restricted circle of the nobility.

The Magistrates:

Elections were held annually in the summer; magistrates entered office on 1 January, except for the tribunes, who did so on 10 December. There were some minor, optional magistracies; but at about twenty-eight a man could become one of the twenty quaestors, with primarily financial duties, and so enter the Senate. Later he might become one of the four aediles, concerned with the administration of the city, or the ten Tribunes of the People. This last office also provided an alternative way into the Senate. A survival of an earlier age of strife, its holders might not be patricians and were supposed to defend the interests of the People. They could veto any proposal before Senate or People; they could preside over the tribal assembly (minus its patrician members) and put legislation to it; Sulla temporarily limited their rights. In practice many tribunes were aristocrats; some, aristocrats or no, tried to use the People against the Senate and for their own advantage or that of a patron.

After aedileship or tribunate came the praetorship (there were eight praetors at this time). The praetor presided over criminal trials and could command an army; on the expiry of his office he was likely to go as a promagistrate (deputy or equivalent to a magistrate) to govern one of the foreign provinces. The Senate might extend his year here to two or three. After two full years from the end of his praetorship he could become one of the two consuls, the highest magistrates in Rome; as before, he would probably follow this with a provincial command. From the ex-consuls or 'consulars' were chosen the two censors, theoretically elected every five years for eighteen months, to take a census, assign citizens to their place in the centuriate assembly, revise the rolls of the Senate, etc. This was an office of much authority, though without the right to command troops. The principle of collegiality at Rome allowed all magistrates to block their colleagues' (and juniors') actions.

In a sense Rome was ruled not by magistrates but ex-magistrates; the ex-consuls speaking first in the Senate were immensely influential (though after Sulla none had the permanent position of 'Leader of the Senate'); much power also rested with those members of the oligarchy, mostly great nobles, who held priesthoods and could declare actions invalid on religious grounds.

The Equites:

Men outside the Senate with property over a certain sum (capital, not income) were known as *equites*, cavalry. Since senators were not supposed to engage in trade or take state contracts, numerous *equites* were engaged in these activities. Some corporate feeling developed in this class, though many *equites* were quiet country gentlemen; at several periods juries were drawn exclusively or partly from it, and thus it had a certain hold over such members of the Senate as might appear in the criminal courts charged with bribery, violence or extortion. Clashes between *equites* and Senate or members thereof often arose largely in or over the provinces, where *equites* collected taxes and had many business ventures. The *equites* of course might have sympathetic allies in the Senate.

Political Life:

It is possible to talk of optimates, leading conservatives asserting the supremacy of the Senate and the *status quo* (more generally of *boni*, the 'good' or *bien pensants*); and of *populares* (usually independent or competing individuals, rather than a party) exploiting the power of the tribal assemblies against it; and the *equites* might sometimes seem to have an intermediate role, ready to ally with the Senate against revolution, and with the People when the Senate crossed their interests. In practice personal ties of all kinds, and especially the institution of clientship, by which individuals or whole communities put themselves in the protection of prominent men, often cut across these horizontal divisions. If in addition to acquiring a great personal following a wealthy man either exploited the grievances of the People or flung his army in the scale, the State, with limited funds and no real police force, was in danger (citizens paid no direct taxes and the provinces, except those of the East, now did little more than pay for their administration and defence). Nonetheless, the Romans, great traditionalists, found it difficult to criticize their system.

ROMAN NOMENCLATURE

The Roman citizen was consciously distinguished from other men by his possession of 'the three names': the given forename or *praenomen*, of which surprisingly few were in common use: the name proper, or *nomen*, usually ending in -ius, identifying the *gens* or family in a wide sense; and the surname, *cognomen*, serving to distinguish either two branches of the family, or two families of the same name – or else being personal and descriptive. In fact many hereditary *cognomina* were (often unflattering) nicknames in origin. Sometimes several *cognomina* might be used, sometimes none at all (e.g. C. Marius). A man adopted into a new family kept his old *nomen* in a special adjectival form, as a *cognomen*: thus Octavius, after his adoption by Caesar, was C. Julius Caesar Octavianus.

Cicero refers to other Romans sometimes by name, sometimes by surname, and sometimes by both together, whichever seemed to be most convenient. In the Senate, the archaic custom of using only forename and name persisted, so that Cicero was M. Tullius. Official documents however would use all three names, plus the forenames of father and grandfather, and the tribe. In the index below, *nomen* or family name is the prime indicator of alphabetic order, but the main surnames are cross-referenced. Where praenomen is missing, it is not known.

Women used only the feminine form of the family name, without either forename or surname, so that Cicero's daughter was necessarily Tullia. Several daughters would be distinguished as Prima, Secunda, Tertia and so on. Slaves bore a single name, often Greek; on liberation they took their master's family name, and, usually, his forename; thus Tiro became M. Tullius Tiro. Greeks had a single name, and were often further identified, not very adequately, by their father's name or by their city of origin.

Common first names and their usual abbreviations:

A. – Aulus	P. – Publius
Ap. – Appius	Q. – Quintus
C. – Gaius	Ser. – Servius
Cn. – Gnaeus	Sex. – Sextus
D. – Decimus	Sp. – Spurius
L. – Lucius	T. – Titus
M. – Marcus	Ti. – Tiberius
M'. – Manius	

DESCRIPTIVE INDEX OF PERSONS

327

Archimedes, Greek scientist and mathematician, of Syracuse, 3rd century, 33–4, 212

Ariobarzanes, King of Cappadocia in Asia Minor, 168, 178, 251

Aristotle, Greek philosopher of 4th century B.C., 19, 48, 135, 147–8, 150, 215, 233–5, 239, 241, 248, 258

Q. Asconius Pedianus, scholar of 1st century A.D., some of whose commentaries on Cicero's speeches survive, 51, 55, 58, 139

C. Asinius Pollio, Caesarian, governor of Spain 44–3, joined Antony. Later wrote history of the years 60–42, 250, 260, 279–80, 287–8, 292, 295

Attica, nickname of Atticus' little daughter, 168, 197, 223–4, 297

Augustus, see Julius

C. Aurelius Cotta, consul in 75, modified Sulla's law on tribunate, takes Academic role in On the Nature of the Gods, 43, 242–3

L. Aurelius Cotta, his brother, praetor in 70, passed law on composition of the juries, consul in 65, 43

Balbus, see (1) Cornelius, (2) Lucilius
Bibulus, see Calpurnius
Brutus, see Junius
Bursa, see Munatius

L. Caecilius Metellus, governed Sicily in 70, 41, 47

Q. Caecilius Metellus Celer, served under his brother-in-law Pompey, as praetor in 63 prominent in trial of Rabirius, but helped suppress the conspiracy. As consul in 60 opposed Pompey (who had divorced his sister) and Caesar. Died in 59, probably not poisoned by his wife Clodia, 68, 91, 93–4, 103–4, 143

Q. Caecilius Metellus Creticus, as consul-designate in 70 supported Verres, 41

Q. Caecilius Metellus Nepos, brother of Celer, also served Pompey in the East, to whom he fled on suspension of his tribunate in 62. Consul in 57, he was persuaded not to oppose Cicero's return, 71, 77, 86, 89, 90–1, 93, 120, 123

Q. Caecilius Metellus Scipio, Pompey's father-in-law and colleague as consul in 52, 140

A. Caecina, distinguished Etruscan, writer, opponent of Caesar, 218–9

M. Caelius Rufus, pupil of Cicero, who defended him on charge of violence in 56; tribune in 52, aedile in 50, praetor in 48, when he was killed in a rising against Caesar, 46, 139, 143, 166, 170, 180–1, 183–6, 189, 191, 197–8, 201, 208

Caerellia, elderly lady correspondent of Cicero, with a liking for gossip and philosophy, 252

Caesar, see Julius

M. Calpurnius Bibulus, unfortunately a contemporary of Caesar and so his colleague in most magistracies, notably as consul in 59. Governed Syria 51–50, commanded Pompey's fleet in Civil War. A consistent optimate, son-in-law to Cato, 103, 105, 107, 110–1, 138, 141, 169–72, 186, 208, 252

C. Calpurnius Piso Frugi, quaestor in 58, but gave up his post abroad to work for the recall of his father-in-law Cicero; before whose return he died, 47, 112–3, 115, 144

influential, though Cicero regarded him as 'inert' and felt betrayed by him in *57*, 18, 22, 31, 37, 40–2, 45, 49–50, 53, 57, 68, 71–2, 77, 89, 96, 112, 114, 116, 118, 126, 131, 139–40, 166, 186, 211, 237, 249, 282

Isocrates, Greek orator of 4th century, 148

C. Julius Caesar. His aunt Julia married Marius. Pontifex Maximus in *63*, praetor *62*, governed Spain *61–0*, consul *59*, governed Gaul and Illyricum *58–49*, dictator *49–44*; assassinated; 15, 17, 20, 30, 38, 40, 52, 55, 58, 61–4, 66–9, 70–1, 80, 82–5, 88–91, 93–5, 98, 104–12, 114–6, 120, 127–135, 138–9, 141, 145, 157–8, 160–1, 166, 169–71, 175, 179, 182–98, 200–2, 204–11, 213–4, 218–23, 245–8, 251–64, 266, 269, 273, 281, 290–2

C. Julius Caesar Octavianus, born C. Octavius, great-nephew of Caesar. Master of Horse designate for *43*; adopted in Caesar's will; recognized as pro-praetor Jan. *43*, consul in August and with Antony and Lepidus one of Triumviri; later Emperor Augustus, 73, 133, 152, 157–8, 161, 168, 255–6, 260–1, 264, 269–70, 273–6, 278–9, 281–2, 284–94, 296–9

L. Julius Caesar, uncle of Antony, consul in *64*; honoured by Caesar; opposed Antony in *43*, 281

Julia, (1) wife of Marius, aunt of Caesar, 5; (2) daughter of Caesar and wife of Pompey, 38, 110, 133, 220

M. Junius Brutus, nephew to Cato, son to Servilia; married a daughter of Ap. Claudius and then Cato's daughter Porcia. Fought for Pompey, pardoned by Caesar, but led conspirators in the Ides. Urban praetor in *44*, proconsul of Crete and then of Macedonia and the East *43–2*; fell at Philippi. Author of works on ethical philosophy, 20, 71, 85, 112, 141, 177–80, 202, 209, 211–4, 216, 226, 228, 230–1, 238–40, 248, 250–3, 257–60, 262–70, 272, 279, 281–5, 287–91, 293, 295–7

D. Junius Brutus Albinus, remote cousin of M. Brutus, one of the Liberators, proconsul of Cisalpine Gaul *44–3*; died in flight from Antony, 258, 262, 264, 266–7, 270, 274–6, 278–80, 284–8, 291–2, 296

D. Junius Silanus, Servilia's husband, consul in *62*, 71, 83–4

T. Labienus, tribune in *63*, co-operating with Caesar, perhaps on instructions from Pompey; fought for Caesar in Gaul *58–49*, for Pompey *49–5*. From Picenum, perhaps Pompey's man throughout, 66–9, 87, 185, 200, 202

C. Laelius, often known as Sapiens (the Wise), a close friend of Scipio Aemilianus, being slightly his elder and his advisor on political matters, 92, 111, 149, 152, 246, 276

Lentulus, *see* Cornelius

Lepidus, *see* Aemilius

L. Licinius Crassus, the greatest orator of Cicero's youth, he was consul in *95*, censor in *92*, died in *91* while supporting Livius Drusus, 6, 8, 10, 12–5, 17, 24, 43, 147–8, 156, 162

M. Licinius Crassus Dives, not a close relation of the above. Crushed Spartacus' slave revolt *72–1*, consul with Pompey in *70*, censor in *65*, from *60* in alliance with Pompey and Caesar, consul again in *55*, governor of Syria *54–3*, where he was defeated and killed by the Parthians,

GEOGRAPHICAL INDEX